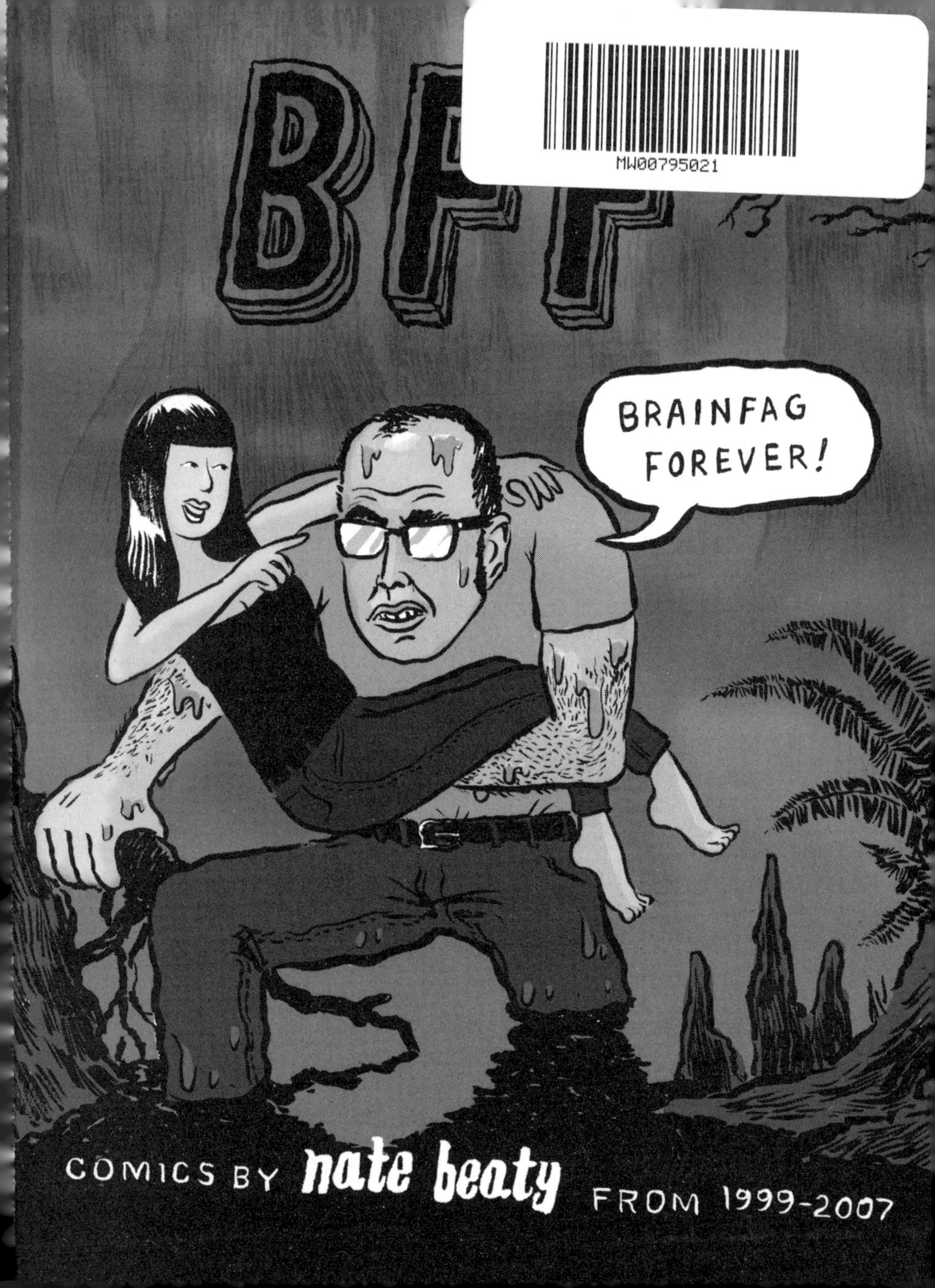
BFF
BRAINFAG FOREVER!
COMICS BY nate beaty FROM 1999-2007

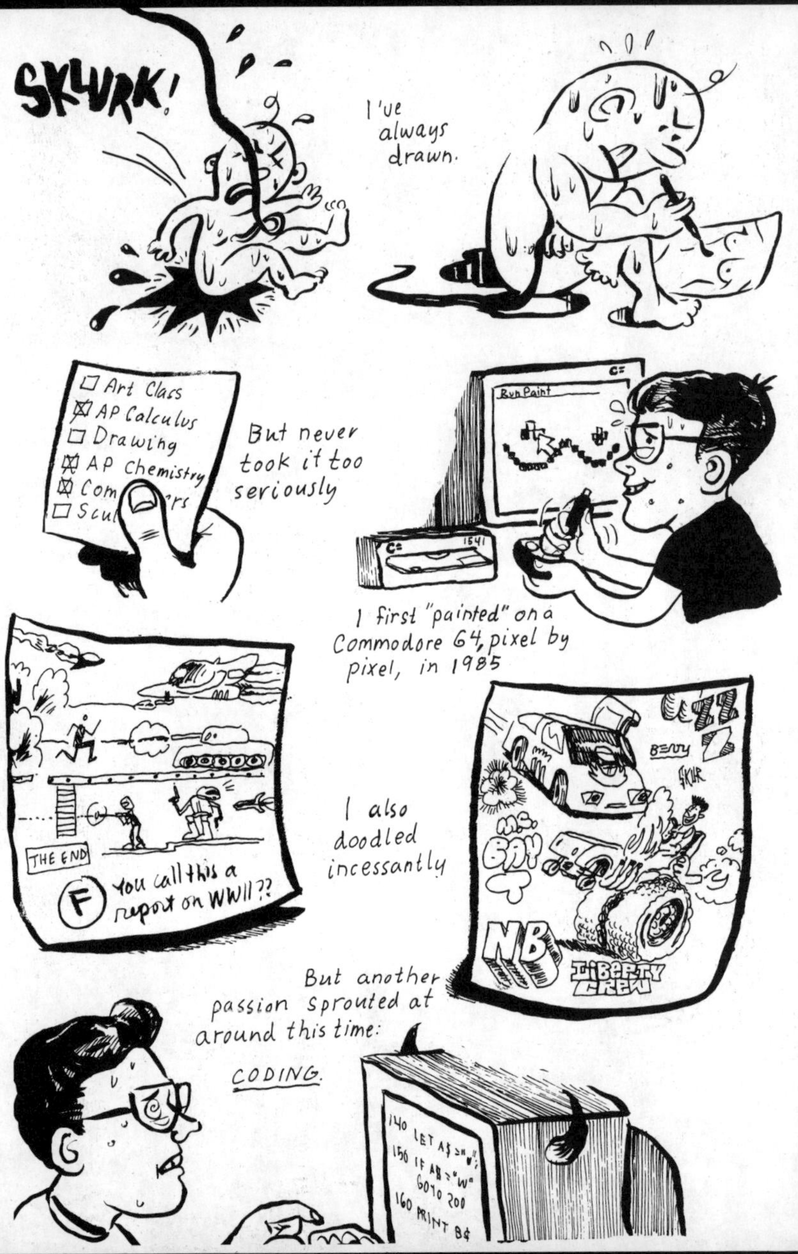
SKLURK!
I've always drawn.
Art Class
AP Calculus
Drawing
AP Chemistry
But never took it too seriously
C=
1541
I first "painted" on a Commodore 64, pixel by pixel, in 1985
THE END
F
You call this a report on WWII??
I also doodled incessantly
NB
LIBERTY CREW
But another passion sprouted at around this time:
CODING.
160 PRINT B$

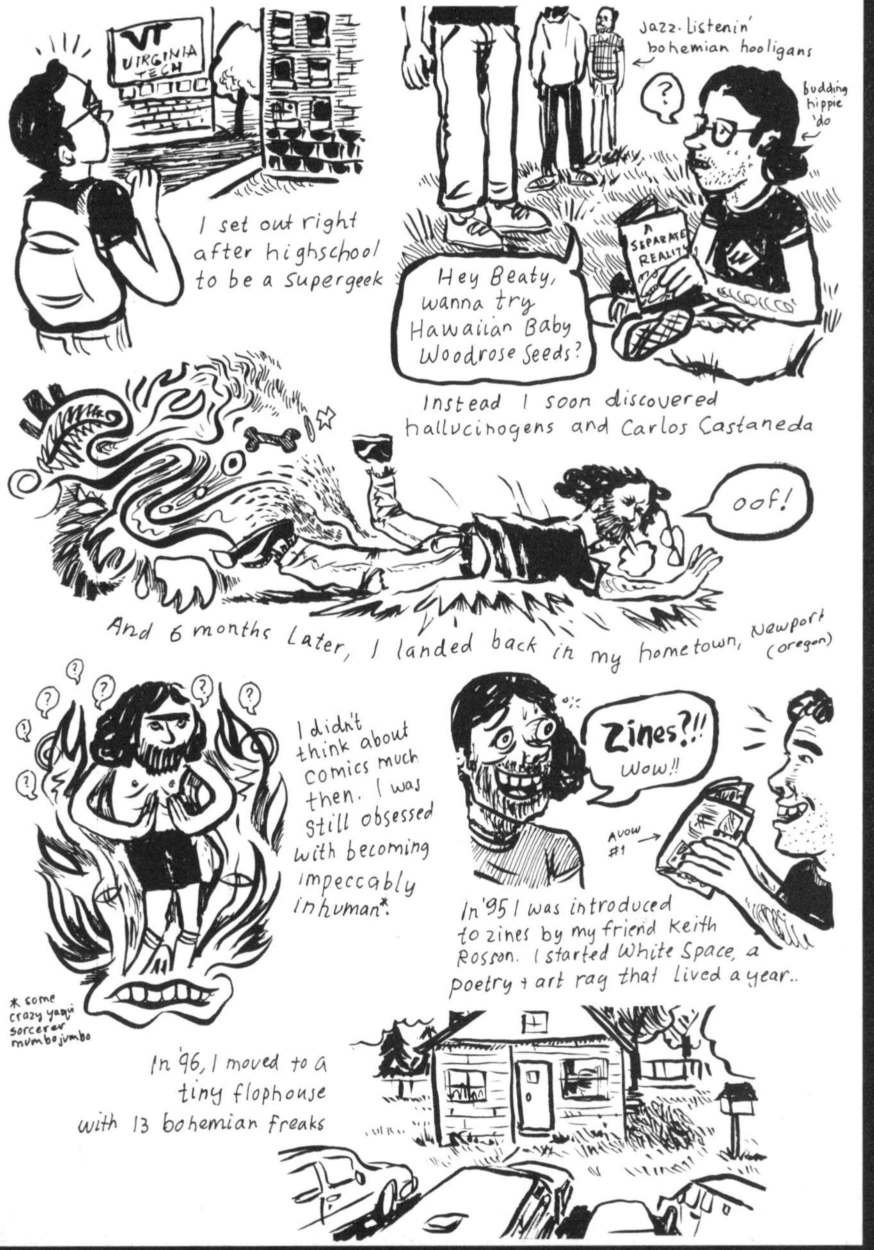
VT VIRGINIA TECH
I set out right after highschool to be a supergeek
Jazz-listenin' bohemian hooligans
budding hippie 'do
?
A SEPARATE REALITY
Hey Beaty, wanna try Hawaiian Baby Woodrose Seeds?
Instead I soon discovered hallucinogens and Carlos Castaneda
oof!
And 6 months later, I landed back in my hometown, Newport (oregon)
I didn't think about comics much then. I was still obsessed with becoming impeccably inhuman*.
* some crazy yaqui sorcerer mumbojumbo
Zines?!! Wow!!
AVOW #1
In '95 I was introduced to zines by my friend Keith Rosson. I started White Space, a poetry + art rag that lived a year..
In '96, I moved to a tiny flophouse with 13 bohemian freaks

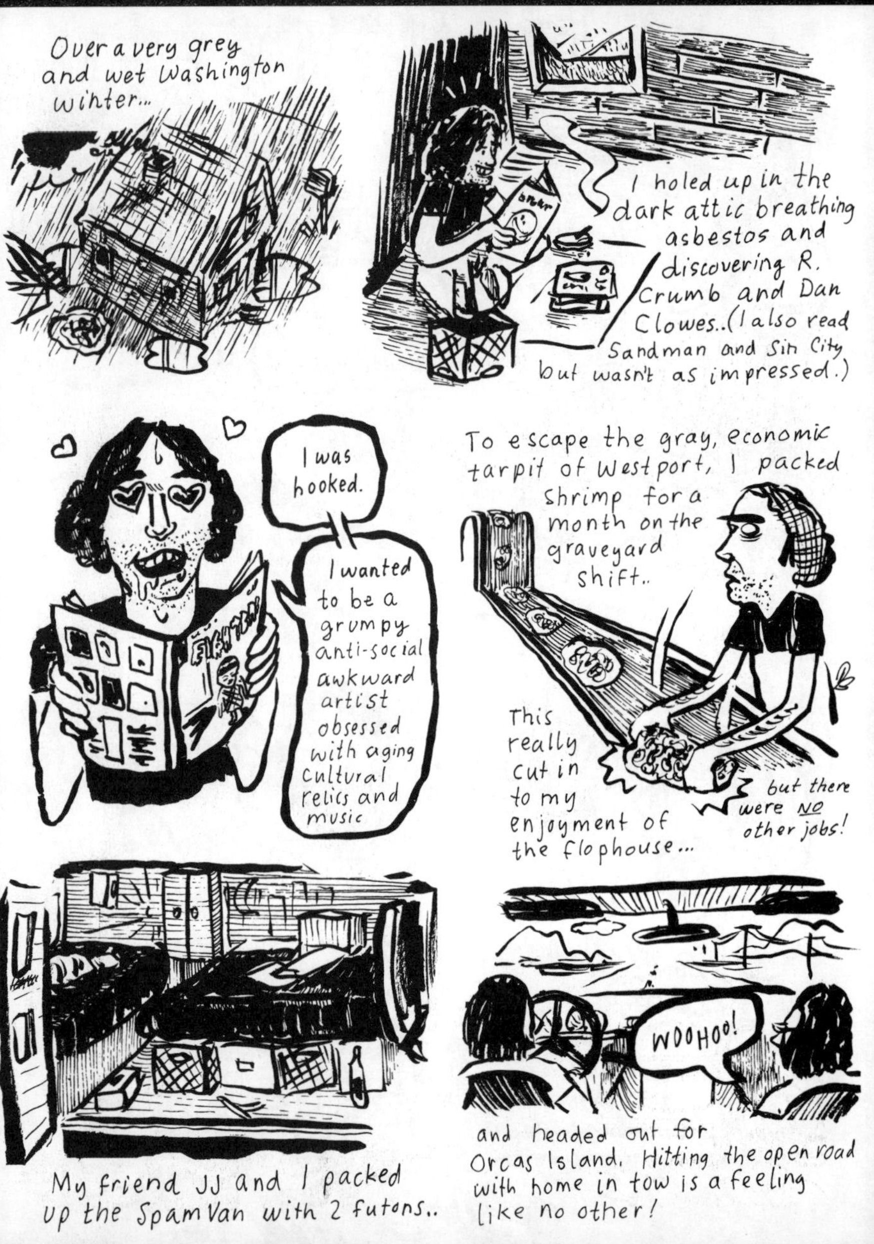
Over a very grey and wet Washington winter...
I holed up in the dark attic breathing asbestos and discovering R. Crumb and Dan Clowes..(I also read Sandman and Sin City but wasn't as impressed.)
I was hooked.
I wanted to be a grumpy anti-social awkward artist obsessed with aging cultural relics and music
To escape the gray, economic tarpit of Westport, I packed shrimp for a month on the graveyard shift..
This really cut in to my enjoyment of the flophouse...
but there were NO other jobs!
My friend JJ and I packed up the SpamVan with 2 futons..
WOOHOO!
and headed out for Orcas Island. Hitting the open road with home in tow is a feeling like no other!

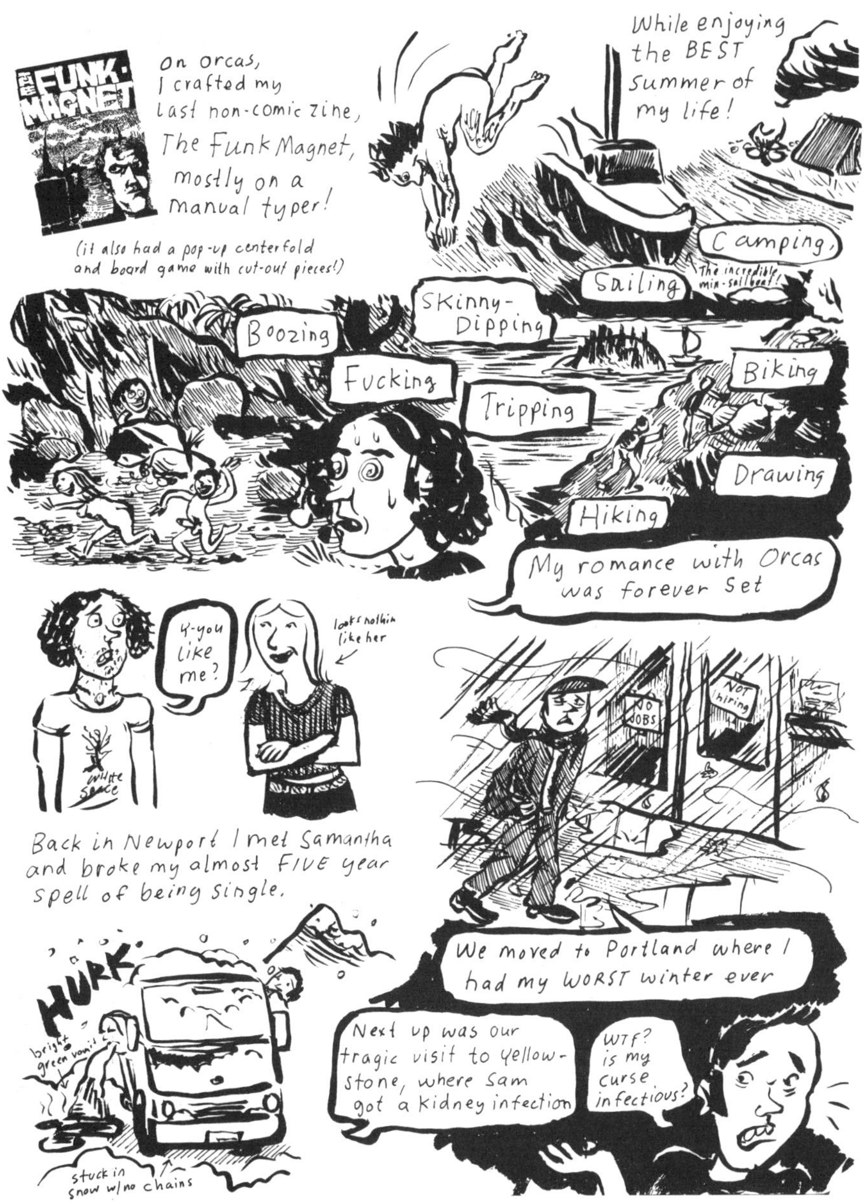

THE FUNK MAGNET
On Orcas, I crafted my last non-comic zine, The Funk Magnet, mostly on a manual typer!
(it also had a pop-up centerfold and board game with cut-out pieces!)
While enjoying the BEST summer of my life!
Camping,
The incredible min-sailboat!
Sailing
Skinny-Dipping
Boozing
Fucking
Tripping
Biking
Drawing
Hiking
My romance with Orcas was forever set
K-you like me?
looks nothin like her
White Space
Back in Newport I met Samantha and broke my almost FIVE year spell of being single.
NO JOBS
NOT hiring
We moved to Portland where I had my WORST winter ever
HURK
bright green vomit
stuck in snow w/no chains
Next up was our tragic visit to Yellowstone, where Sam got a kidney infection
WTF? is my curse infectious?

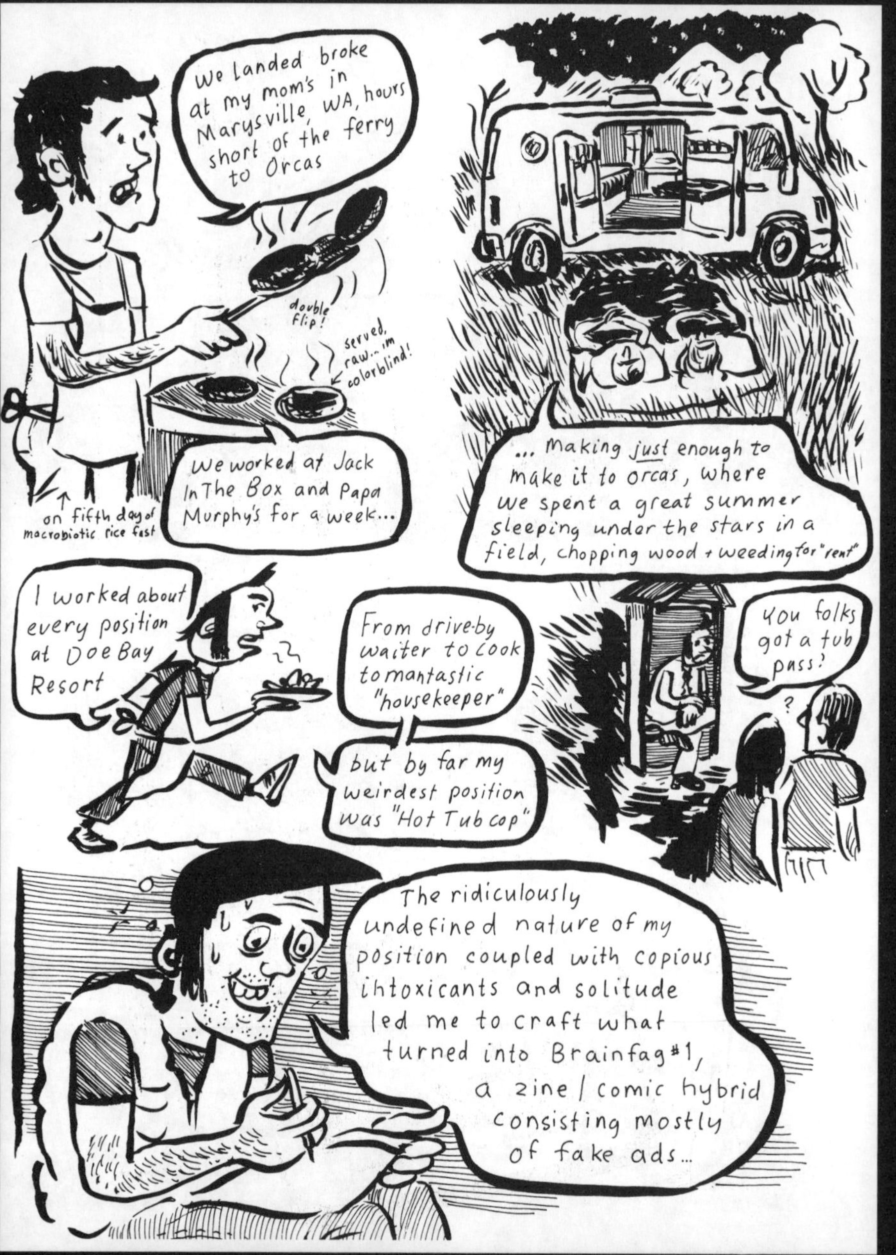
We landed broke at my mom's in Marysville, WA, hours short of the ferry to Orcas
double flip!
served, raw... im colorblind!
on fifth day of macrobiotic rice fast
We worked at Jack In The Box and Papa Murphy's for a week...
... Making just enough to make it to orcas, where we spent a great summer sleeping under the stars in a field, chopping wood + weeding for "rent"
I worked about every position at Doe Bay Resort
From drive-by waiter to cook to mantastic "housekeeper"
but by far my weirdest position was "Hot Tub cop"
You folks got a tub pass?
?
The ridiculously undefined nature of my position coupled with copious intoxicants and solitude led me to craft what turned into Brainfag #1, a zine / comic hybrid consisting mostly of fake ads...

it's the
BRAIN FAG

mystical and methodical,

brought to
you by
natron 46.

(A TUMBLING
FESTIVAL OF IDEAS
AND IMAGES
DESIGNED TO
ALLEVIATE THE
PAIN + CONFUSION
OF EVERYDAY
EXISTENCE.

Smith-Corona

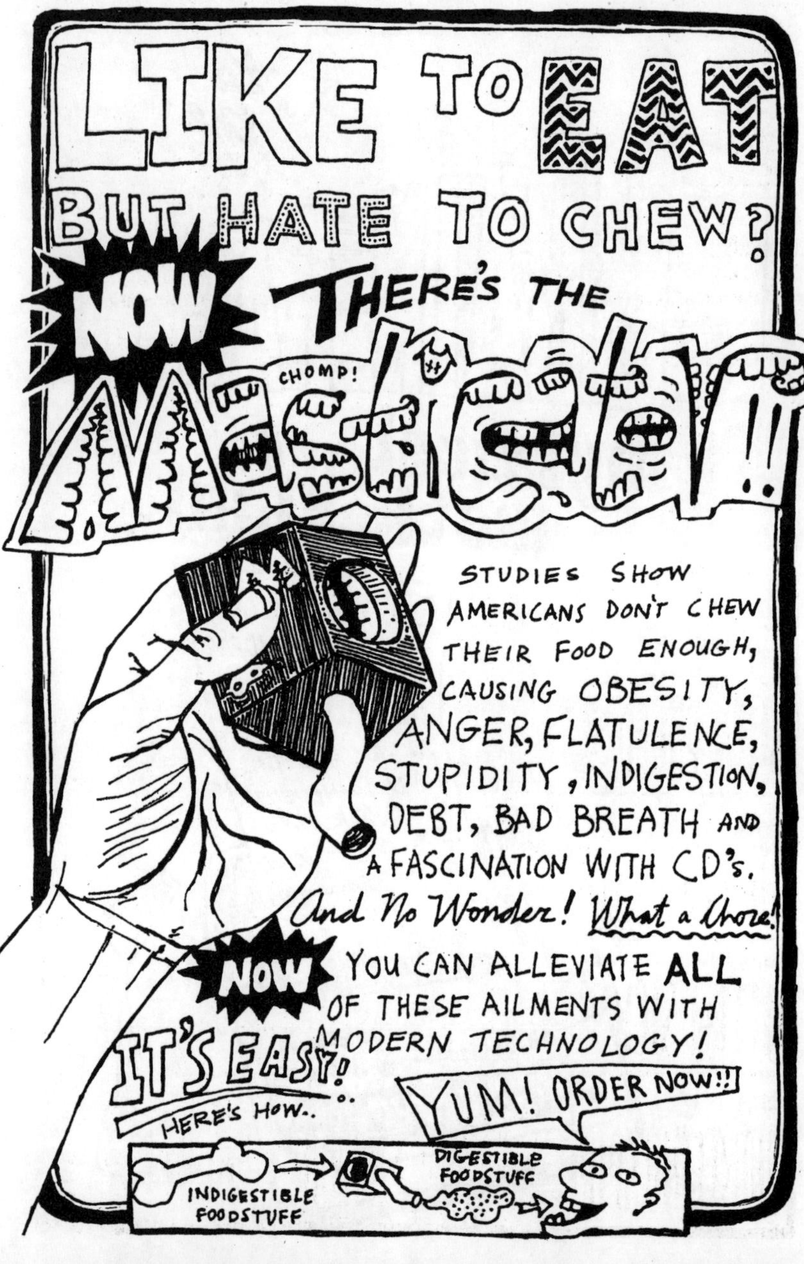
LIKE TO EAT
BUT HATE TO CHEW?
NOW THERE'S THE
CHOMP!
Masticator!!
STUDIES SHOW AMERICANS DON'T CHEW THEIR FOOD ENOUGH, CAUSING OBESITY, ANGER, FLATULENCE, STUPIDITY, INDIGESTION, DEBT, BAD BREATH AND A FASCINATION WITH CD's.
And No Wonder! What a Chore!
NOW YOU CAN ALLEVIATE ALL OF THESE AILMENTS WITH MODERN TECHNOLOGY!
IT'S EASY!
HERE'S HOW..
YUM! ORDER NOW!!
INDIGESTIBLE FOODSTUFF
DIGESTIBLE FOODSTUFF

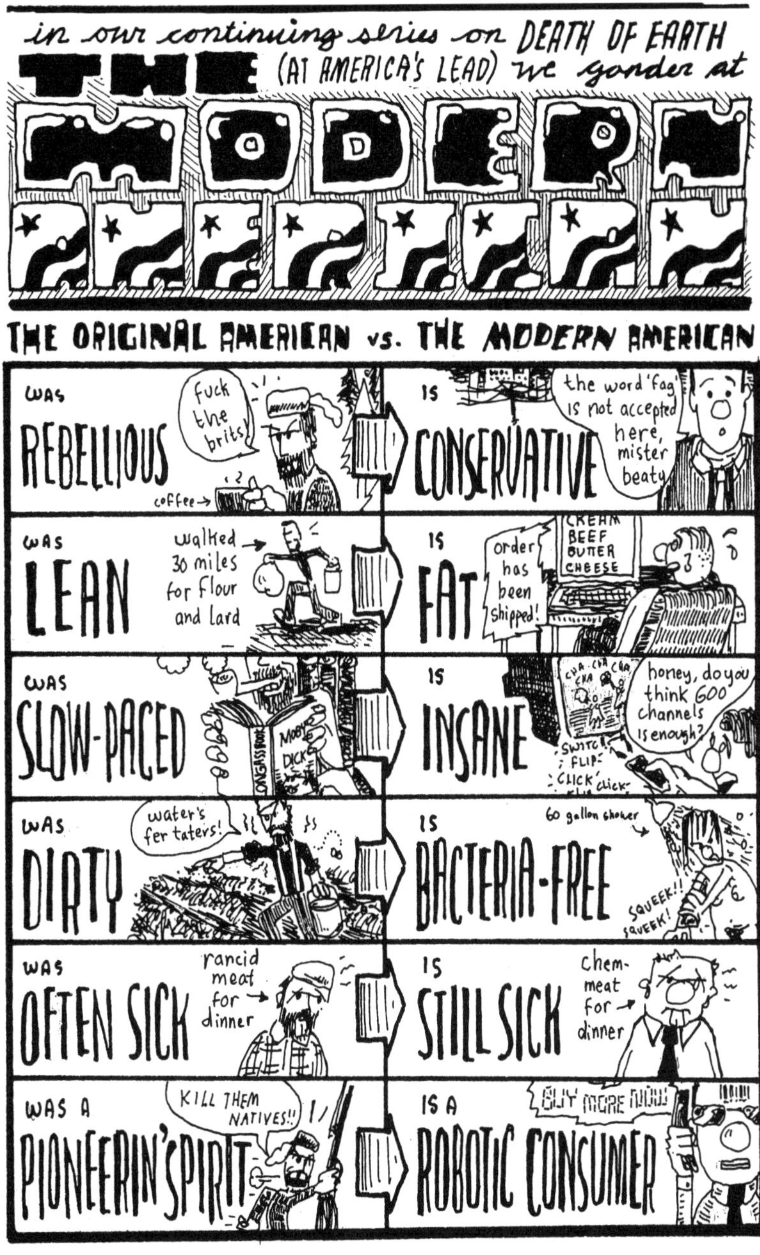
in our continuing series on DEATH OF EARTH
(AT AMERICA'S LEAD) we gander at
THE MODERN AMERICAN
THE ORIGINAL AMERICAN vs. THE MODERN AMERICAN
WAS REBELLIOUS
fuck the brits!
coffee→
IS CONSERVATIVE
the word 'fag' is not accepted here, mister beaty
WAS LEAN
walked → 30 miles for flour and lard
IS FAT
order has been shipped!
CREAM BEEF BUTTER CHEESE
WAS SLOW-PACED
LONGASS BOOK
MOBY DICK
IS INSANE
CHA CHA CHA CHA
honey, do you think 600 channels is enough?
FLIP
CLICK
CLICK
WAS DIRTY
water's fer taters!
IS BACTERIA-FREE
60 gallon shower
SQUEEK!! SQUEEK!
WAS OFTEN SICK
rancid meat for → dinner
IS STILL SICK
chem-meat for → dinner
WAS A PIONEERIN' SPIRIT
KILL THEM NATIVES!!
IS A ROBOTIC CONSUMER
BUY MORE NOW
!!!!!

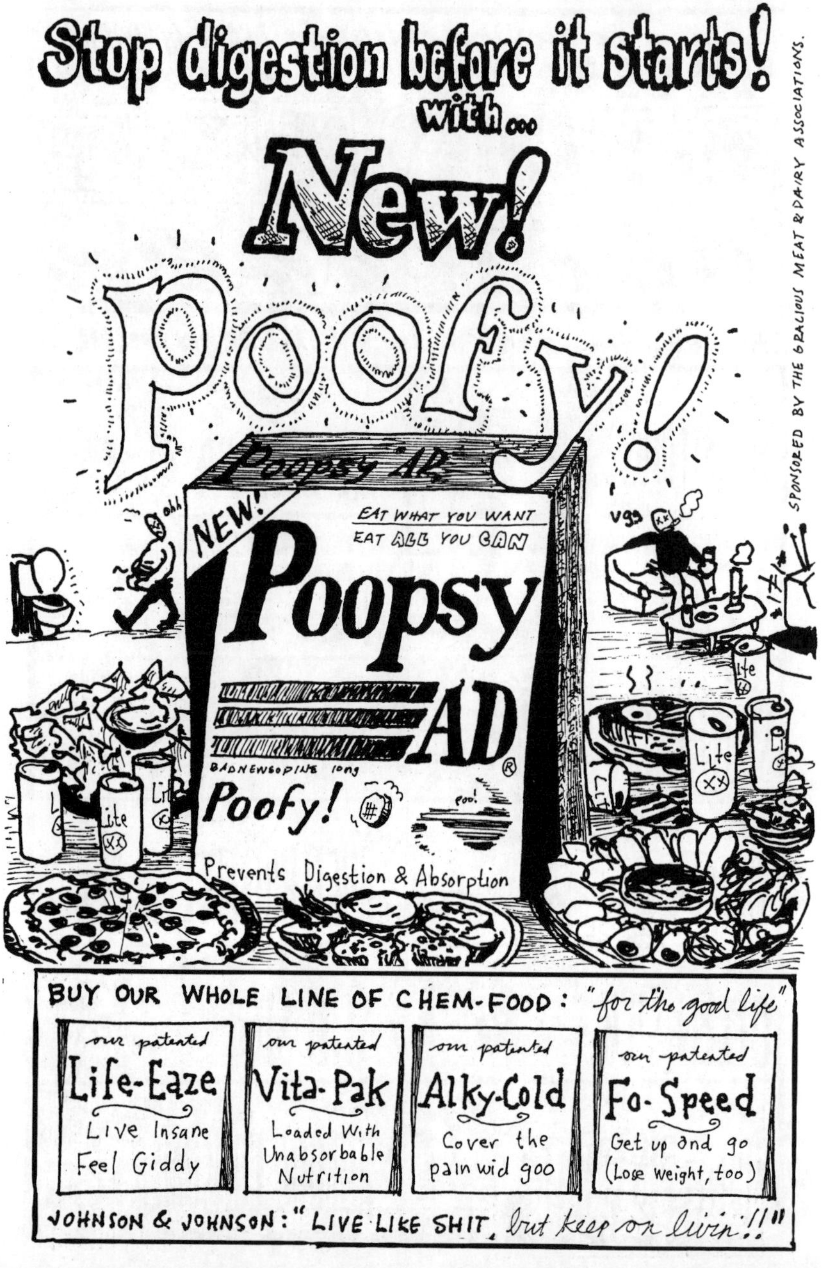
Stop digestion before it starts!
with...
New!
Poofy!
Poopsy AD
NEW!
EAT WHAT YOU WANT
EAT ALL YOU CAN
Poopsy
AD
Poofy!
Prevents Digestion & Absorption
ohh
Lite
SPONSORED BY THE GRACIOUS MEAT & DAIRY ASSOCIATIONS.
BUY OUR WHOLE LINE OF CHEM-FOOD: "for the good life"
our patented
Life-Eaze
Live Insane
Feel Giddy
our patented
Vita-Pak
Loaded With
Unabsorbable
Nutrition
our patented
Alky-Cold
Cover the
pain wid goo
our patented
Fo-Speed
Get up and go
(Lose weight, too)
JOHNSON & JOHNSON: "LIVE LIKE SHIT, but keep on livin'!!"

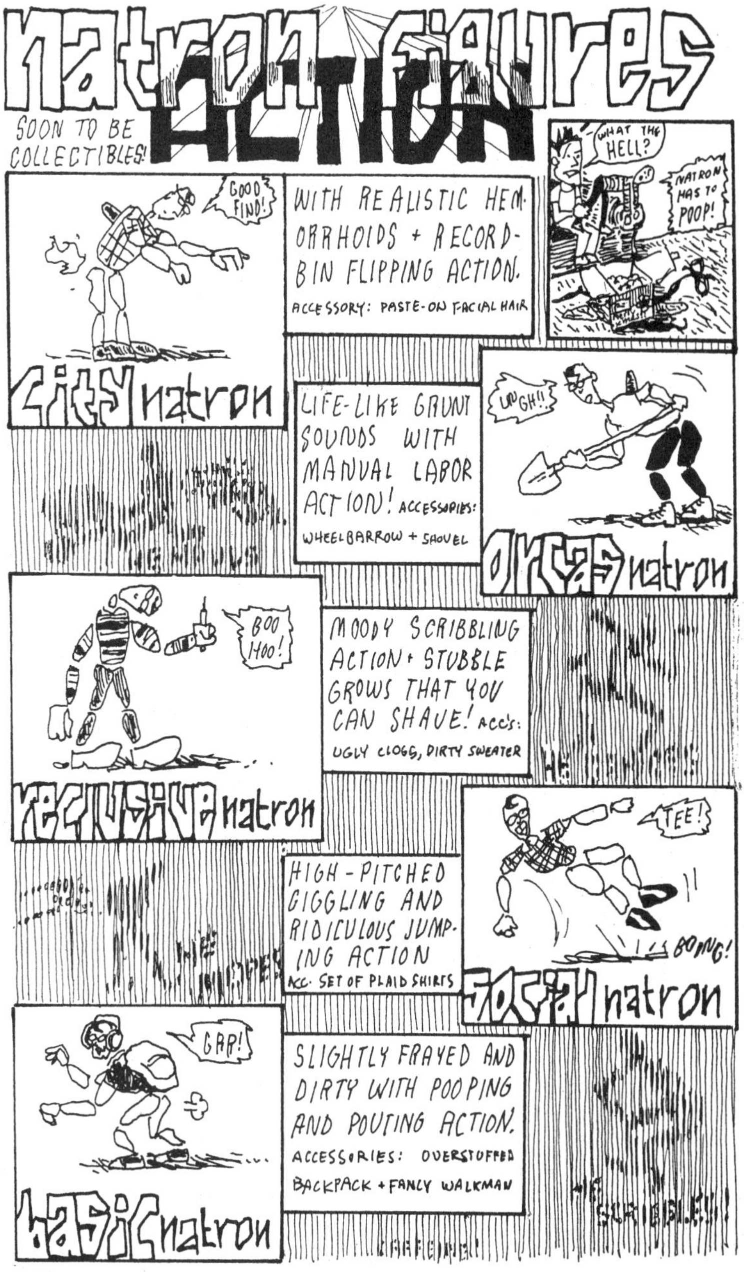
natron ACTION figures
SOON TO BE COLLECTIBLES!
GOOD FIND!
WITH REALISTIC HEMORRHOIDS + RECORD-BIN FLIPPING ACTION.
ACCESSORY: PASTE-ON FACIAL HAIR
WHAT THE HELL?
NATRON HAS TO POOP!
city natron
LIFE-LIKE GRUNT SOUNDS WITH MANUAL LABOR ACTION! ACCESSORIES: WHEELBARROW + SHOVEL
UNGH!!
orcas natron
BOO HOO!
MOODY SCRIBBLING ACTION + STUBBLE GROWS THAT YOU CAN SHAVE! ACC'S: UGLY CLOGS, DIRTY SWEATER
reclusive natron
TEE!
HIGH-PITCHED GIGGLING AND RIDICULOUS JUMPING ACTION
ACC. SET OF PLAID SHIRTS
BOING!
social natron
GAR!
SLIGHTLY FRAYED AND DIRTY WITH POOPING AND POUTING ACTION.
ACCESSORIES: OVERSTUFFED BACKPACK + FANCY WALKMAN
basic natron

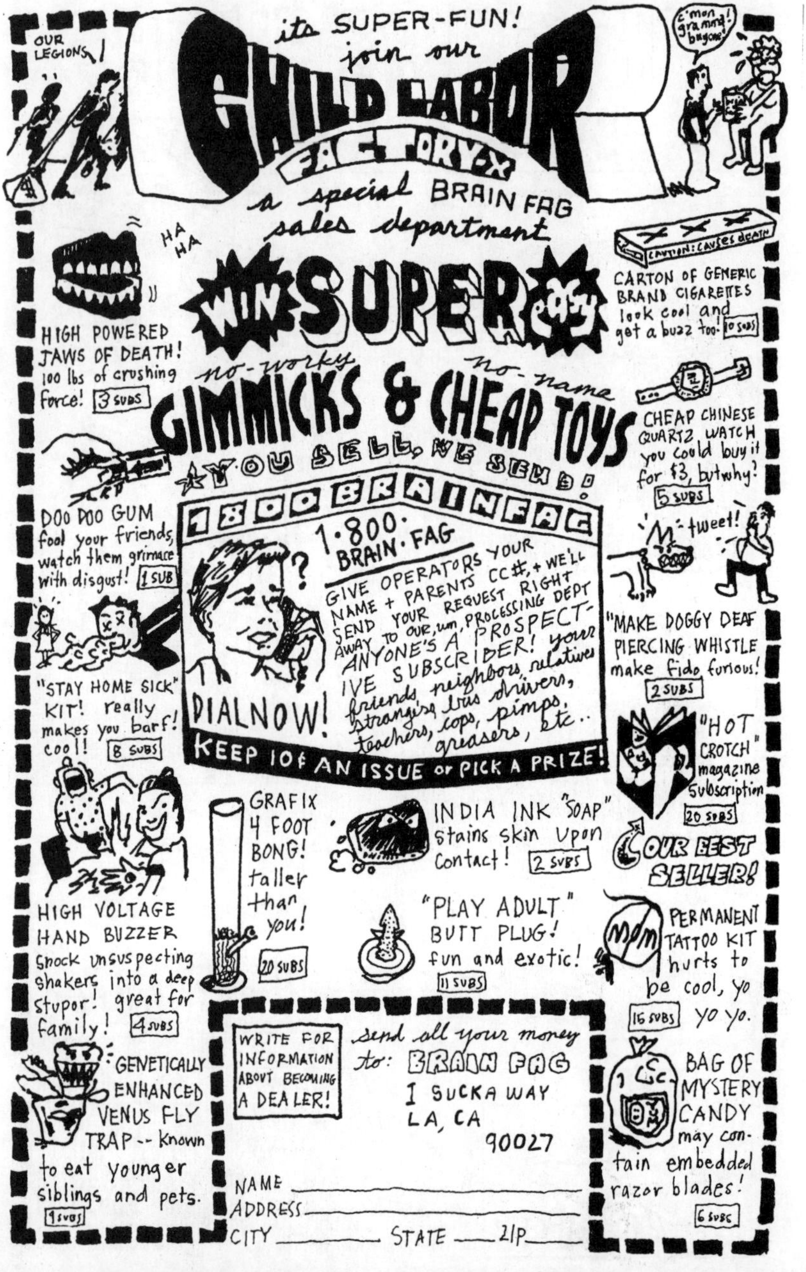

its SUPER-FUN!
join our
CHILD LABOR
FACTORY-X
a special BRAIN FAG
sales department
OUR LEGIONS!
c'mon gramma! buy one!
HA HA
WIN SUPER easy
no-worky no-name
GIMMICKS & CHEAP TOYS
YOU SELL, WE SEND!
HIGH POWERED JAWS OF DEATH! 100 lbs of crushing force! 3 SUBS
CAUTION: CAUSES DEATH
CARTON OF GENERIC BRAND CIGARETTES look cool and get a buzz too! 10 SUBS
CHEAP CHINESE QUARTZ WATCH you could buy it for $3, but why? 5 SUBS
DOO DOO GUM fool your friends, watch them grimace with disgust! 1 SUB
1800BRAINFAG
1·800· BRAIN·FAG
GIVE OPERATORS YOUR NAME + PARENTS CC#, + WE'LL SEND YOUR REQUEST RIGHT AWAY TO OUR, um, PROCESSING DEPT
ANYONE'S A PROSPECTIVE SUBSCRIBER! your friends, neighbors, relatives, strangers, bus drivers, teachers, cops, pimps, greasers, etc..
DIALNOW!
KEEP 10¢ AN ISSUE or PICK A PRIZE!
tweet!
"MAKE DOGGY DEAF PIERCING WHISTLE make fido furious! 2 SUBS
"STAY HOME SICK" KIT! really makes you barf! cool! 8 SUBS
"HOT CROTCH" magazine subscription 20 SUBS
OUR BEST SELLER!
GRAFIX 4 FOOT BONG! taller than you! 20 SUBS
INDIA INK "SOAP" stains skin upon contact! 2 SUBS
HIGH VOLTAGE HAND BUZZER shock unsuspecting shakers into a deep stupor! great for family! 4 SUBS
"PLAY ADULT" BUTT PLUG! fun and exotic! 11 SUBS
MOM
PERMANENT TATTOO KIT hurts to be cool, yo yo yo. 15 SUBS
GENETICALLY ENHANCED VENUS FLY TRAP -- known to eat younger siblings and pets. 9 SUBS
WRITE FOR INFORMATION ABOUT BECOMING A DEALER!
send all your money to: BRAIN FAG
I SUCKA WAY
LA, CA
90027
NAME
ADDRESS
CITY STATE ZIP
BAG OF MYSTERY CANDY may contain embedded razor blades! 6 SUBS

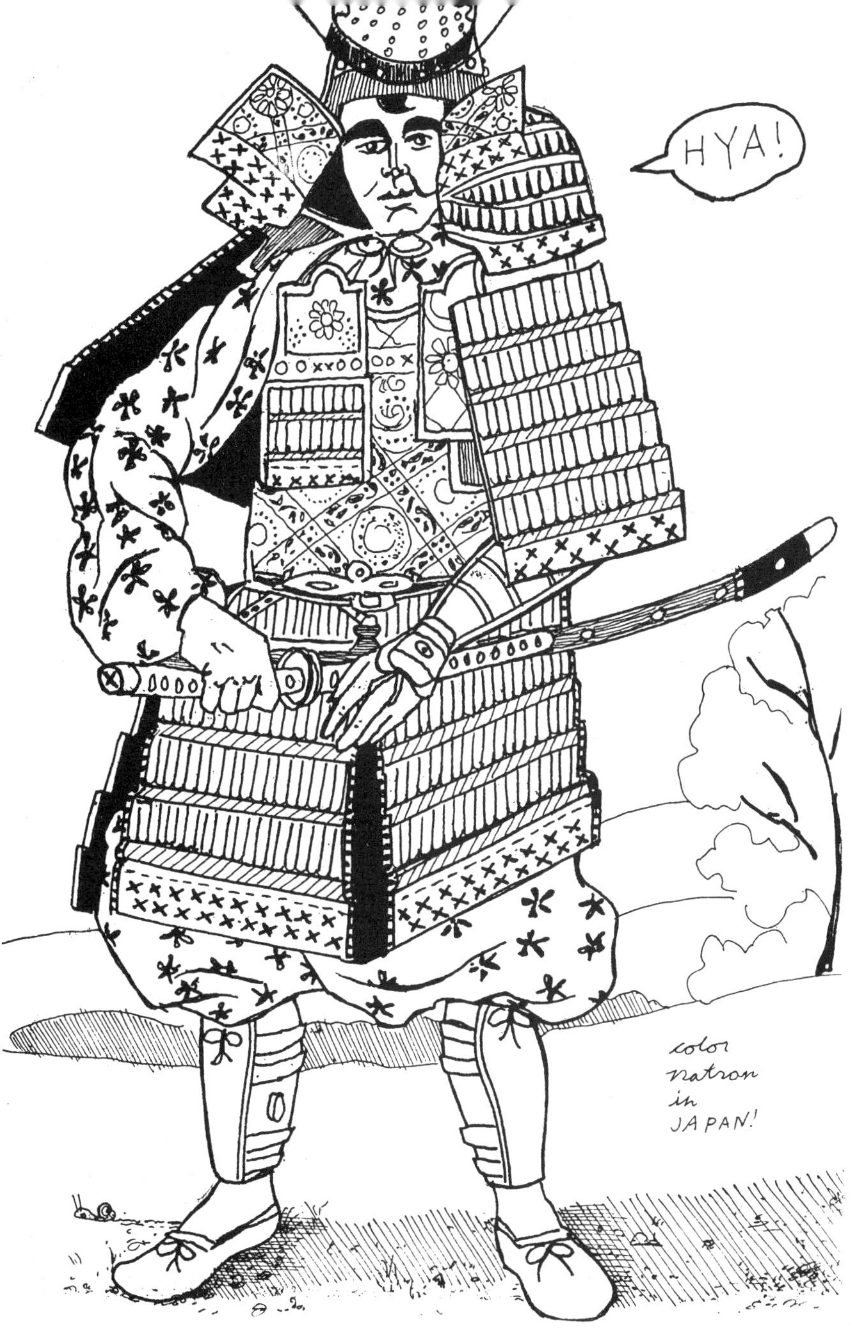
HYA!
color
natron
in
JAPAN!

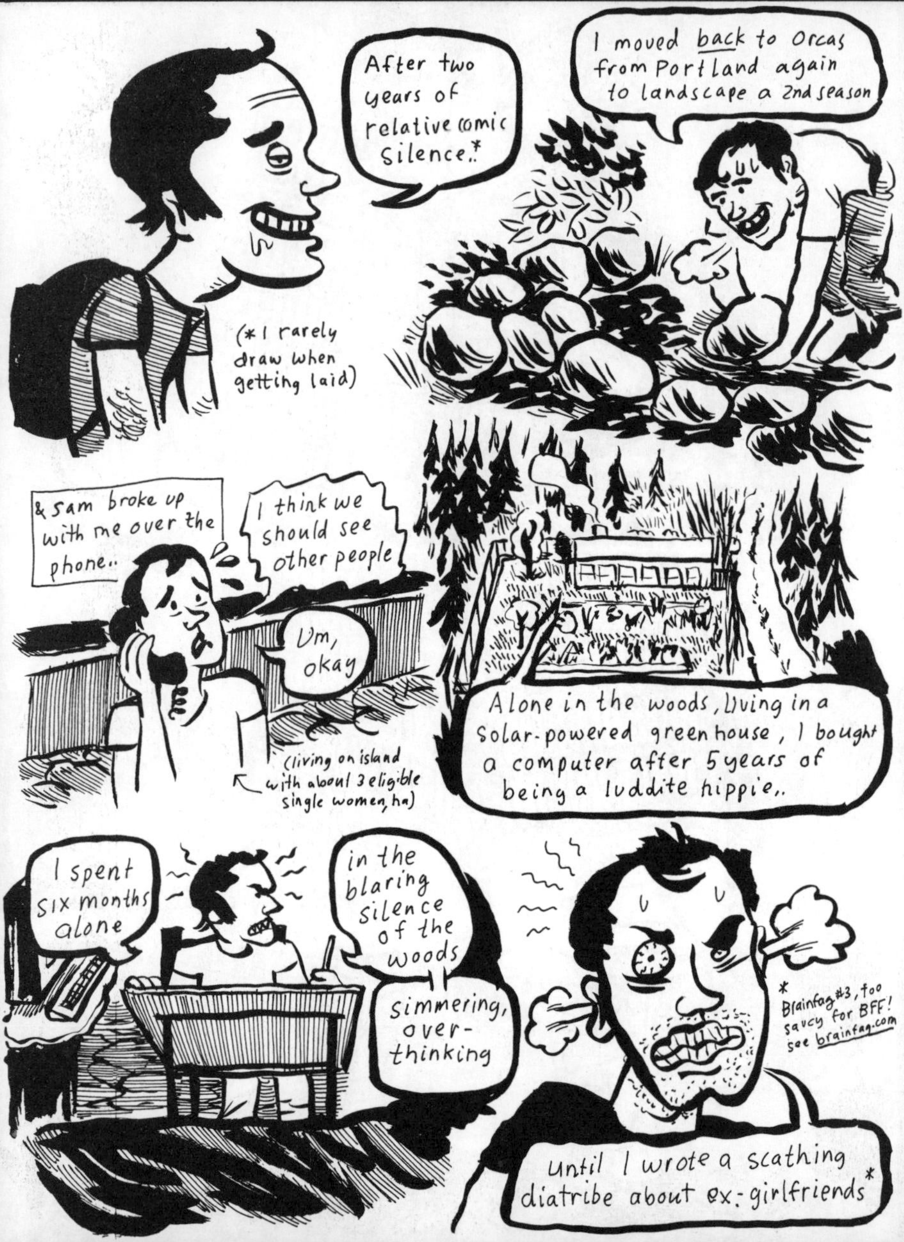
After two years of relative comic silence.*
(*I rarely draw when getting laid)
I moved back to Orcas from Portland again to landscape a 2nd season
& Sam broke up with me over the phone..
I think we should see other people
Um, okay
(living on island with about 3 eligible single women, ha)
Alone in the woods, living in a solar-powered greenhouse, I bought a computer after 5 years of being a luddite hippie..
I spent six months alone
in the blaring silence of the woods
simmering, over-thinking
Until I wrote a scathing diatribe about ex-girlfriends*
* Brainfag #3, too saucy for BFF! see brainfag.com

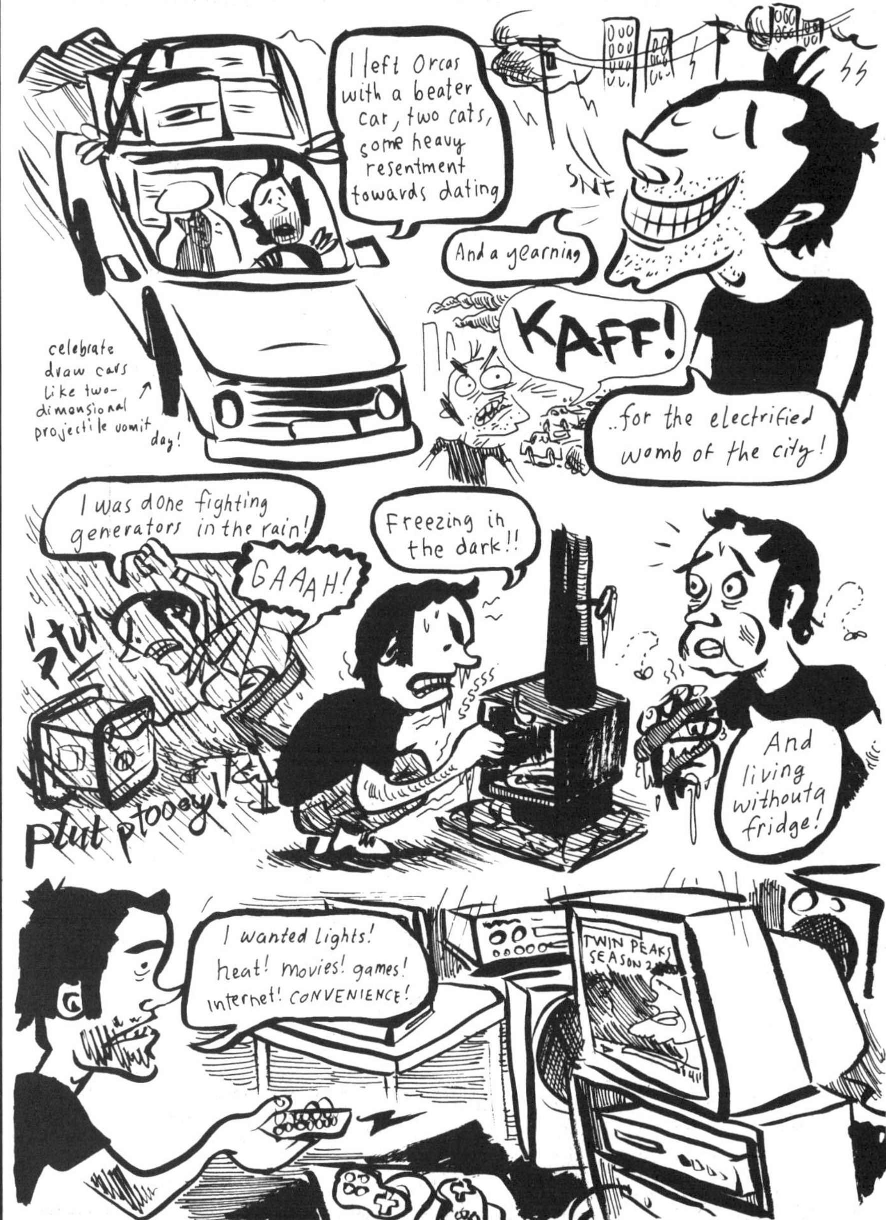
I left Orcas with a beater car, two cats, some heavy resentment towards dating
SNF
And a yearning
KAFF!
..for the electrified womb of the city!
celebrate draw cars like two-dimensional projectile vomit day!
I was done fighting generators in the rain!
GAAAH!
ptut
ptut ptooey!
Freezing in the dark!!
SSSSS
And living withouta fridge!
I wanted lights! heat! movies! games! internet! CONVENIENCE!
TWIN PEAKS SEASON 2

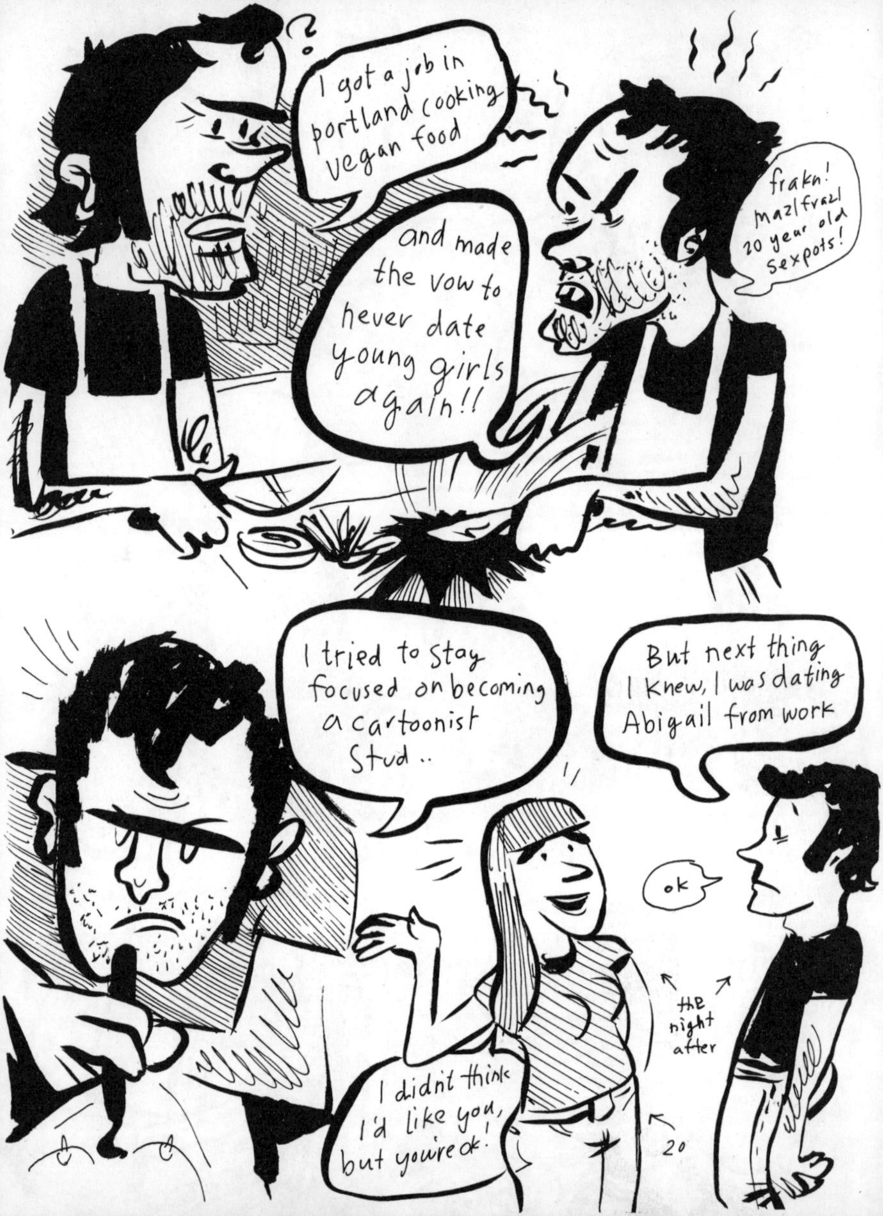
I got a job in portland cooking vegan food
and made the vow to never date young girls again!!
frakn! mazlfrazl 20 year old sexpots!
I tried to stay focused on becoming a cartoonist stud ..
But next thing I knew, I was dating Abigail from work
I didn't think I'd like you, but you're ok!
ok
the night after

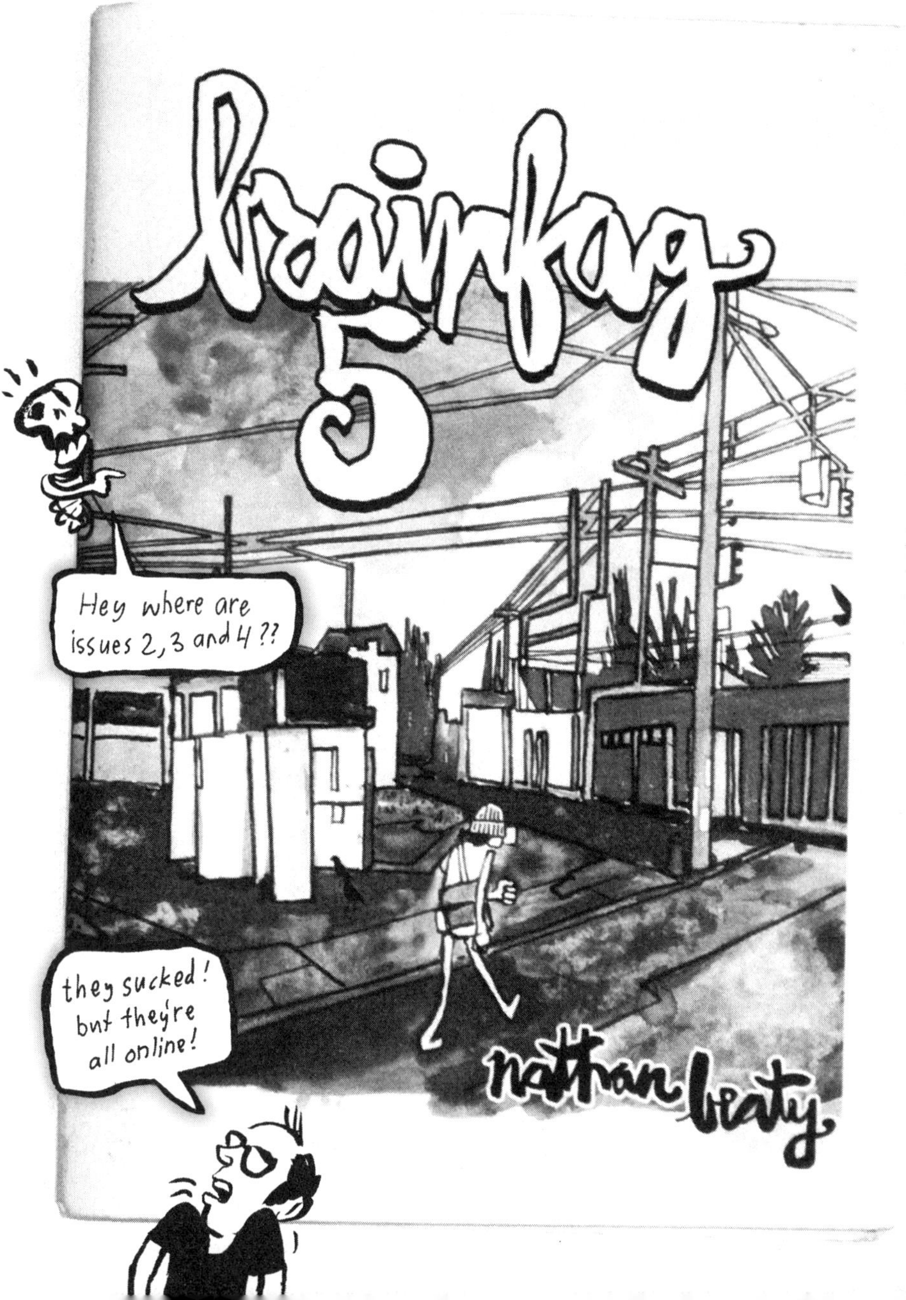
brainfag
5
Hey where are issues 2, 3 and 4 ??
they sucked! but they're all online!
nathan beaty

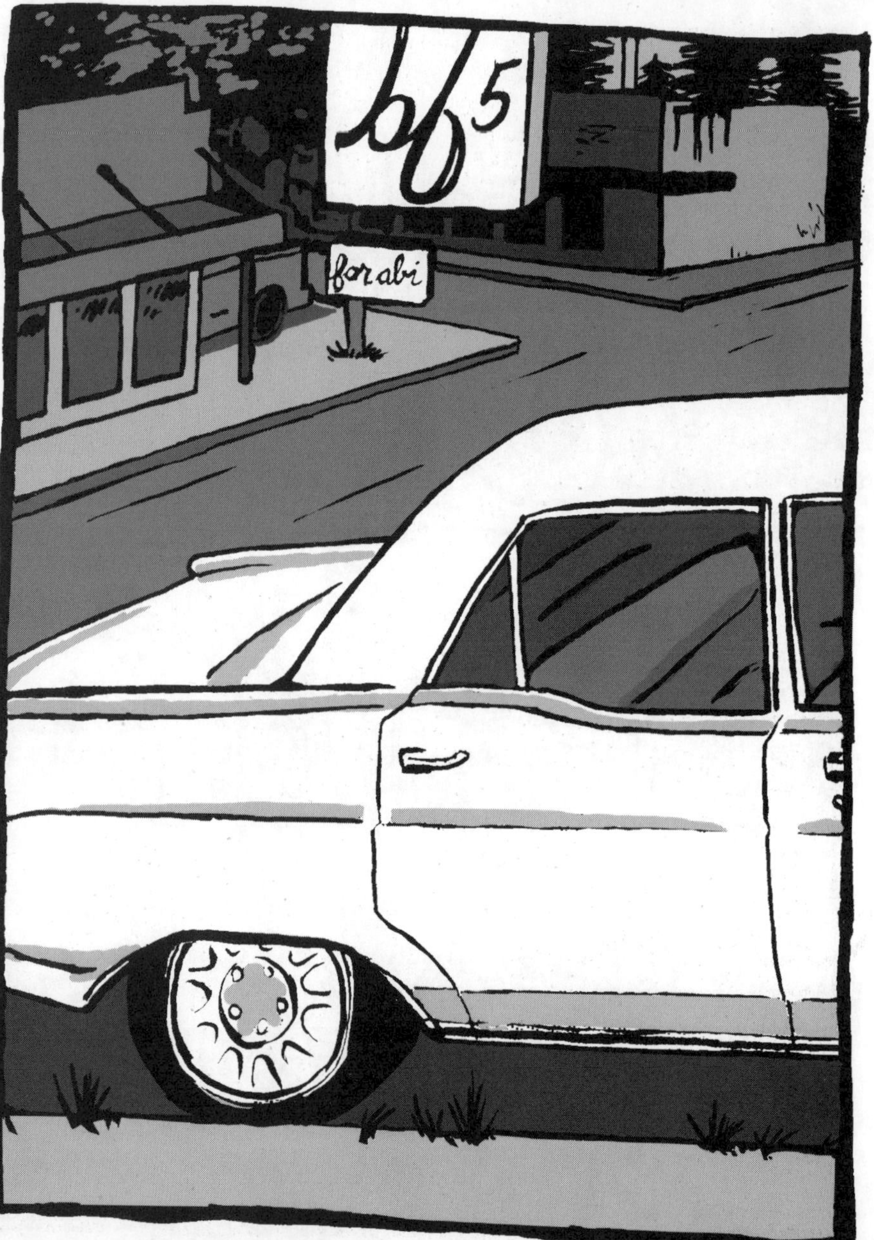
for abi

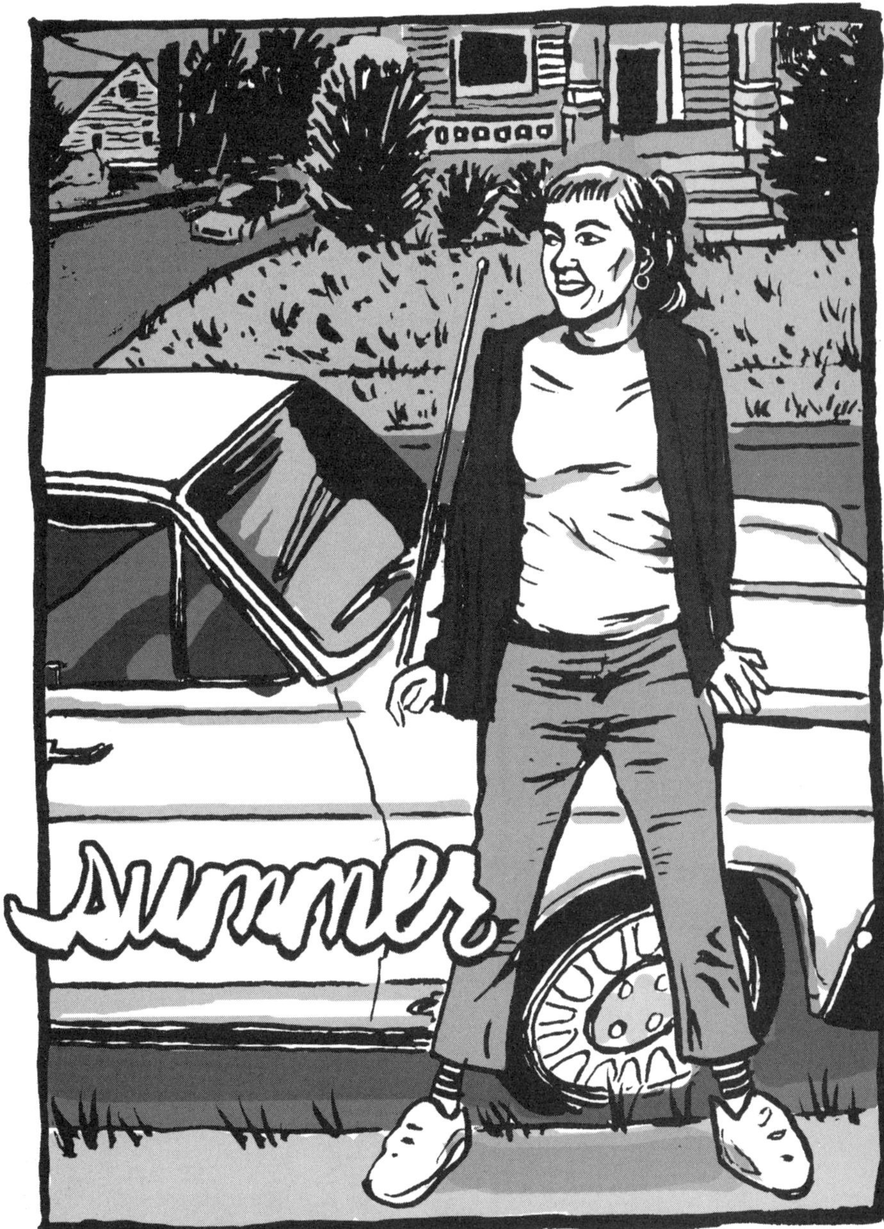
summer

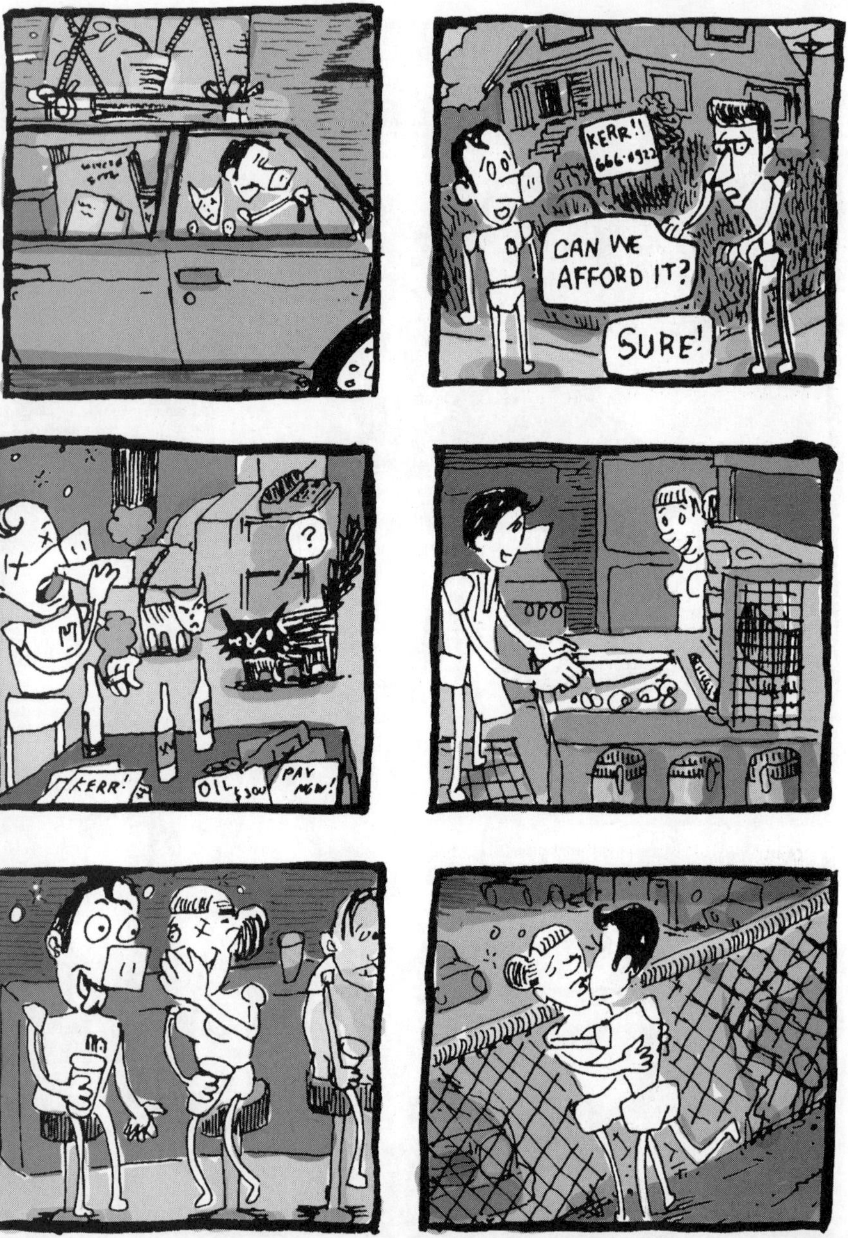
KERR!!
666·8922
CAN WE AFFORD IT?
SURE!
?
KERR!
OIL
PAY NOW!

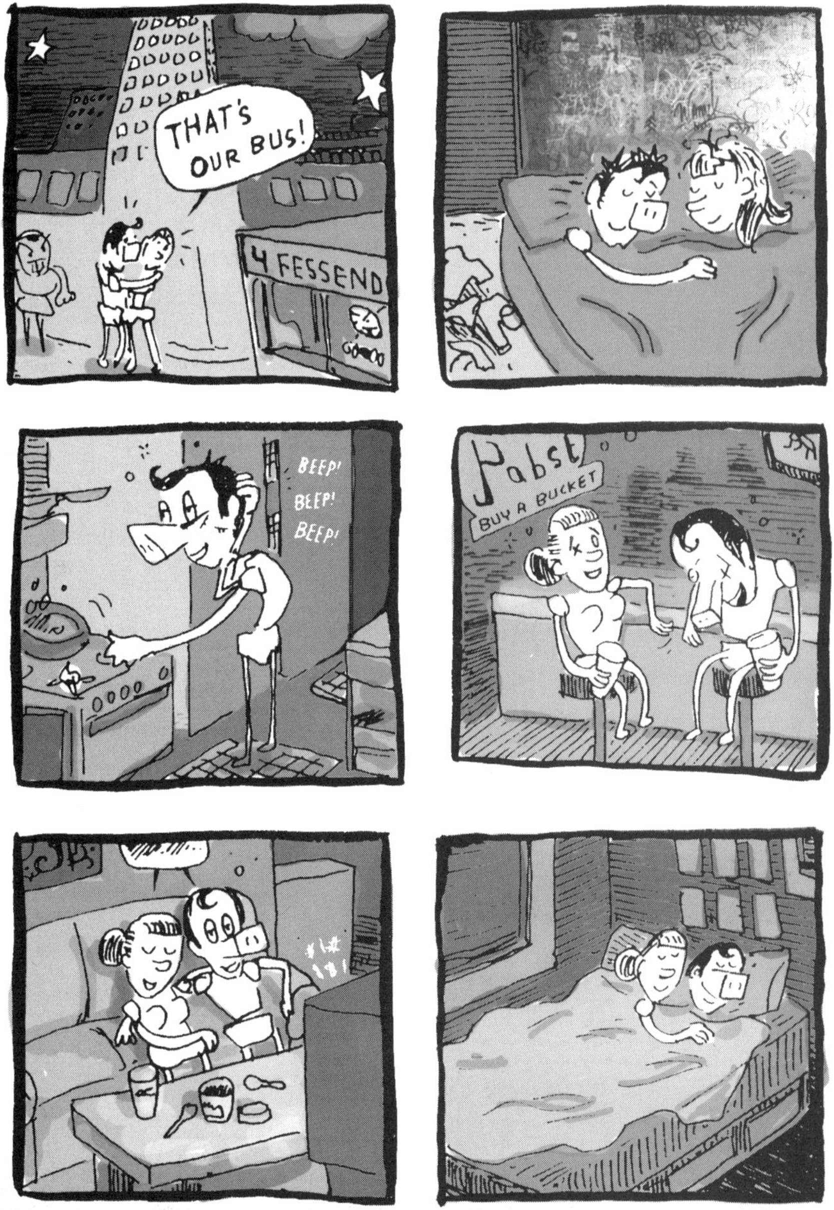
THAT'S OUR BUS!
4 FESSEND
BEEP!
BEEP!
BEEP!
Pabst
BUY A BUCKET

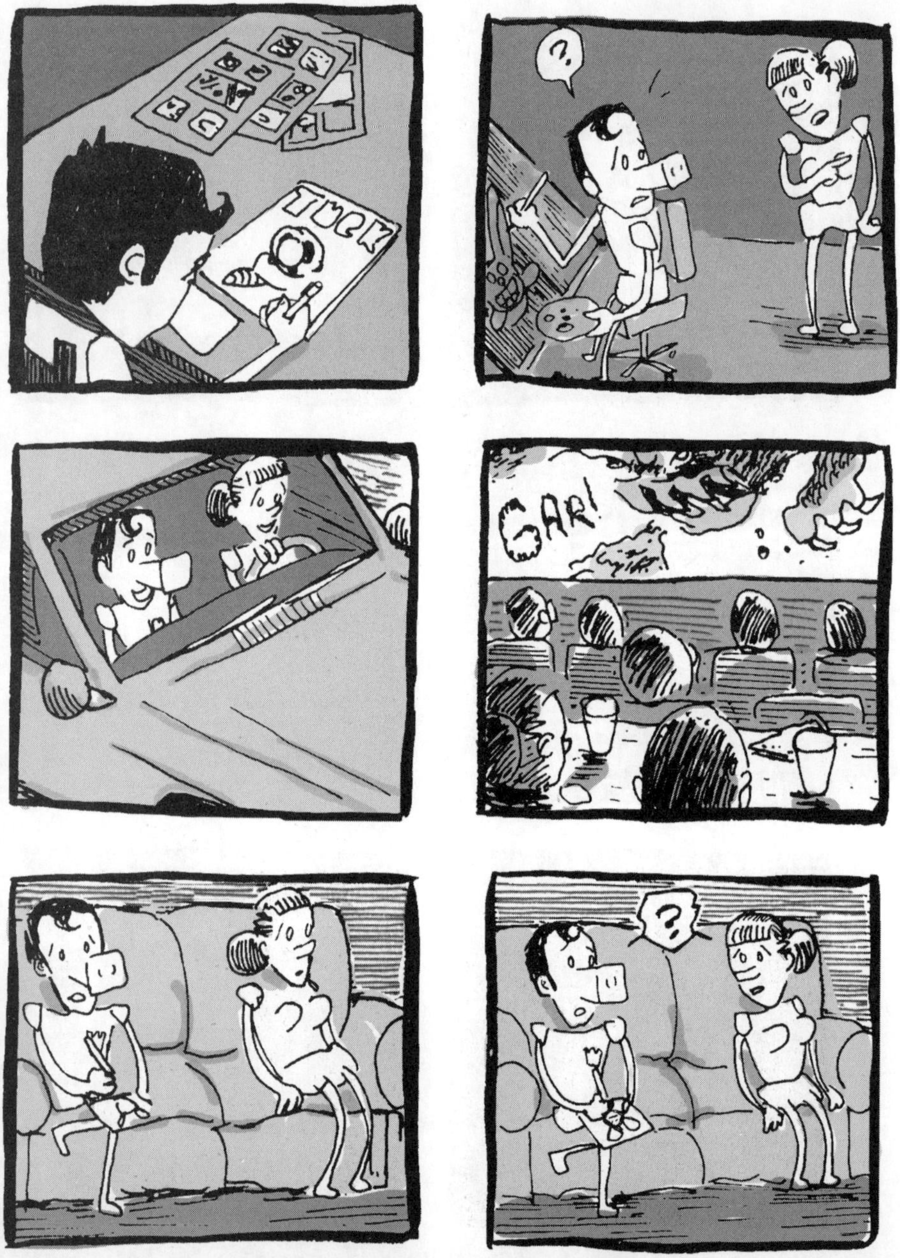
TUCK
?
GAR!
?

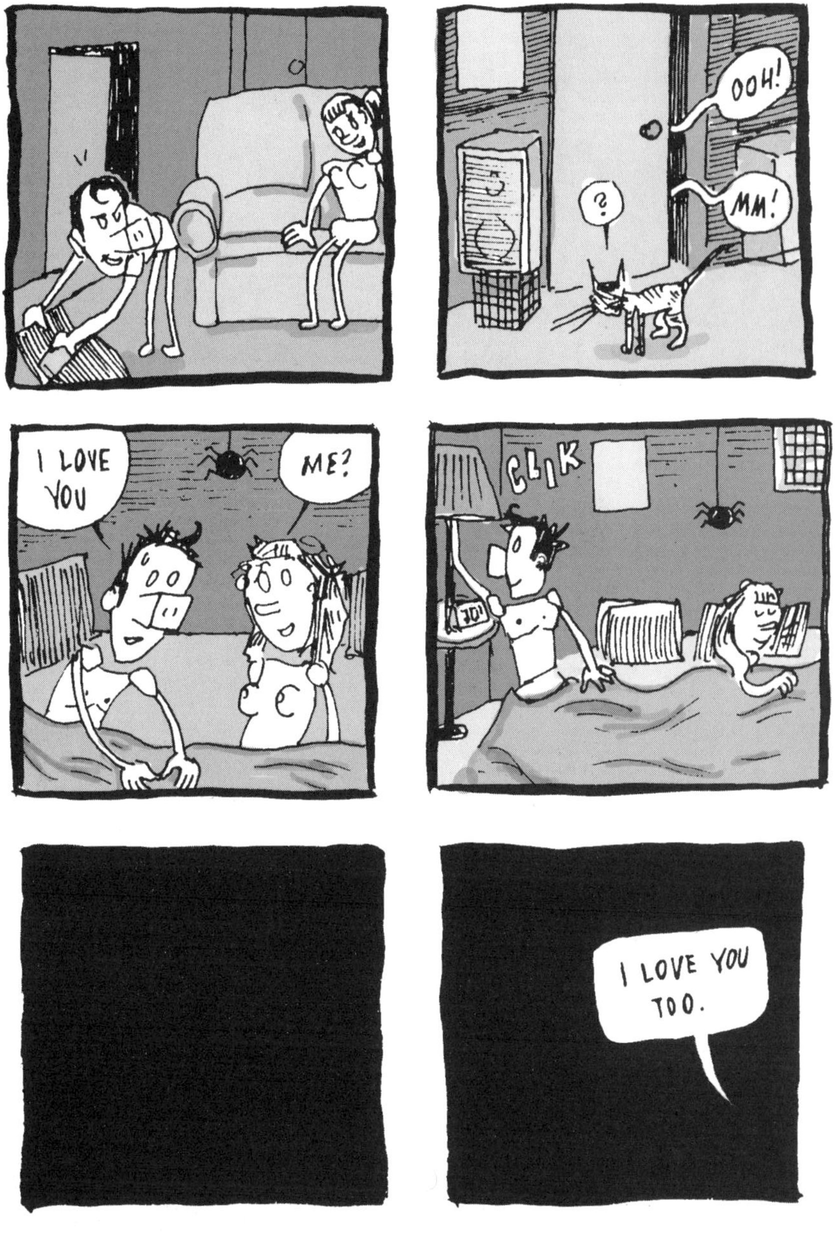
OOH!
?
MM!
I LOVE YOU
ME?
CLIK
I LOVE YOU TOO.

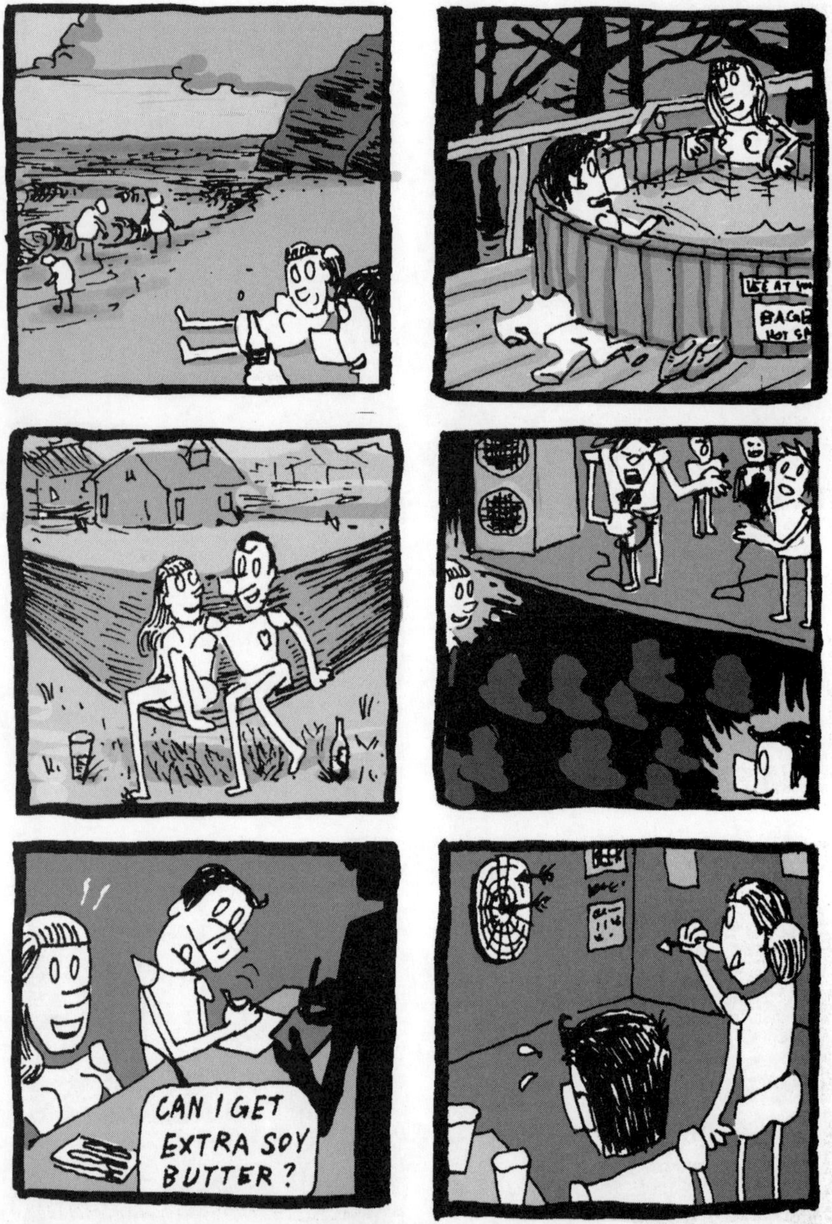
CAN I GET EXTRA SOY BUTTER?

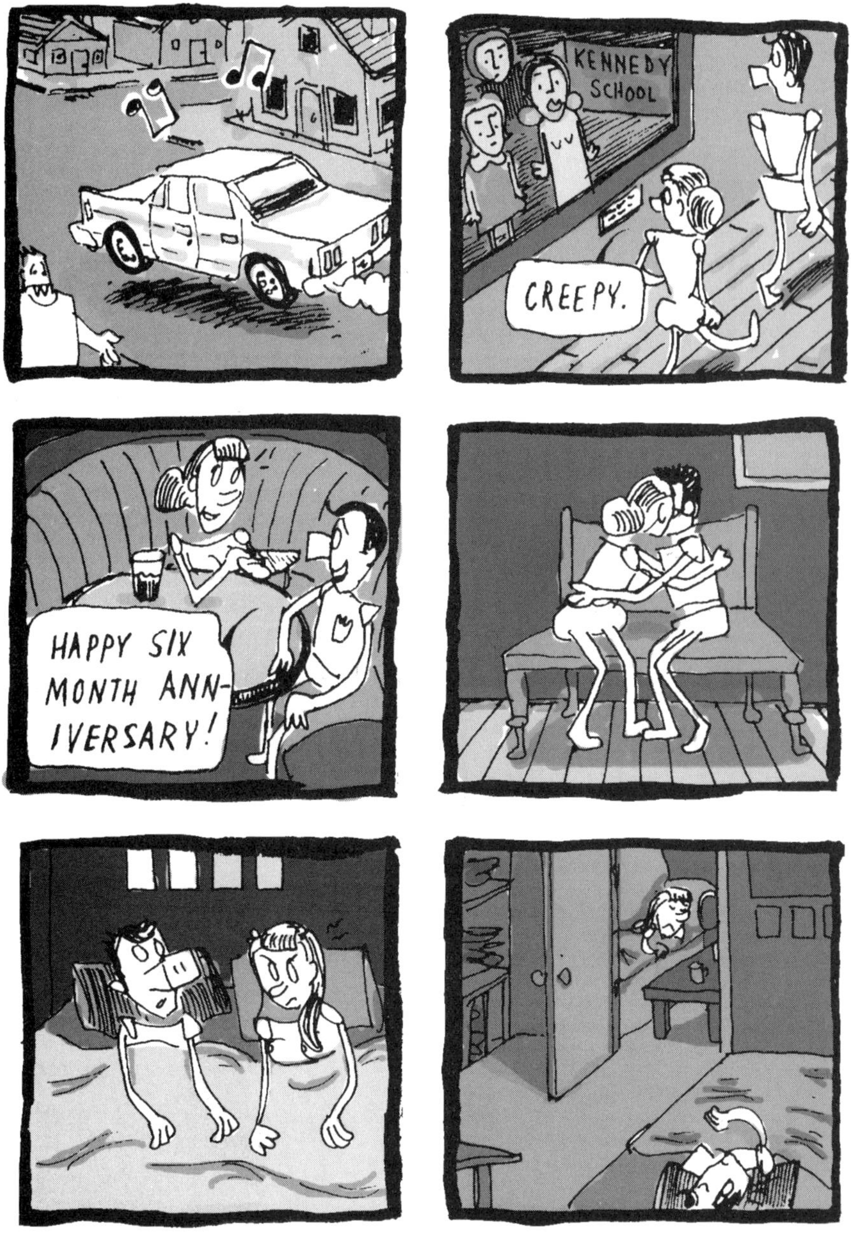
KENNEDY SCHOOL
CREEPY.
HAPPY SIX MONTH ANNIVERSARY!

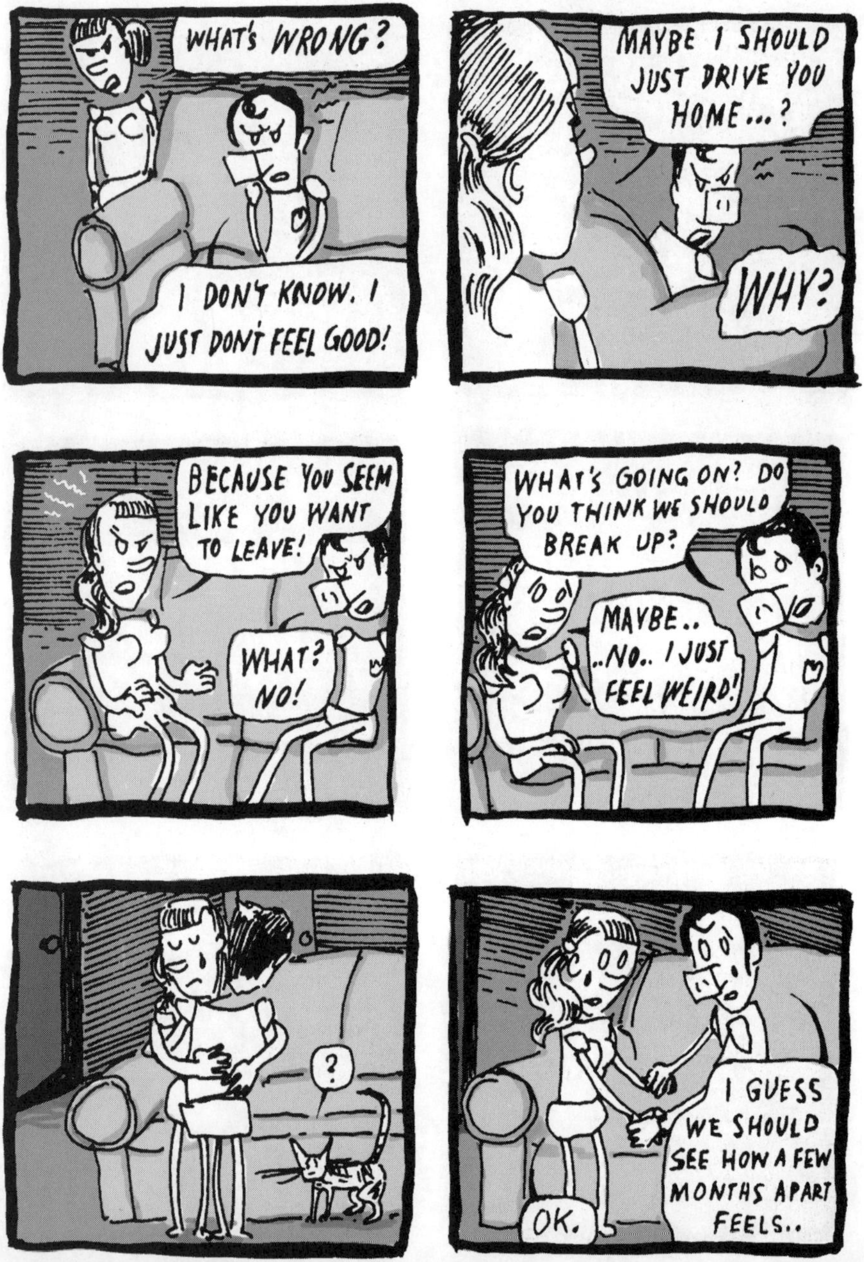
WHAT'S WRONG?
I DON'T KNOW. I JUST DON'T FEEL GOOD!
MAYBE I SHOULD JUST DRIVE YOU HOME...?
WHY?
BECAUSE YOU SEEM LIKE YOU WANT TO LEAVE!
WHAT? NO!
WHAT'S GOING ON? DO YOU THINK WE SHOULD BREAK UP?
MAYBE.. ..NO.. I JUST FEEL WEIRD!
?
I GUESS WE SHOULD SEE HOW A FEW MONTHS APART FEELS..
OK.

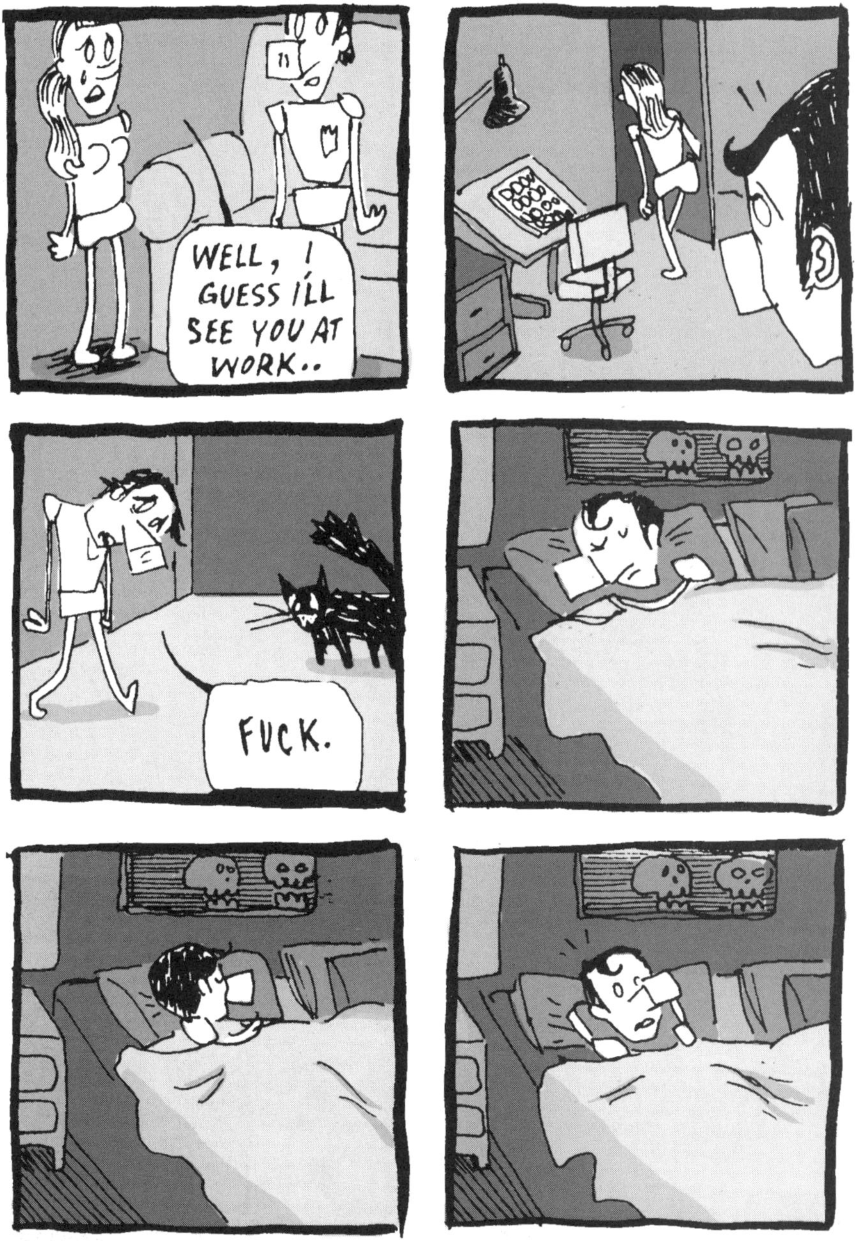
WELL, I GUESS I'LL SEE YOU AT WORK..
FUCK.

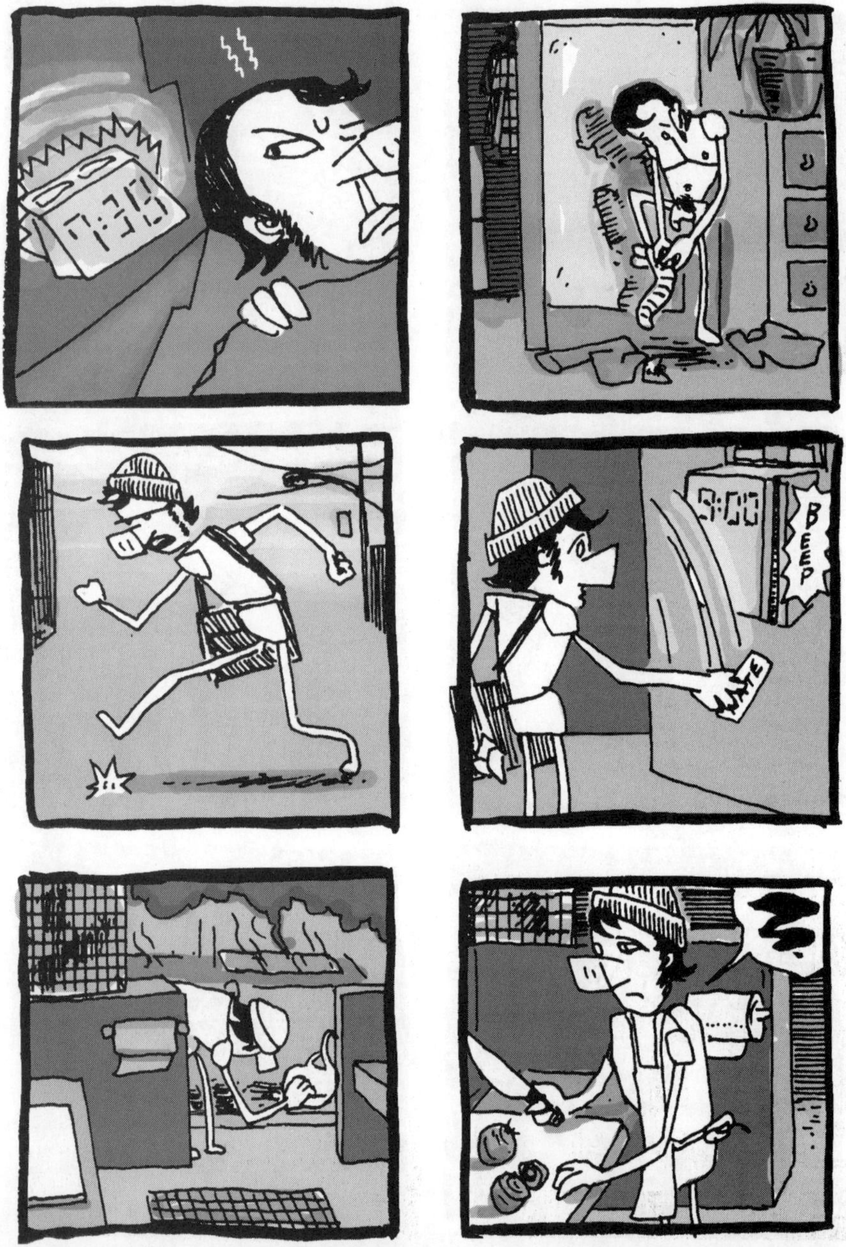
7:38
9:00
BEEP

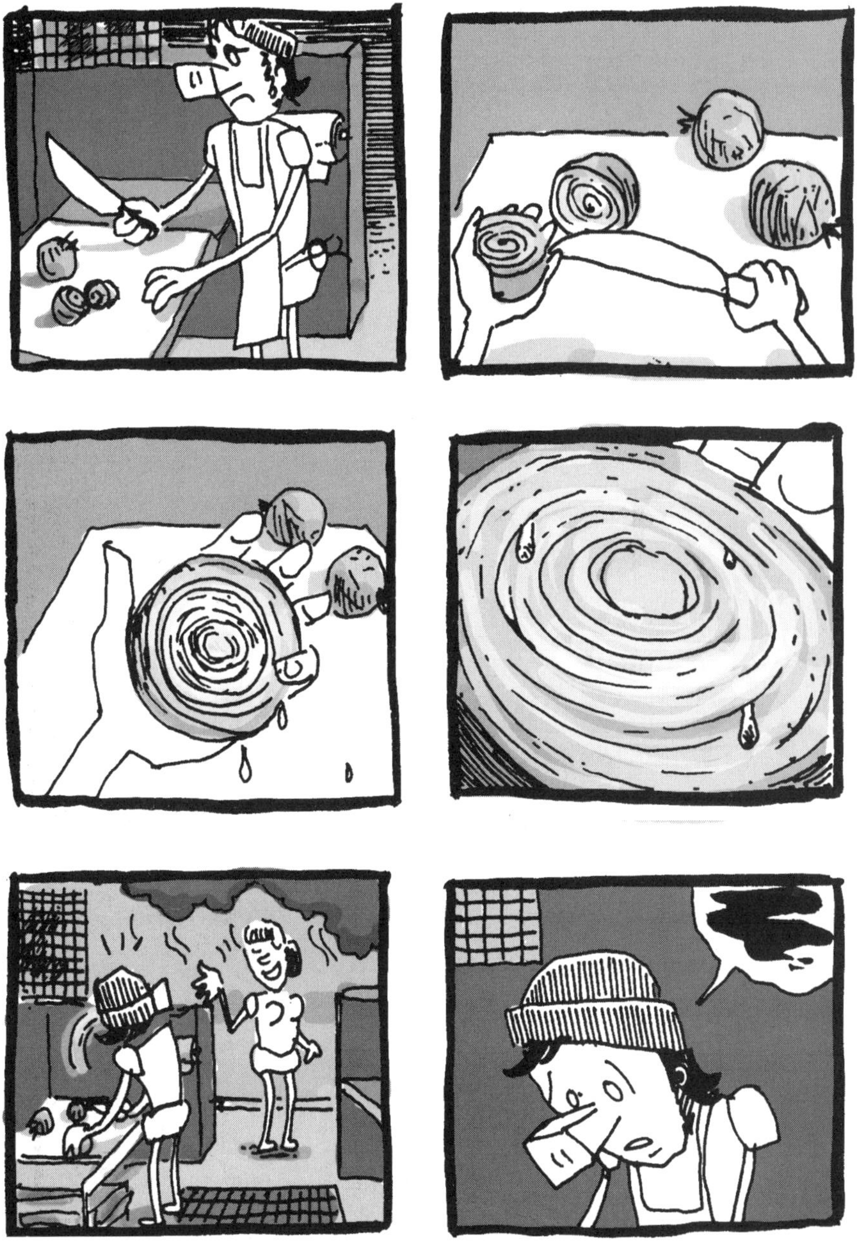

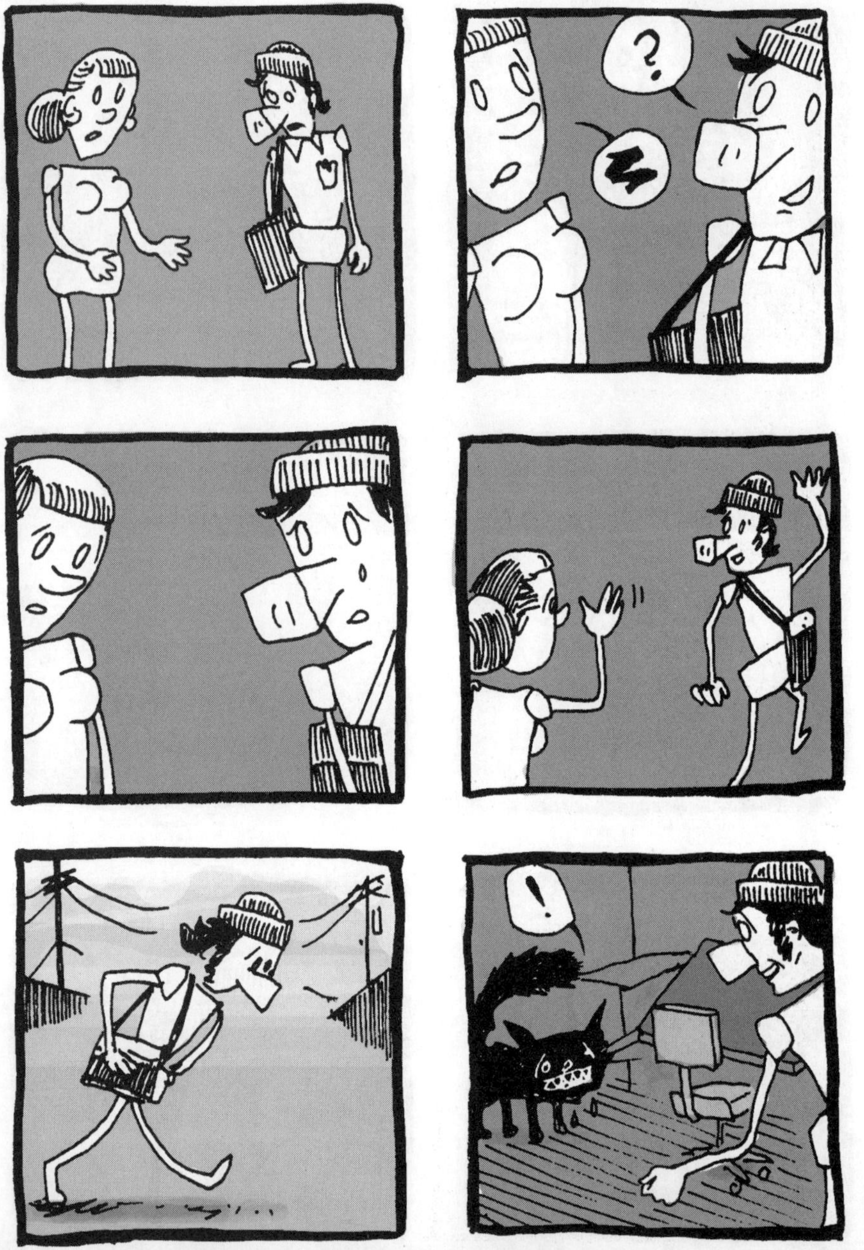
?
!

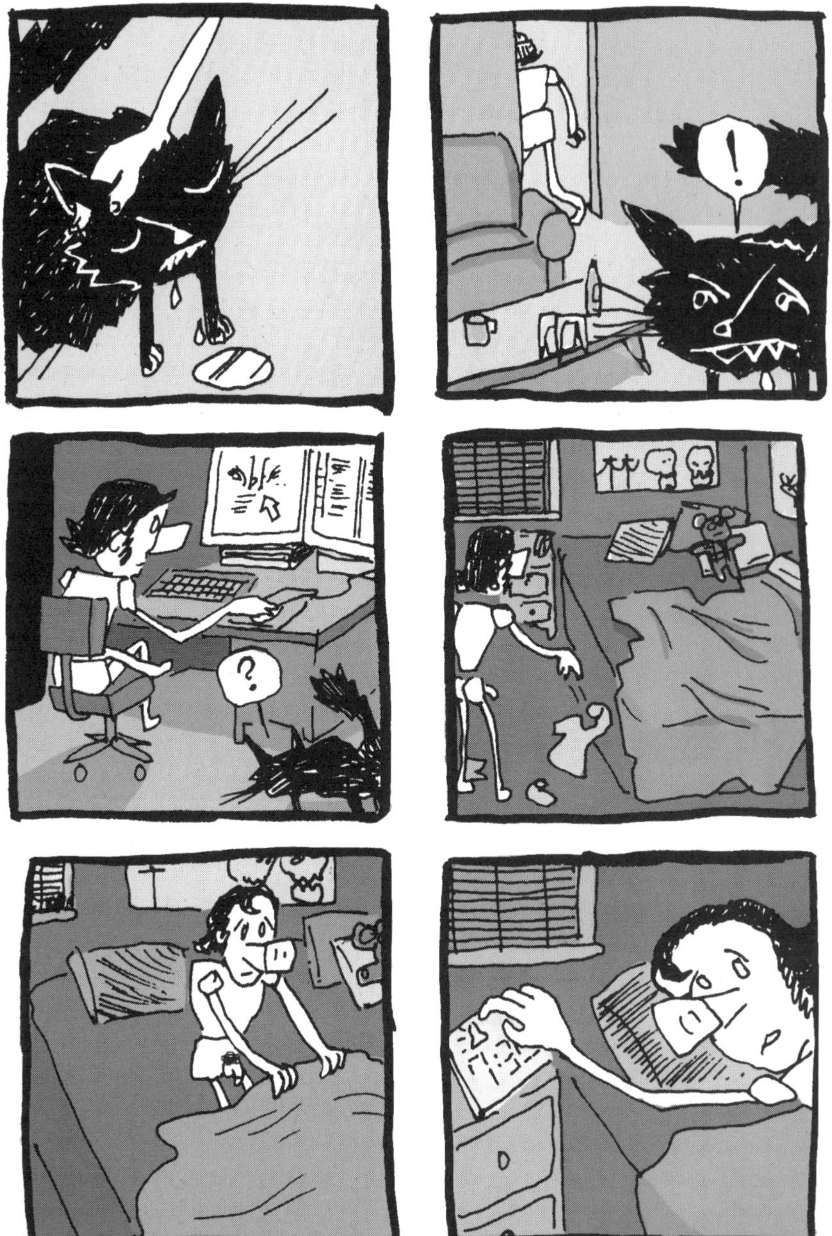
!
?

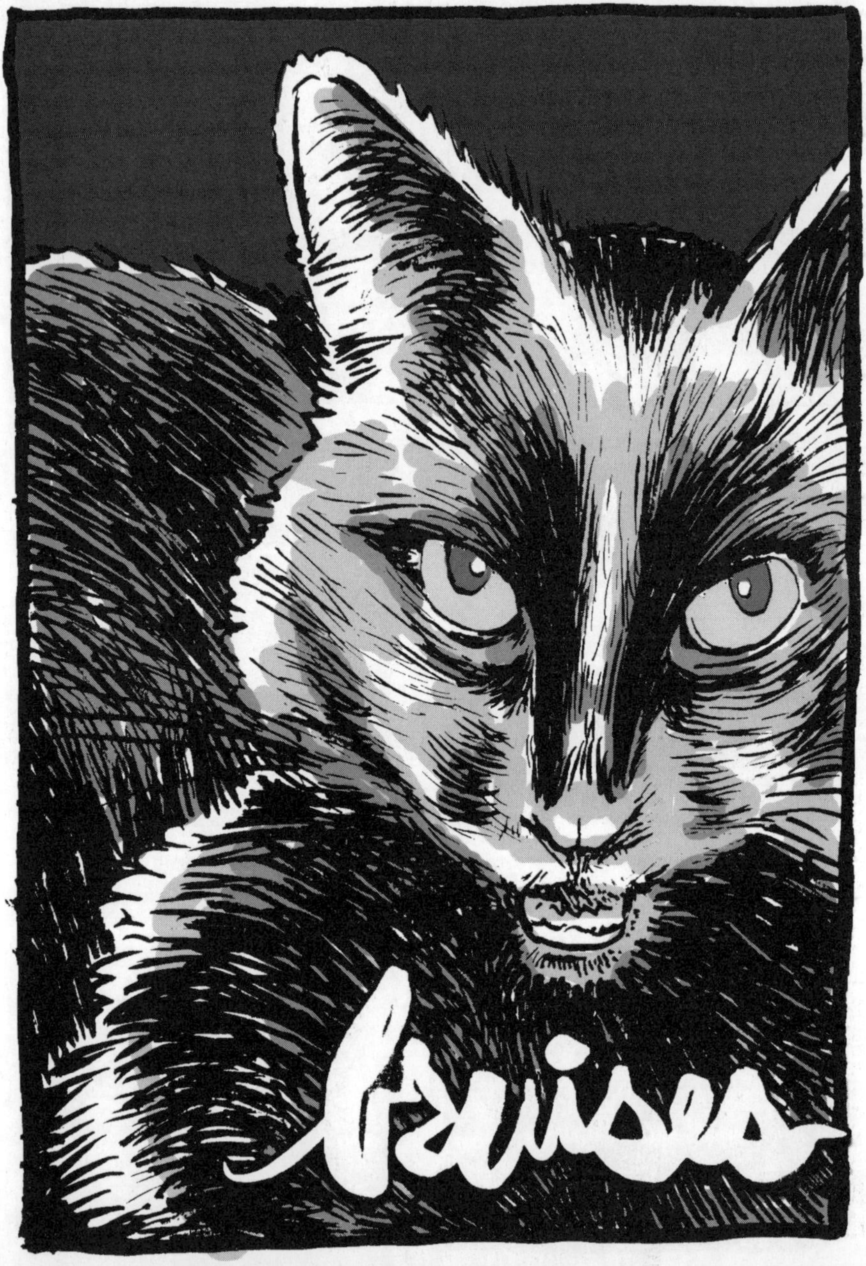
bruises

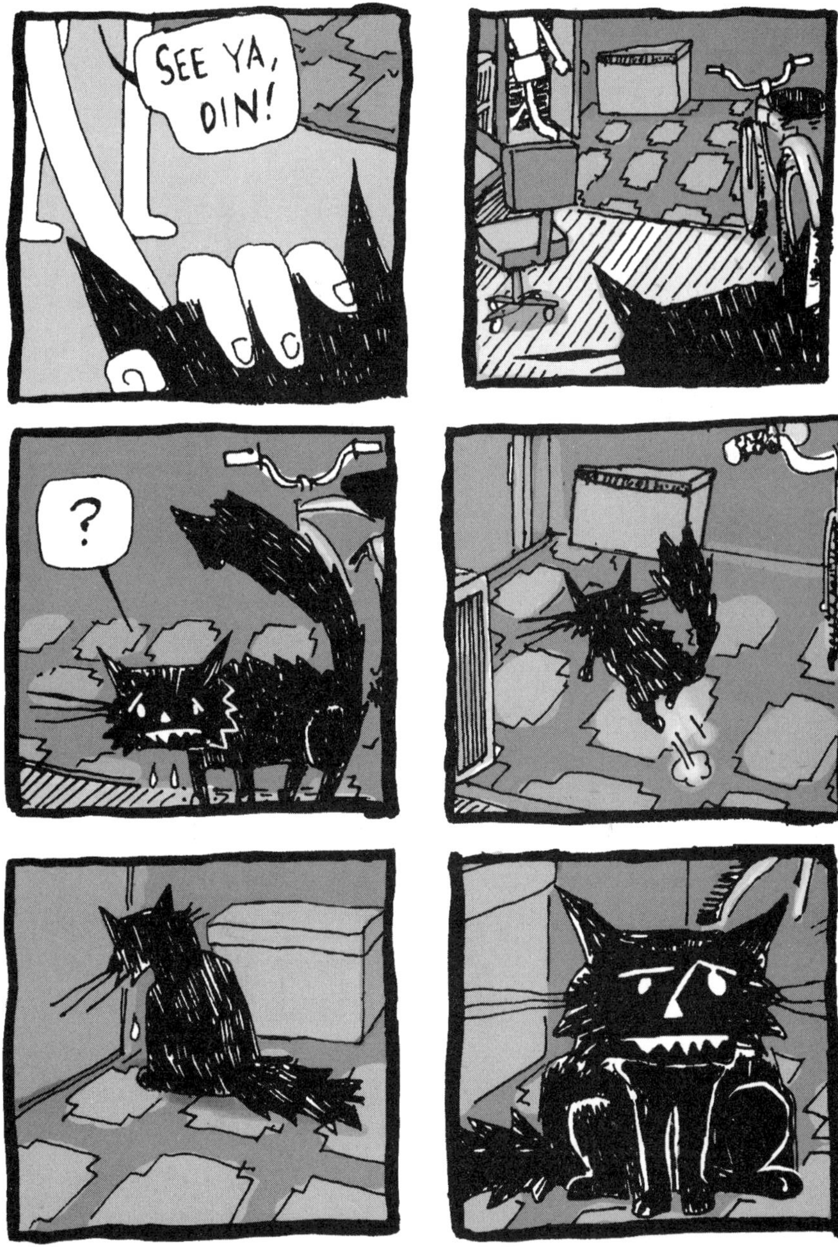
SEE YA, DIN!
?

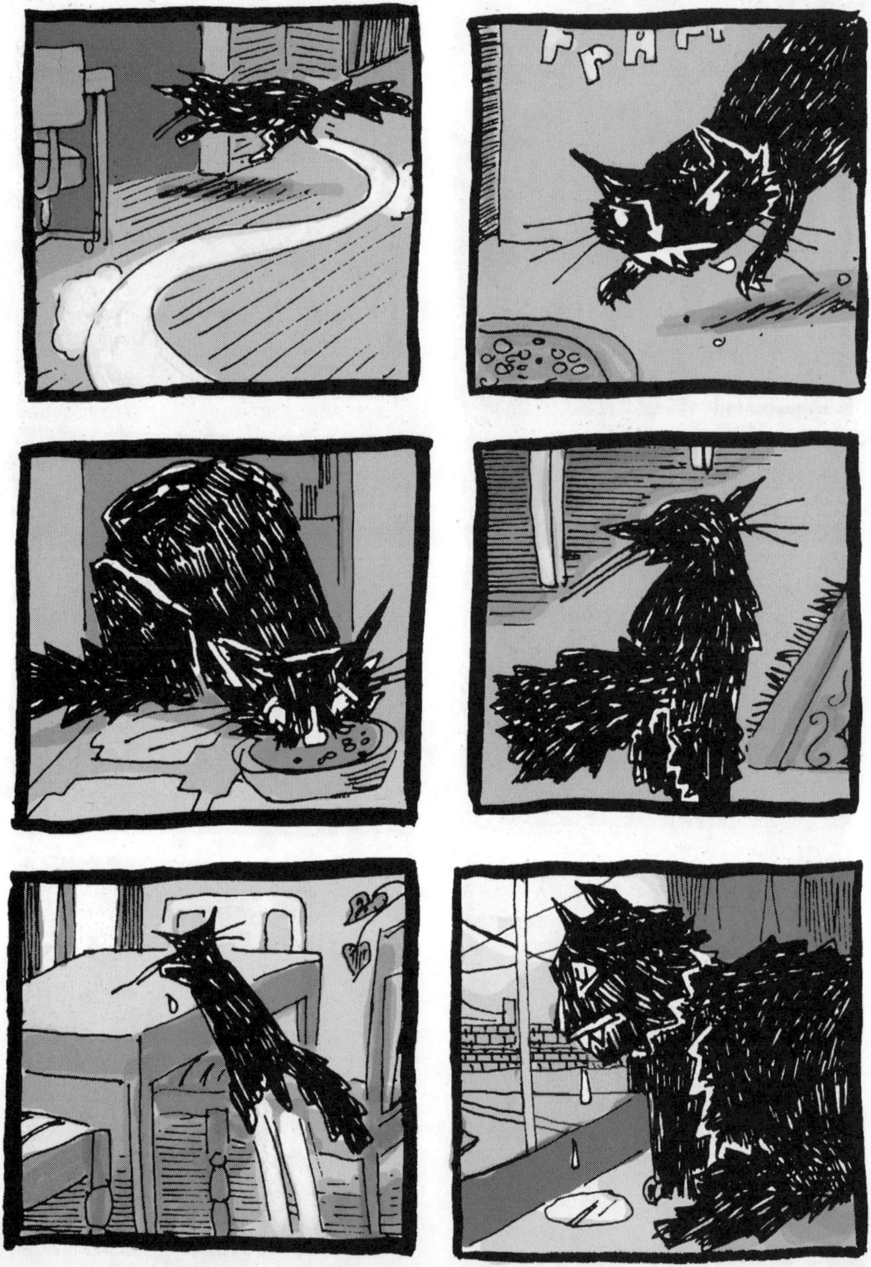

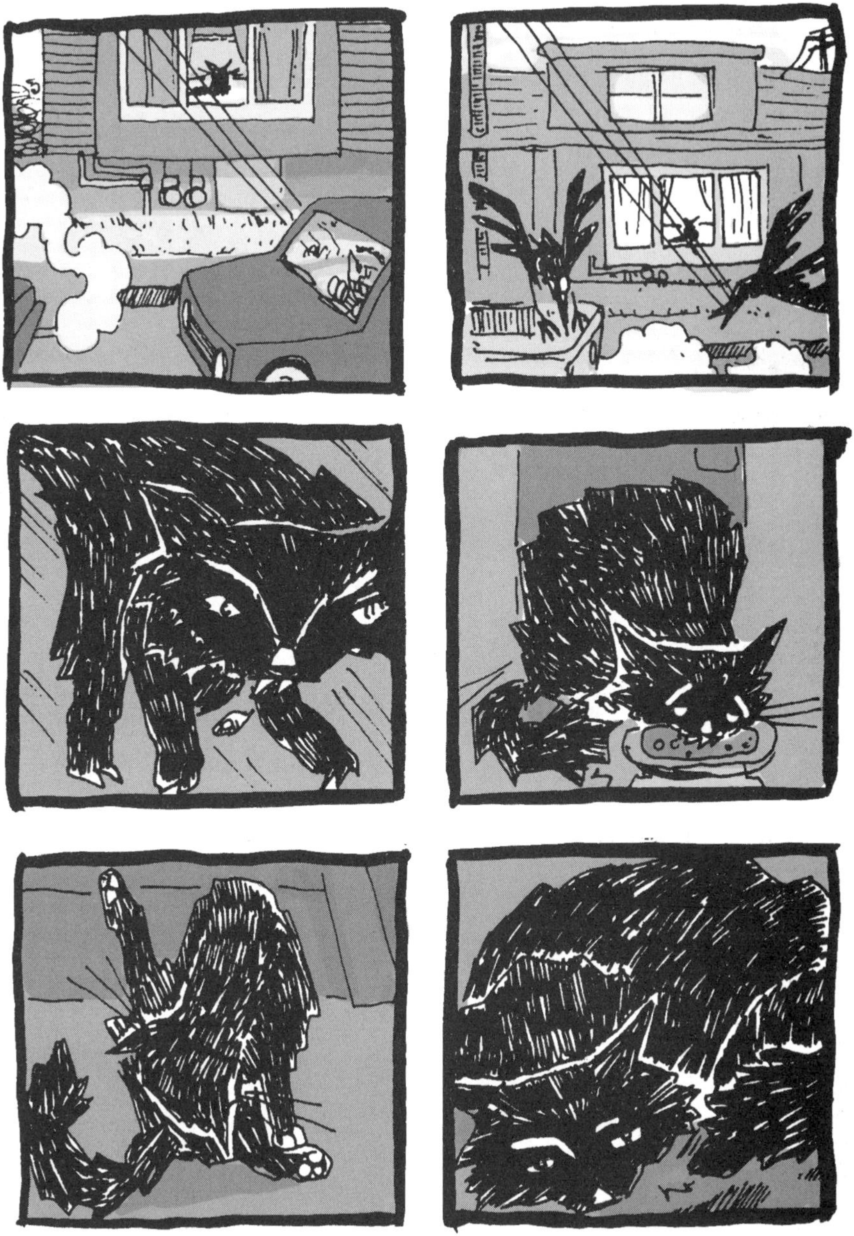

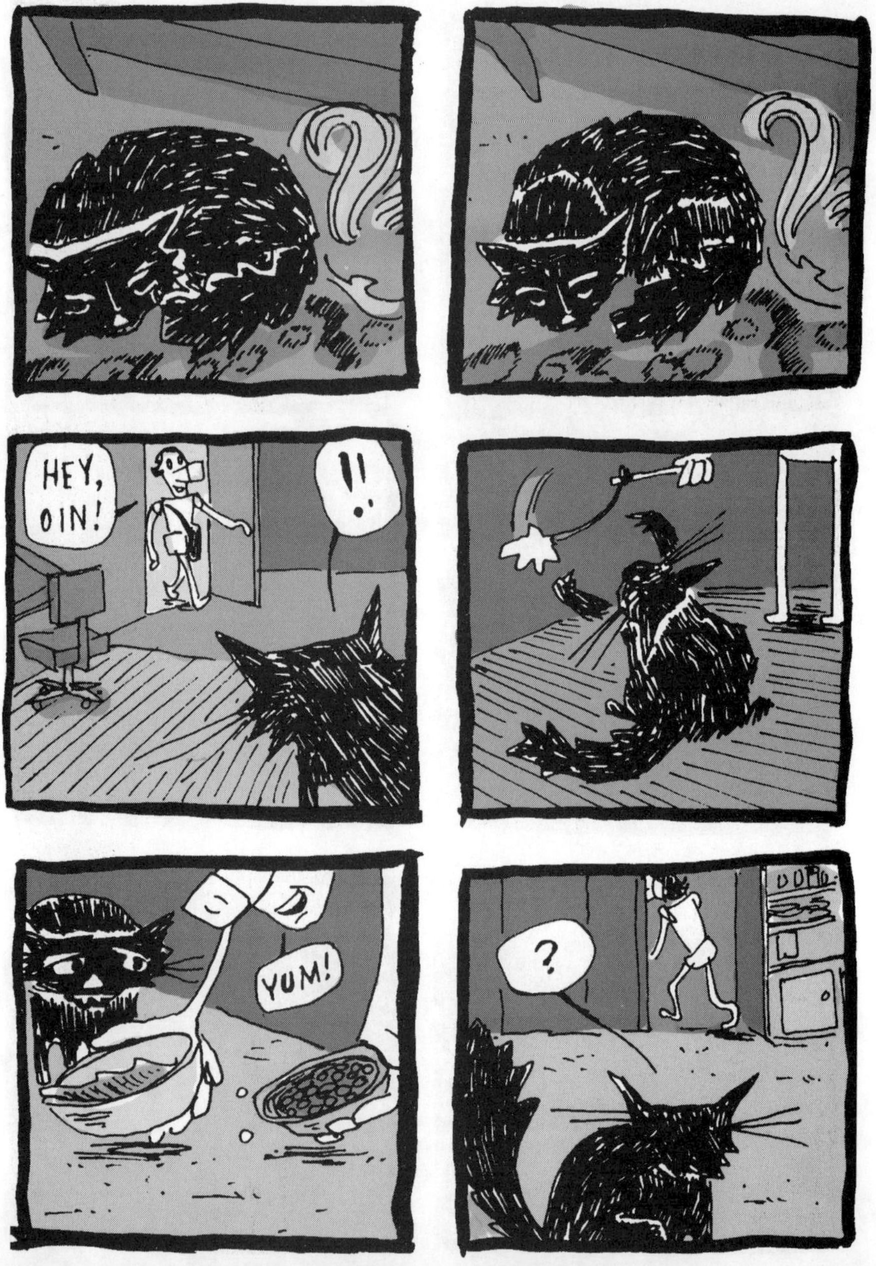
HEY, OIN!
!!
YUM!
?

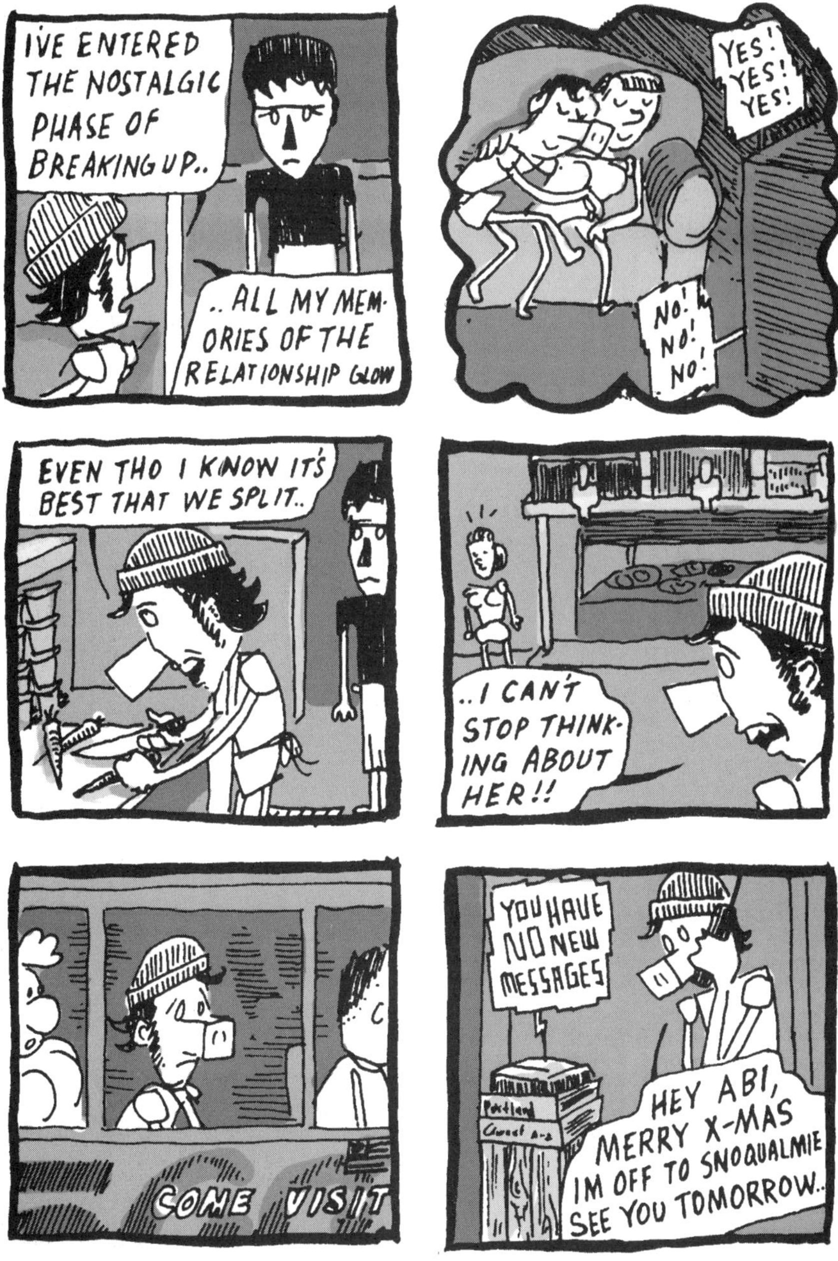
IVE ENTERED THE NOSTALGIC PHASE OF BREAKING UP..
..ALL MY MEMORIES OF THE RELATIONSHIP GLOW
YES! YES! YES!
NO! NO! NO!
EVEN THO I KNOW IT'S BEST THAT WE SPLIT..
..I CAN'T STOP THINKING ABOUT HER!!
COME VISIT
YOU HAVE NO NEW MESSAGES
Portland
HEY ABI, MERRY X-MAS IM OFF TO SNOQUALMIE SEE YOU TOMORROW..

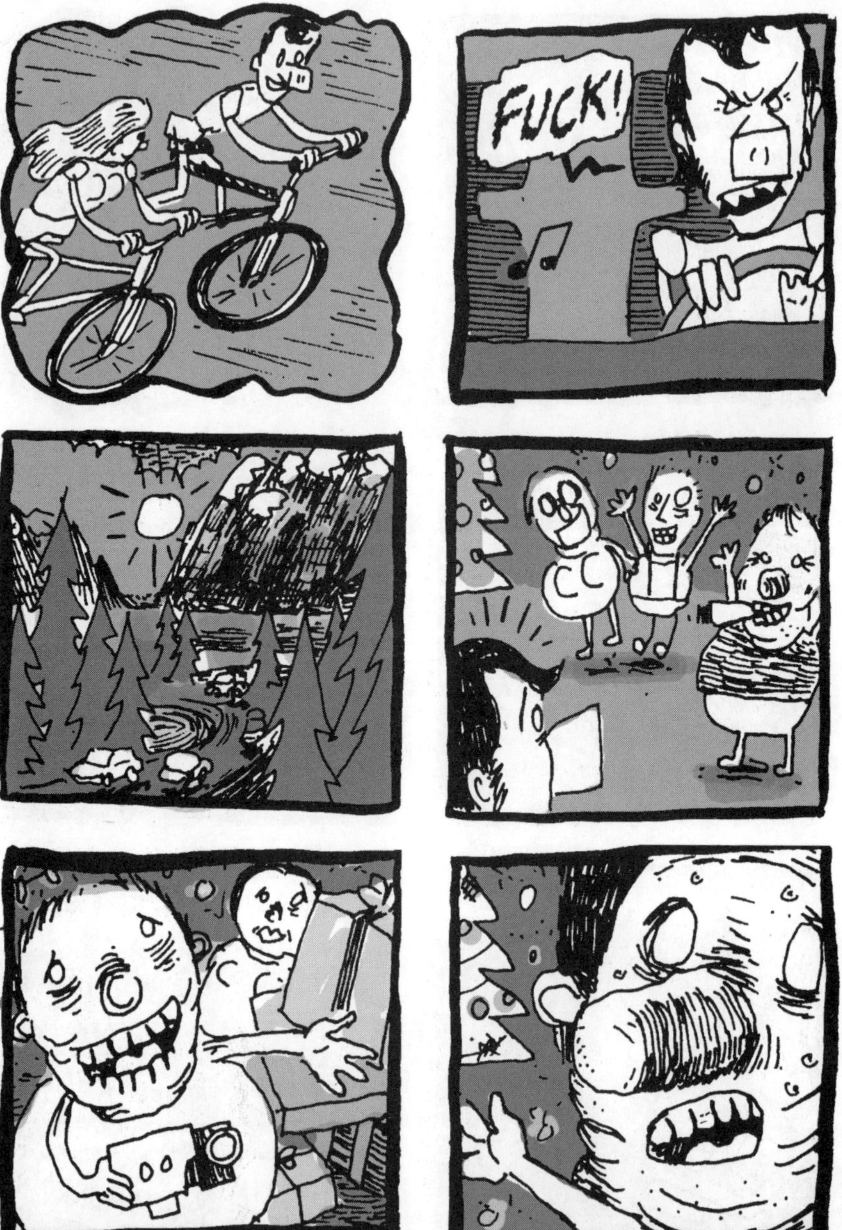
FUCK!

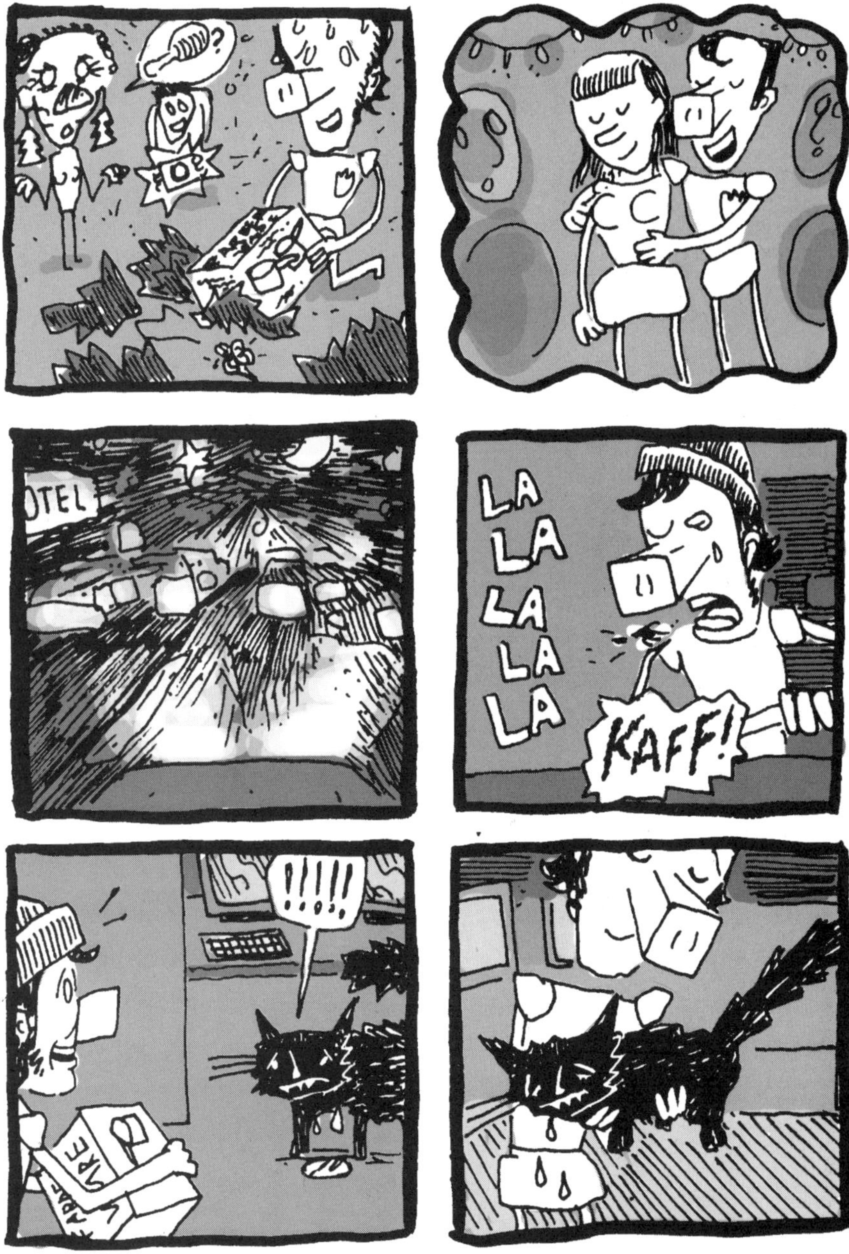
?
OTEL
LA LA LA LA LA LA
KAFF!
!!!!!

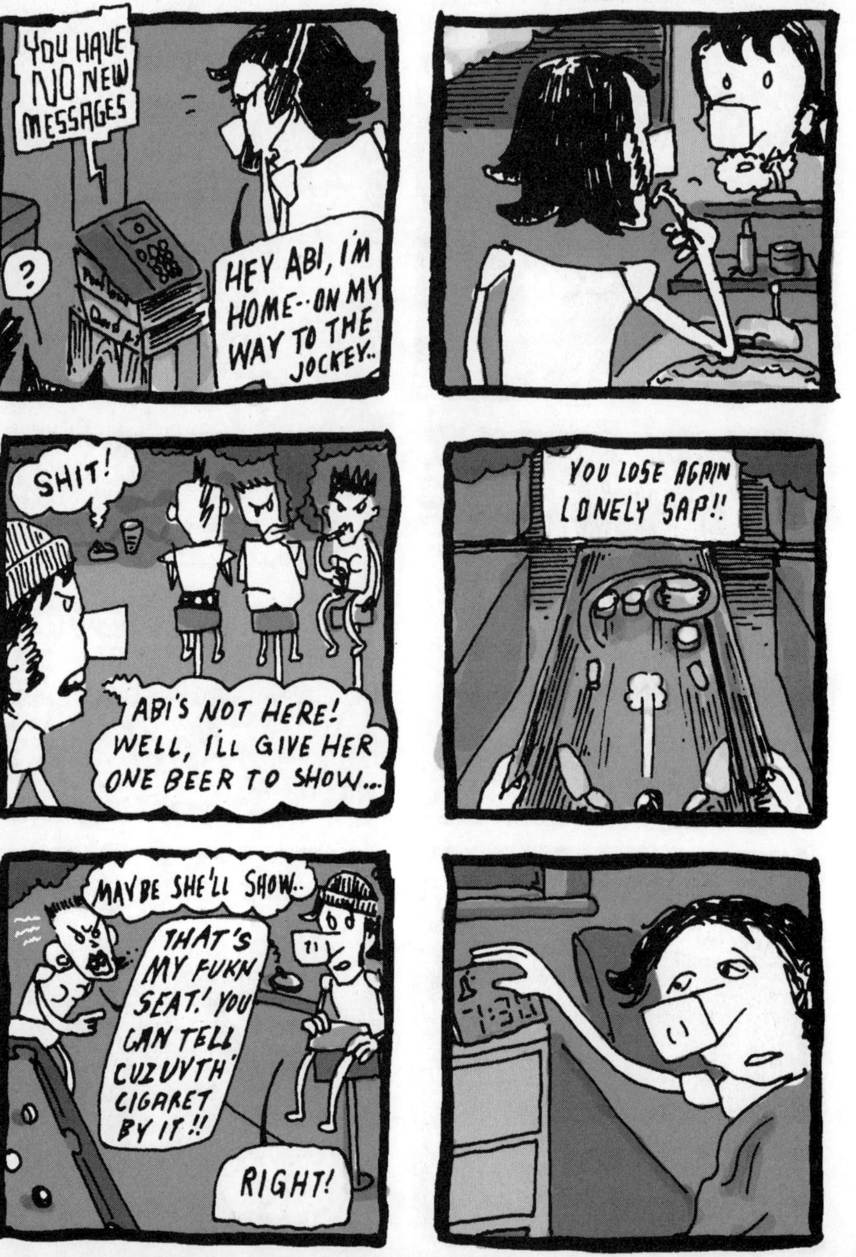
YOU HAVE NO NEW MESSAGES
?
HEY ABI, I'M HOME.. ON MY WAY TO THE JOCKEY..
SHIT!
ABI'S NOT HERE! WELL, I'LL GIVE HER ONE BEER TO SHOW...
YOU LOSE AGAIN LONELY SAP!!
MAYBE SHE'LL SHOW..
THAT'S MY FUKN SEAT! YOU CAN TELL CUZ UVTH' CIGARET BY IT!!
RIGHT!

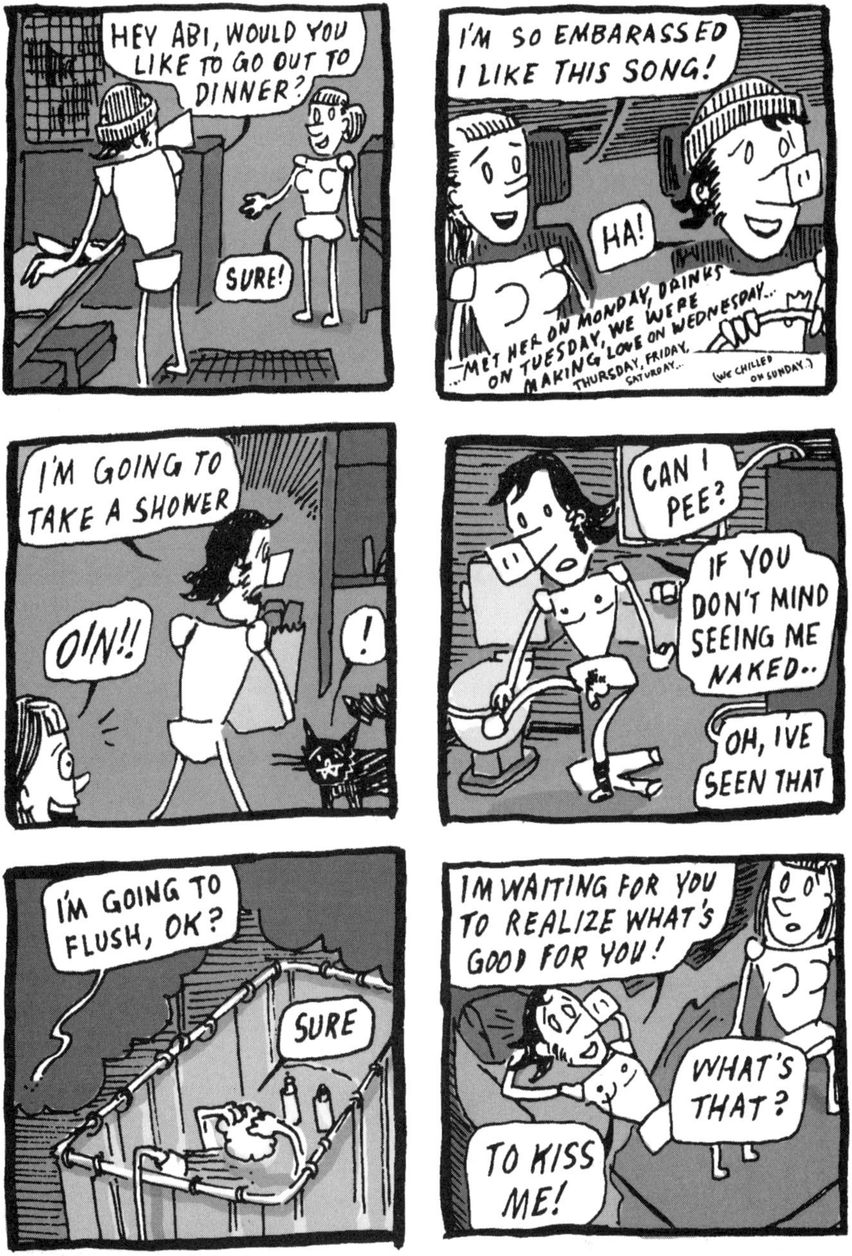
HEY ABI, WOULD YOU LIKE TO GO OUT TO DINNER?
SURE!
I'M SO EMBARASSED I LIKE THIS SONG!
HA!
...MET HER ON MONDAY, DRINKS ON TUESDAY, WE WERE MAKING LOVE ON WEDNESDAY... THURSDAY, FRIDAY, SATURDAY...
(WE CHILLED ON SUNDAY.)
I'M GOING TO TAKE A SHOWER
OIN!!
!
CAN I PEE?
IF YOU DON'T MIND SEEING ME NAKED..
OH, I'VE SEEN THAT
I'M GOING TO FLUSH, OK?
SURE
IM WAITING FOR YOU TO REALIZE WHAT'S GOOD FOR YOU!
WHAT'S THAT?
TO KISS ME!

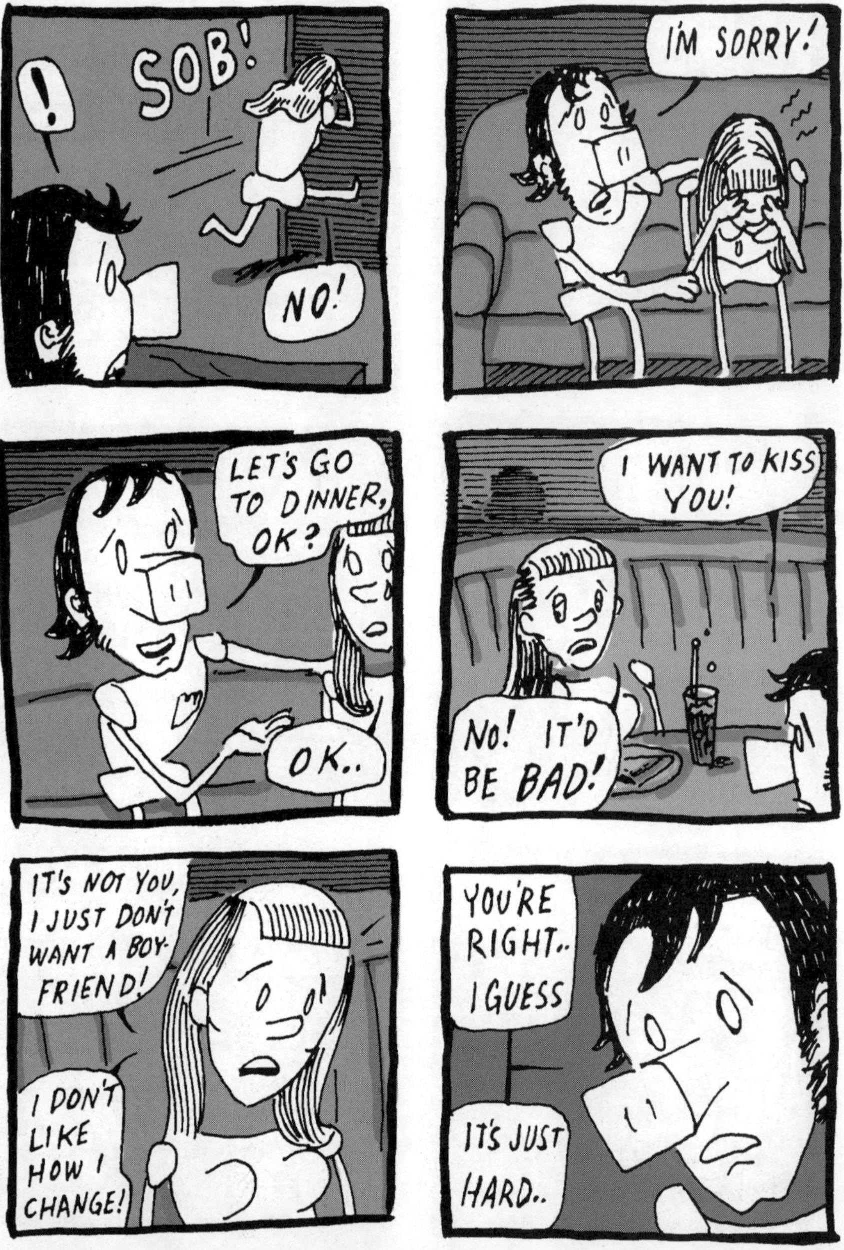
!
SOB!
NO!
I'M SORRY!
LET'S GO TO DINNER, OK?
OK..
I WANT TO KISS YOU!
NO! IT'D BE BAD!
IT'S NOT YOU, I JUST DON'T WANT A BOY-FRIEND!
I DON'T LIKE HOW I CHANGE!
YOU'RE RIGHT.. I GUESS
IT'S JUST HARD..

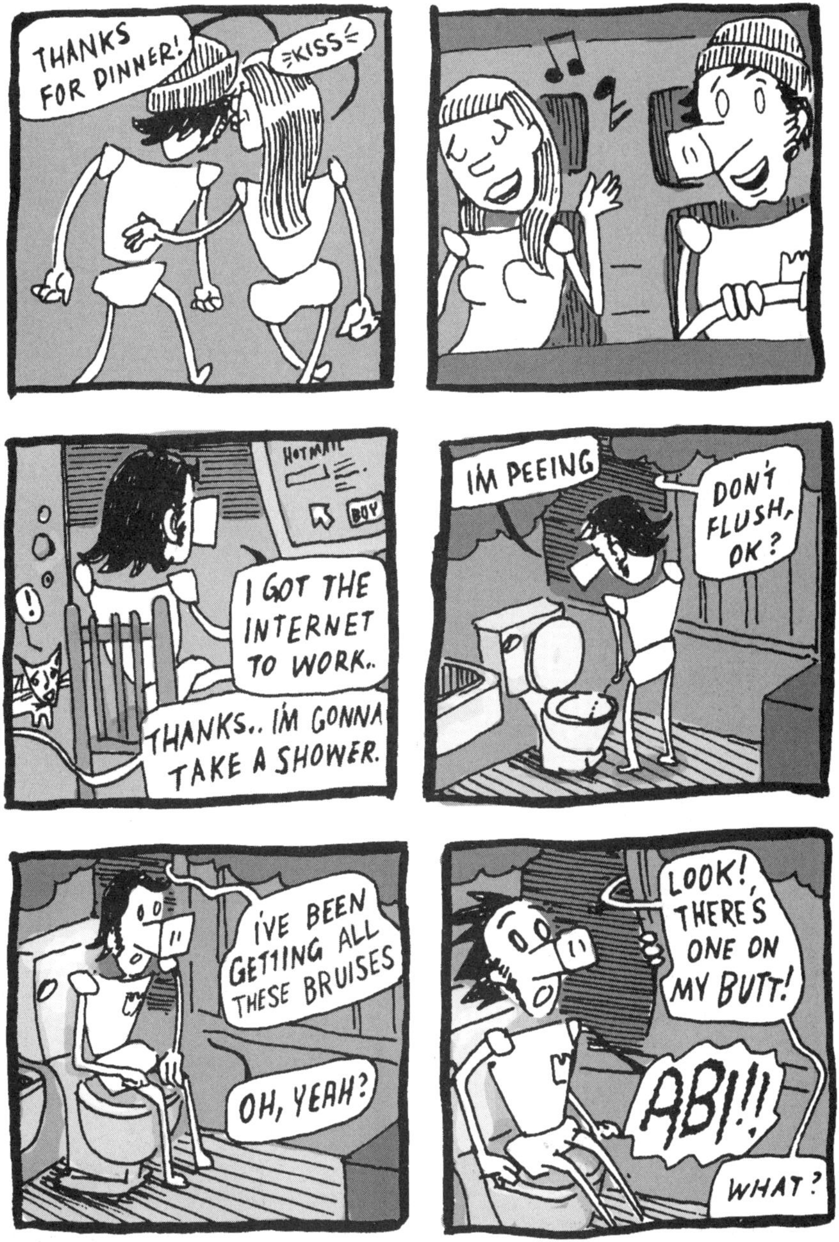

THANKS FOR DINNER!
KISS
I GOT THE INTERNET TO WORK..
THANKS.. I'M GONNA TAKE A SHOWER.
HOTMAIL
BUY
I'M PEEING
DON'T FLUSH, OK?
I'VE BEEN GETTING ALL THESE BRUISES
OH, YEAH?
LOOK! THERE'S ONE ON MY BUTT!
ABI!!
WHAT?

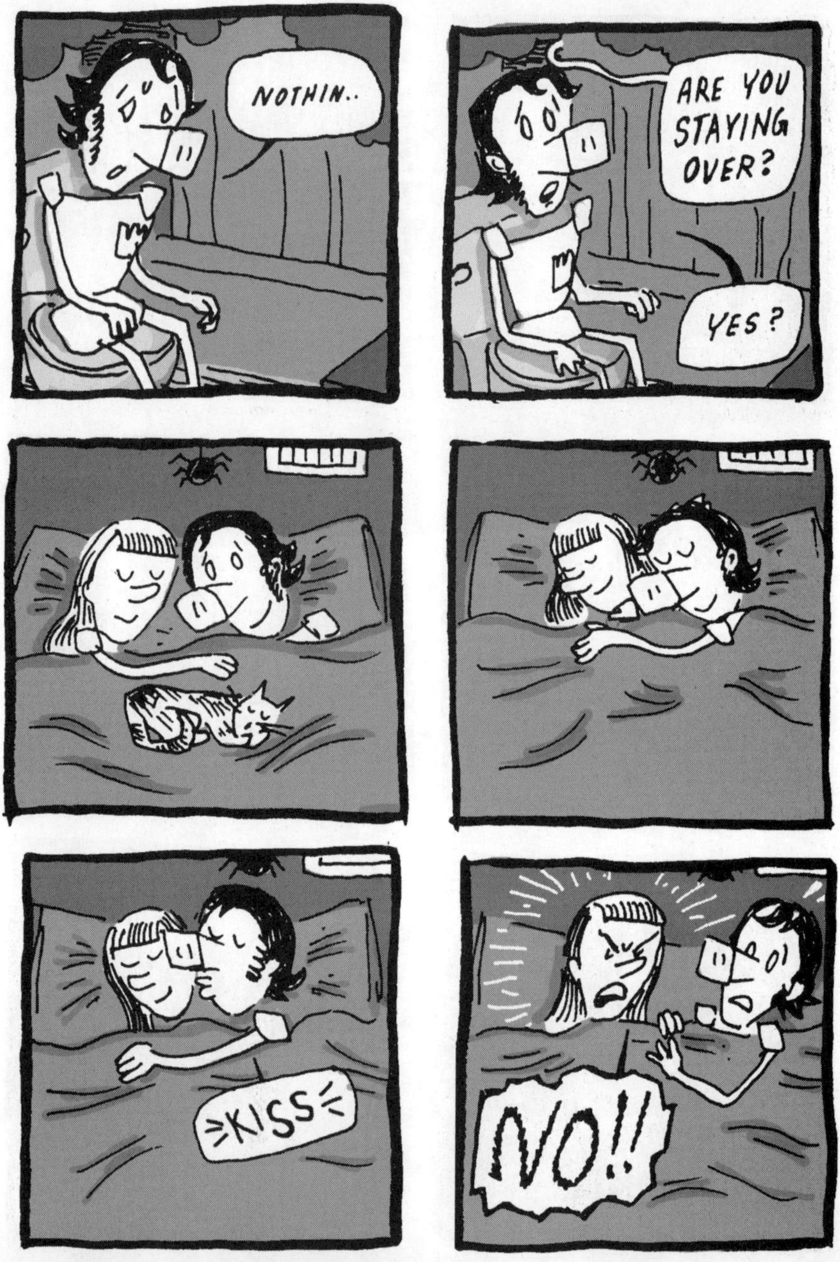
NOTHIN..
ARE YOU STAYING OVER?
YES?
KISS
NO!!

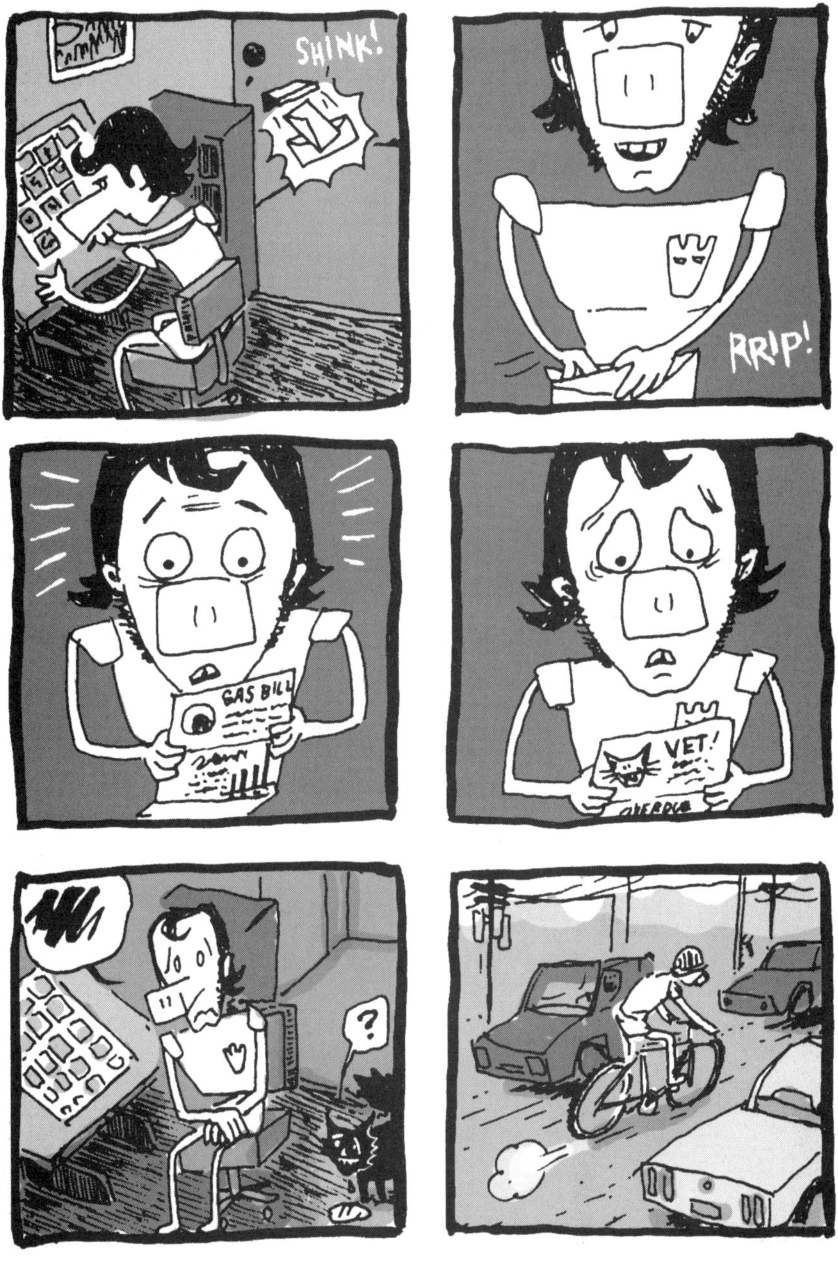
SHINK!
RRIP!
GAS BILL
VET!
?

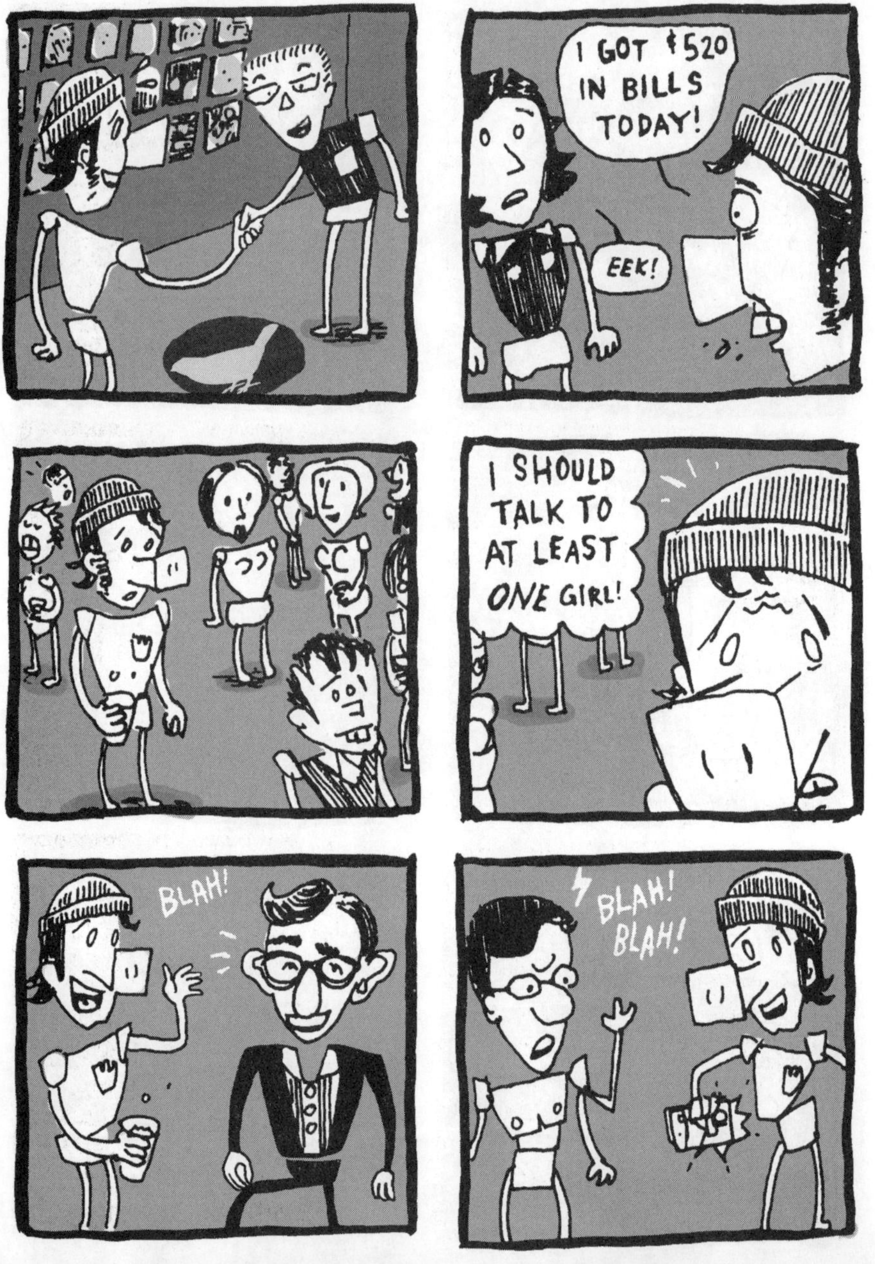
I GOT $520 IN BILLS TODAY!
EEK!
I SHOULD TALK TO AT LEAST ONE GIRL!
BLAH!
BLAH! BLAH!

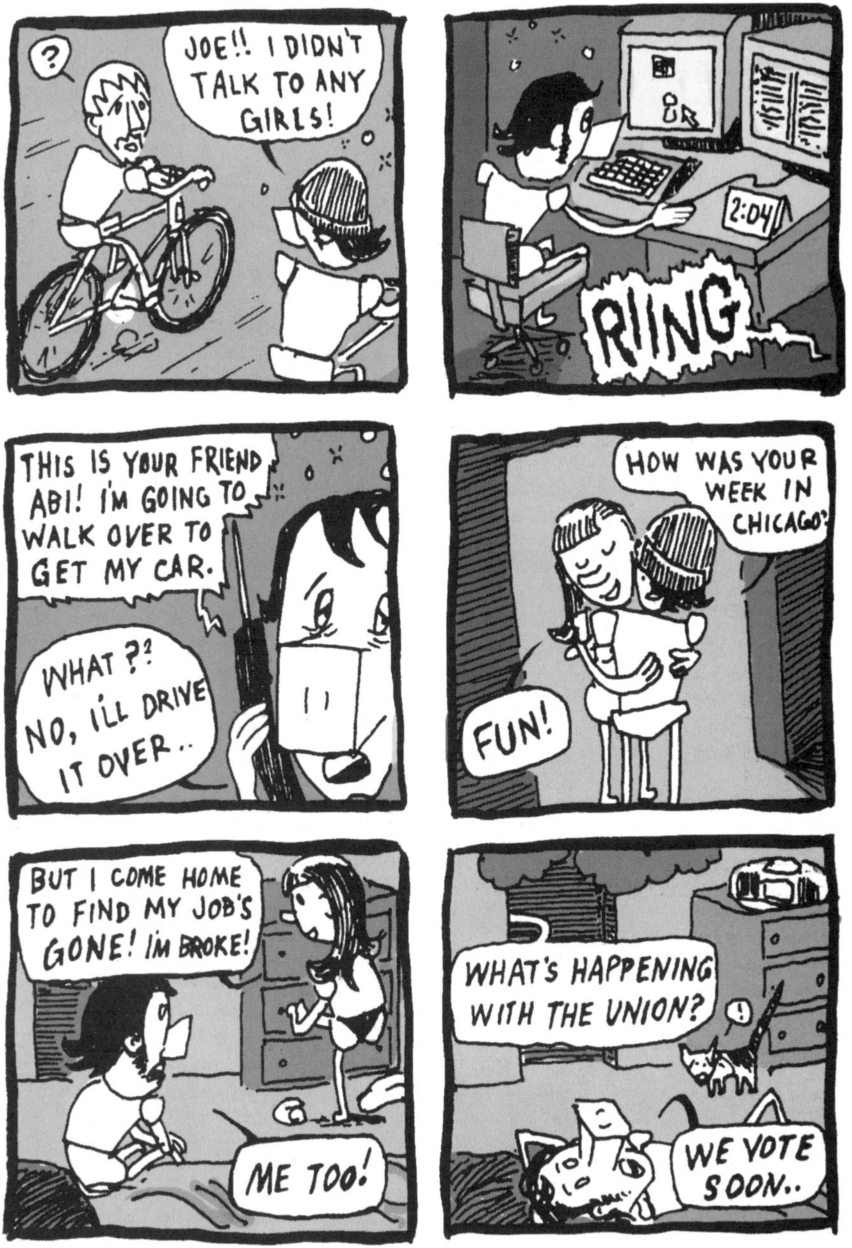
?
JOE!! I DIDN'T TALK TO ANY GIRLS!
2:04
RIING
THIS IS YOUR FRIEND ABI! I'M GOING TO WALK OVER TO GET MY CAR.
WHAT ?? NO, I'LL DRIVE IT OVER..
HOW WAS YOUR WEEK IN CHICAGO?
FUN!
BUT I COME HOME TO FIND MY JOB'S GONE! I'M BROKE!
ME TOO!
WHAT'S HAPPENING WITH THE UNION?
!
WE VOTE SOON..

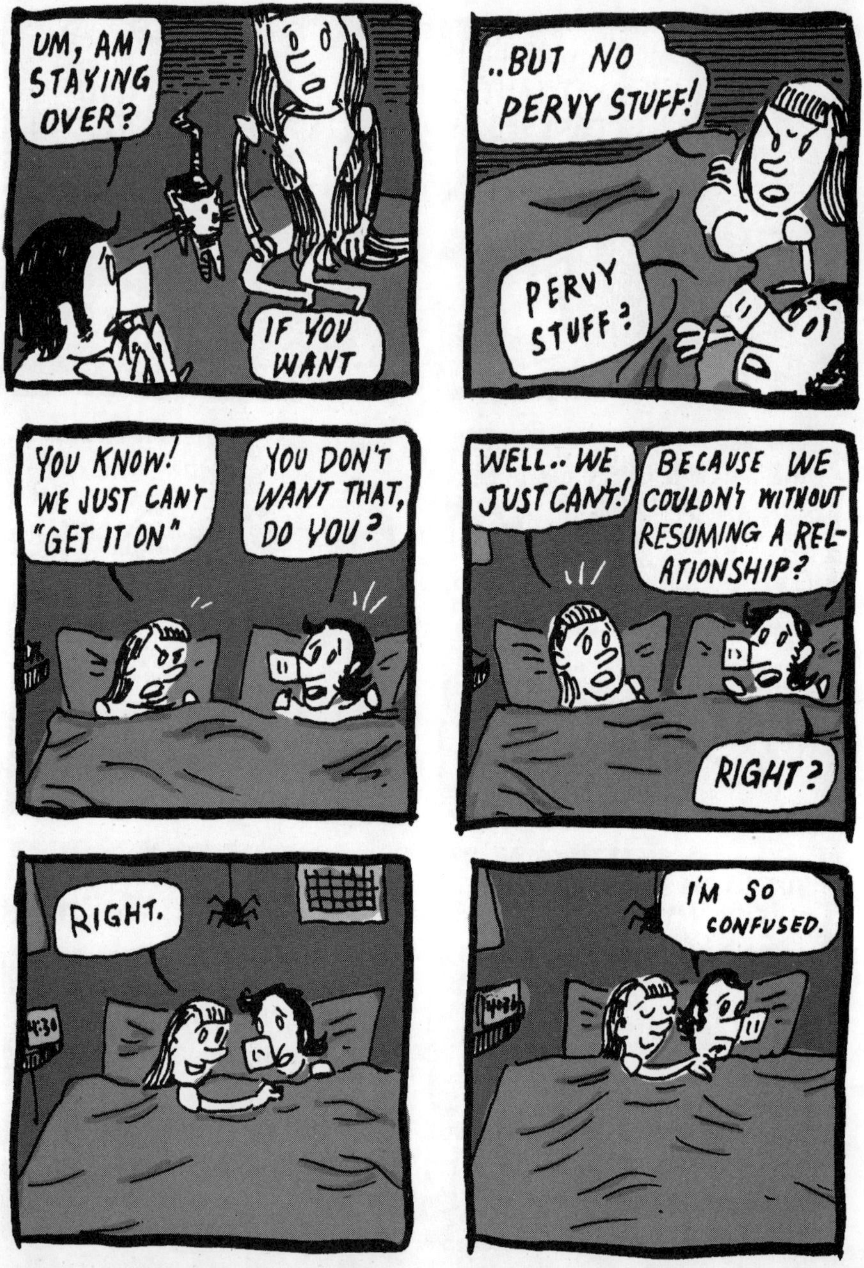
UM, AM I STAYING OVER?
IF YOU WANT
..BUT NO PERVY STUFF!
PERVY STUFF?
YOU KNOW! WE JUST CAN'T "GET IT ON"
YOU DON'T WANT THAT, DO YOU?
WELL.. WE JUST CAN'T!
BECAUSE WE COULDN'T WITHOUT RESUMING A REL-ATIONSHIP?
RIGHT?
RIGHT.
I'M SO CONFUSED.

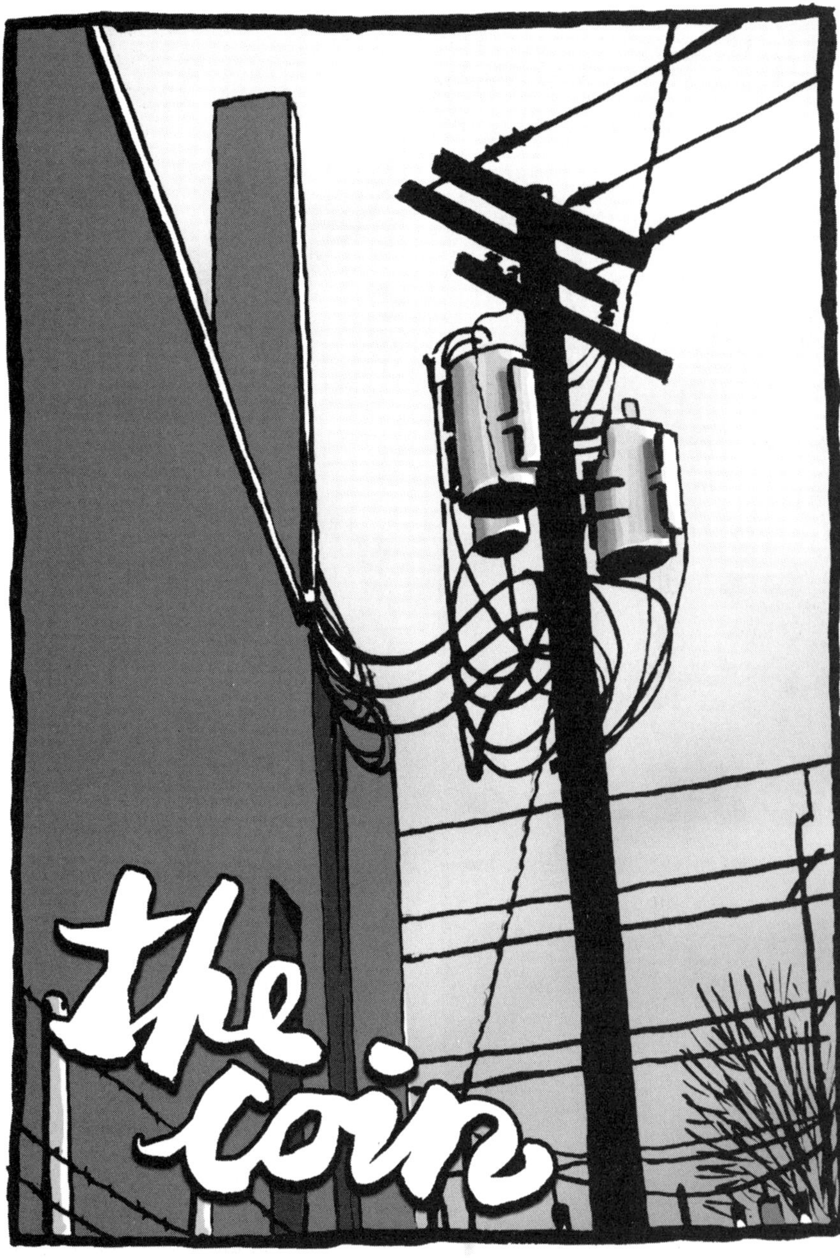
the coin

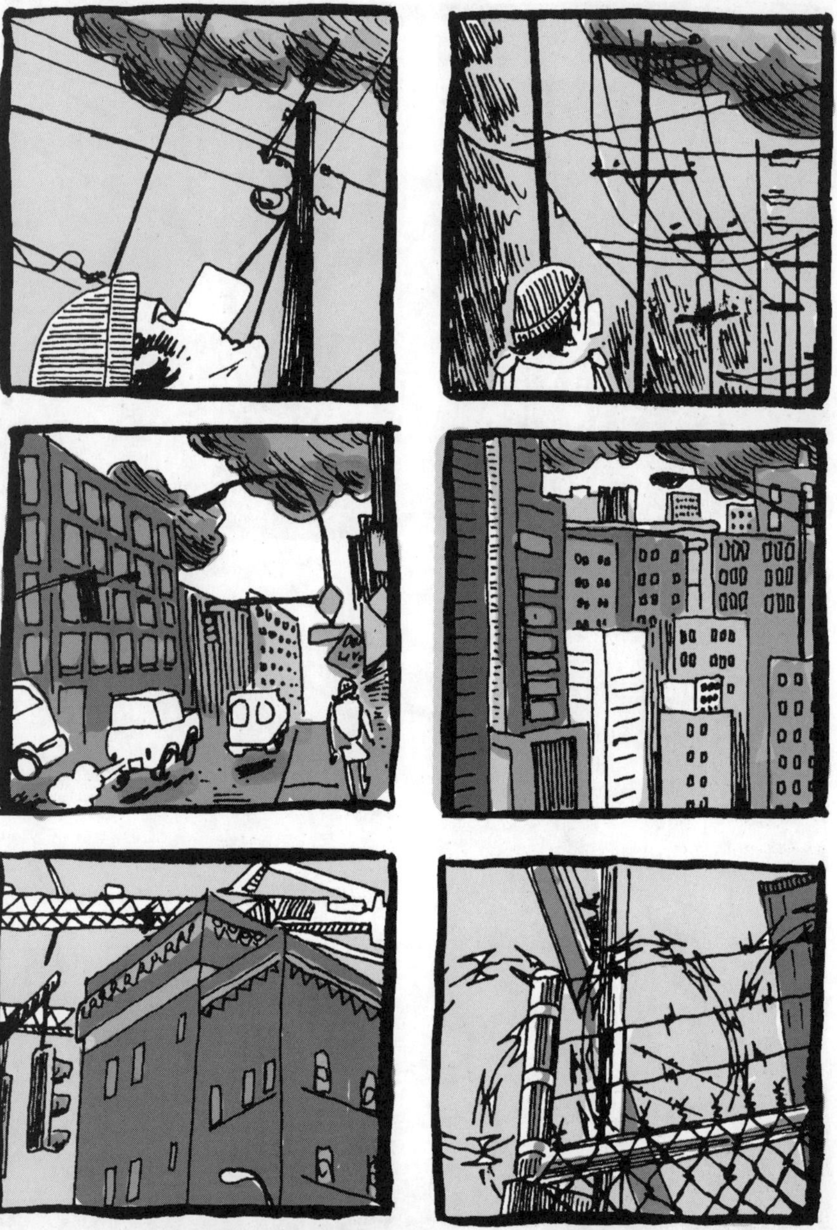

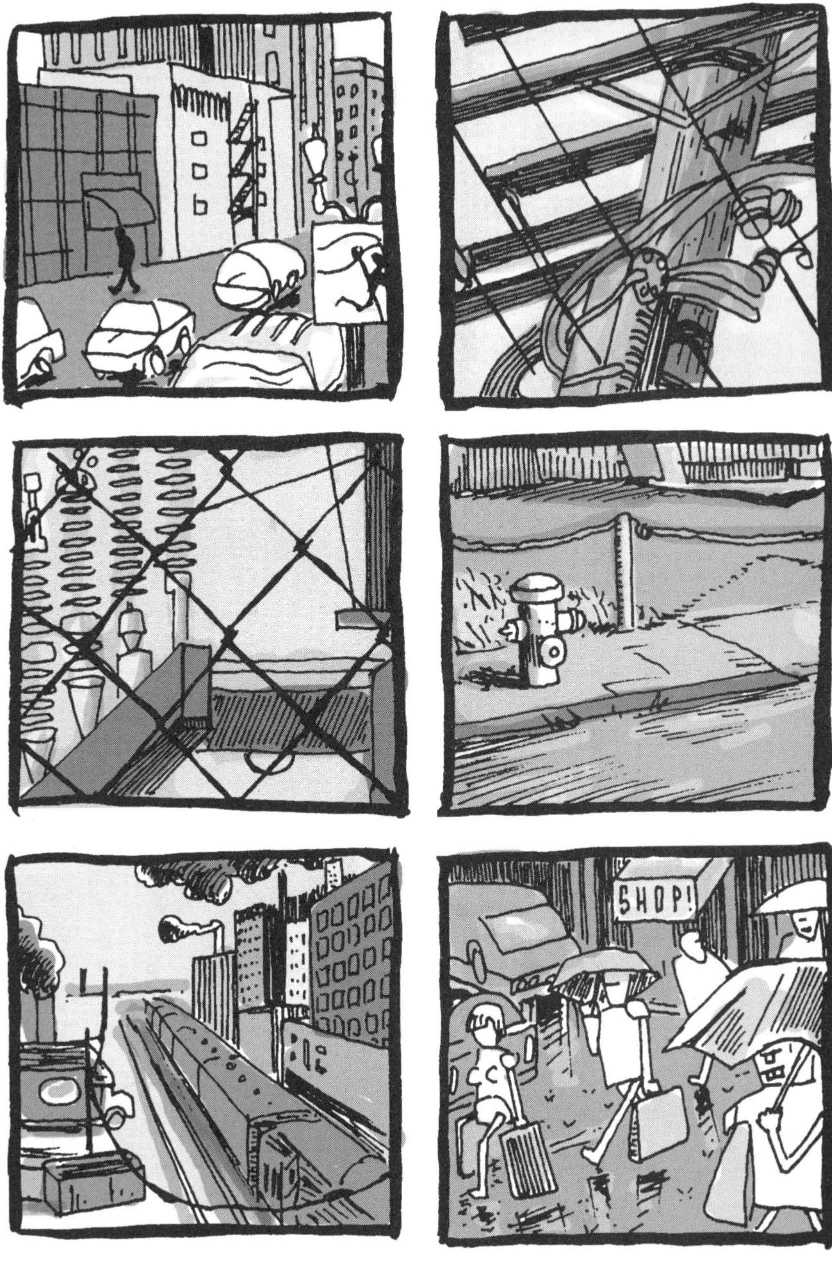
SHOP!

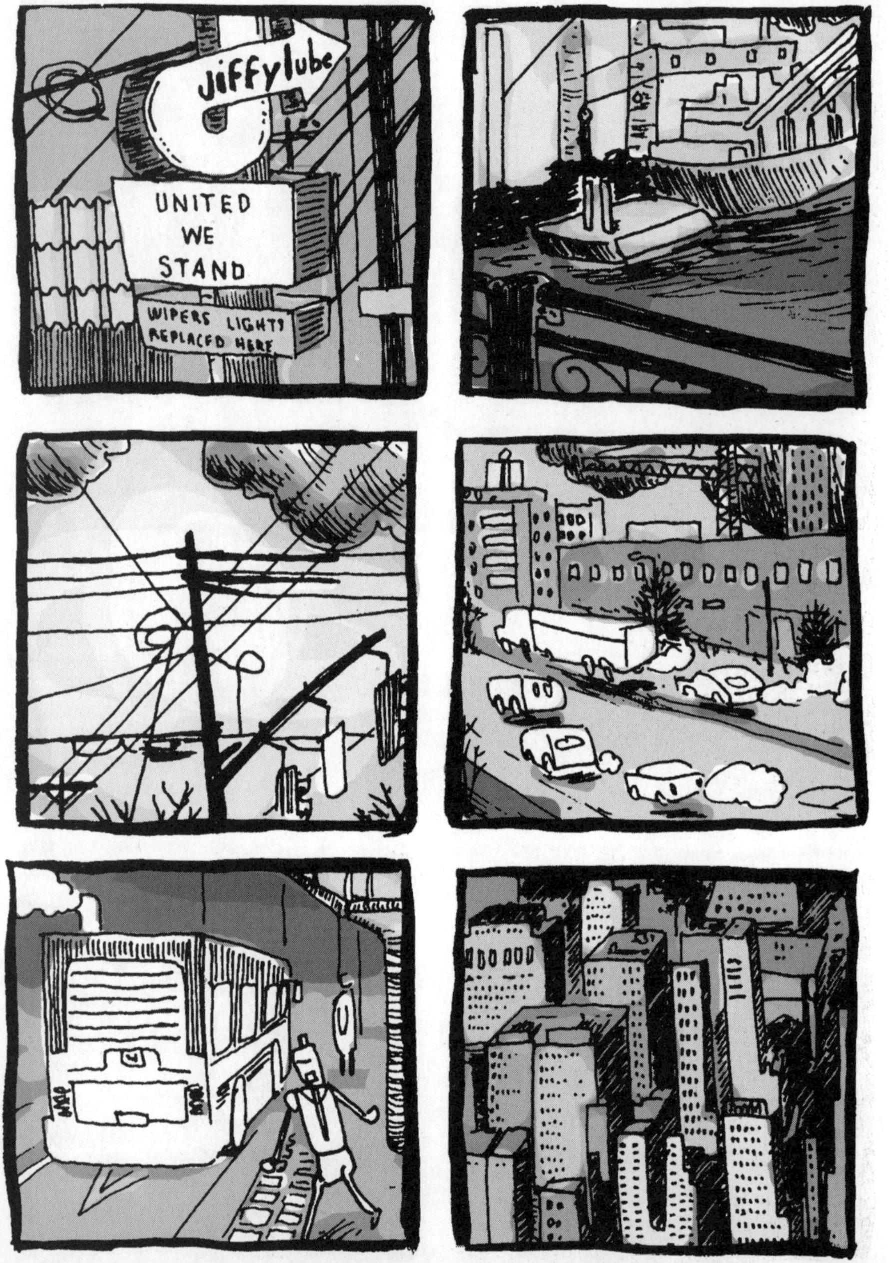
jiffylube
UNITED
WE
STAND
WIPERS LIGHTS
REPLACED HERE

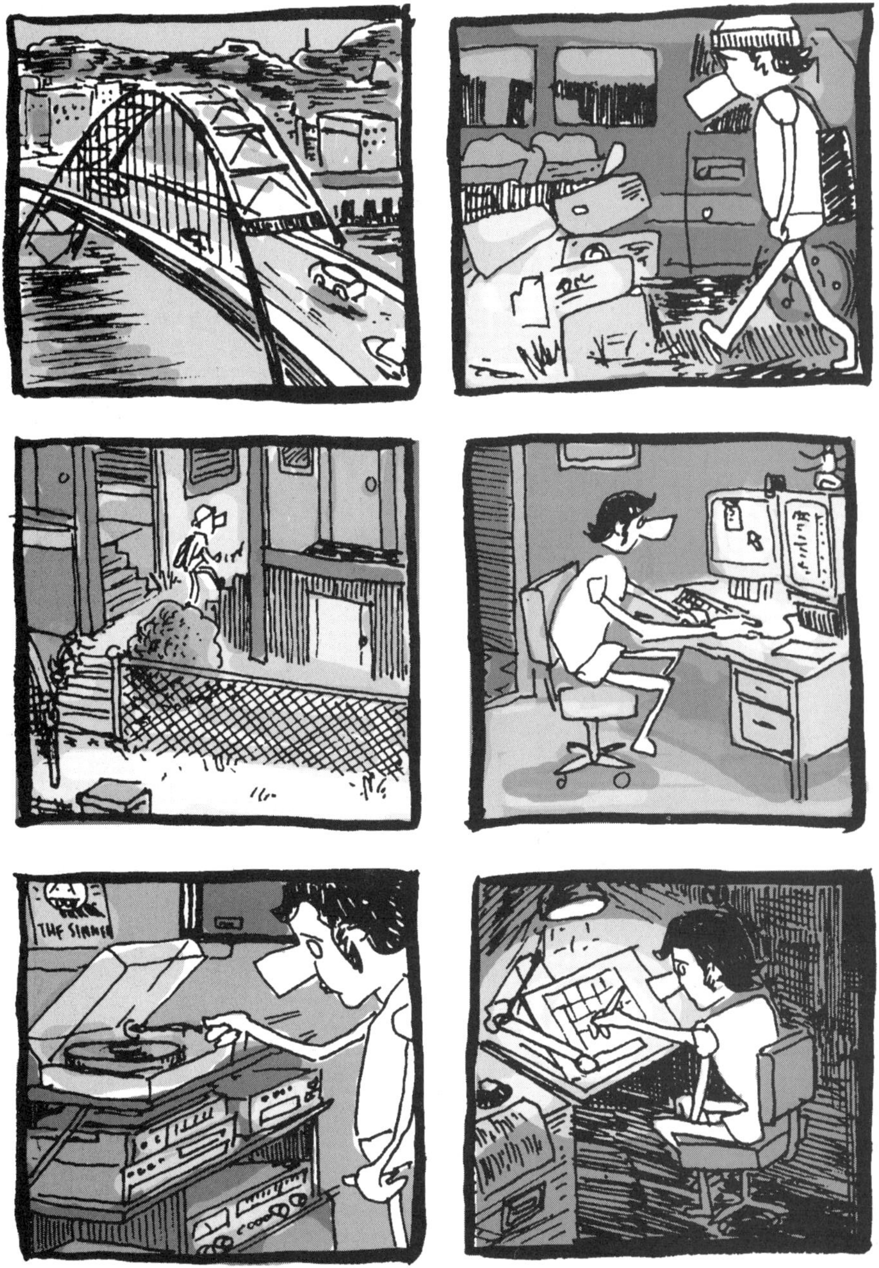
THE SINNER

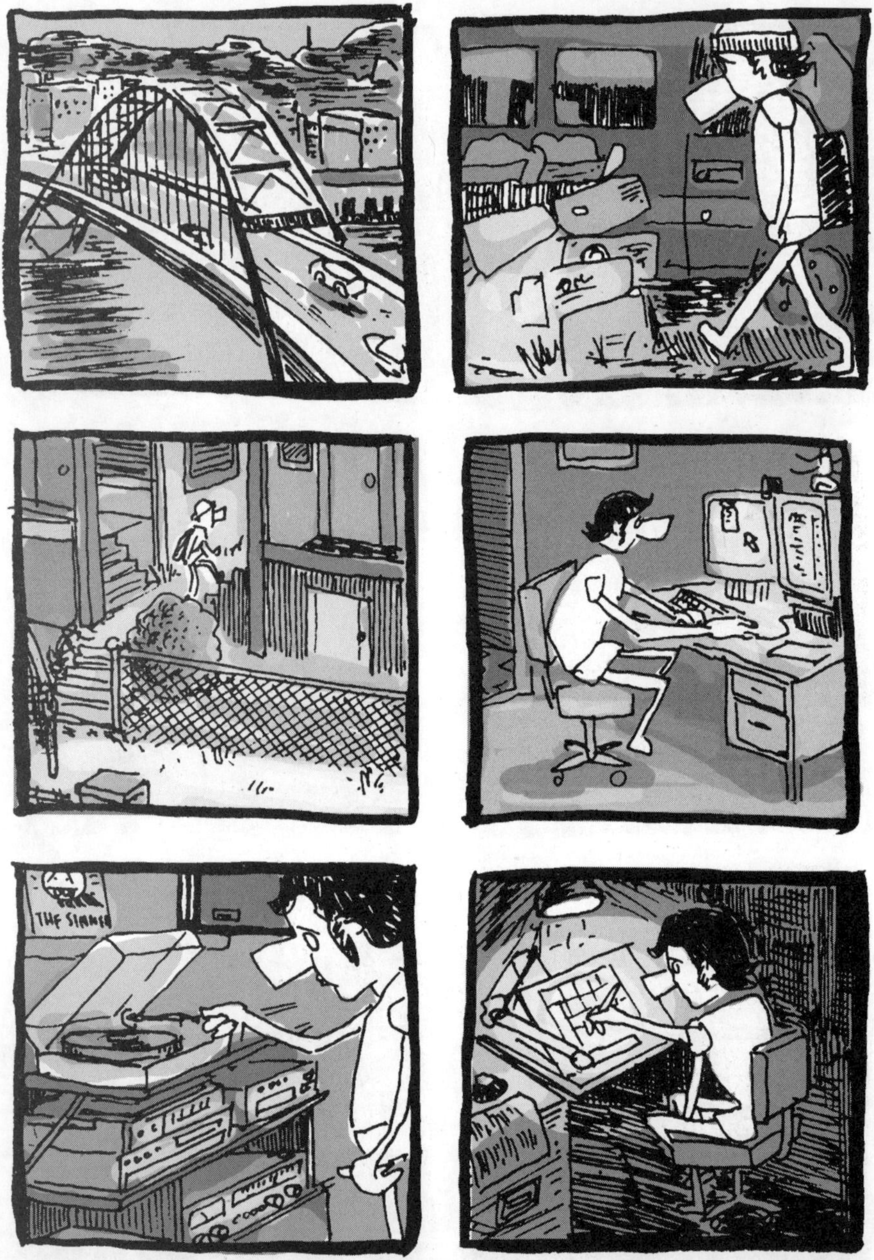

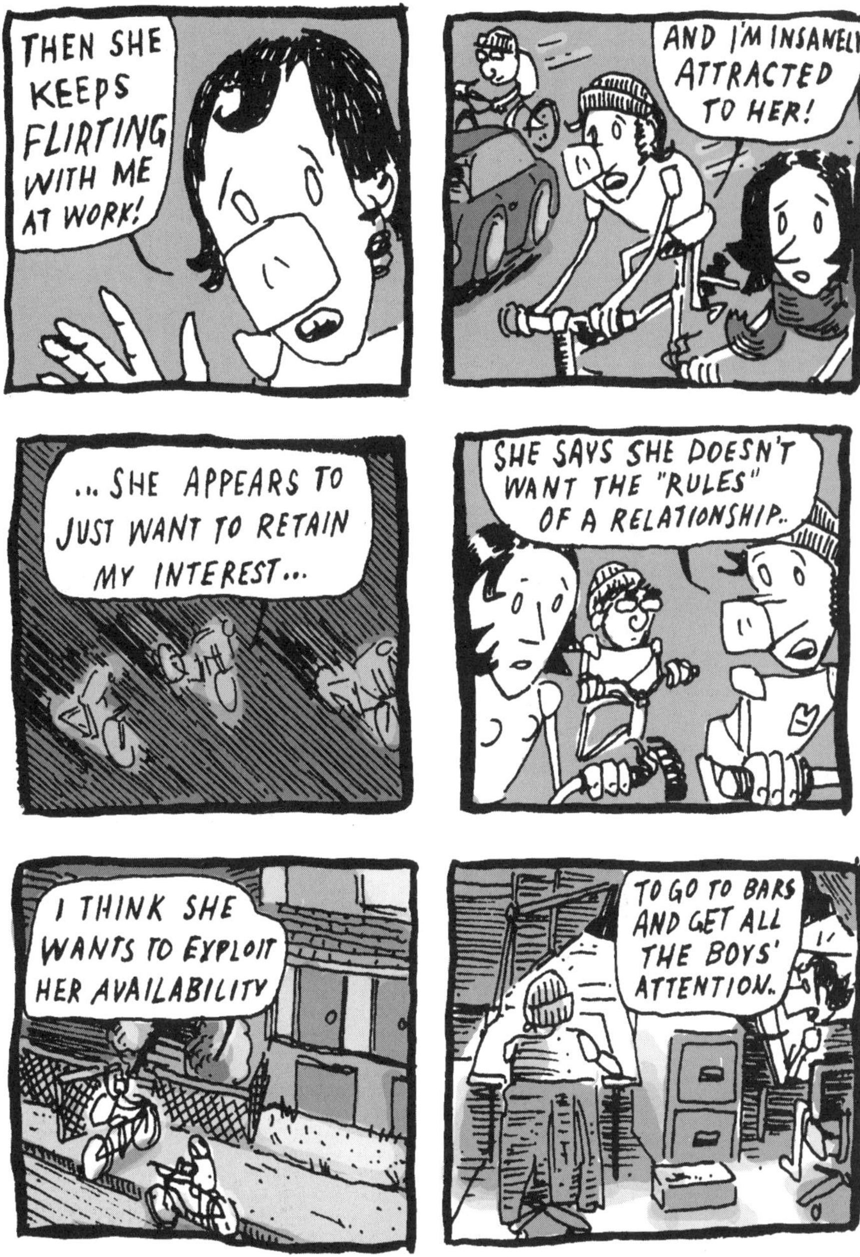
THEN SHE KEEPS FLIRTING WITH ME AT WORK!
AND I'M INSANELY ATTRACTED TO HER!
... SHE APPEARS TO JUST WANT TO RETAIN MY INTEREST...
SHE SAYS SHE DOESN'T WANT THE "RULES" OF A RELATIONSHIP..
I THINK SHE WANTS TO EXPLOIT HER AVAILABILITY
TO GO TO BARS AND GET ALL THE BOYS' ATTENTION..

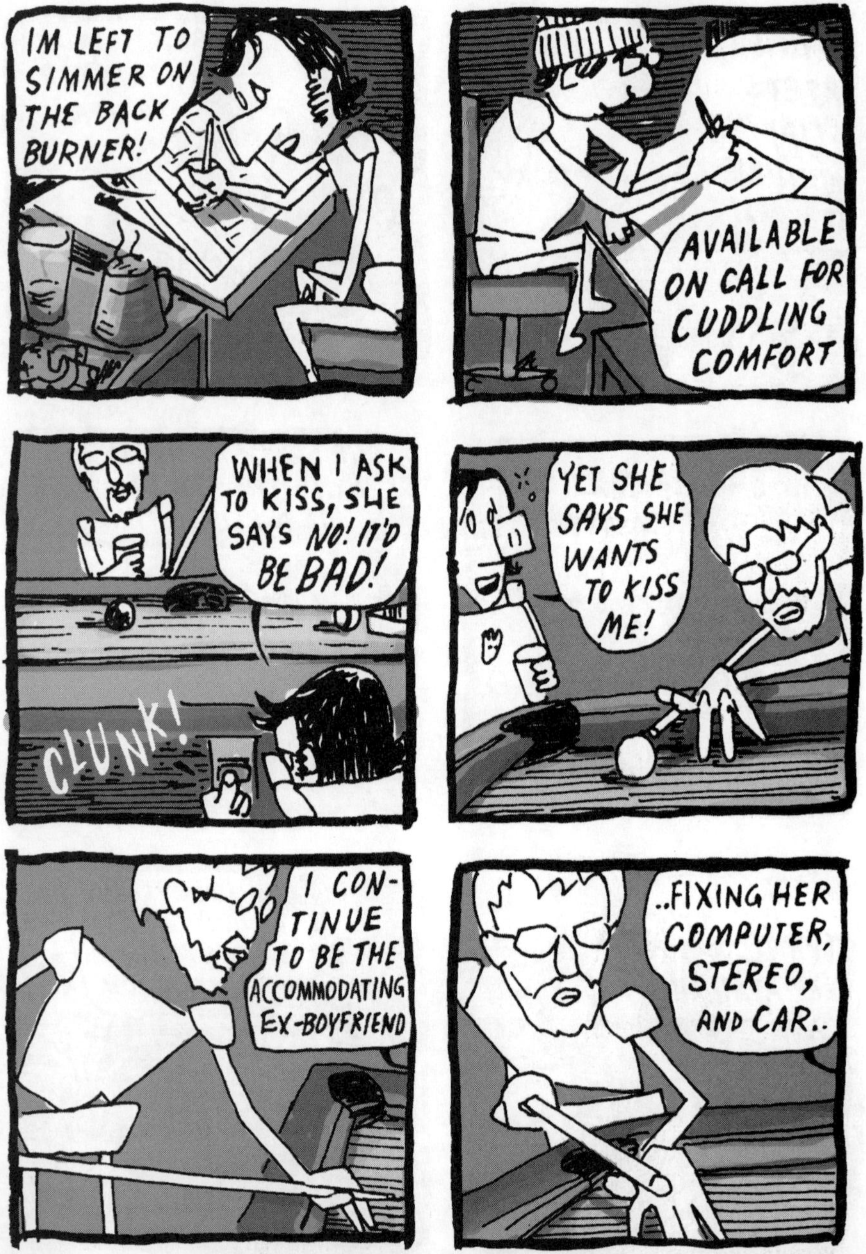
IM LEFT TO SIMMER ON THE BACK BURNER!
AVAILABLE ON CALL FOR CUDDLING COMFORT
WHEN I ASK TO KISS, SHE SAYS NO! IT'D BE BAD!
CLUNK!
YET SHE SAYS SHE WANTS TO KISS ME!
I CONTINUE TO BE THE ACCOMMODATING EX-BOYFRIEND
..FIXING HER COMPUTER, STEREO, AND CAR..

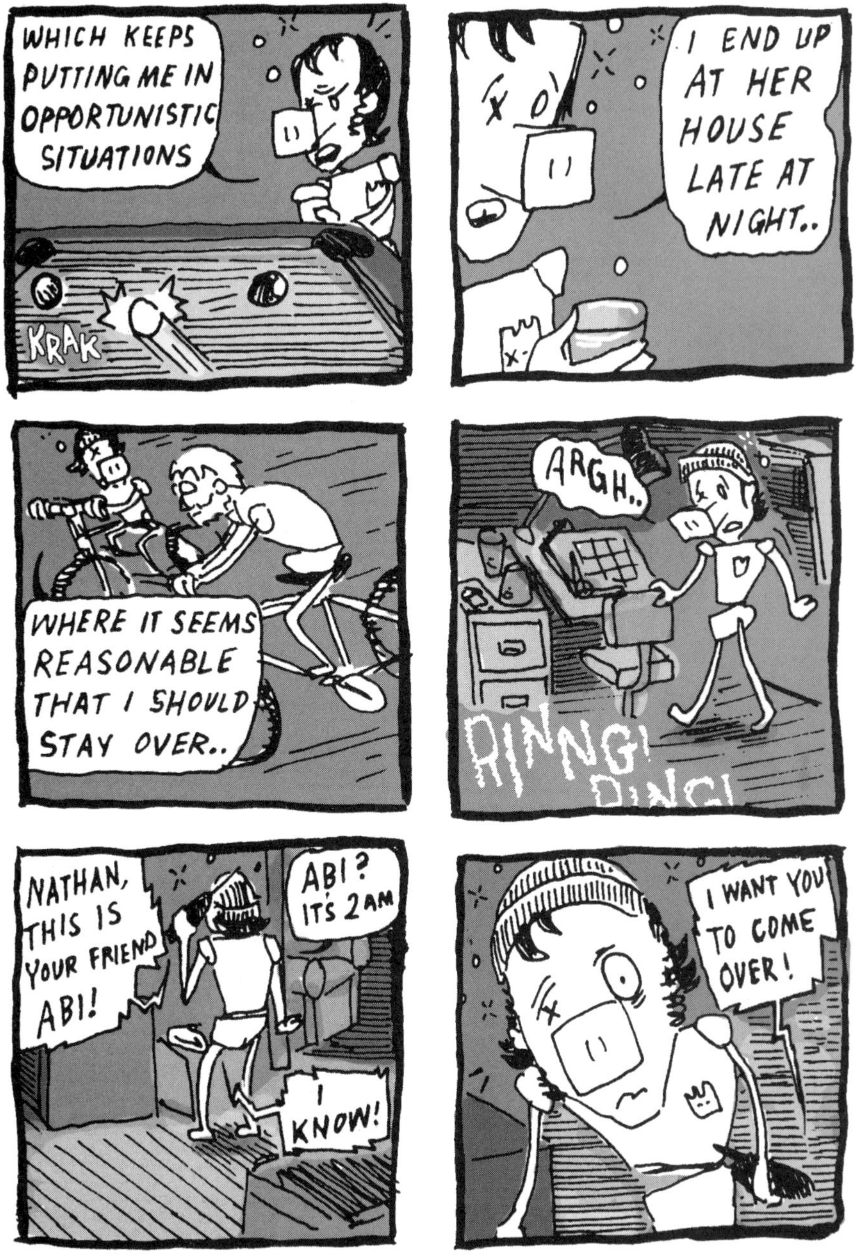
WHICH KEEPS PUTTING ME IN OPPORTUNISTIC SITUATIONS
KRAK
I END UP AT HER HOUSE LATE AT NIGHT..
WHERE IT SEEMS REASONABLE THAT I SHOULD STAY OVER..
ARGH..
RINNG!
NATHAN, THIS IS YOUR FRIEND ABI!
ABI? IT'S 2AM
I KNOW!
I WANT YOU TO COME OVER!

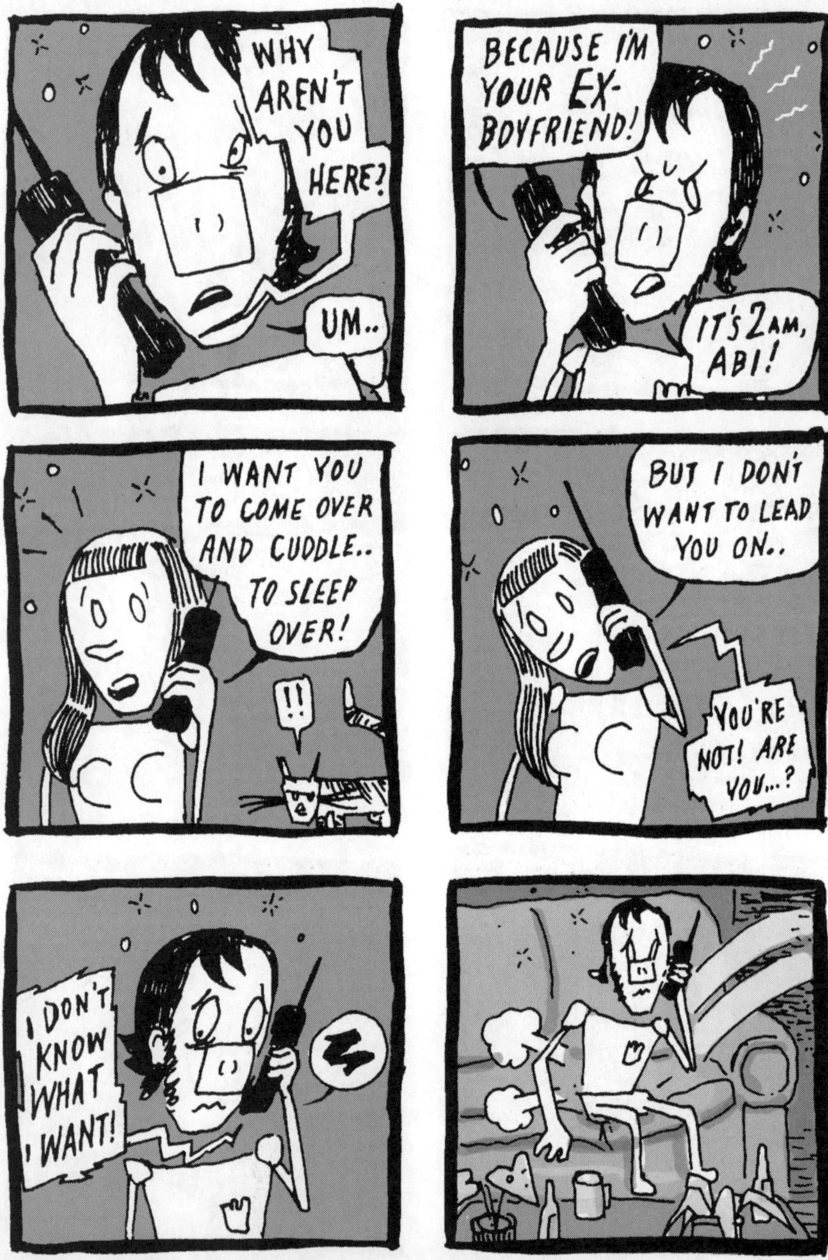
WHY AREN'T YOU HERE?
UM..
BECAUSE I'M YOUR EX-BOYFRIEND!
IT'S 2AM, ABI!
I WANT YOU TO COME OVER AND CUDDLE.. TO SLEEP OVER!
!!
BUT I DON'T WANT TO LEAD YOU ON..
YOU'RE NOT! ARE YOU...?
I DON'T KNOW WHAT I WANT!

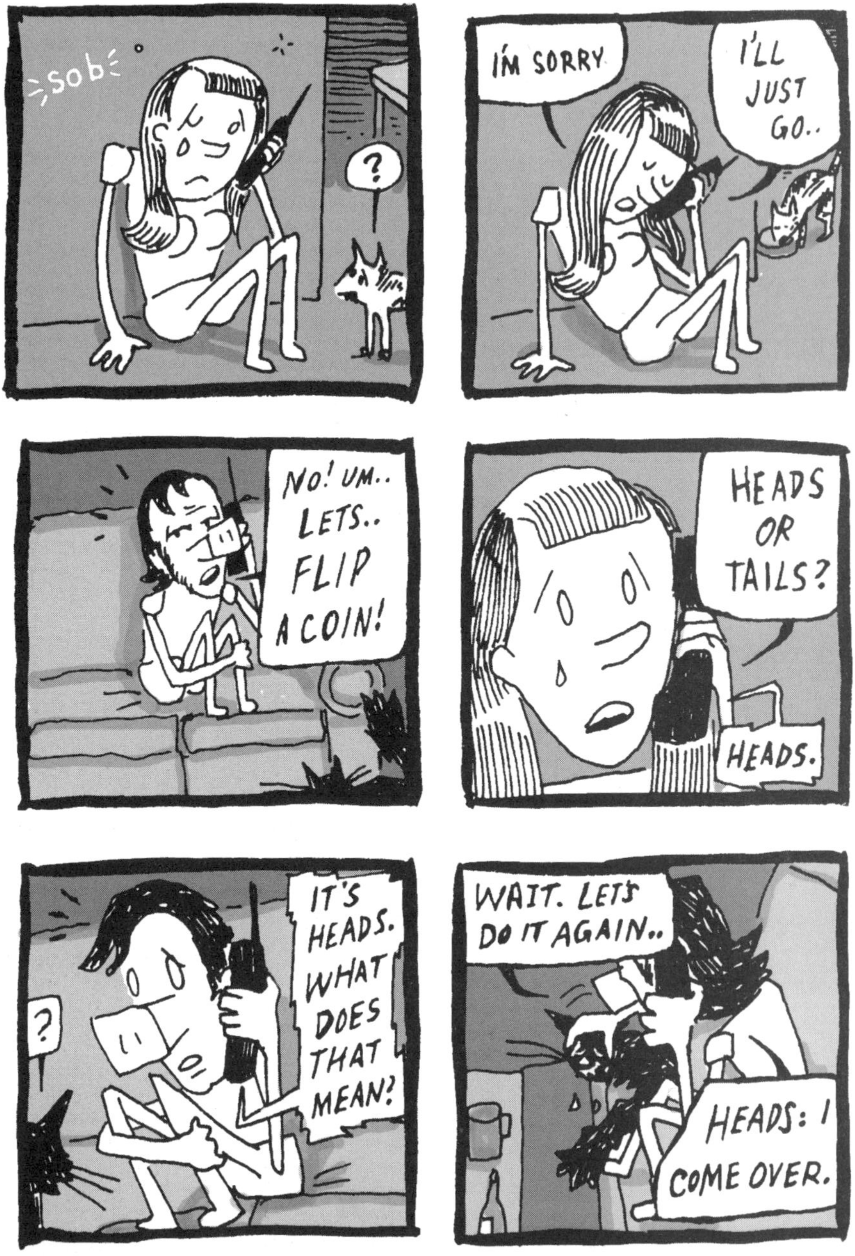
sob
?
I'M SORRY
I'LL JUST GO..
NO! UM.. LETS.. FLIP A COIN!
HEADS OR TAILS?
HEADS.
IT'S HEADS. WHAT DOES THAT MEAN?
?
WAIT. LET'S DO IT AGAIN..
HEADS: I COME OVER.

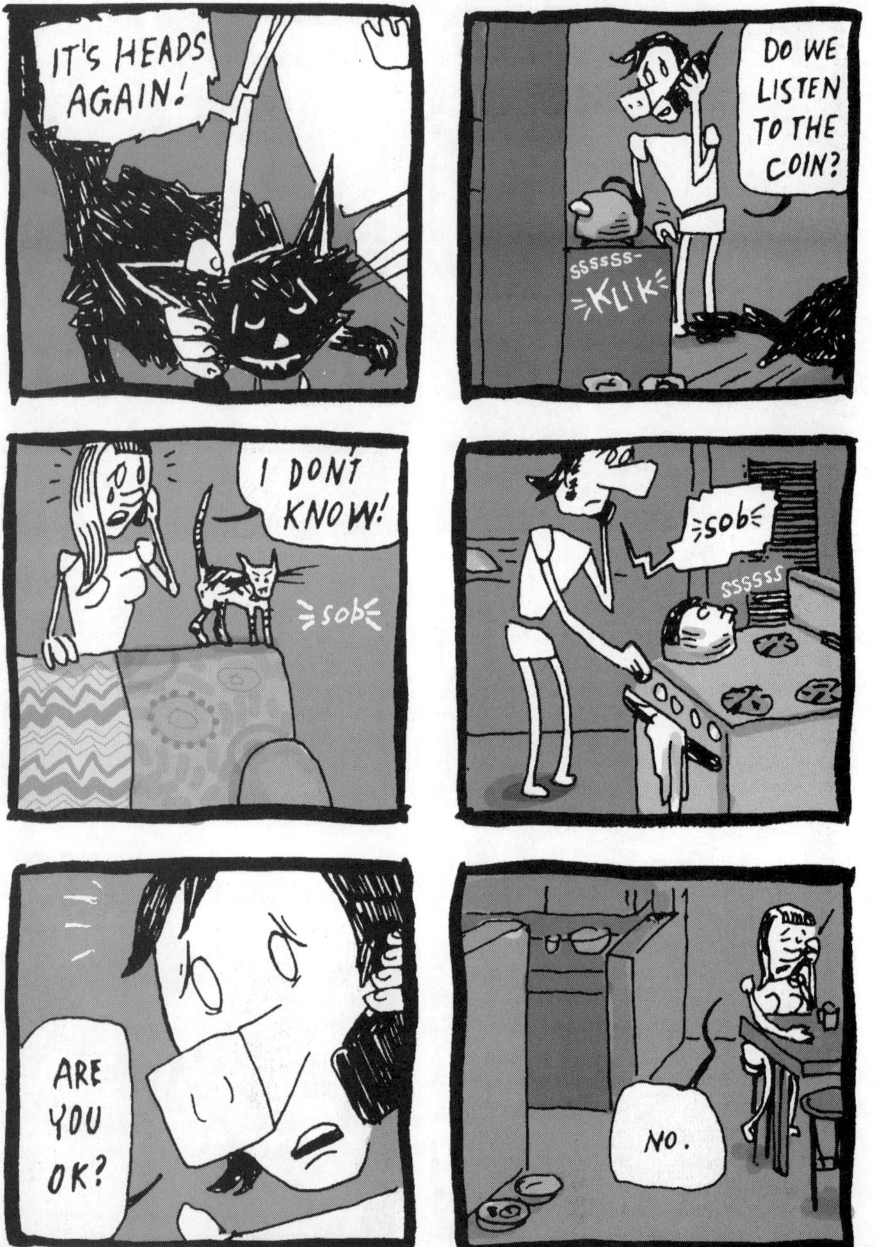
IT'S HEADS AGAIN!
DO WE LISTEN TO THE COIN?
SSSSSS-
KLIK
I DON'T KNOW!
sob
sob
SSSSSS
ARE YOU OK?
NO.

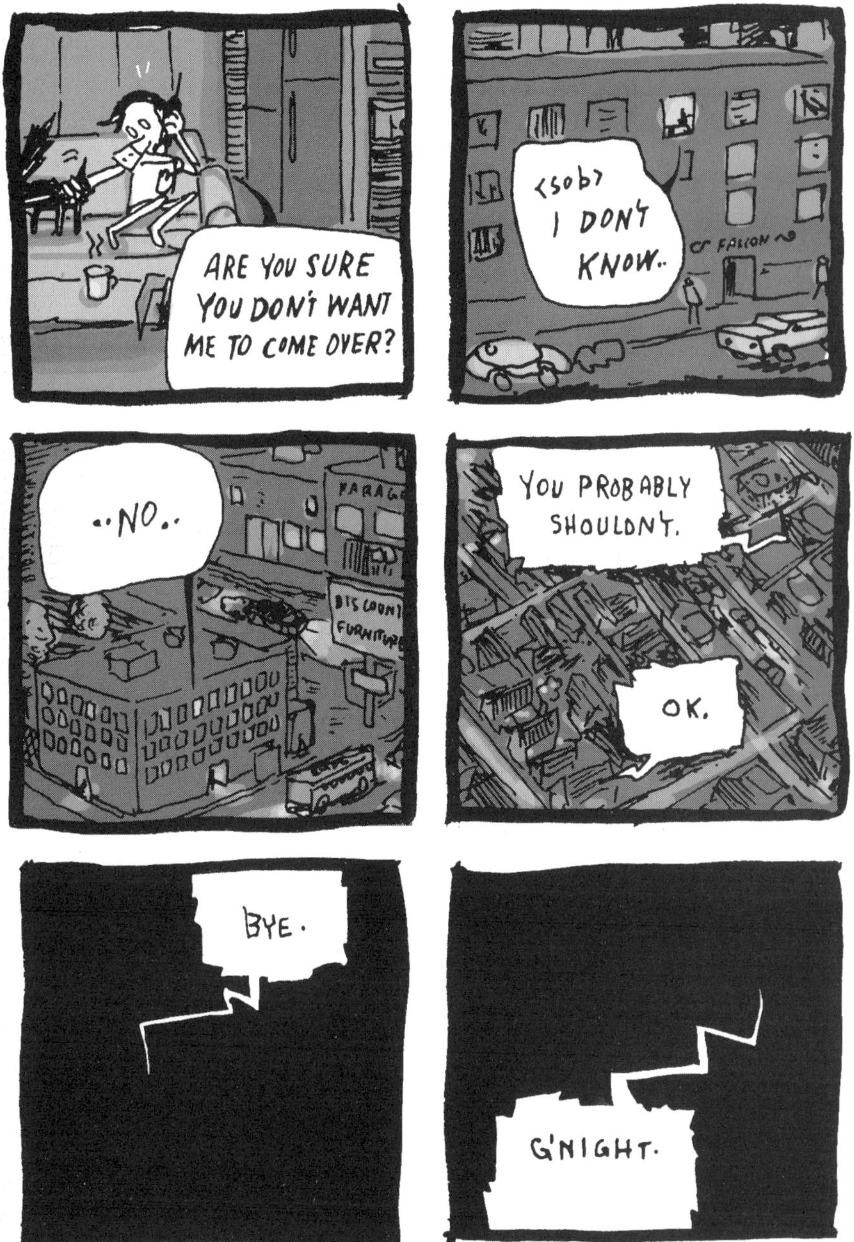

ARE YOU SURE YOU DON'T WANT ME TO COME OVER?
<sob> I DON'T KNOW..
..NO..
YOU PROBABLY SHOULDN'T.
OK.
BYE.
G'NIGHT.

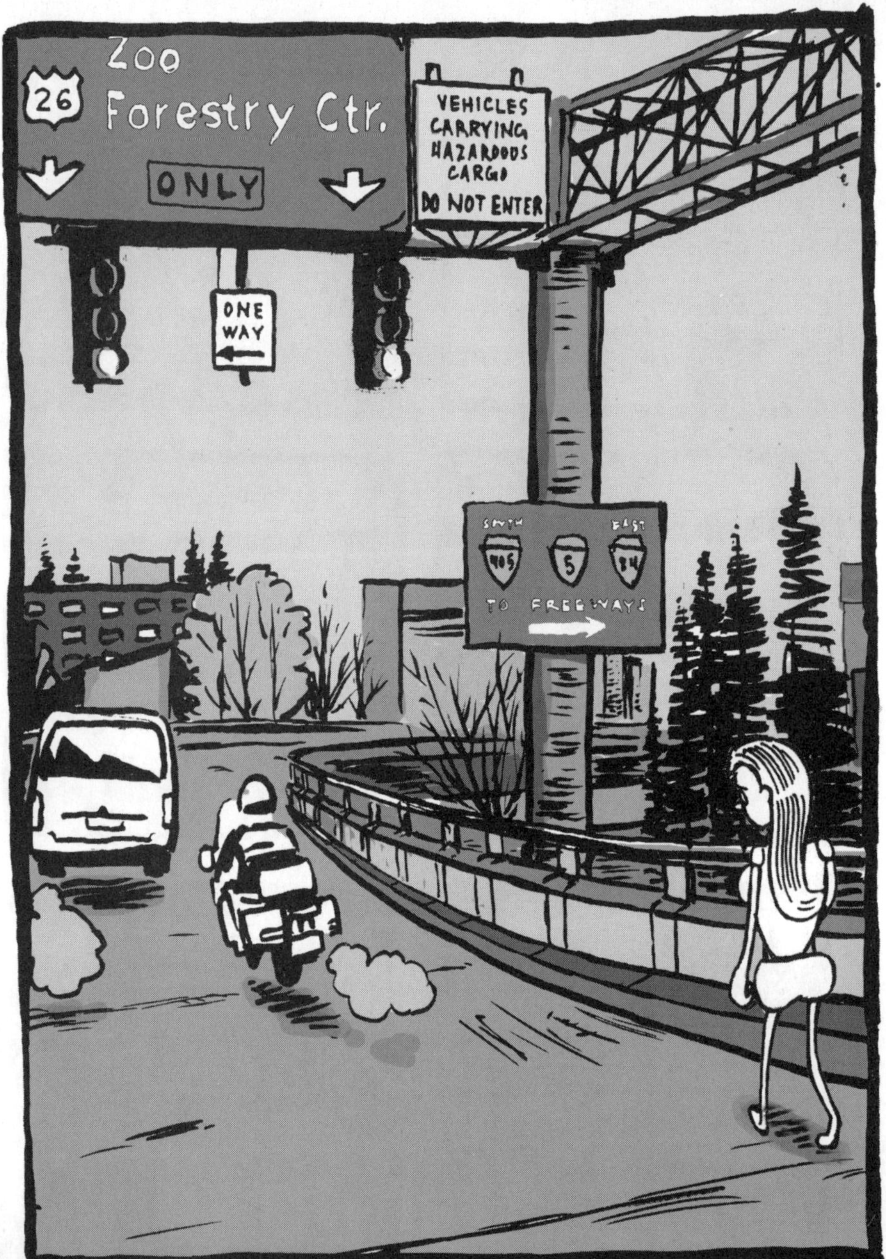
Zoo
26
Forestry Ctr.
ONLY
VEHICLES CARRYING HAZARDOUS CARGO DO NOT ENTER
ONE WAY
EAST
405
5
84
TO FREEWAYS

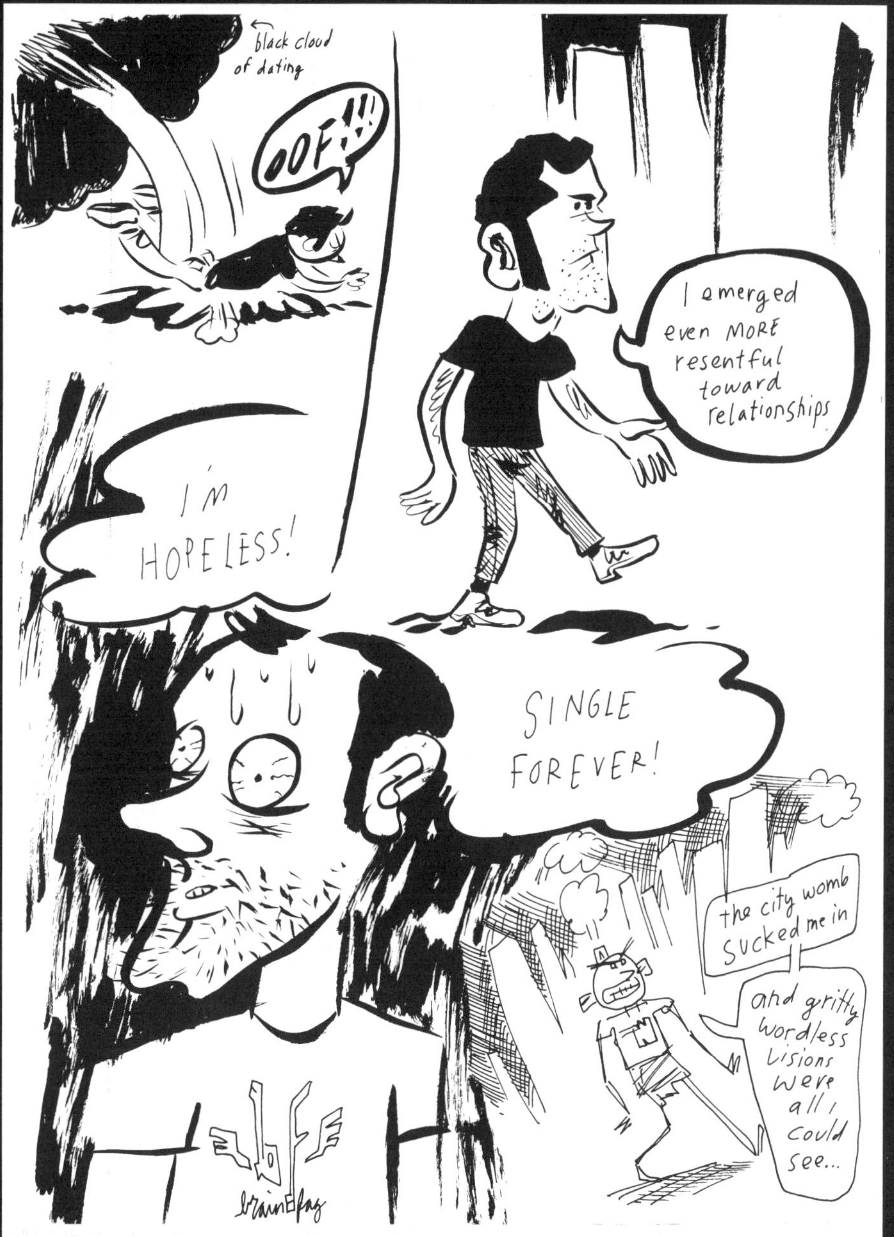
black cloud of dating
OOF!!!
I emerged even MORE resentful toward relationships
I'M HOPELESS!
SINGLE FOREVER!
the city womb sucked me in
and gritty wordless visions were all I could see...
brainfag

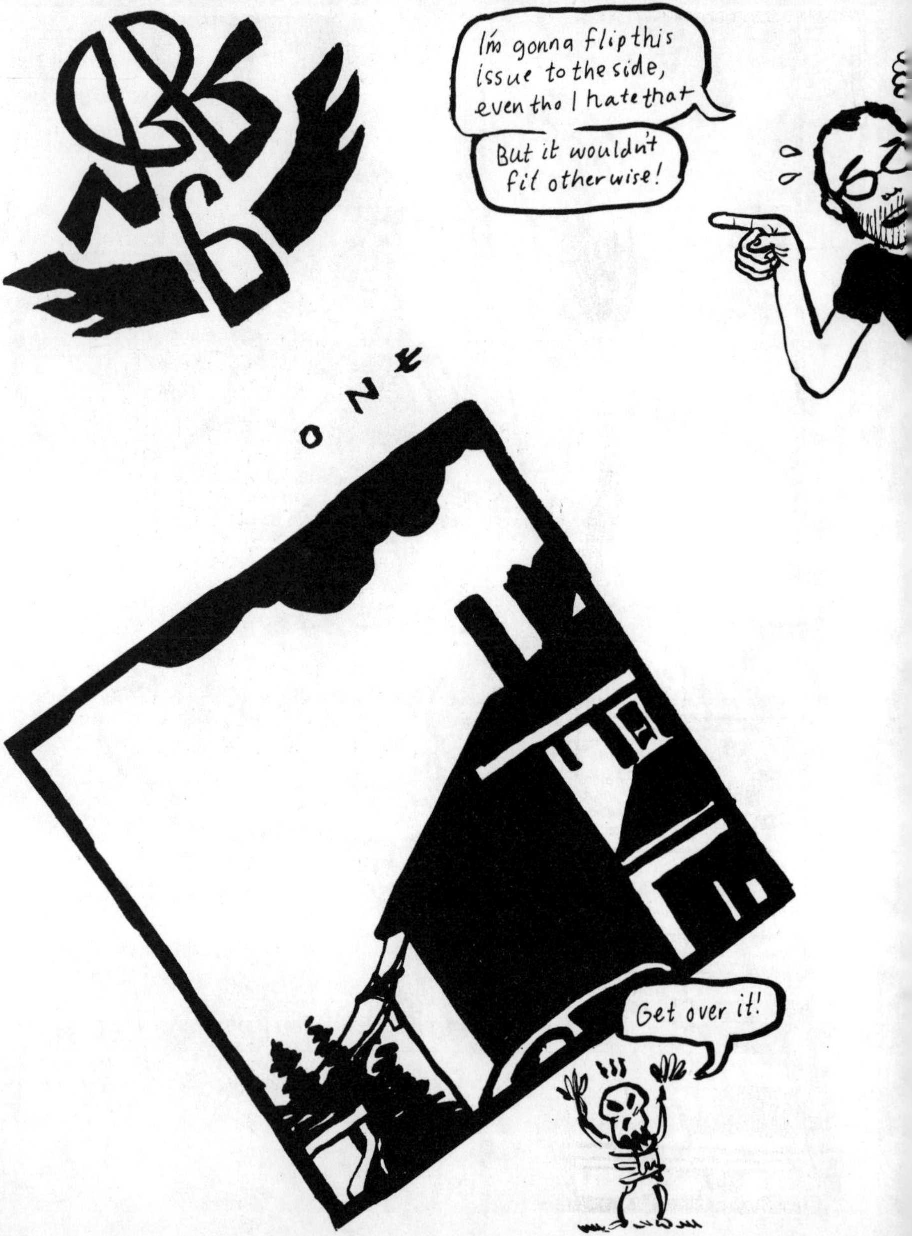
I'm gonna flip this issue to the side, even tho I hate that
But it wouldn't fit otherwise!
ONE
Get over it!

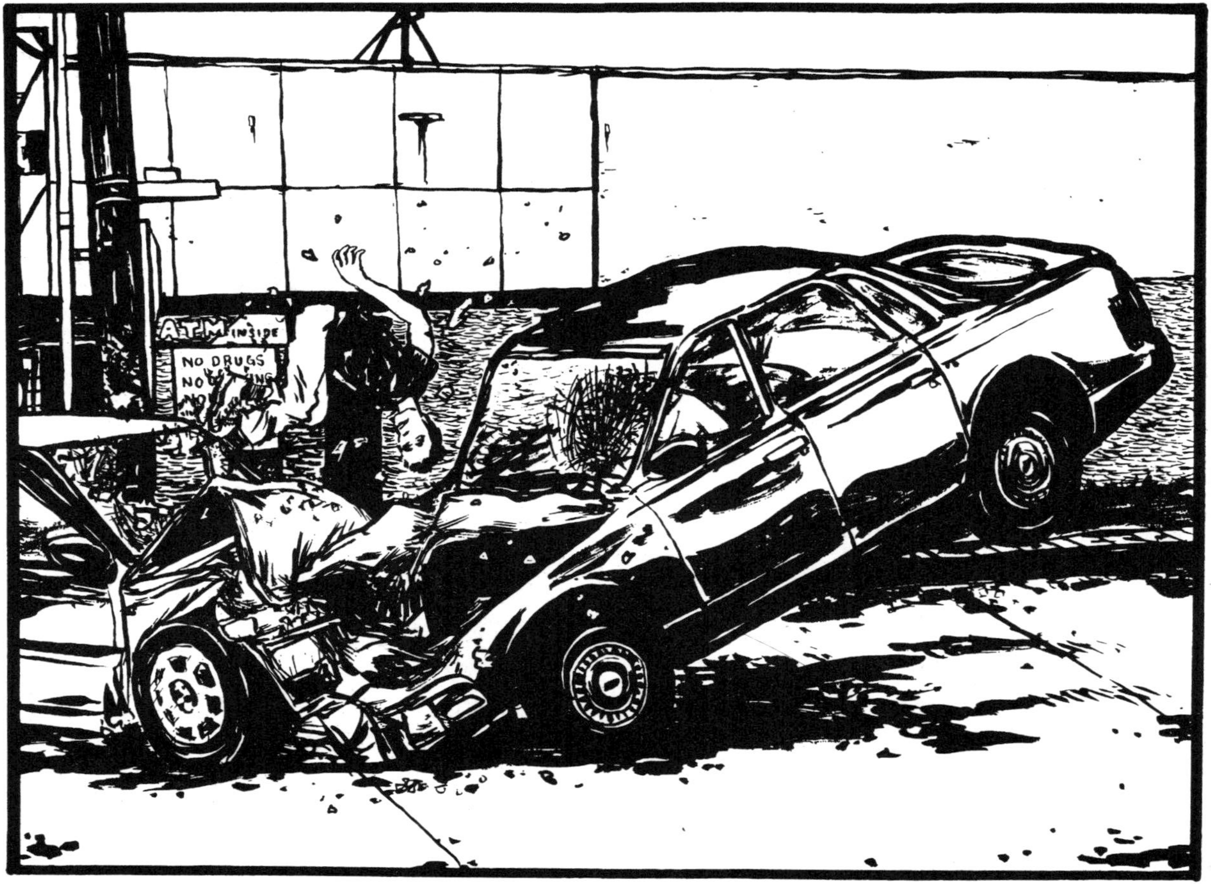
ATM INSIDE
NO DRUGS

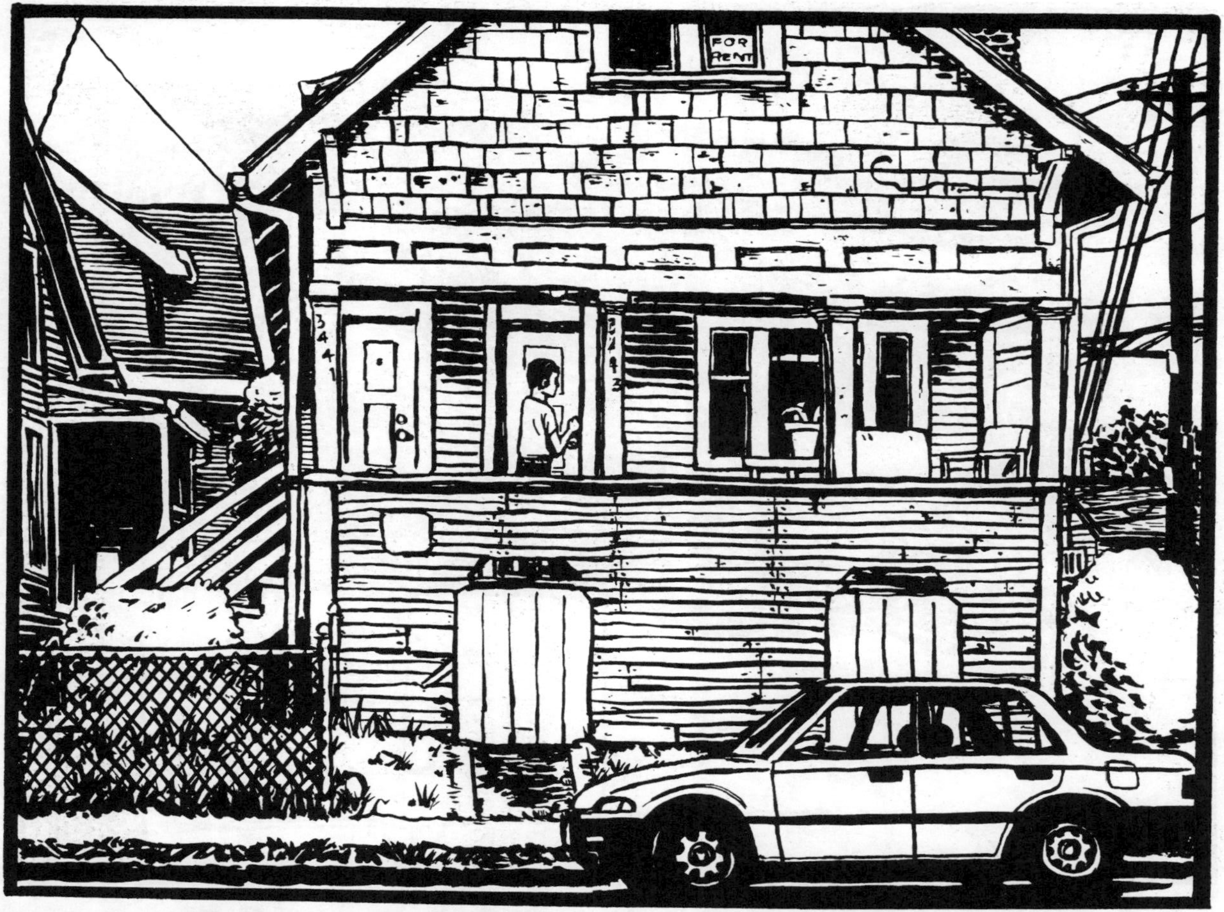
FOR RENT
3441

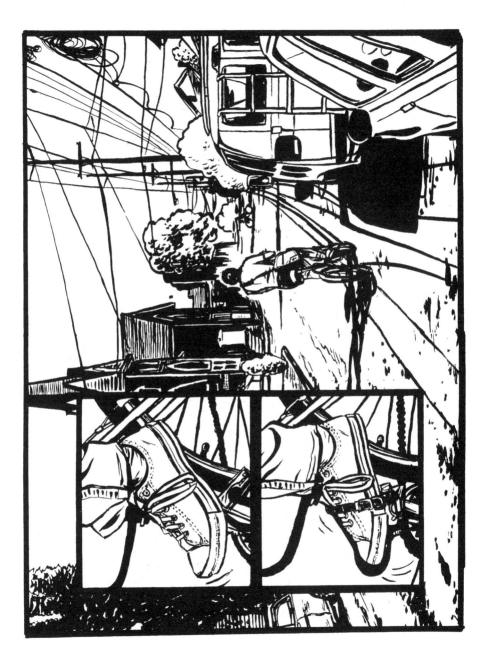

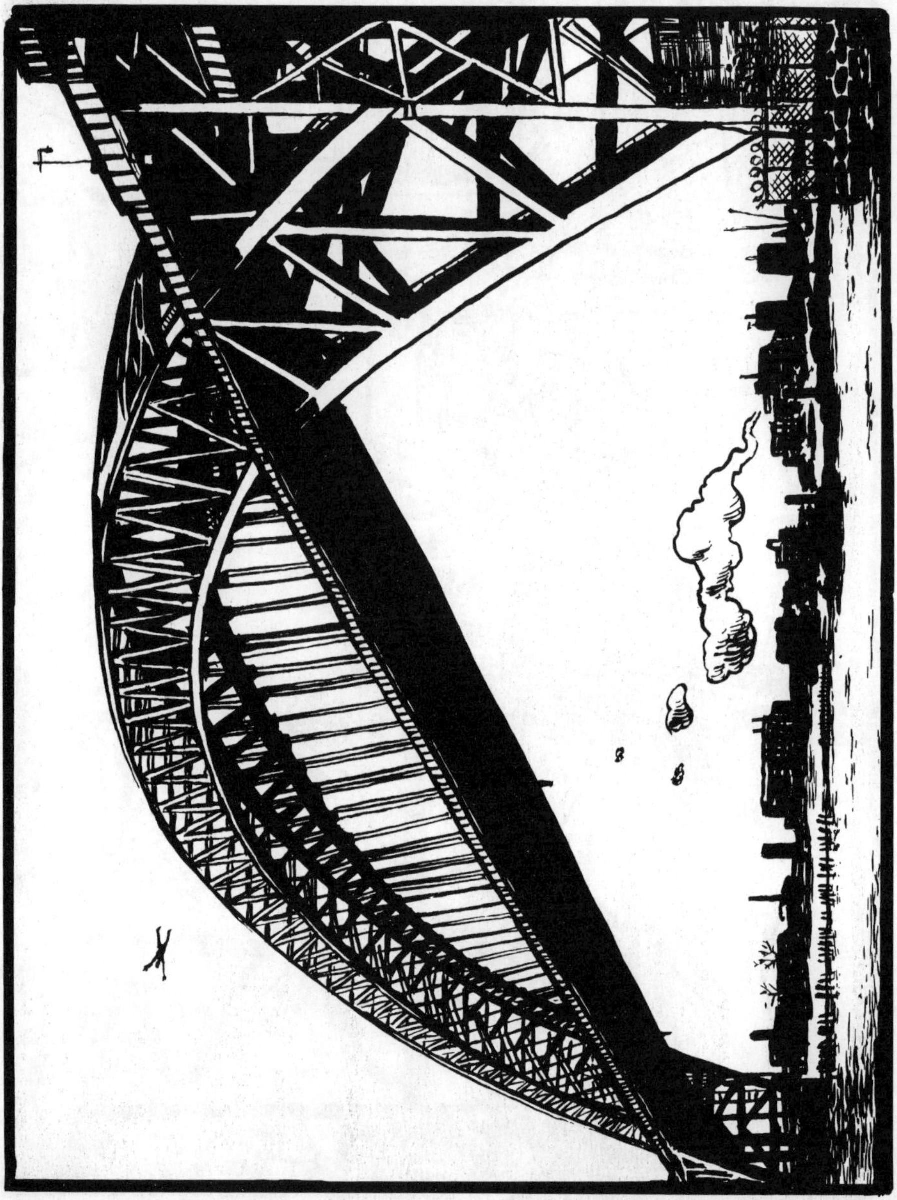

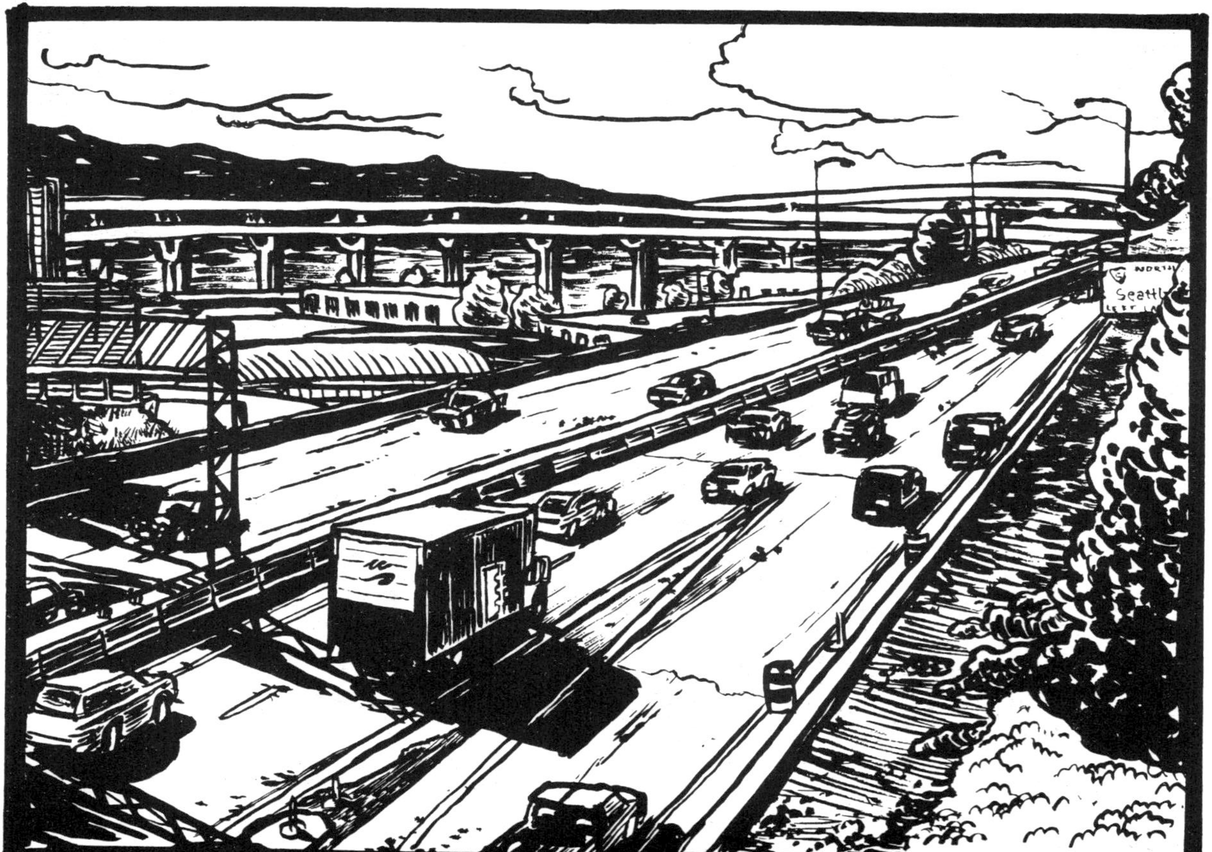
NORTH
Seattl

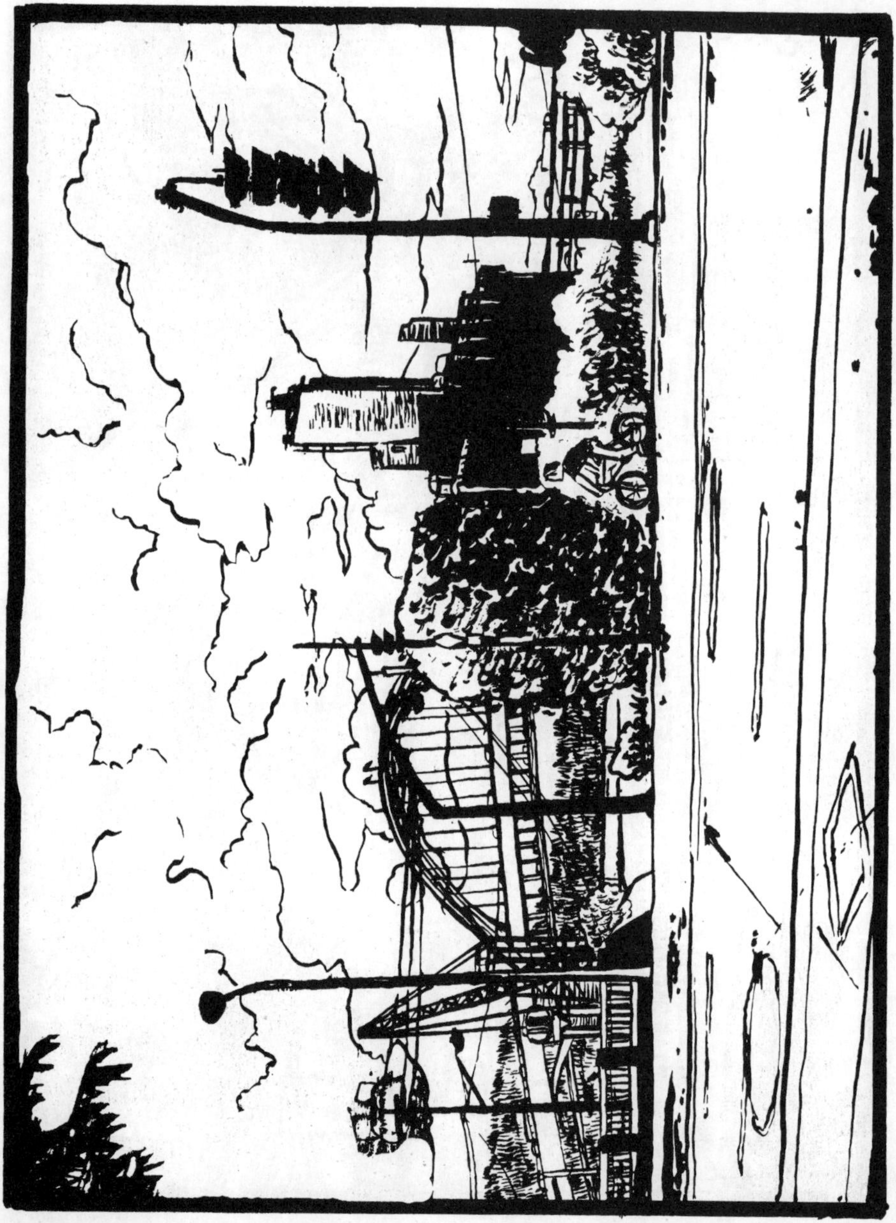

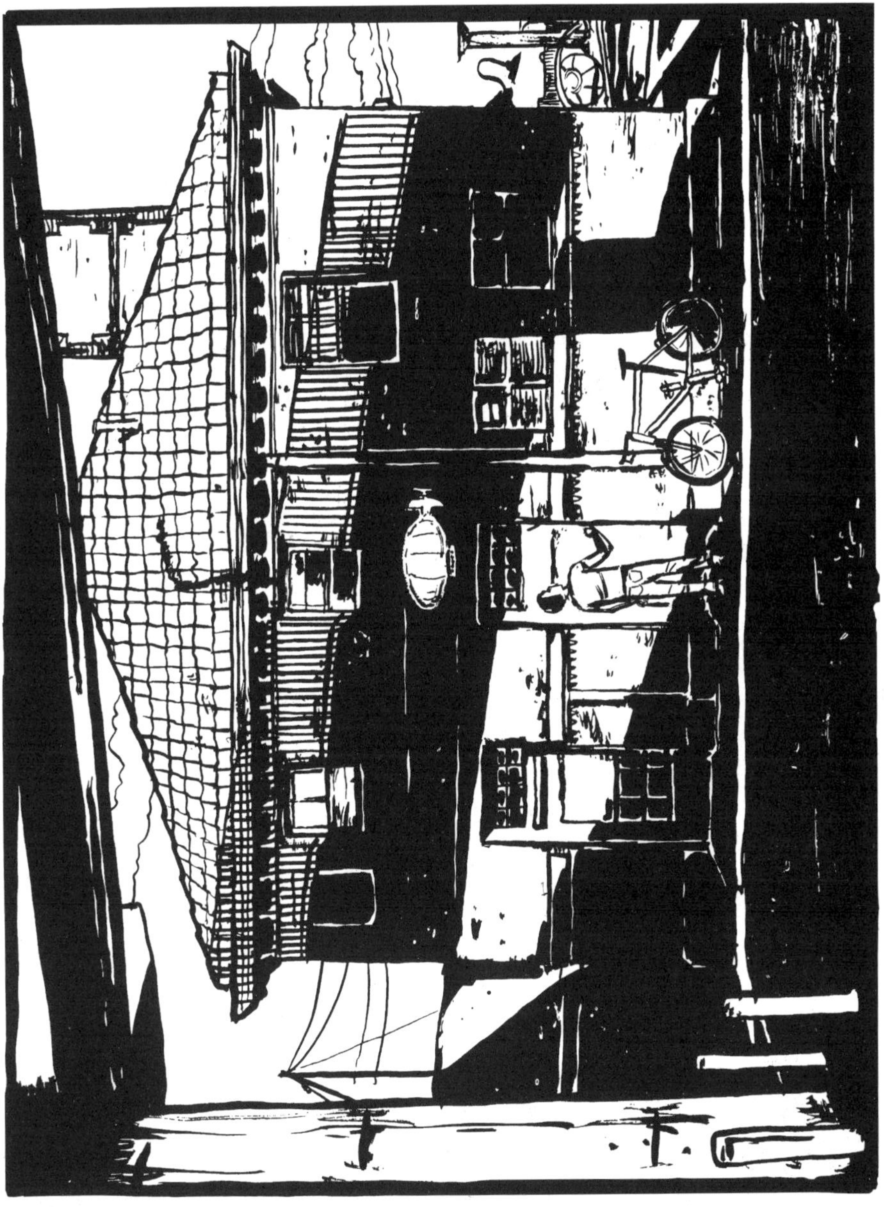

TWO

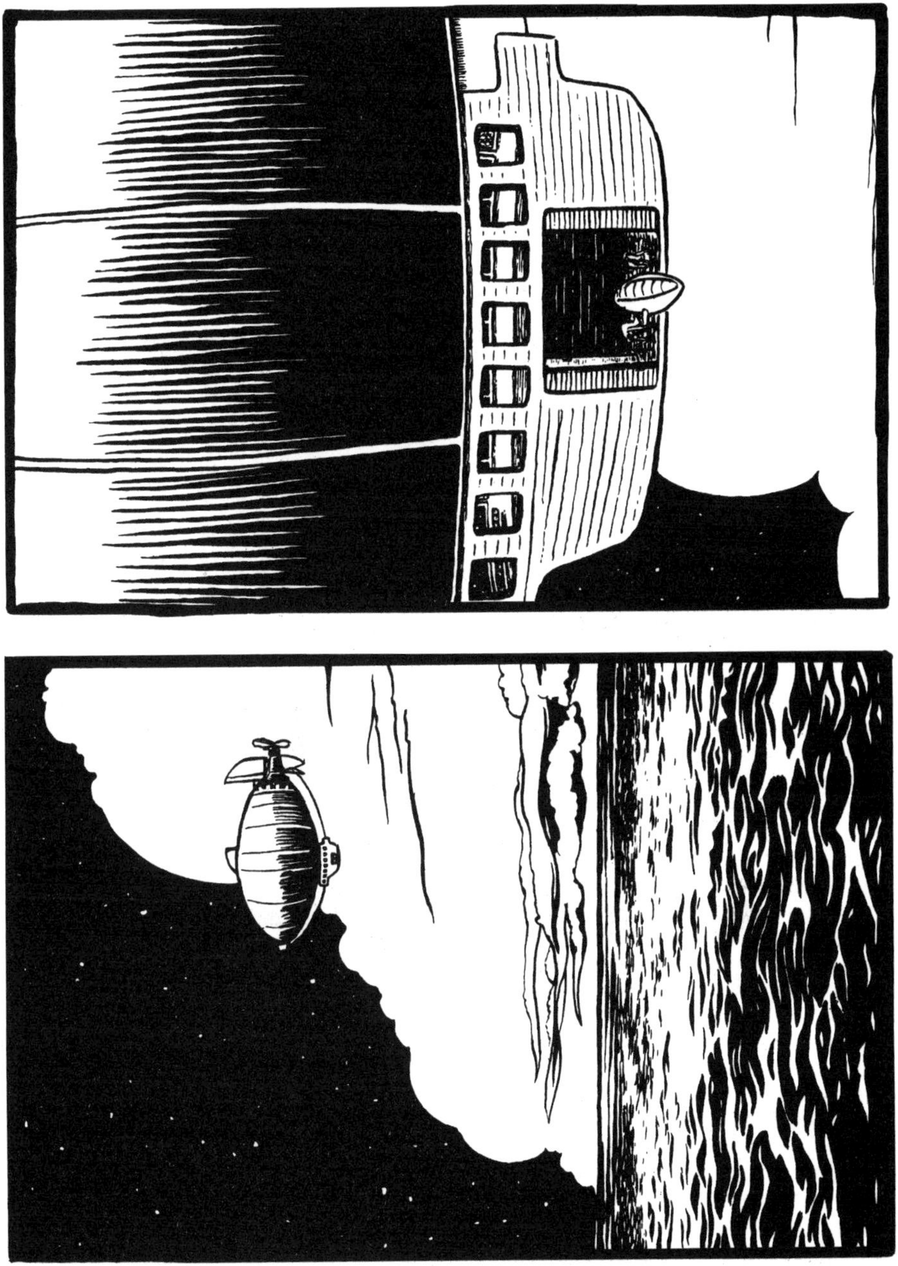

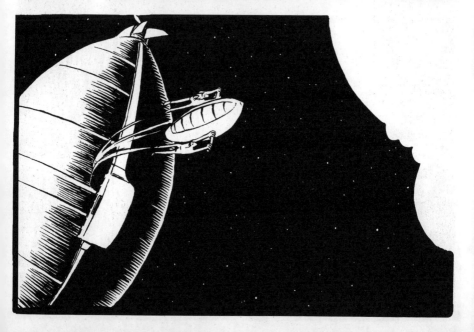

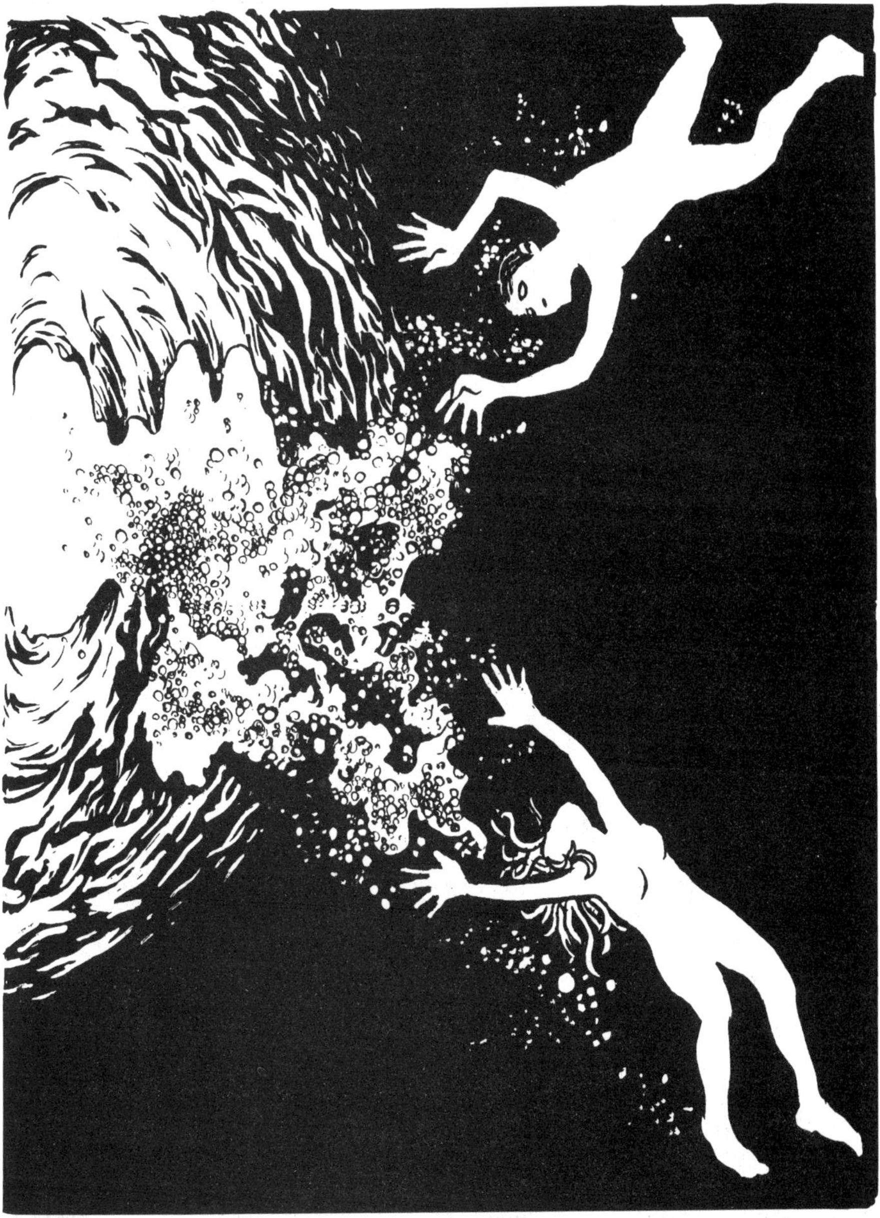

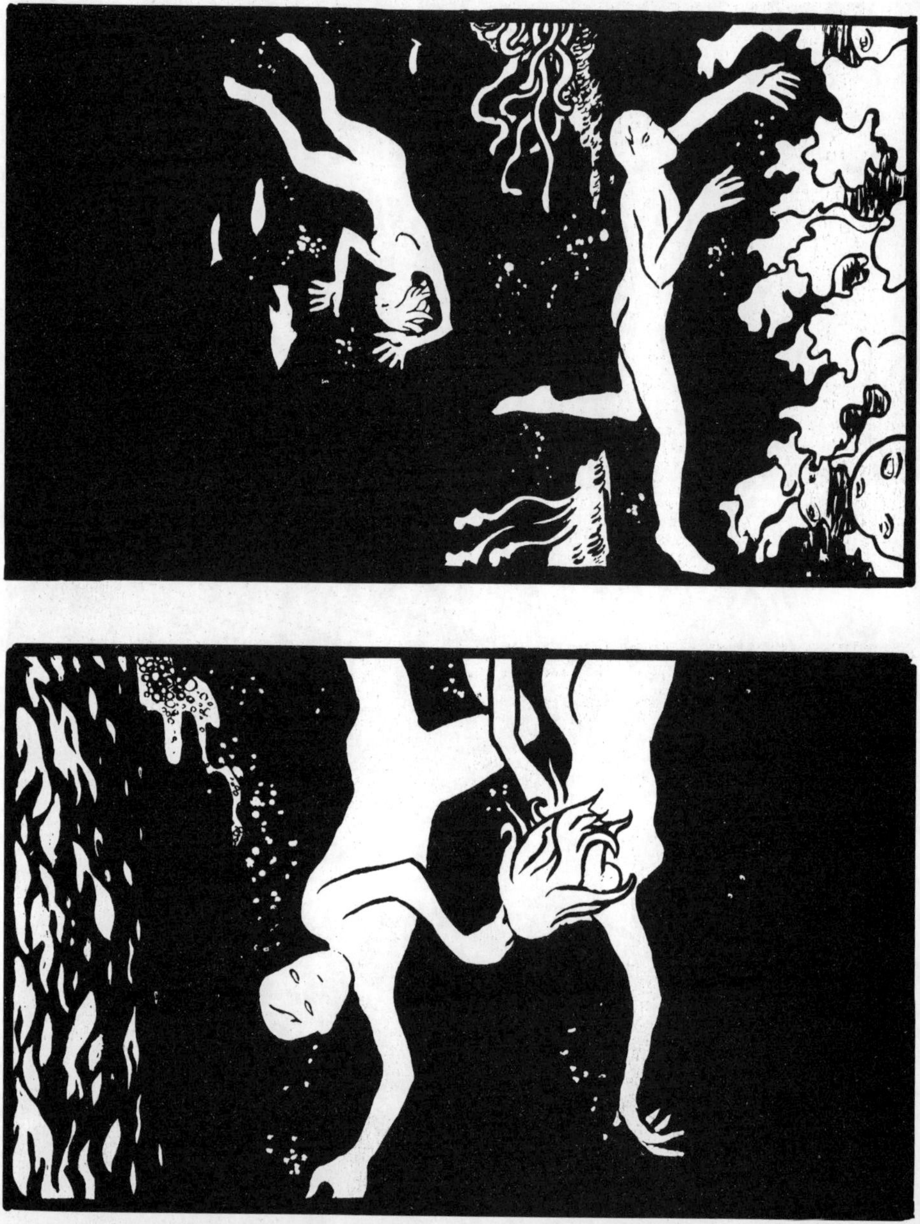

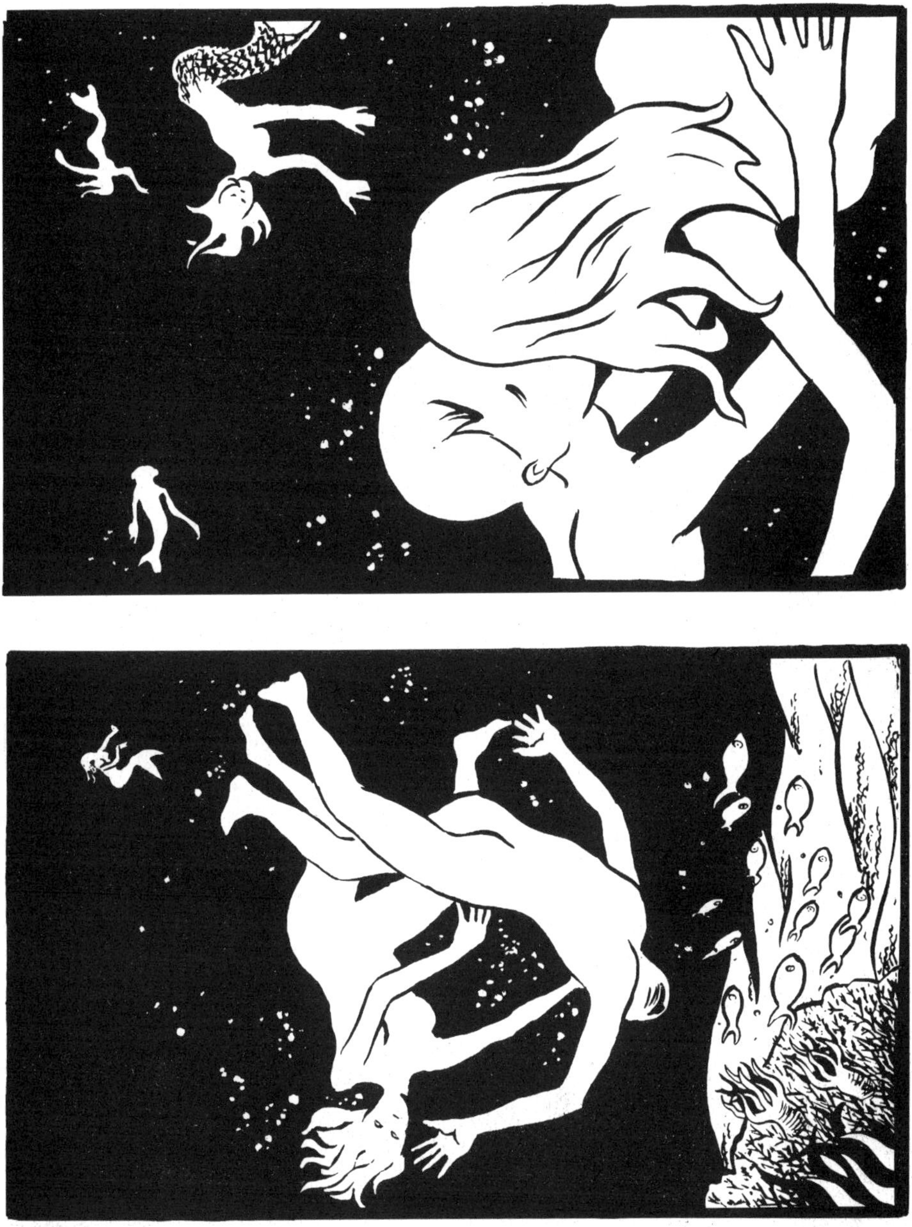

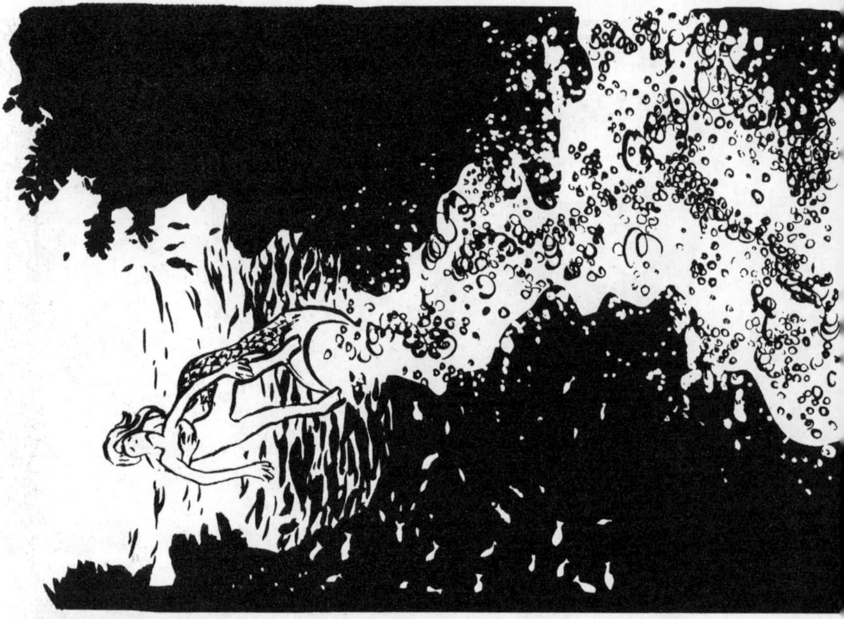

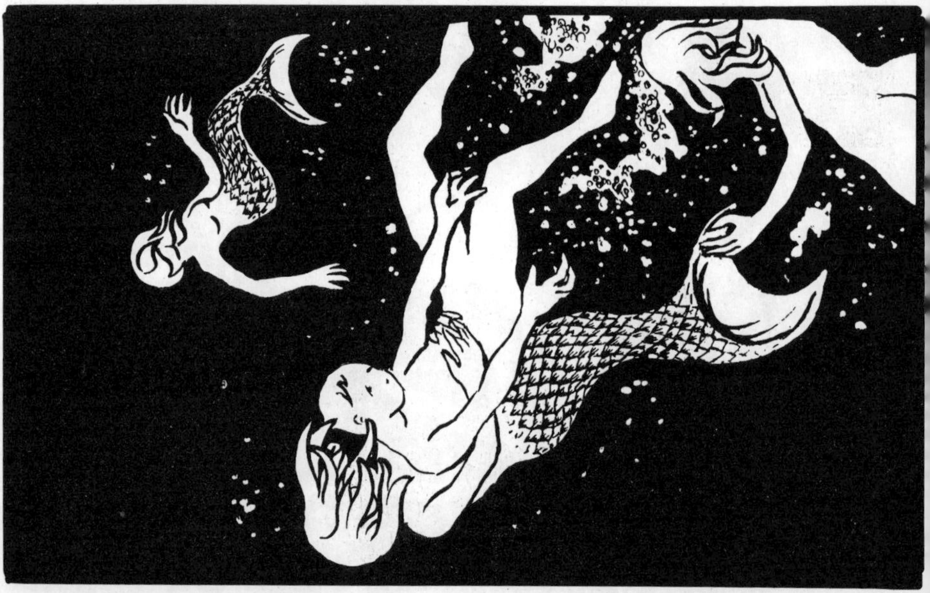

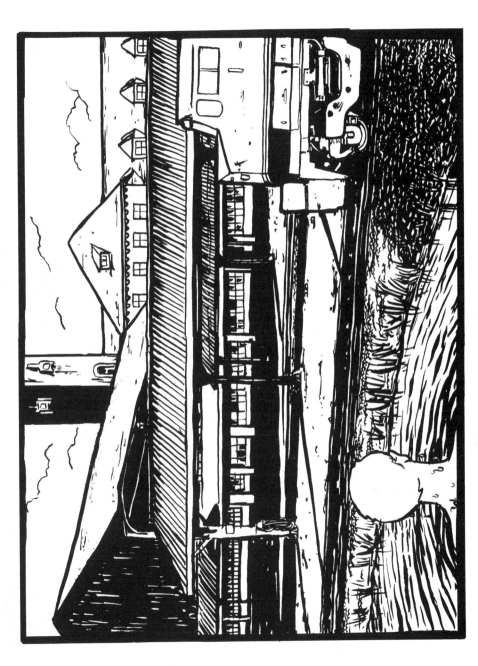

THREE

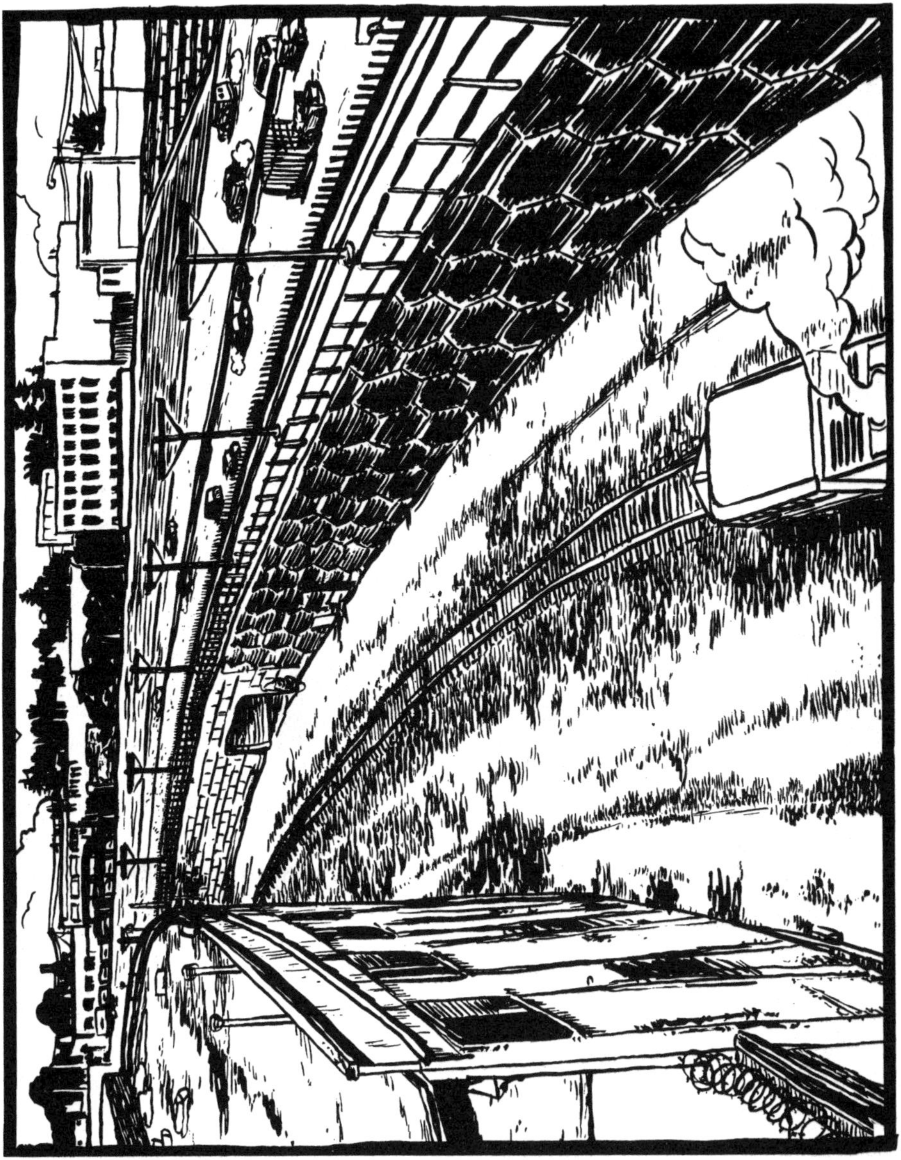

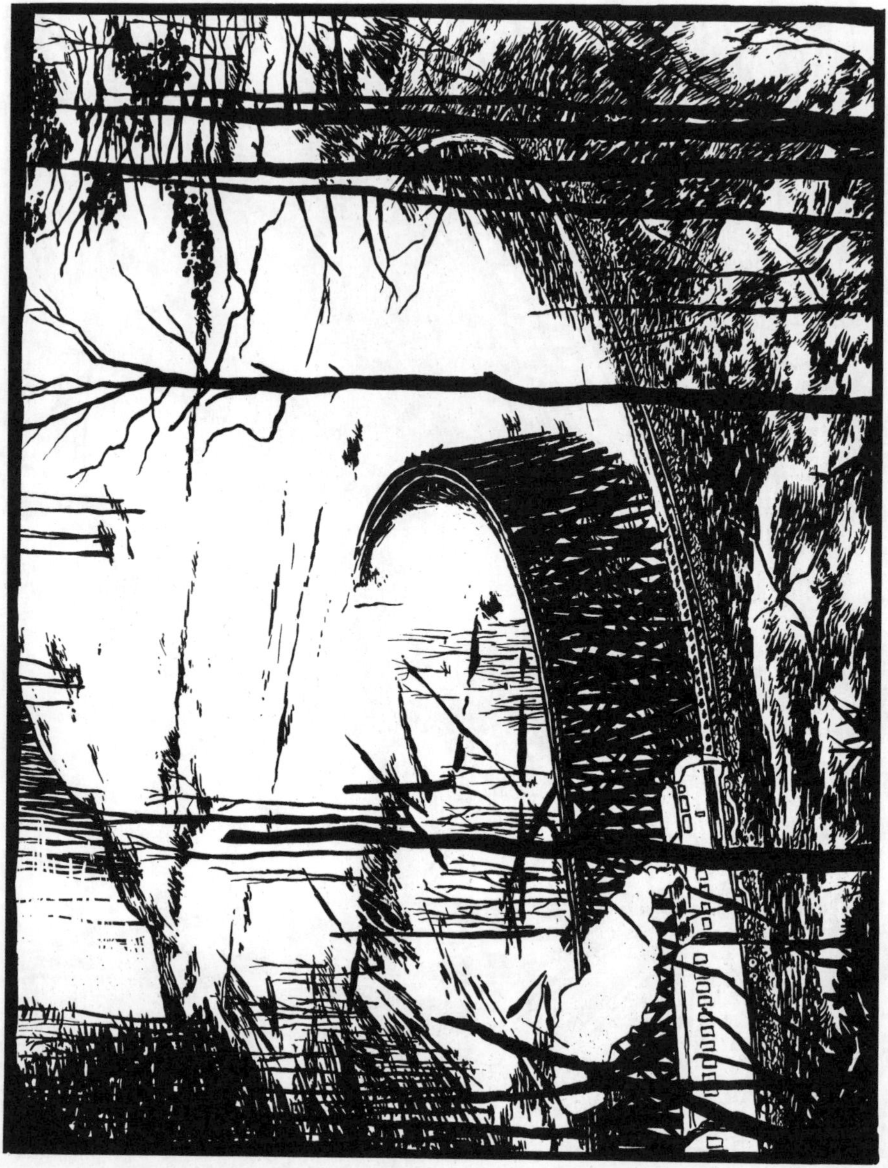

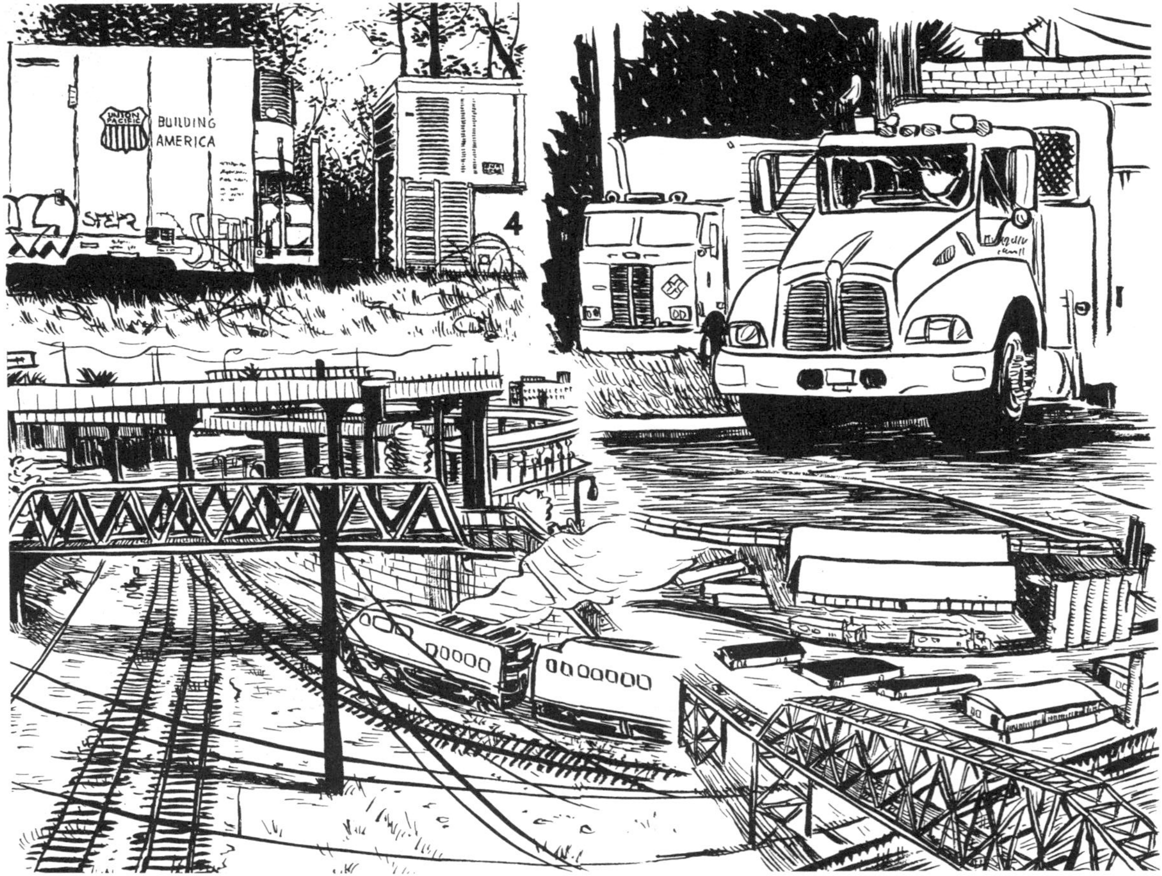
UNION PACIFIC
BUILDING
AMERICA
4

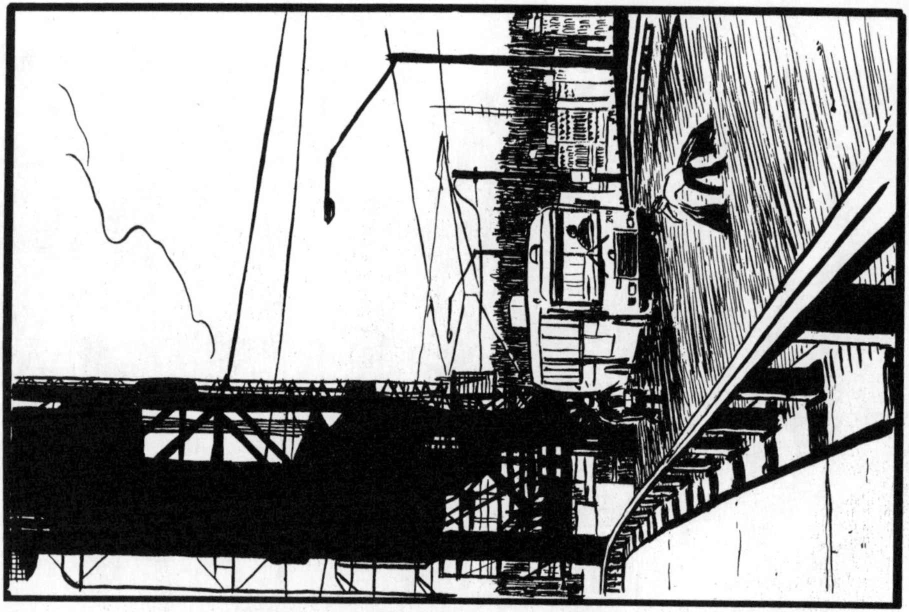

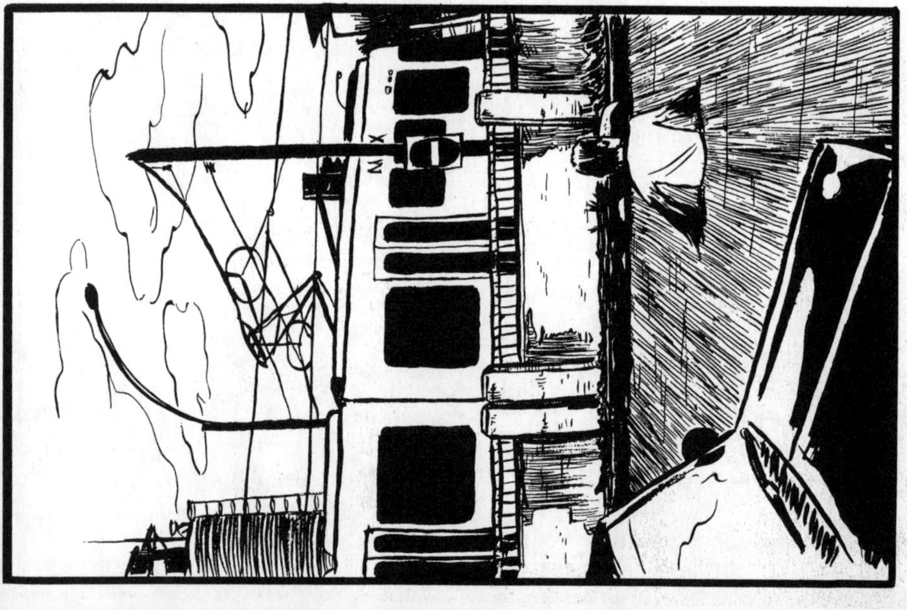

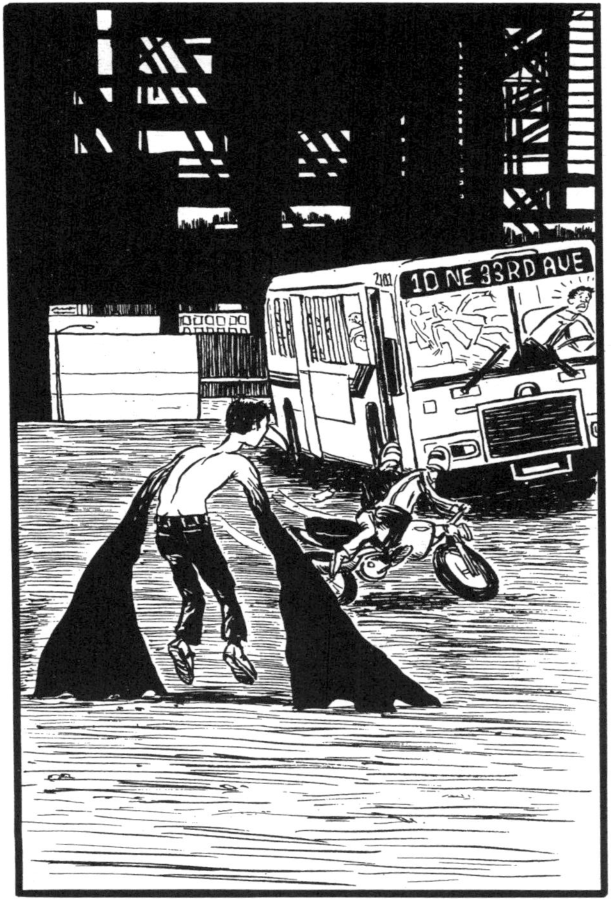
10 NE 33RD AVE
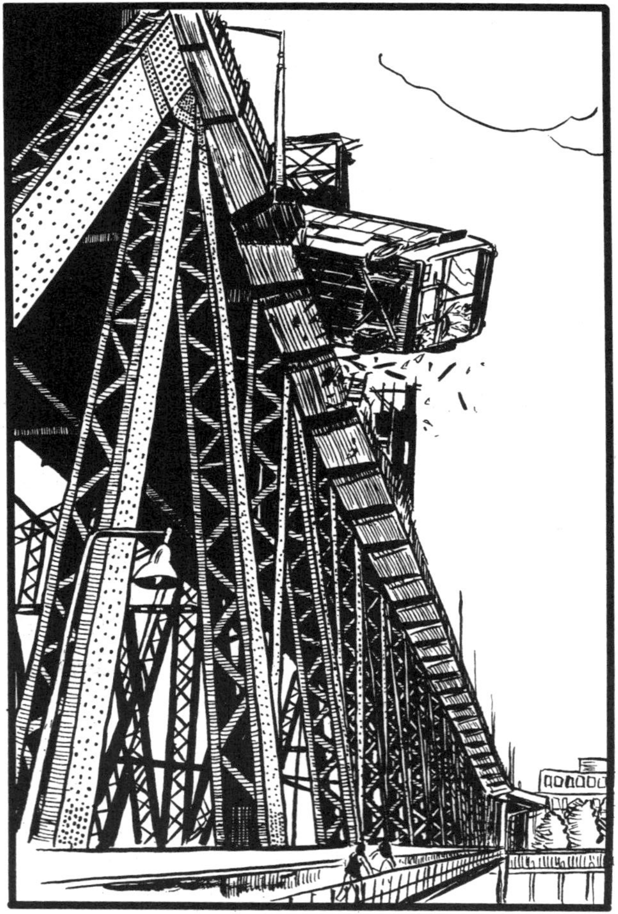

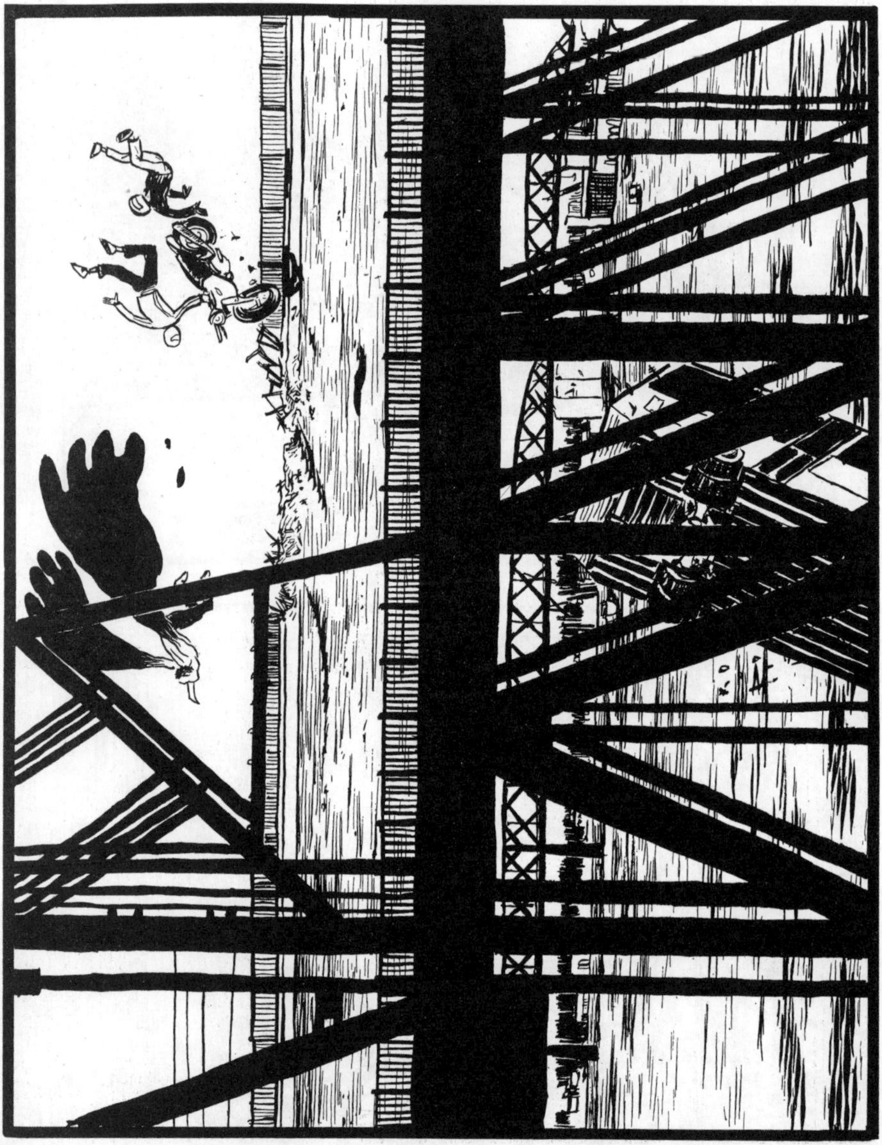

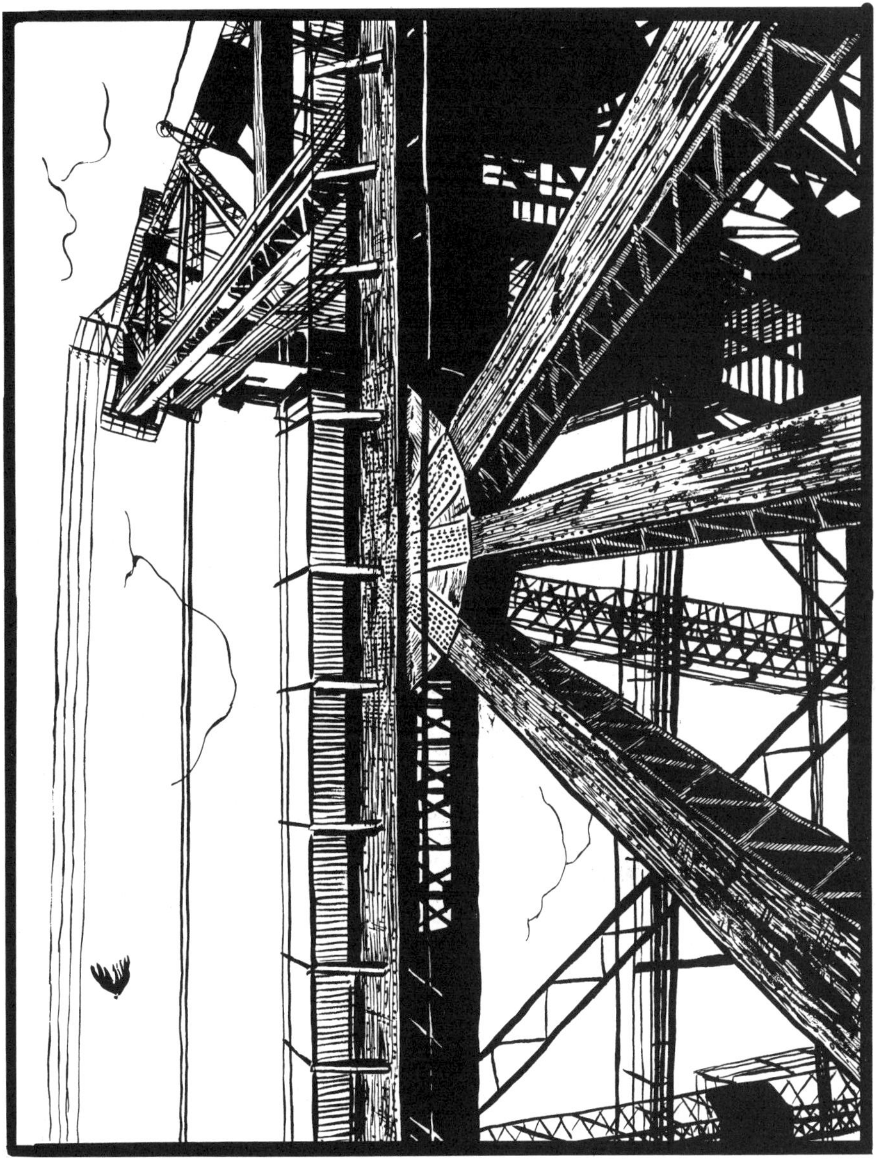

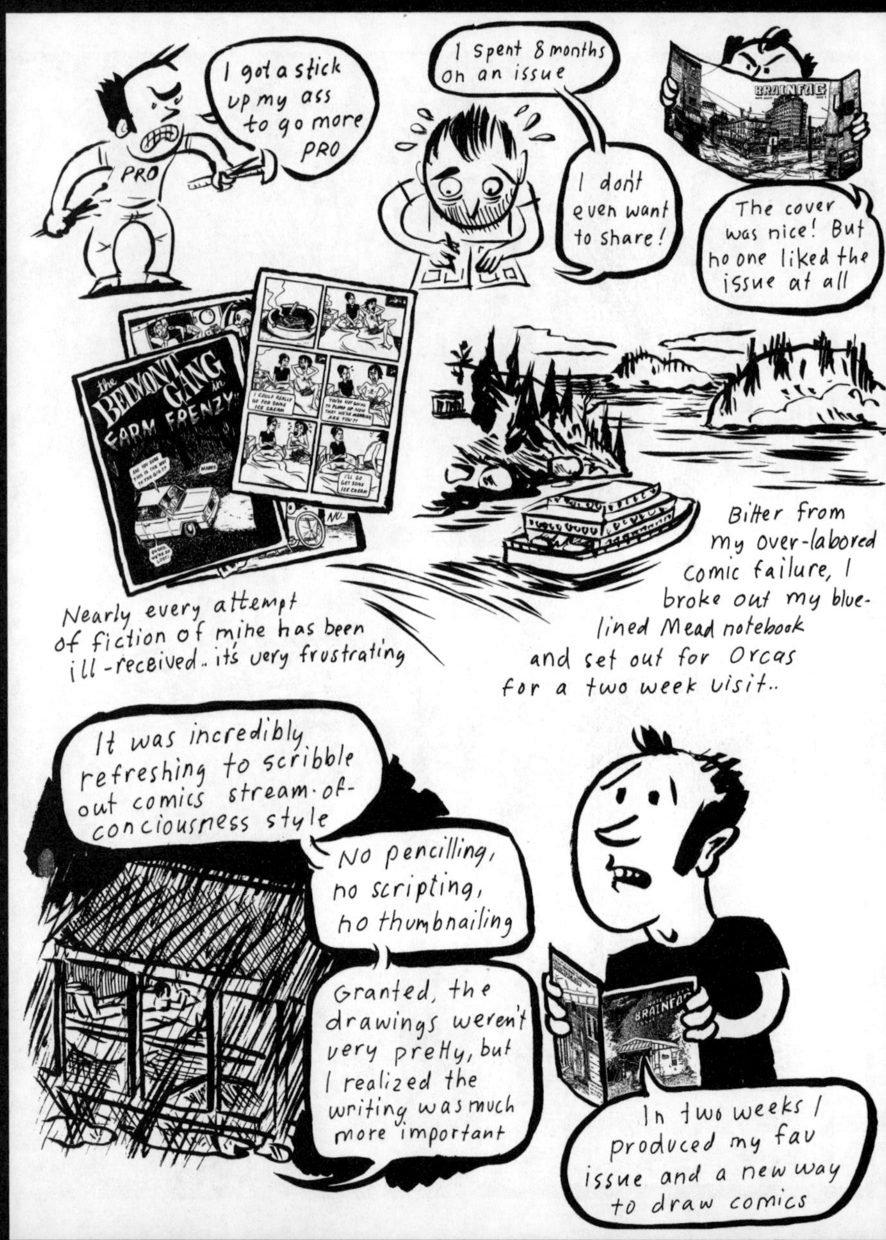

I got a stick up my ass to go more PRO
PRO
I spent 8 months on an issue
I don't even want to share!
BRAINFAG
The cover was nice! But no one liked the issue at all
the BELMONT GANG in FARM FRENZY
Nearly every attempt of fiction of mine has been ill-received.. it's very frustrating
Bitter from my over-labored comic failure, I broke out my blue-lined Mead notebook and set out for Orcas for a two week visit..
It was incredibly refreshing to scribble out comics stream-of-conciousness style
No pencilling, no scripting, no thumbnailing
Granted, the drawings weren't very pretty, but I realized the writing was much more important
BRAINFAG
In two weeks I produced my fav issue and a new way to draw comics

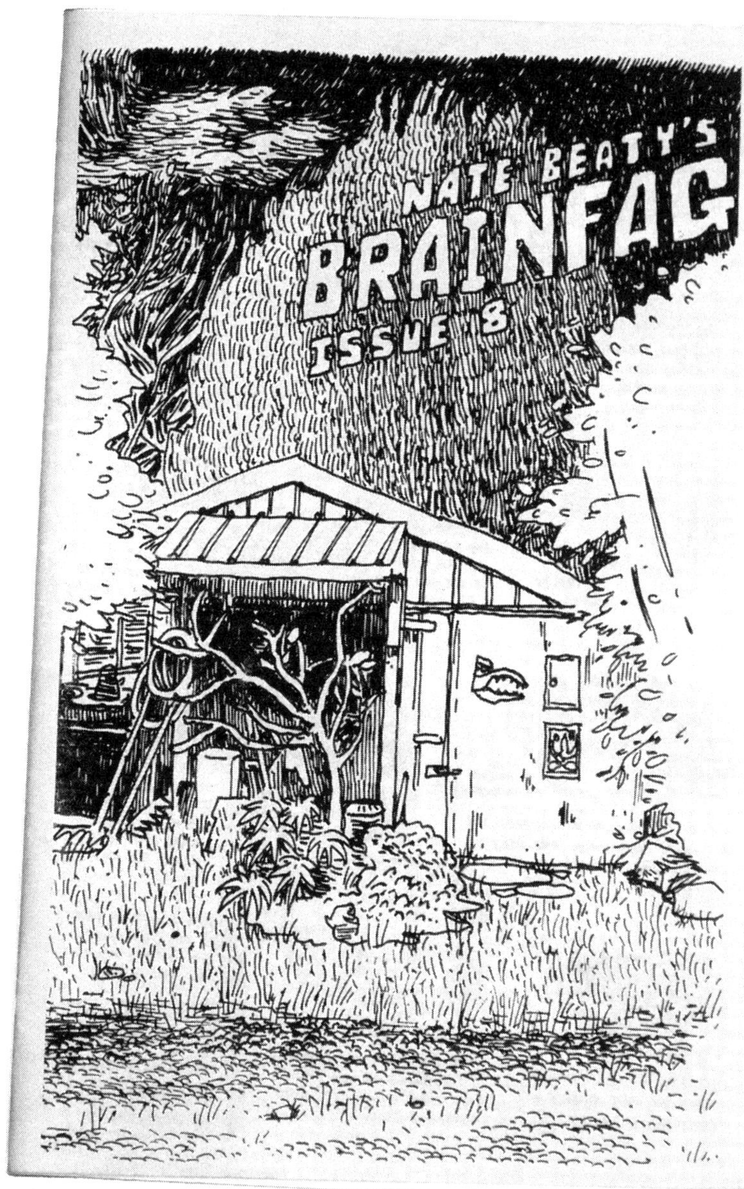
NATE BEATY'S
BRAINFAG
ISSUE 8

A very quick history..

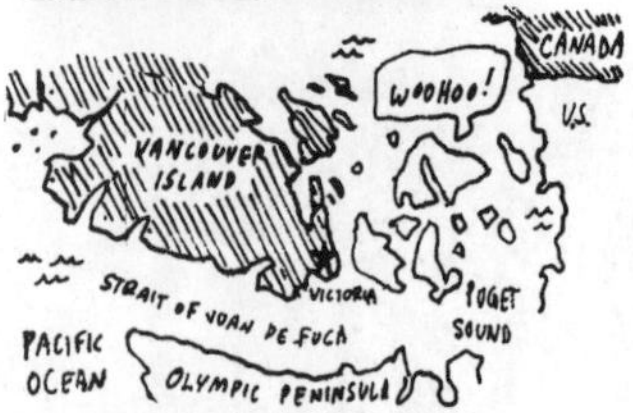
CANADA
U.S.
WOOHOO!
VANCOUVER ISLAND
VICTORIA
STRAIT OF JUAN DE FUCA
PUGET SOUND
PACIFIC OCEAN
OLYMPIC PENINSULA

Once a part of Vancouver Island, Orcas was severed in the last ice age, along with the rest of the gulf and San Juan archipelago

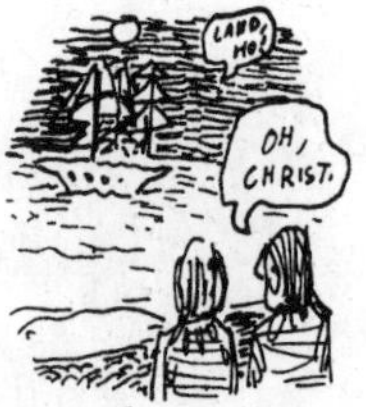
LAND, HO!
OH, CHRIST.

Honkies first appeared in 1841. Lummis native to the area for 12,000 years were "moved" in 1855

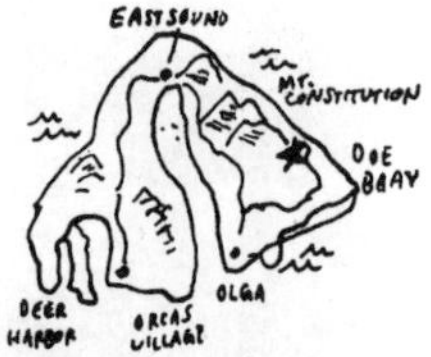
EASTSOUND
MT. CONSTITUTION
DOE BAAY
OLGA
DEER HARBOR
ORCAS VILLAGE

There are now about 3,500 fulltime residents and upwards of 15,000 in the summertime

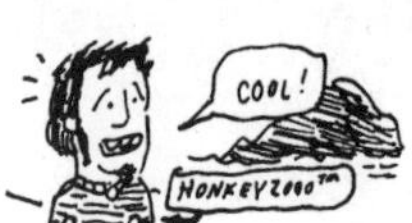
COOL!
HONKEY2000™

I came to visit my friend Mindy in '95 for a weekend and stayed 6 months

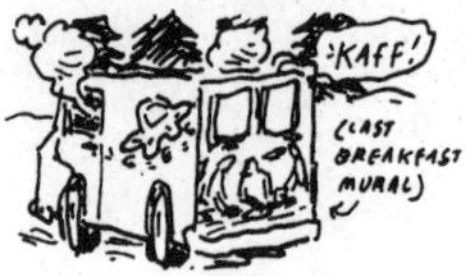
KAFF!
(LAST BREAKFAST MURAL)

JJ and I lived in the Spam Van & worked at Doe Bay Resort for one very fun summer! ①

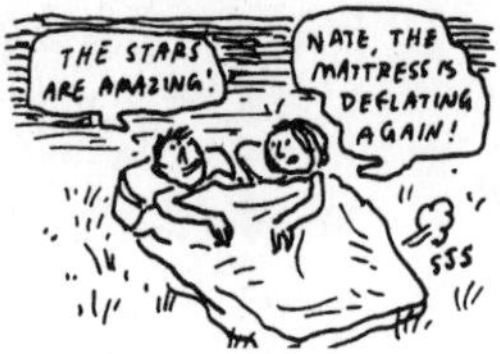
THE STARS ARE AMAZING!
NATE, THE MATTRESS IS DEFLATING AGAIN!
SSS

Two years later, I moved back to the island with my girlfriend Sam ②

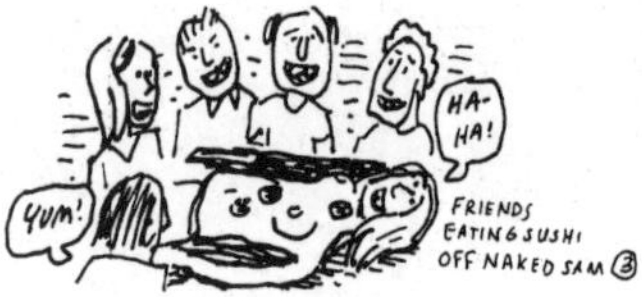
HA-HA!
YUM!
FRIENDS EATING SUSHI OFF NAKED SAM ③

We fit well (too well?) with the younger community and may have become permanent, salty locals, but!

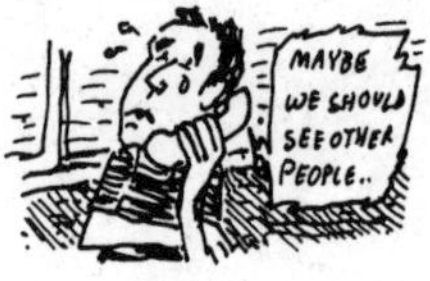
MAYBE WE SHOULD SEE OTHER PEOPLE..

We broke up just as I was starting my second landscaping season with Victor ④

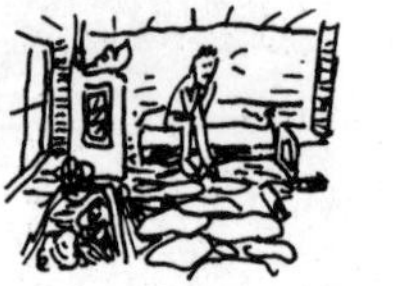

Sam moved back to Portland and I spent 8 months living alone in a greenhouse

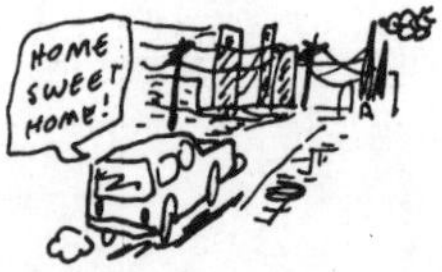
HOME SWEET HOME!

In the winter I moved back to pdx and soon dated Abigail ⑤

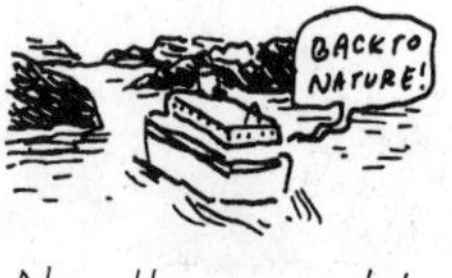
BACK TO NATURE!

Now, three years later, I recently made two working visits in the summer / fall

Our comic begins the night before taking the Greyhound north for my second visit...

① SEE "FUNK MAGNET"
② SEE BRAINFAG 1
③ UM.. LONG STORY?
④ SEE BRAINFAG 3
⑤ SEE BRAINFAG 5

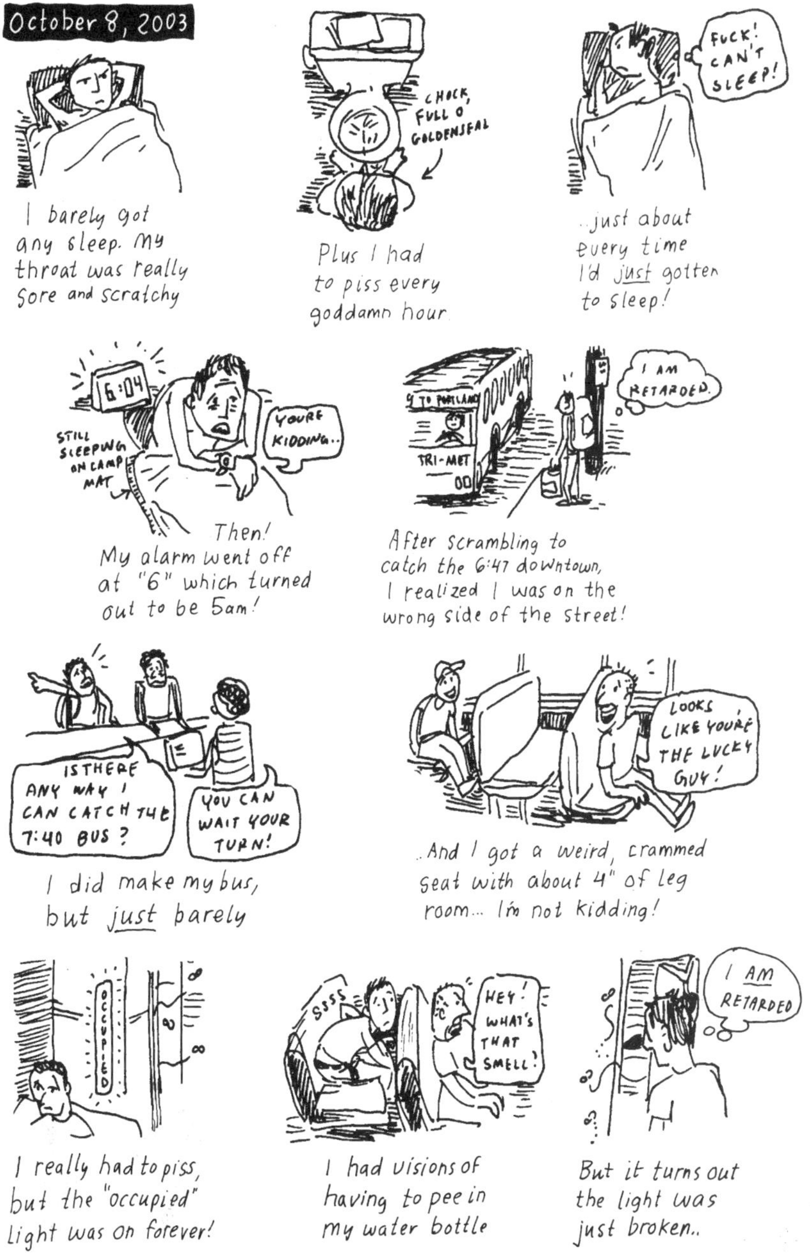

October 8, 2003
I barely got any sleep. My throat was really sore and scratchy
CHOCK, FULL O' GOLDENSEAL
Plus I had to piss every goddamn hour
FUCK! CAN'T SLEEP!
..just about every time I'd just gotten to sleep!
6:04
STILL SLEEPING ON CAMP MAT
YOU'RE KIDDING..
Then! My alarm went off at "6" which turned out to be 5am!
TO PORTLAND
TRI-MET
I AM RETARDED.
After scrambling to catch the 6:47 downtown, I realized I was on the wrong side of the street!
IS THERE ANY WAY I CAN CATCH THE 7:40 BUS?
YOU CAN WAIT YOUR TURN!
I did make my bus, but just barely
LOOKS LIKE YOU'RE THE LUCKY GUY!
..And I got a weird, crammed seat with about 4" of leg room... I'm not kidding!
OCCUPIED
I really had to piss, but the "occupied" light was on forever!
SSSS
HEY! WHAT'S THAT SMELL?
I had visions of having to pee in my water bottle
I AM RETARDED
But it turns out the light was just broken..

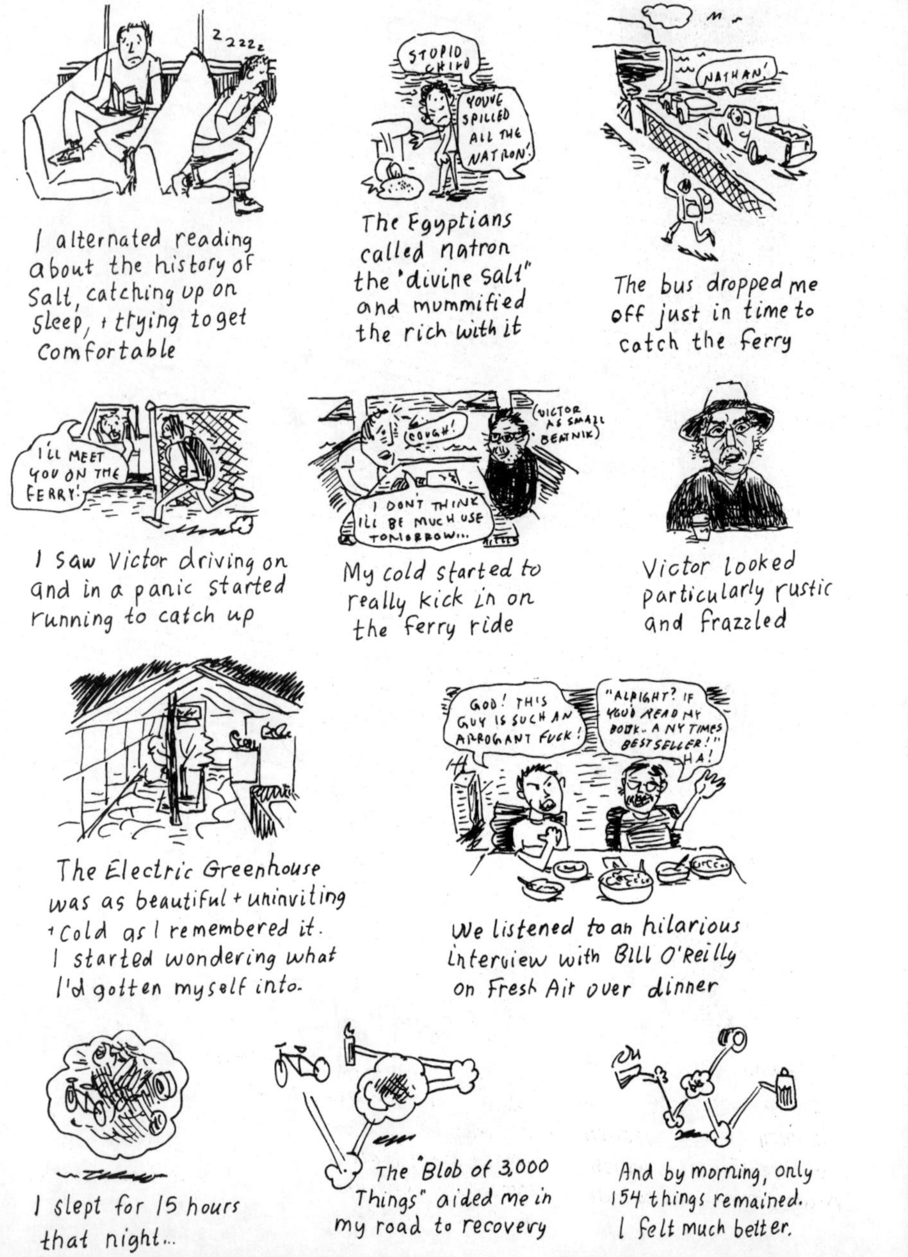
zzzzz
I alternated reading about the history of Salt, catching up on Sleep, + trying to get Comfortable
STUPID CHILD
YOU'VE SPILLED ALL THE NATRON!
The Egyptians called natron the "divine Salt" and mummified the rich with it
NATHAN!
The bus dropped me off just in time to catch the ferry
I'LL MEET YOU ON THE FERRY!
I saw Victor driving on and in a panic started running to catch up
(COUGH!)
(VICTOR AS SMALL BEATNIK)
I DON'T THINK I'LL BE MUCH USE TOMORROW...
My cold started to really kick in on the ferry ride
Victor looked particularly rustic and frazzled
The Electric Greenhouse was as beautiful + uninviting + Cold as I remembered it. I started wondering what I'd gotten myself into.
GOD! THIS GUY IS SUCH AN ARROGANT FUCK!
"ALRIGHT? IF YOU'D READ MY BOOK.. A NY TIMES BESTSELLER!" HA!
We listened to an hilarious interview with Bill O'Reilly on Fresh Air over dinner
I slept for 15 hours that night...
The "Blob of 3,000 Things" aided me in my road to recovery
And by morning, only 154 things remained. I felt much better.

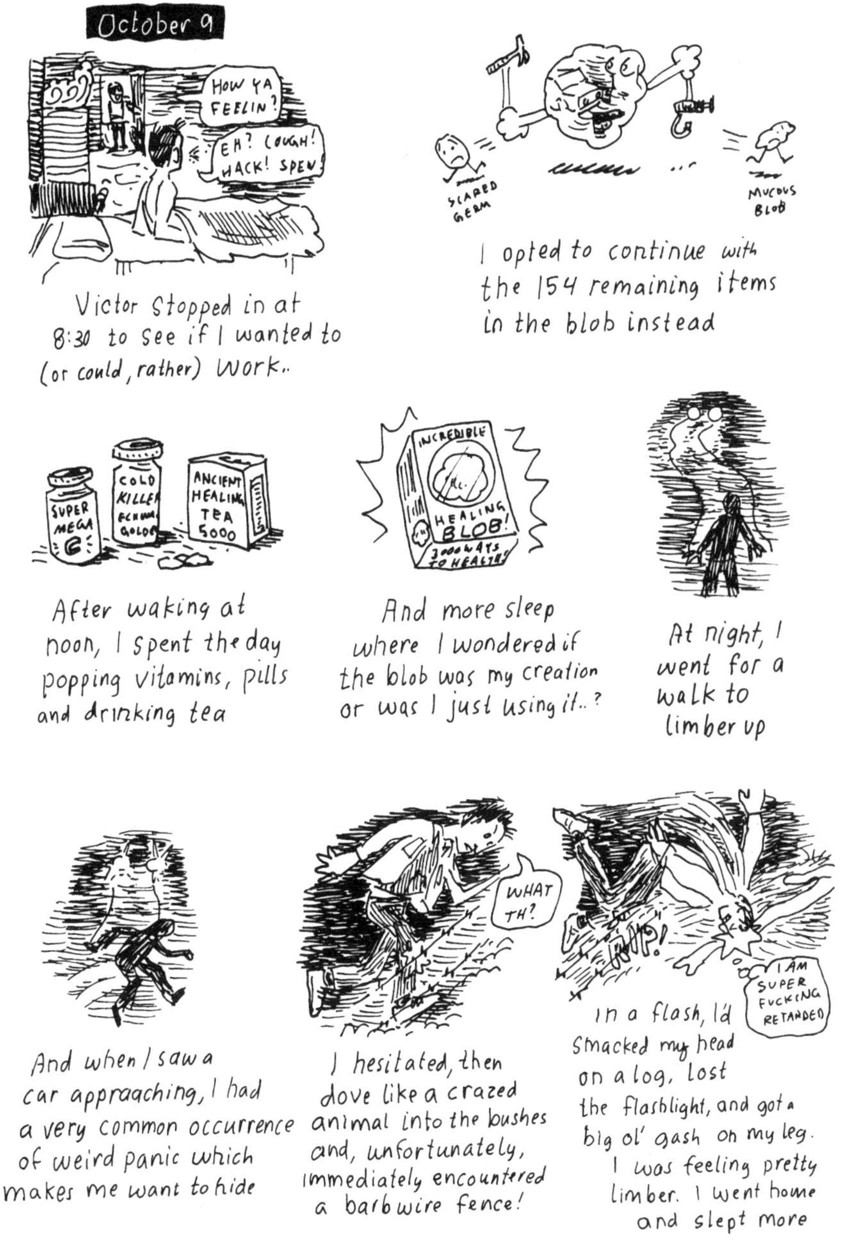
October 9
HOW YA FEELIN?
EH? COUGH! HACK! SPEW!
Victor stopped in at 8:30 to see if I wanted to (or could, rather) work..
SCARED GERM
MUCOUS BLOB
I opted to continue with the 154 remaining items in the blob instead
SUPER MEGA C
COLD KILLER
ANCIENT HEALING TEA 5000
INCREDIBLE
HEALING BLOB!
3000 WAYS TO HEALTH!
After waking at noon, I spent the day popping vitamins, pills and drinking tea
And more sleep where I wondered if the blob was my creation or was I just using it..?
At night, I went for a walk to limber up
And when I saw a car appraaching, I had a very common occurrence of weird panic which makes me want to hide
WHAT TH?
I hesitated, then dove like a crazed animal into the bushes and, unfortunately, immediately encountered a barbwire fence!
I AM SUPER FUCKING RETARDED
In a flash, I'd smacked my head on a log, lost the flashlight, and got a big ol' gash on my leg. I was feeling pretty limber. I went home and slept more

October 10

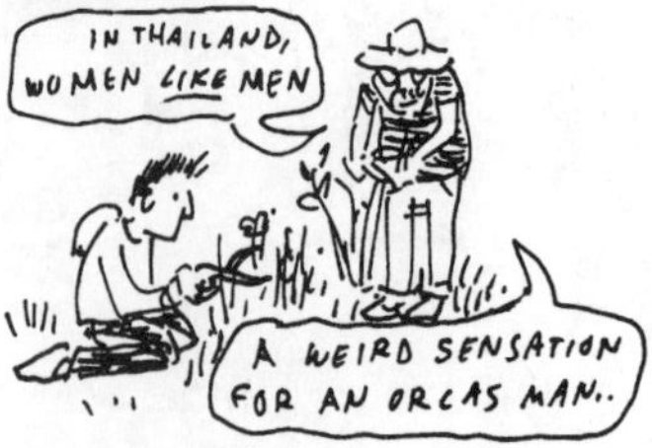
IN THAILAND, WOMEN LIKE MEN
A WEIRD SENSATION FOR AN ORCAS MAN..

A pretty laid back day of pruning and sweeping / raking

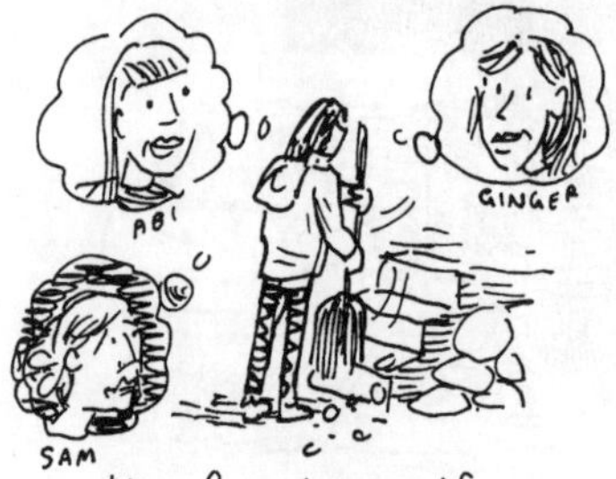
ABI
GINGER
SAM

I've found myself musing over old loves, most likely from visiting old routines.. >SIGH<

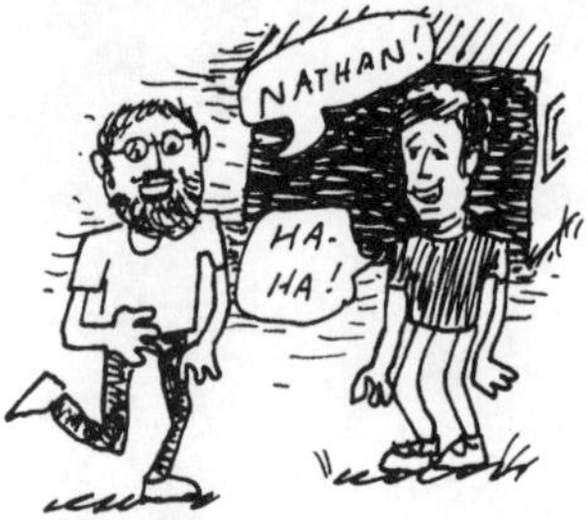
NATHAN!
HA-HA!

In town I saw Alan and Charles. (I see I can only draw myself at this size, ha)

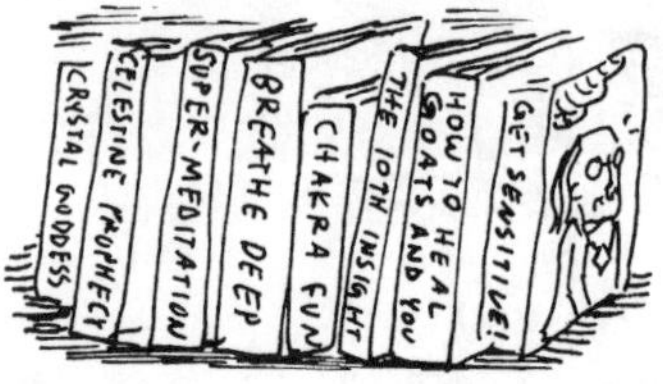
CRYSTAL GODDESS
CELESTINE PROPHECY
SUPER-MEDITATION
BREATHE DEEP
CHAKRA FUN
THE 10TH INSIGHT
HOW TO HEAL GOATS AND YOU
GET SENSITIVE!

Glancing at one person's library, I remembered a lot of why I left Orcas, and how I relate even less now

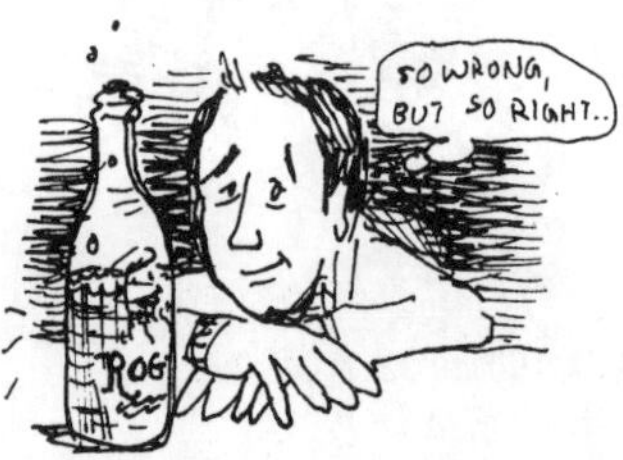
SO WRONG, BUT SO RIGHT..
ROG

At night I thoroughly enjoyed a 24oz. Rogue I think it made me feel a little less sick

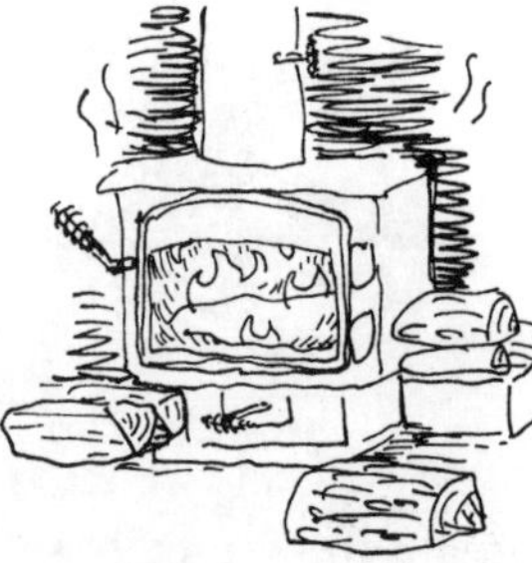

I coaxed a fire out of the woodstove I installed ages ago

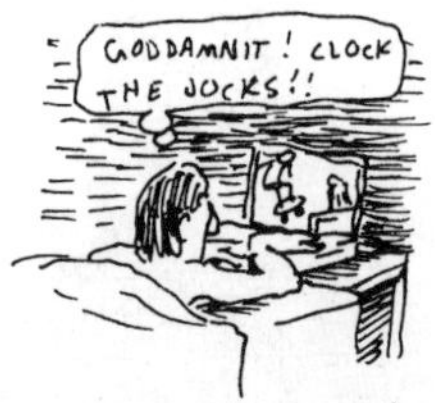
GODDAMNIT! CLOCK THE JOCKS!!

Then I played Tony Hawk 4 out in the secluded beautiful woods of Orcas Island

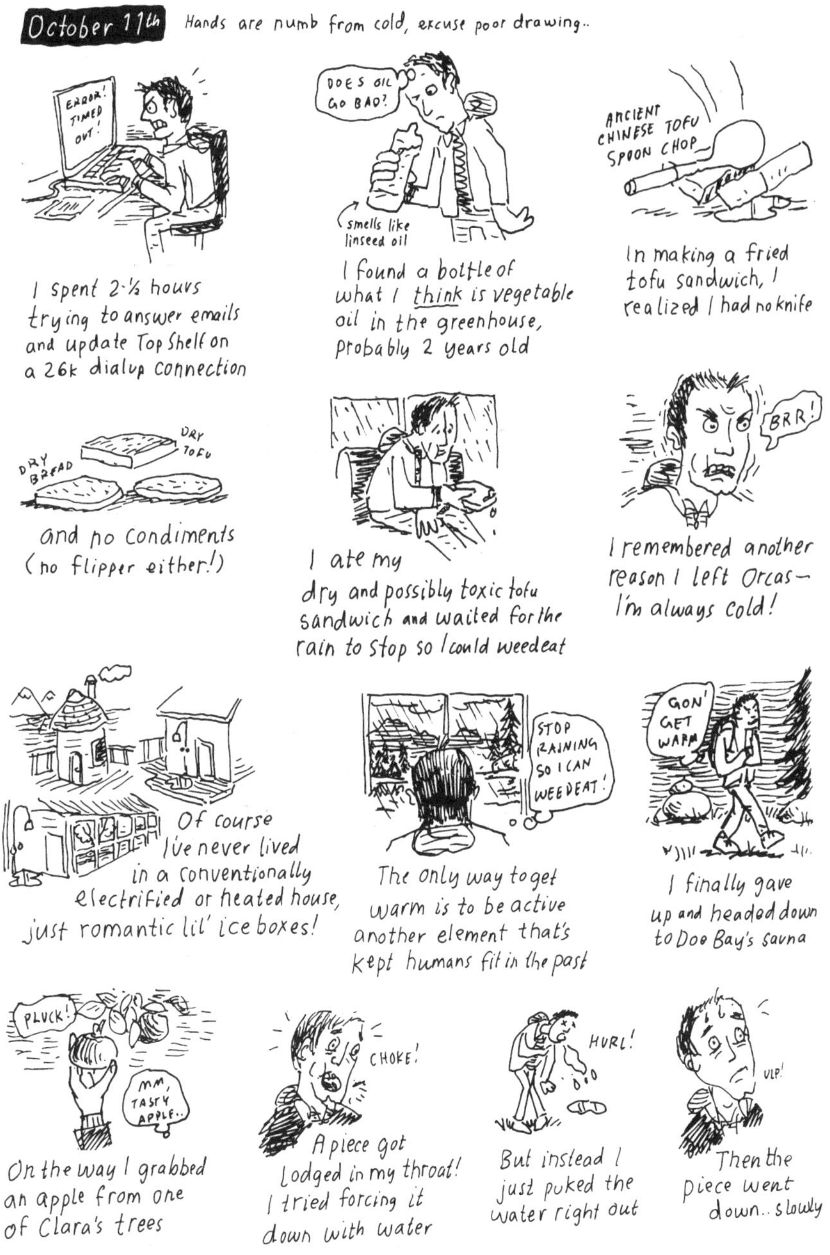
October 11th
Hands are numb from cold, excuse poor drawing..
ERROR! TIMED OUT!
I spent 2½ hours trying to answer emails and update Top Shelf on a 26k dialup connection
DOES OIL GO BAD?
smells like linseed oil
I found a bottle of what I think is vegetable oil in the greenhouse, probably 2 years old
ANCIENT CHINESE TOFU SPOON CHOP
In making a fried tofu sandwich, I realized I had no knife
DRY TOFU
DRY BREAD
and no condiments (no flipper either!)
I ate my dry and possibly toxic tofu sandwich and waited for the rain to stop so I could weedeat
BRR!
I remembered another reason I left Orcas— I'm always cold!
Of course I've never lived in a conventionally electrified or heated house, just romantic lil' ice boxes!
STOP RAINING SO I CAN WEEDEAT!
The only way to get warm is to be active another element that's kept humans fit in the past
GON' GET WARM
I finally gave up and headed down to Doe Bay's sauna
PLUCK!
MM, TASTY APPLE..
On the way I grabbed an apple from one of Clara's trees
CHOKE!
A piece got lodged in my throat! I tried forcing it down with water
HURL!
But instead I just puked the water right out
ULP!
Then the piece went down.. slowly

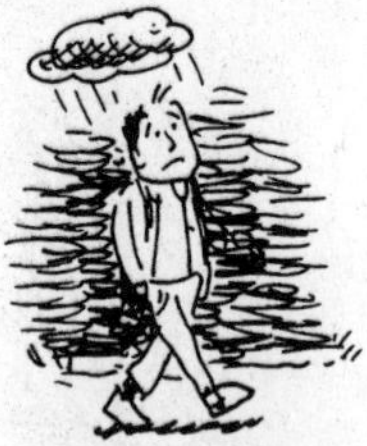

Have I always been a walking catastrophe?

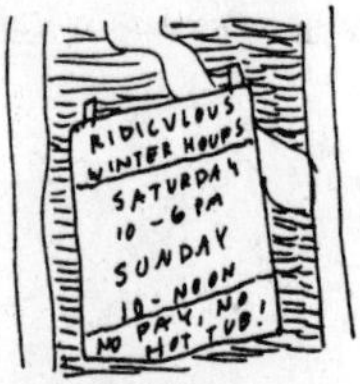
RIDICULOUS WINTER HOURS
SATURDAY 10-6 PM
SUNDAY 10-NOON
NO PAY, NO HOT TUB!

The Doe Bay office was closed. (Shit! I was hoping they still sold beer!)

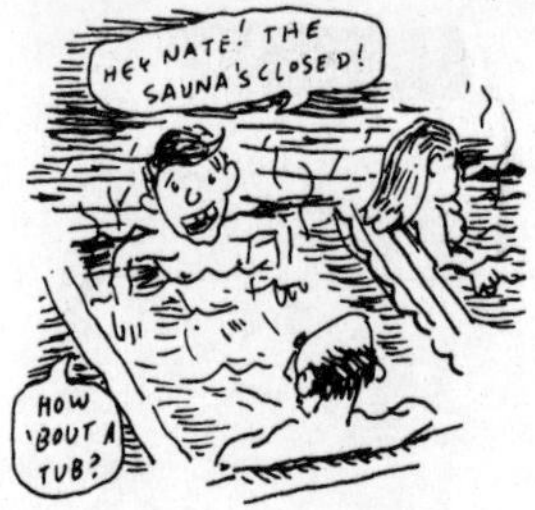
HEY NATE! THE SAUNA'S CLOSED!
HOW 'BOUT A TUB?

Unfortunately, Doe Bay's "springs' are heated and chlorinated heavily - ugh!

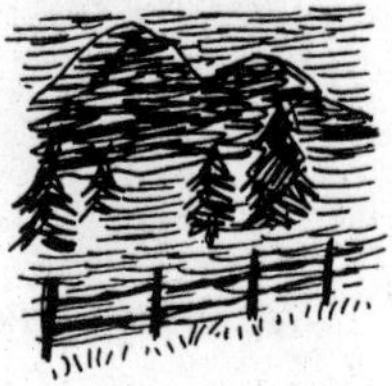

Altho initially really down about the sauna being out for my visit, the walk back was gorgeous

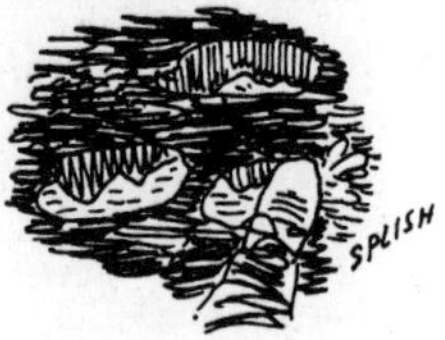
SPLISH

The gray green of northwest nighttime, silence but wind and footsteps

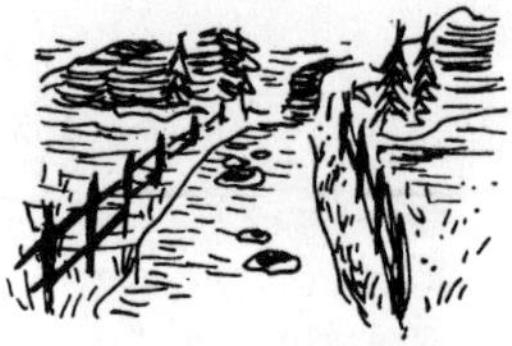

My mind soaked it up and was lost in all my memories of times in my life when walks like this were more common

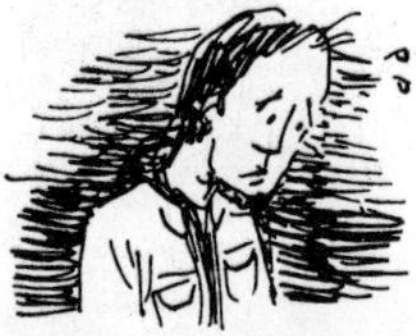

A common theme so far on this trip is a forgotten longing for companionship.. A dangerous thing to my quest for eternal bachelorhood, celibacy and extreme clarity

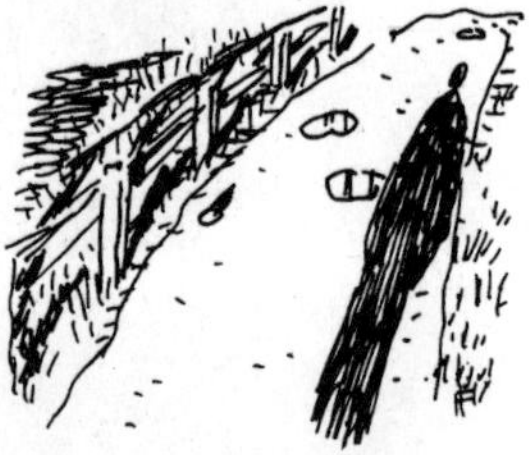

I was amazed at how easily a passing minivan vacuumed up all this peaceful reverie, chewed it up with its mindless motor + piercing headlights. Goddamn you, minivan!!!

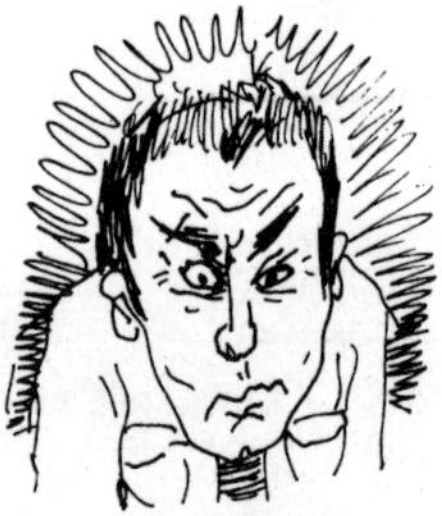

I was just about to cry!!

October 12

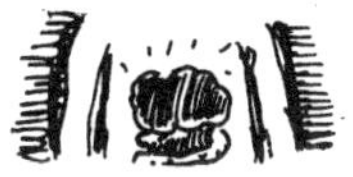

I was awakened at 5am to the roar of a torrential downpour on the corrugated metal + plastic roof + an empty stomach from no dinner (dry fried tofu? pbj?)

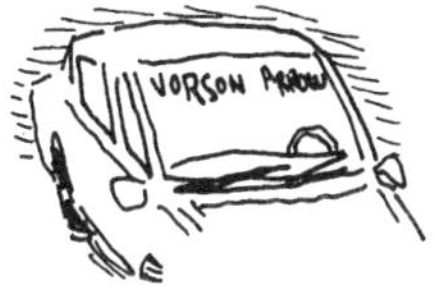
VORSON ARROW

I had been dreaming about my ancient flame, Ginger, + how she painted "vorson arrow" on her car window (?)

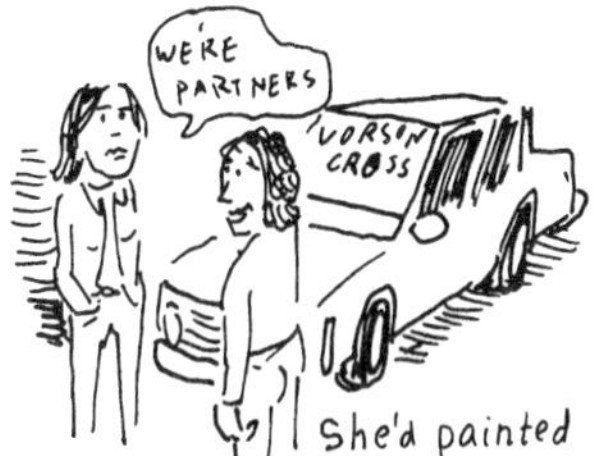
WE'RE PARTNERS
VORSON CROSS

She'd painted on her mom + sister's car also. When asked if it meant anything she smiled and said "we're partners"

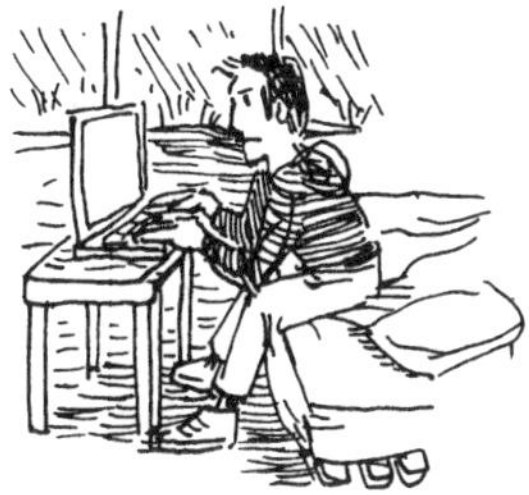

Today would easily fit the term "wash": rain, rain, rain. I spent most of the day programming on my laptop for Top Shelf

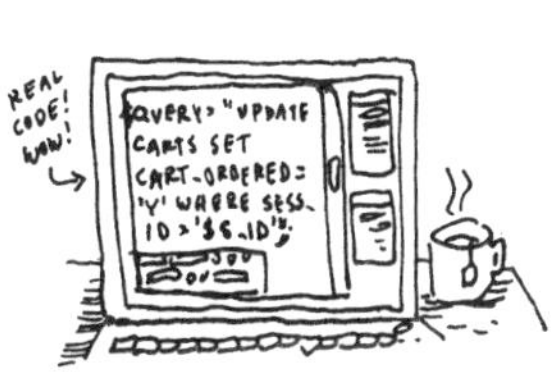
REAL CODE! WOW!
$QUERY = "UPDATE CARTS SET CART_ORDERED = 'Y' WHERE SESS_ID = '$S_ID'";

I did exciting things like set up automated cleanup of outdated cart entries in the database – so sexy.

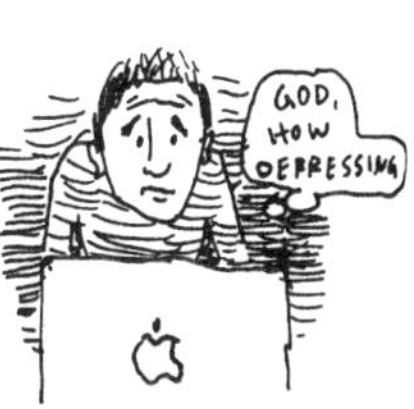
GOD, HOW DEPRESSING

I also read a bunch of old journal entries from february last year

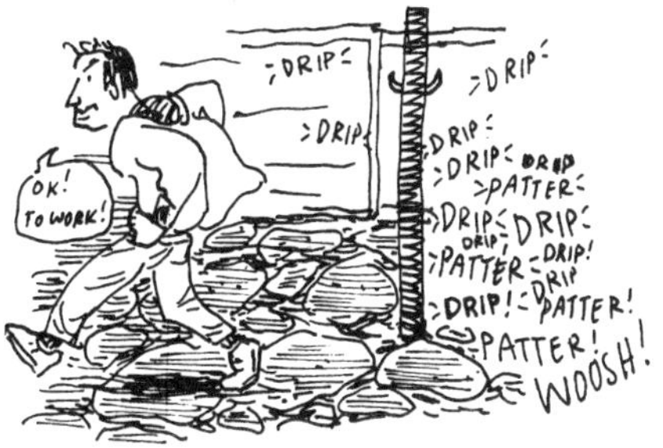
OK! TO WORK!
DRIP
DRIP
DRIP
DRIP
DRIP
DROP
PATTER
DRIP
DRIP
DRIP
PATTER
DRIP!
DRIP
DRIP!
PATTER!
PATTER!
WOOSH!

Every time it'd stop raining just enough for me to get my hopes up and head out the door, it'd slowly creep back to a downpour

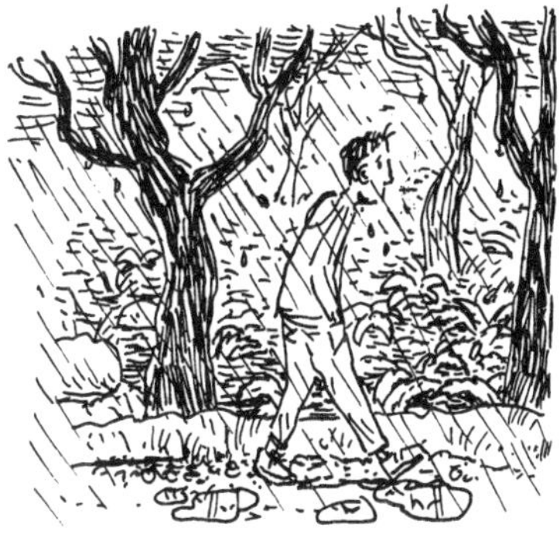

I eventually gave up and went for a long walk in the rain

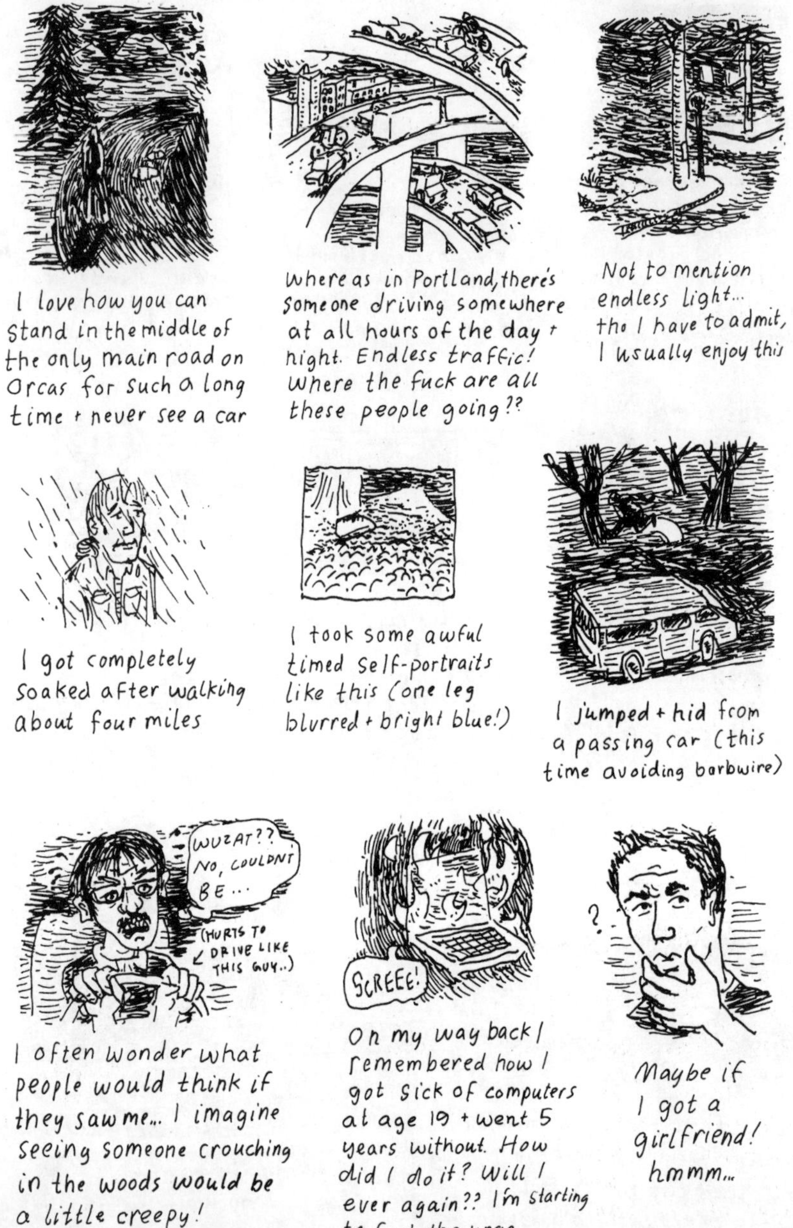
I love how you can stand in the middle of the only main road on Orcas for such a long time + never see a car
Where as in Portland, there's someone driving somewhere at all hours of the day + night. Endless traffic! Where the fuck are all these people going??
Not to mention endless light... tho I have to admit, I usually enjoy this
I got completely soaked after walking about four miles
I took some awful timed self-portraits like this (one leg blurred + bright blue!)
I jumped + hid from a passing car (this time avoiding barbwire)
WUZAT?? NO, COULDNT BE...
(HURTS TO DRIVE LIKE THIS GUY..)
I often wonder what people would think if they saw me... I imagine seeing someone crouching in the woods would be a little creepy!
SCREEE!
On my way back I remembered how I got sick of computers at age 19 + went 5 years without. How did I do it? Will I ever again?? I'm starting to feel the urge.
?
Maybe if I got a girlfriend! hmmm...

I shot up at 5AM suddenly convinced the "bod oil" had gotten to me and this was it!!

But I calmed myself down. Since when was I an hypochondriac? I wondered

CAUTION: TERRIBLE POSTURE

I spent a good portion of the day stuck in this position

RATTA RATTA RATTA

Staring at this.

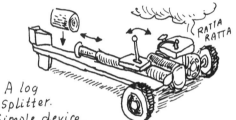

RATTA RATTA

A log splitter. Simple device.. Drop in a log, move the lever + wham-o. We sawed + split a good 3 to 4 cords + hauled 'em to various homes, including mine..

We split up on the new area of Victor's property, way up the hill — which has one of the most beautiful and surreal views of the San Juans

After work I spent an hour emailing + uploading my updates to Top Shelf

Then I went for a walk and climbed an apple tree in the near pitch black of night.

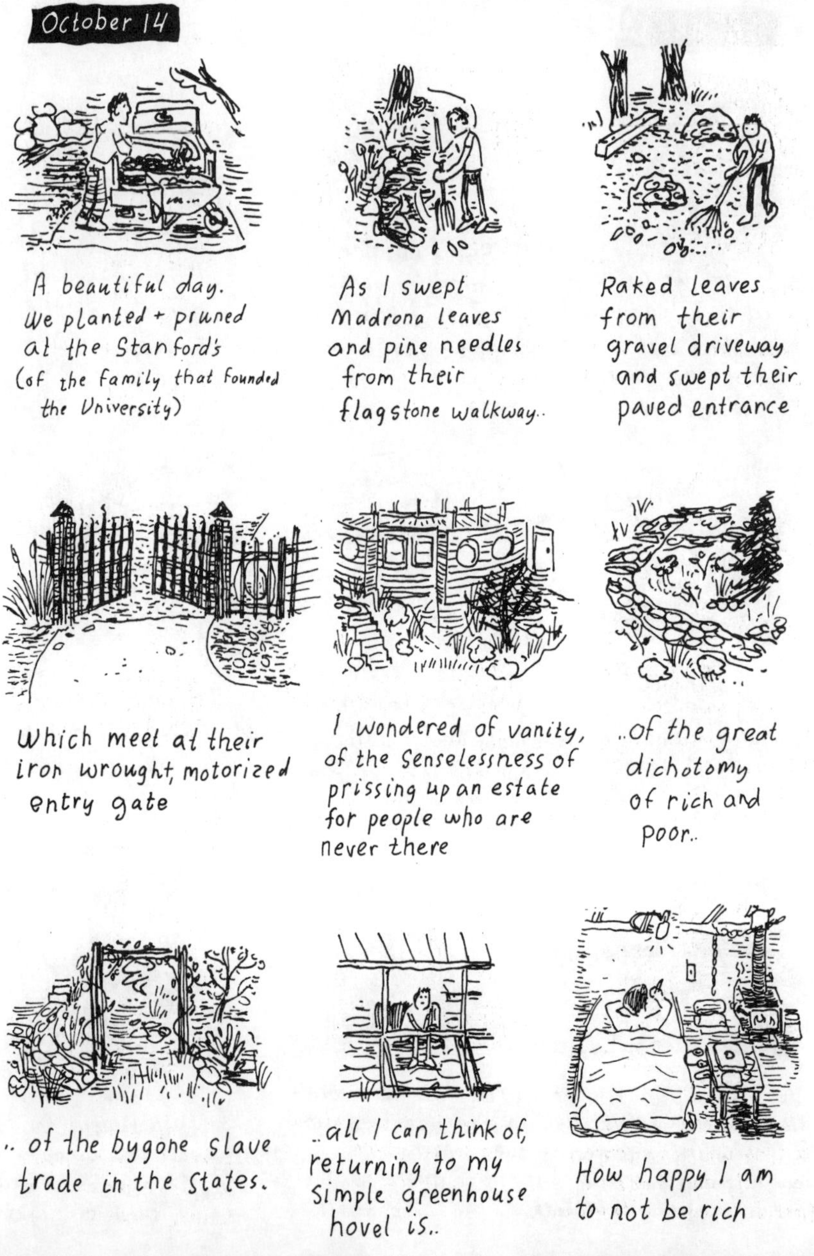
October 14
A beautiful day. We planted + pruned at the Stanford's (of the family that founded the University)
As I swept Madrona leaves and pine needles from their flagstone walkway..
Raked leaves from their gravel driveway and swept their paved entrance
Which meet at their iron wrought, motorized entry gate
I wondered of vanity, of the senselessness of prissing up an estate for people who are never there
..Of the great dichotomy of rich and poor..
.. of the bygone slave trade in the States.
..all I can think of, returning to my simple greenhouse hovel is..
How happy I am to not be rich

October 15

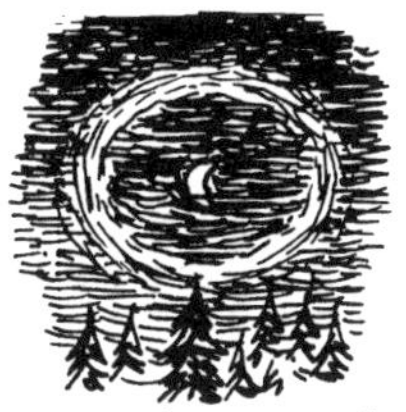

When I got up to pee in the middle of the night there was a huge ring around the moon.

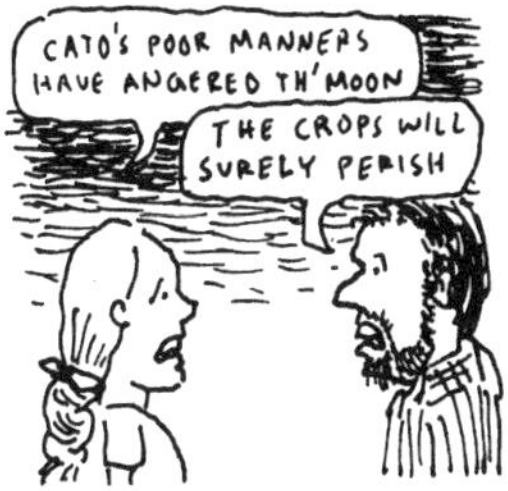
CATO'S POOR MANNERS HAVE ANGERED TH' MOON
THE CROPS WILL SURELY PERISH

I'm sure these types of phenomena set off the superstitions of older cultures like wildfire

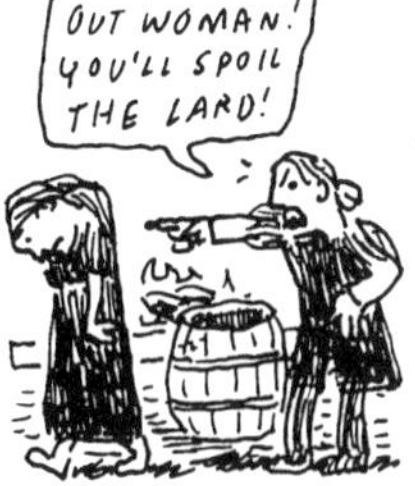
OUT WOMAN! YOU'LL SPOIL THE LARD!

Like how menstruating women weren't allowed to salt meat for curing in medieval France; they were believed to be "curing in salt" themselves

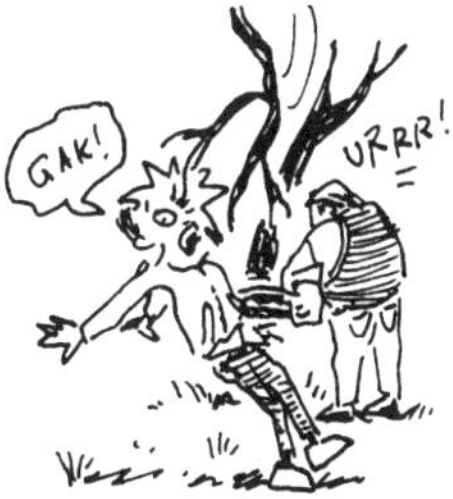
GAK!
URRR!

Almost immediately after starting work today, a Madrona branch fell smack dab into my eyeball

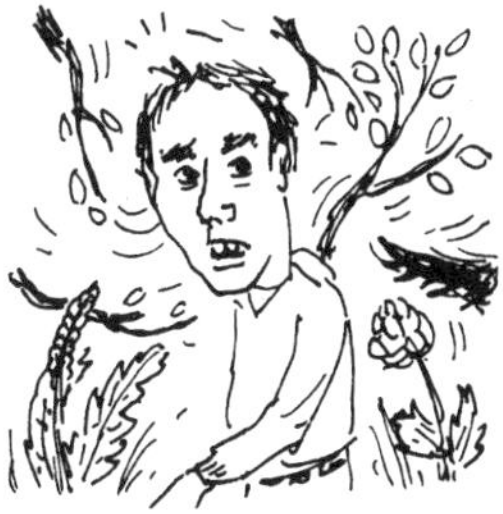

For the rest of the day I was paranoid that every plant + tree was out to get my eye

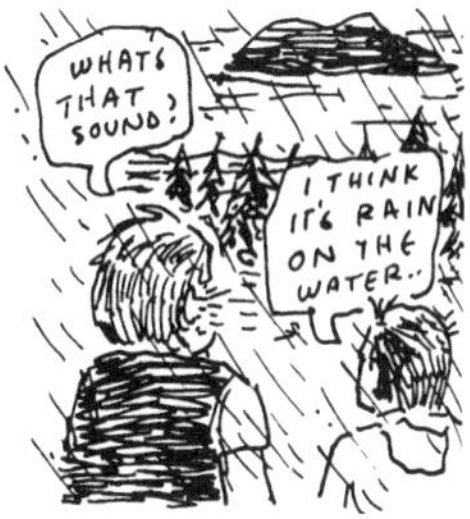
WHAT'S THAT SOUND?
I THINK IT'S RAIN ON THE WATER..

Almost immediately came workday-destroying rain. You could hear the hard rain approaching on the Puget Sound

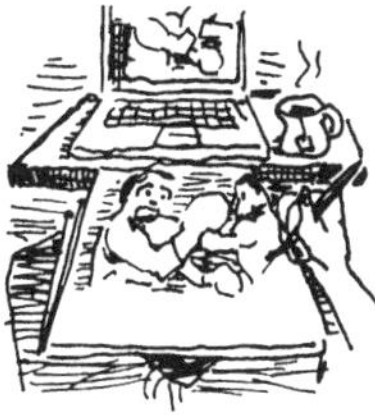

I drew some boxers for my unending project for Willy and made my first lil' movies with iMovie

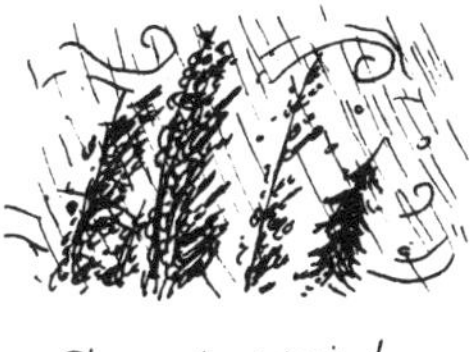

The rain + wind picked up at night to near-storm proportions

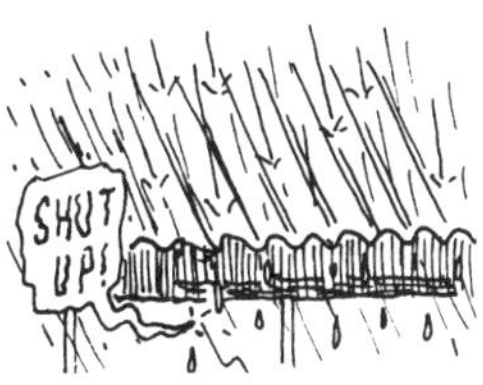
SHUT UP!

The rain on the metal roof of the greenhouse was so loud I could barely sleep!

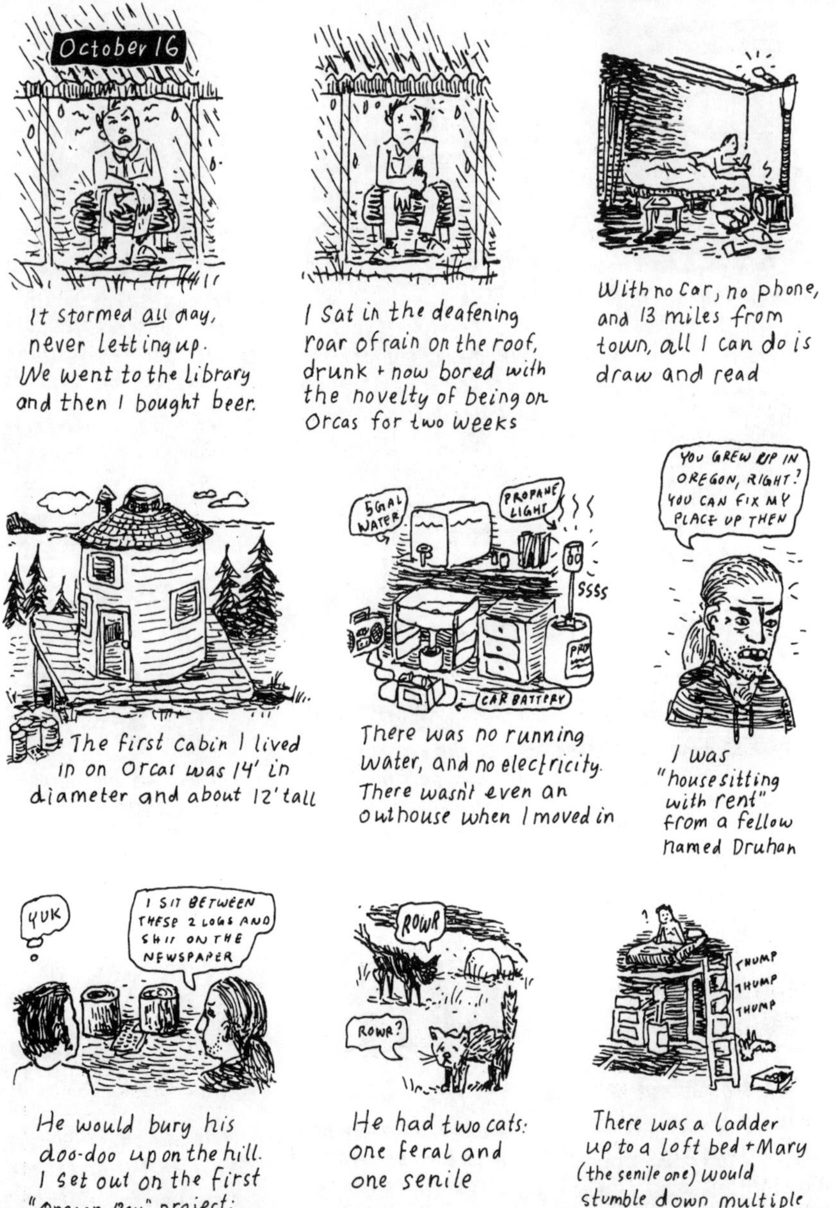

October 16
It stormed all day, never letting up. We went to the library and then I bought beer.
I sat in the deafening roar of rain on the roof, drunk + now bored with the novelty of being on Orcas for two weeks
With no car, no phone, and 13 miles from town, all I can do is draw and read
The first cabin I lived in on Orcas was 14' in diameter and about 12' tall
5 GAL WATER
PROPANE LIGHT
SSSS
PRO
CAR BATTERY
There was no running water, and no electricity. There wasn't even an outhouse when I moved in
YOU GREW UP IN OREGON, RIGHT? YOU CAN FIX MY PLACE UP THEN
I was "housesitting with rent" from a fellow named Druhan
YUK
I SIT BETWEEN THESE 2 LOGS AND SHIT ON THE NEWSPAPER
He would bury his doo-doo up on the hill. I set out on the first "Oregon Boy" project: an outhouse
ROWR
ROWR?
He had two cats: one feral and one senile
?
THUMP
THUMP
THUMP
There was a ladder up to a loft bed + Mary (the senile one) would stumble down multiple times every night

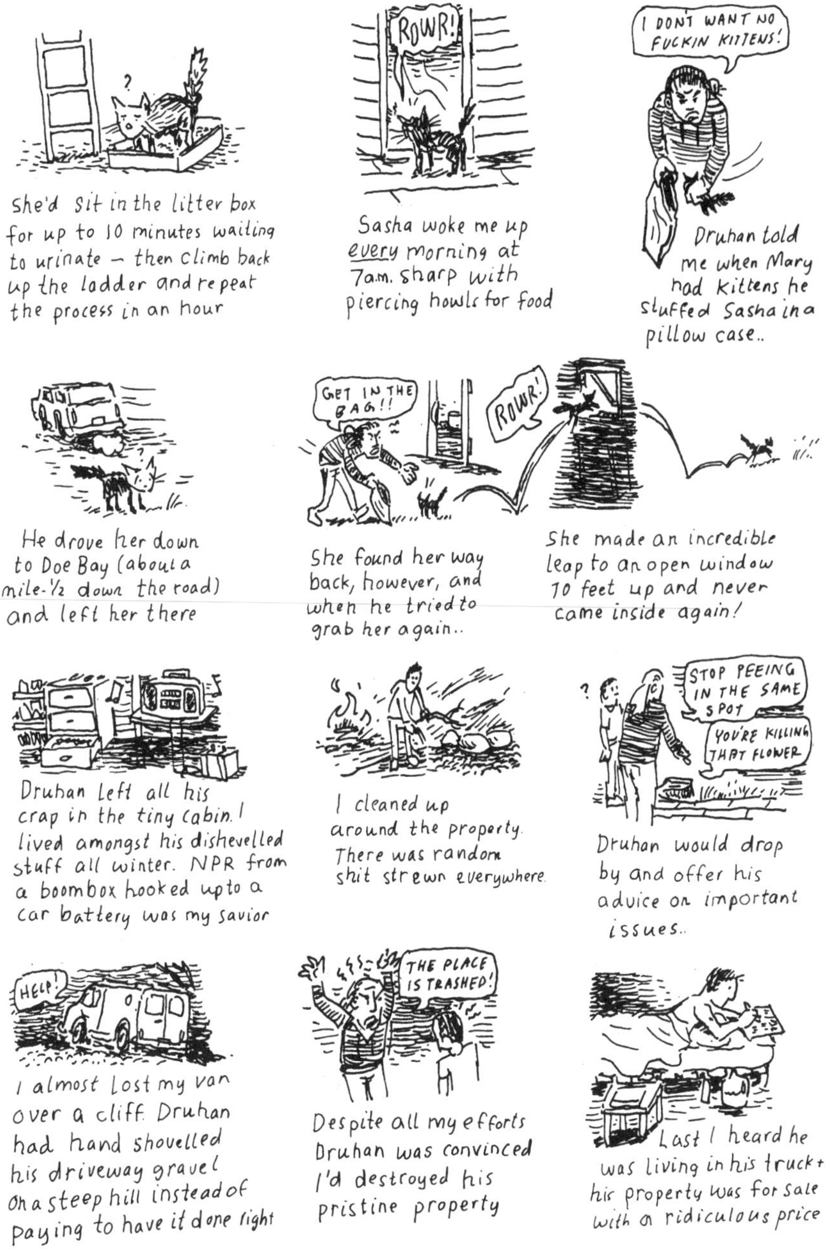
She'd sit in the litter box for up to 10 minutes waiting to urinate – then climb back up the ladder and repeat the process in an hour
ROWR!
Sasha woke me up every morning at 7a.m. sharp with piercing howls for food
I DON'T WANT NO FUCKIN KITTENS!
Druhan told me when Mary had kittens he stuffed Sasha in a pillow case..
He drove her down to Doe Bay (about a mile-½ down the road) and left her there
GET IN THE BAG!!
She found her way back, however, and when he tried to grab her again..
ROWR!
She made an incredible leap to an open window 10 feet up and never came inside again!
Druhan left all his crap in the tiny cabin. I lived amongst his dishevelled stuff all winter. NPR from a boombox hooked up to a car battery was my savior
I cleaned up around the property. There was random shit strewn everywhere.
STOP PEEING IN THE SAME SPOT
YOU'RE KILLING THAT FLOWER
Druhan would drop by and offer his advice on important issues..
HELP!
I almost lost my van over a cliff. Druhan had hand shovelled his driveway gravel on a steep hill instead of paying to have it done right
THE PLACE IS TRASHED!
Despite all my efforts Druhan was convinced I'd destroyed his pristine property
Last I heard he was living in his truck + his property was for sale with a ridiculous price

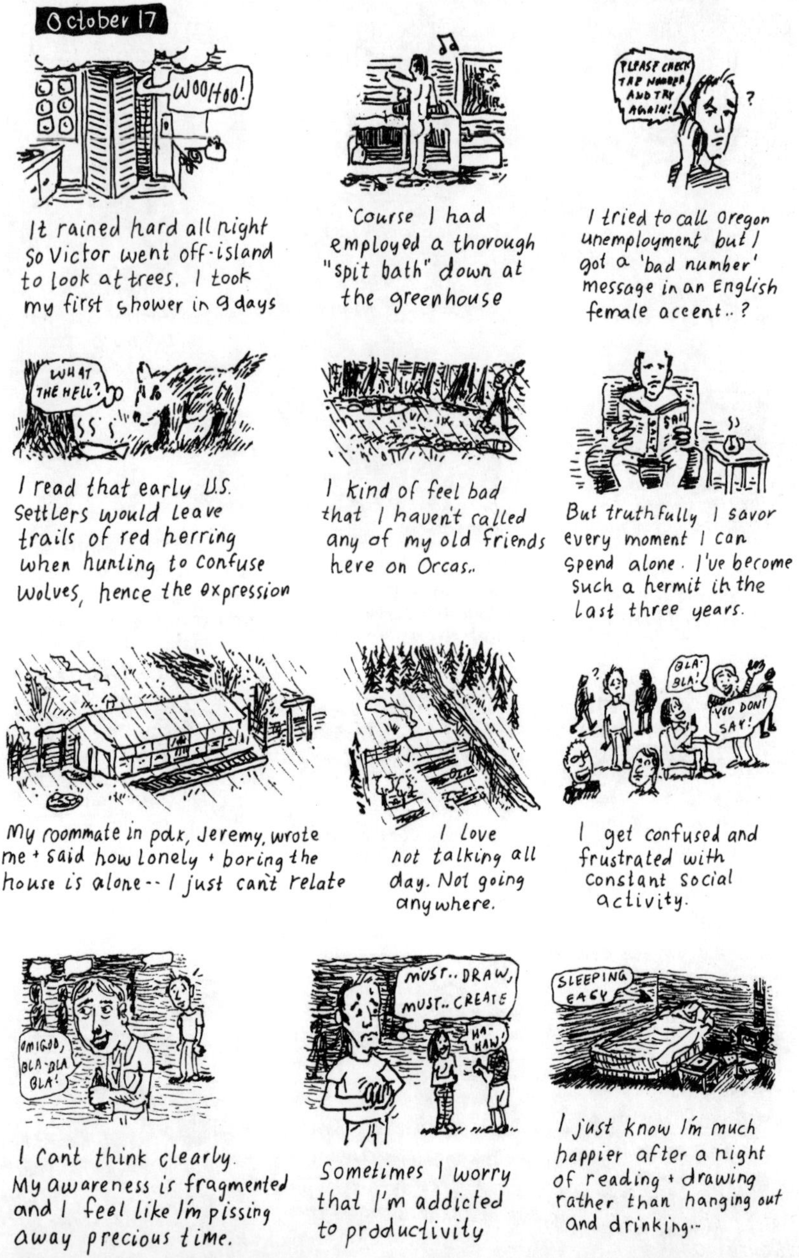
October 17
WOO!HOO!
It rained hard all night so Victor went off-island to look at trees. I took my first shower in 9 days
'Course I had employed a thorough "spit bath" down at the greenhouse
PLEASE CHECK THE NUMBER AND TRY AGAIN!
?
I tried to call Oregon unemployment but I got a 'bad number' message in an English female accent..?
WHAT THE HELL?
I read that early U.S. settlers would leave trails of red herring when hunting to confuse wolves, hence the expression
I kind of feel bad that I haven't called any of my old friends here on Orcas..
SALT
But truthfully I savor every moment I can spend alone. I've become such a hermit in the last three years.
My roommate in pdx, Jeremy, wrote me + said how lonely + boring the house is alone-- I just can't relate
I love not talking all day. Not going anywhere.
BLA-BLA!
YOU DON'T SAY!
I get confused and frustrated with constant social activity.
OMIGOD, BLA-BLA BLA!
I can't think clearly. My awareness is fragmented and I feel like I'm pissing away precious time.
MUST.. DRAW, MUST.. CREATE
HA-HAW!
Sometimes I worry that I'm addicted to productivity
SLEEPING EASY
I just know I'm much happier after a night of reading + drawing rather than hanging out and drinking..

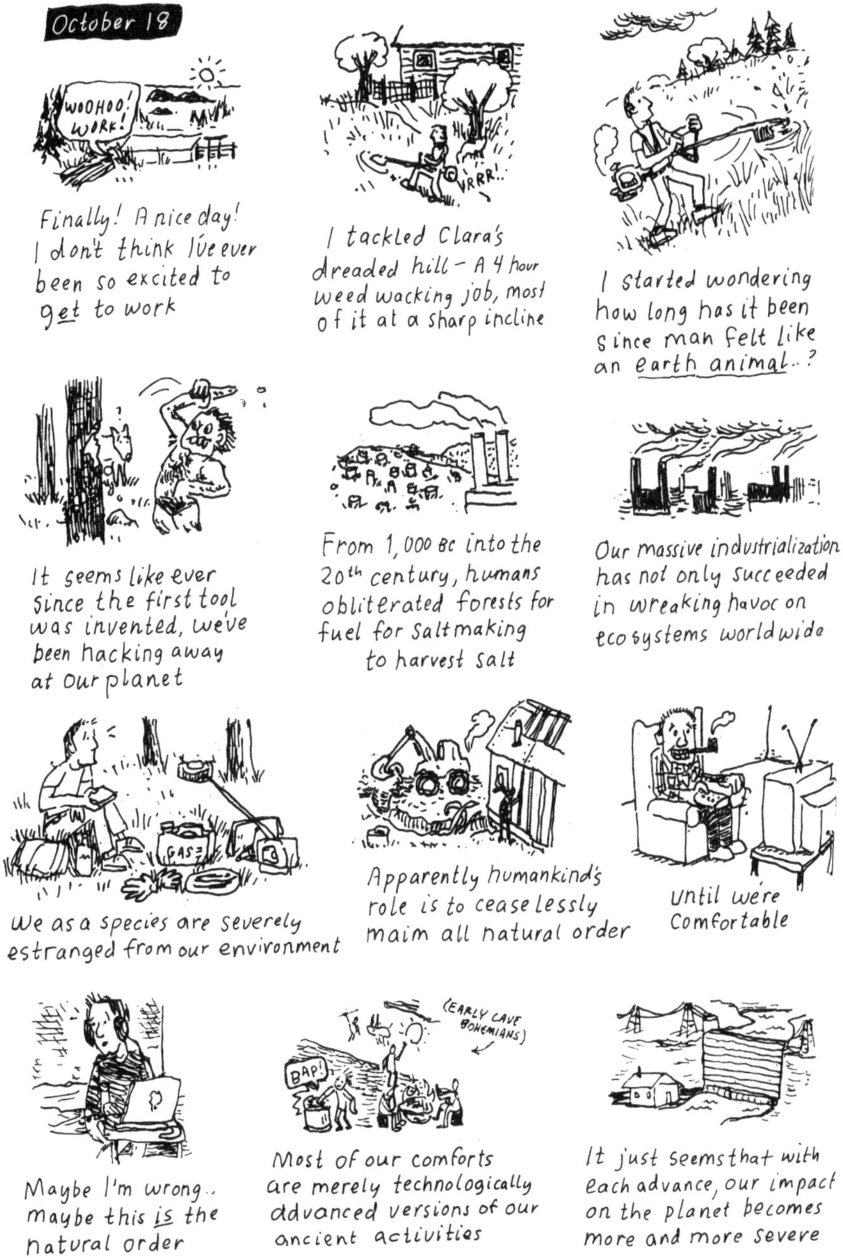
October 18
WOOHOO! WORK!
Finally! A nice day! I don't think I've ever been so excited to get to work
VRRR..
I tackled Clara's dreaded hill - A 4 hour weed wacking job, most of it at a sharp incline
I started wondering how long has it been since man felt like an earth animal..?
It seems like ever since the first tool was invented, we've been hacking away at our planet
From 1,000 BC into the 20th century, humans obliterated forests for fuel for saltmaking to harvest salt
Our massive industrialization has not only succeeded in wreaking havoc on ecosystems worldwide
GAS
We as a species are severely estranged from our environment
Apparently humankind's role is to ceaselessly maim all natural order
Until we're comfortable
Maybe I'm wrong.. maybe this is the natural order
(EARLY CAVE BOHEMIANS)
BAP!
Most of our comforts are merely technologically advanced versions of our ancient activities
It just seems that with each advance, our impact on the planet becomes more and more severe

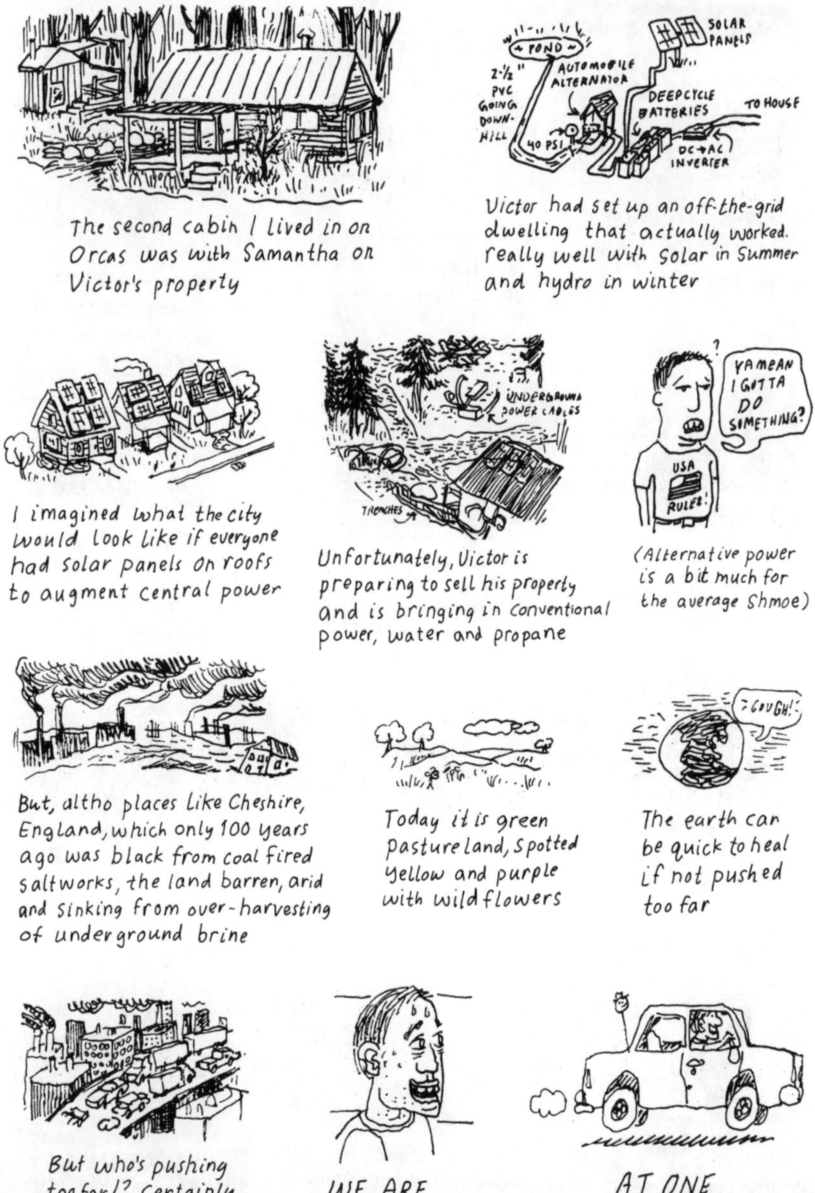
POND
2-1/2" PVC GOING DOWN-HILL
AUTOMOBILE ALTERNATOR
SOLAR PANELS
DEEPCYCLE BATTERIES
TO HOUSE
40 PSI
DC→AC INVERTER
The second cabin I lived in on Orcas was with Samantha on Victor's property
Victor had set up an off-the-grid dwelling that actually worked. really well with solar in summer and hydro in winter
I imagined what the city would look like if everyone had solar panels on roofs to augment central power
UNDERGROUND POWER CABLES
TRENCHES
Unfortunately, Victor is preparing to sell his property and is bringing in conventional power, water and propane
YA MEAN I GOTTA DO SOMETHING?
USA RULEZ!
(Alternative power is a bit much for the average shmoe)
But, altho places like Cheshire, England, which only 100 years ago was black from coal fired saltworks, the land barren, arid and sinking from over-harvesting of underground brine
Today it is green pasture land, spotted yellow and purple with wildflowers
COUGH!
The earth can be quick to heal if not pushed too far
But who's pushing too far!? Certainly not us!
WE ARE HUMANS!
AT ONE WITH EARTH!

October 9

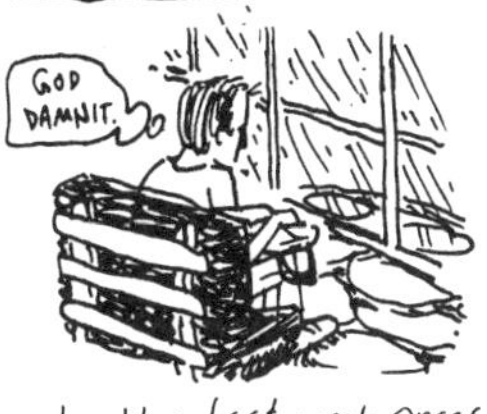
GOD DAMNIT.

In the last week, Orcas has had 1/3 of its annual rainfall

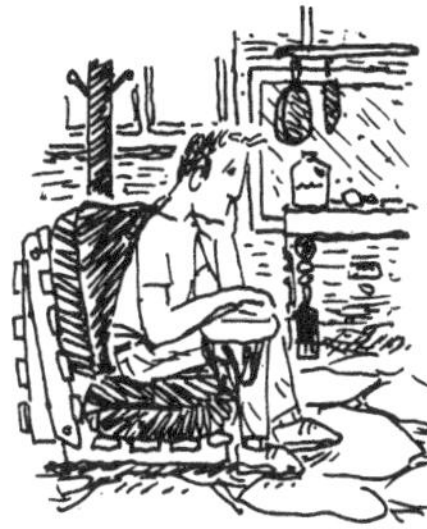

I seriously doubt if I'll ever find rain on a metal roof romantic again

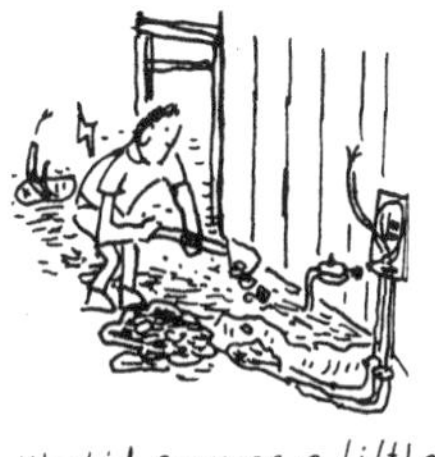

We did squeeze a little work in today, hooking up propane + an electrical box plus lots of backfilling

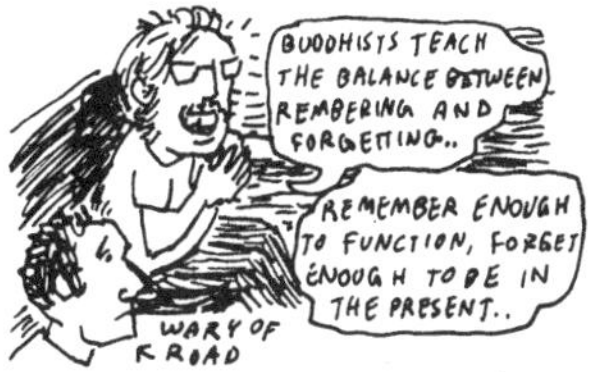
BUDDHISTS TEACH THE BALANCE BETWEEN REMBERING AND FORGETTING..
REMEMBER ENOUGH TO FUNCTION, FORGET ENOUGH TO BE IN THE PRESENT..
WARY OF K ROAD

Then we drove to Alan's for his weekly Sunday Sauna

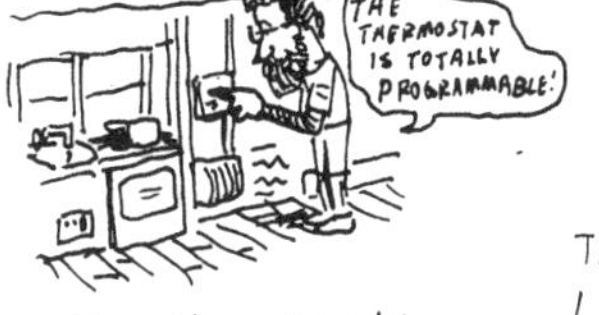
THE THERMOSTAT IS TOTALLY PROGRAMMABLE!

Alan showed us his super-fancy, recently completed bus-house

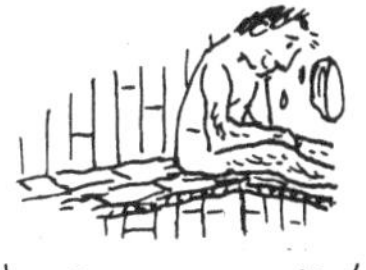

The sauna was great. I was glad to get a soak in on this visit.

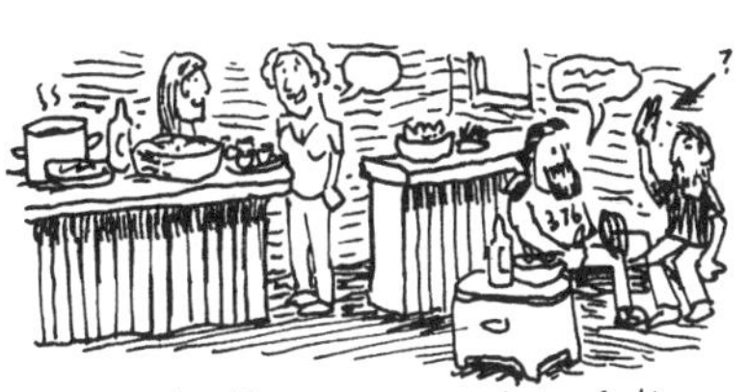

Later in the evening a lot of the locals showed up -- there was lots of great food + many beautiful girls

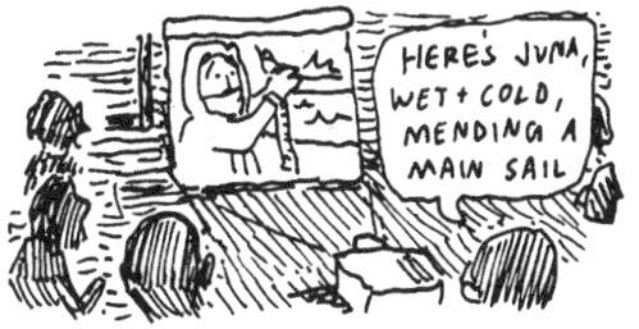
HERE'S JUNA, WET + COLD, MENDING A MAIN SAIL

Victor brought his projector so Matt + Juna could show slides of their sailing trip from Mexico to Hawaii – It took nearly a month each way..

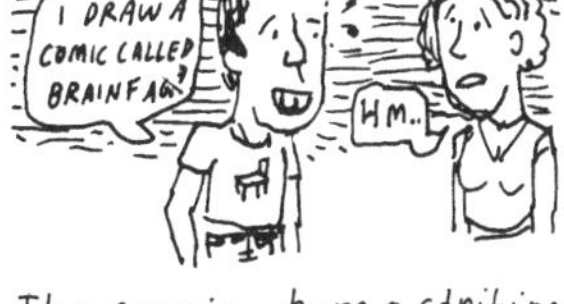
I DRAW A COMIC CALLED BRAINFAG?
HM..

The evening bore a striking resemblance to what I drew about social situations recently

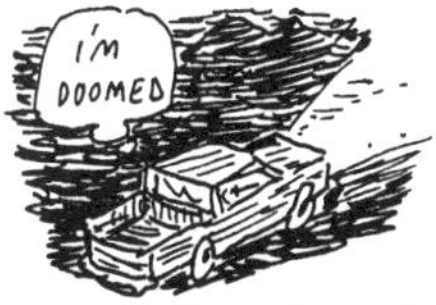
I'M DOOMED

As we drove home, I contemplated the impossibility of meeting a girl..

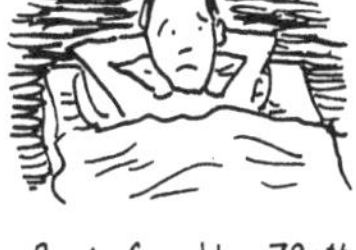

And for the 720th time in a row, I went to sleep ..alone.. again!

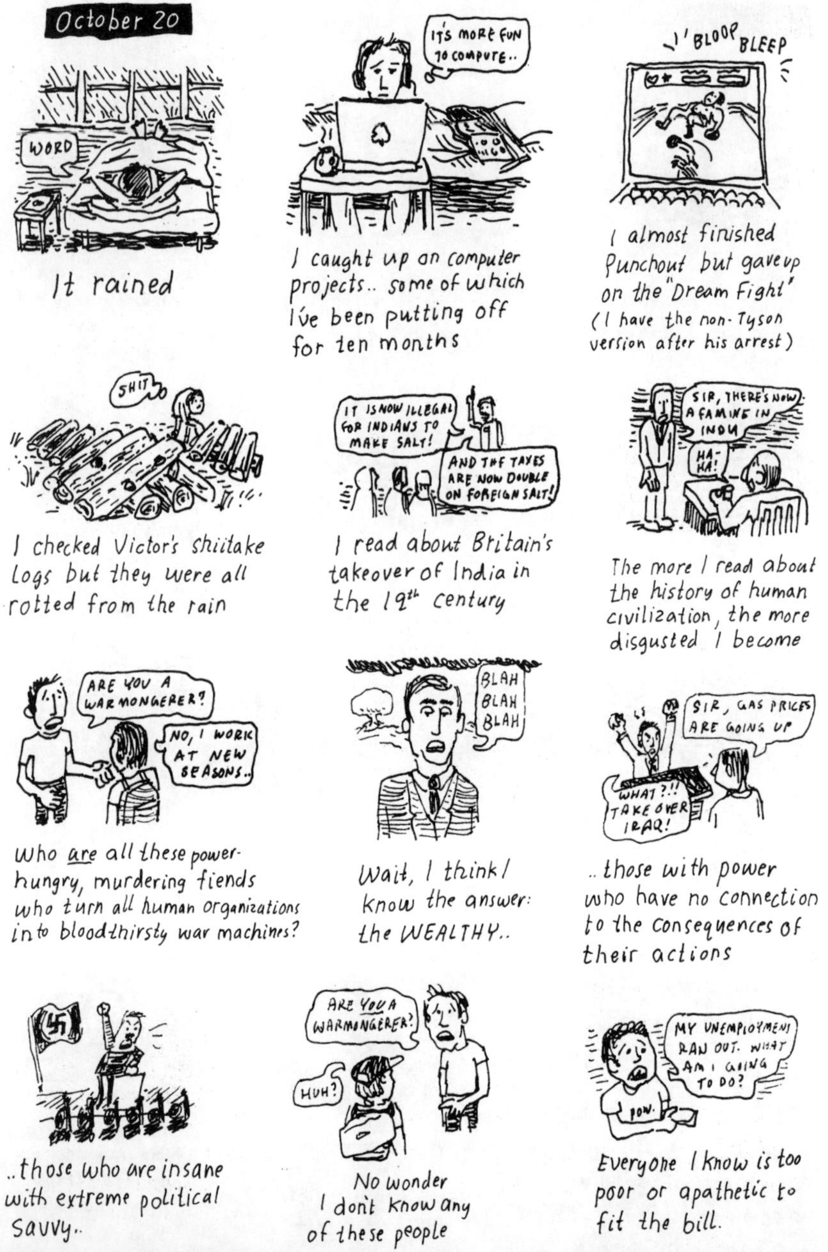
October 20
WORD
It rained
IT'S MORE FUN TO COMPUTE..
I caught up on computer projects.. some of which I've been putting off for ten months
BLOOP BLEEP
I almost finished Punchout but gave up on the "Dream Fight"
(I have the non-Tyson version after his arrest)
SHIT
I checked Victor's shiitake logs but they were all rotted from the rain
IT IS NOW ILLEGAL FOR INDIANS TO MAKE SALT!
AND THE TAXES ARE NOW DOUBLE ON FOREIGN SALT!
I read about Britain's takeover of India in the 19th century
SIR, THERE'S NOW A FAMINE IN INDIA
HA-HA!
The more I read about the history of human civilization, the more disgusted I become
ARE YOU A WARMONGERER?
NO, I WORK AT NEW SEASONS..
Who are all these power-hungry, murdering fiends who turn all human organizations into bloodthirsty war machines?
BLAH BLAH BLAH
Wait, I think I know the answer: the WEALTHY..
SIR, GAS PRICES ARE GOING UP
WHAT?!! TAKE OVER IRAQ!
..those with power who have no connection to the consequences of their actions
..those who are insane with extreme political savvy..
ARE YOU A WARMONGERER?
HUH?
No wonder I don't know any of these people
MY UNEMPLOYMENT RAN OUT. WHAT AM I GOING TO DO?
Everyone I know is too poor or apathetic to fit the bill.

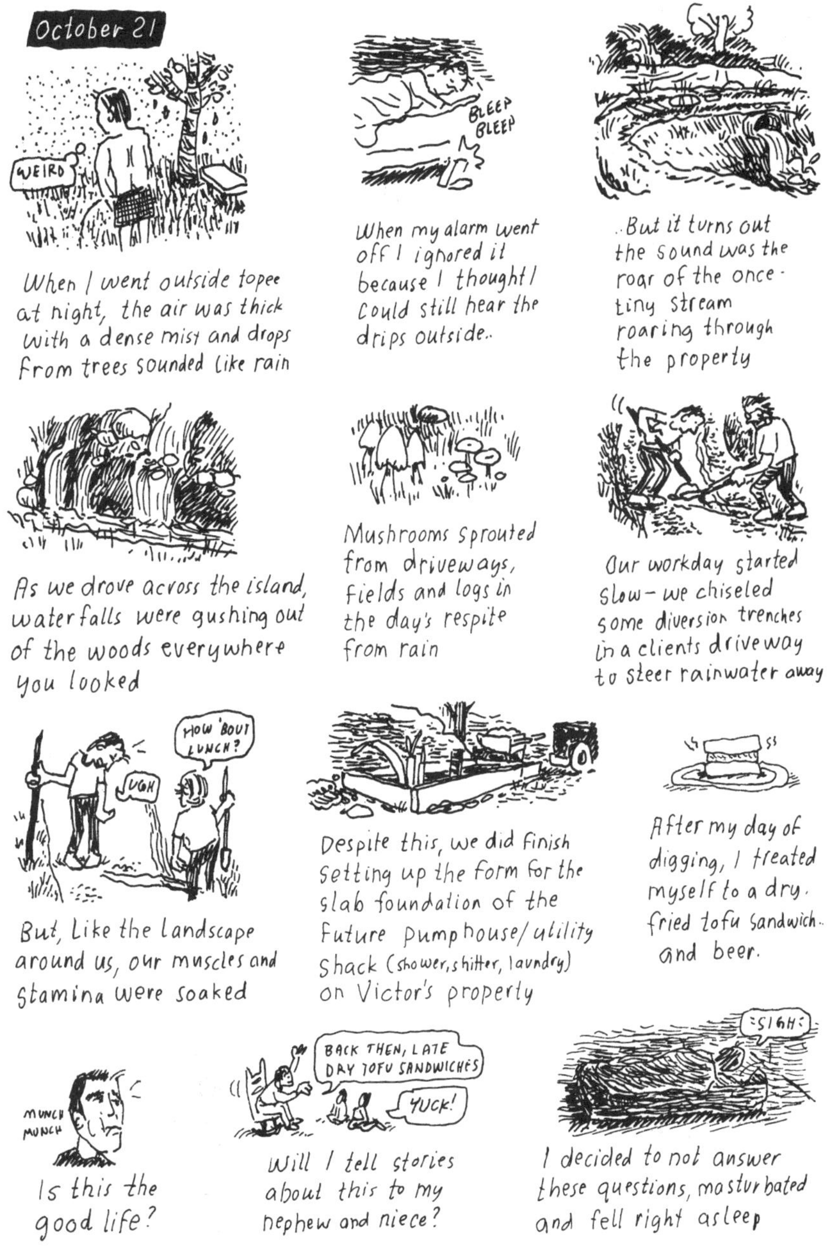
October 21
WEIRD
When I went outside to pee at night, the air was thick with a dense mist and drops from trees sounded like rain
BLEEP BLEEP
When my alarm went off I ignored it because I thought I could still hear the drips outside..
..But it turns out the sound was the roar of the once-tiny stream roaring through the property
As we drove across the island, waterfalls were gushing out of the woods everywhere you looked
Mushrooms sprouted from driveways, fields and logs in the day's respite from rain
Our workday started slow - we chiseled some diversion trenches in a clients driveway to steer rainwater away
HOW 'BOUT LUNCH?
UGH
But, like the landscape around us, our muscles and stamina were soaked
Despite this, we did finish setting up the form for the slab foundation of the future pump house/utility shack (shower, shitter, laundry) on Victor's property
After my day of digging, I treated myself to a dry-fried tofu sandwich.. and beer.
MUNCH MUNCH
Is this the good life?
BACK THEN, LATE DAY TOFU SANDWICHES
YUCK!
Will I tell stories about this to my nephew and niece?
SIGH
I decided to not answer these questions, masturbated and fell right asleep

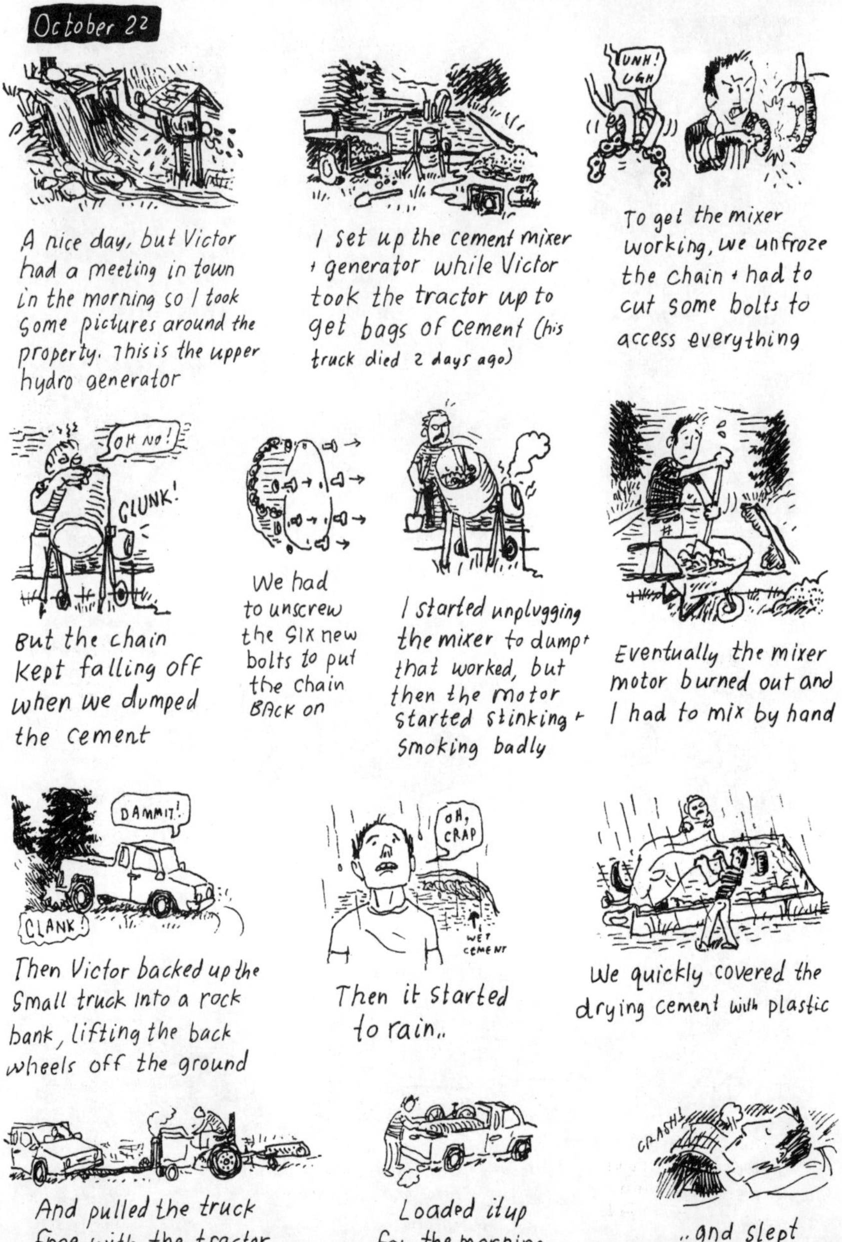
October 22
A nice day, but Victor had a meeting in town in the morning so I took some pictures around the property. This is the upper hydro generator
I set up the cement mixer + generator while Victor took the tractor up to get bags of cement (his truck died 2 days ago)
UNH! UGH
To get the mixer working, we unfroze the chain + had to cut some bolts to access everything
OH NO!
CLUNK!
But the chain kept falling off when we dumped the cement
We had to unscrew the SIX new bolts to put the chain BACK on
I started unplugging the mixer to dump + that worked, but then the motor started stinking + smoking badly
Eventually the mixer motor burned out and I had to mix by hand
DAMMIT!
CLANK!
Then Victor backed up the small truck into a rock bank, lifting the back wheels off the ground
OH, CRAP
WET CEMENT
Then it started to rain..
We quickly covered the drying cement with plastic
And pulled the truck free with the tractor
Loaded it up for the morning
CRASH!
..and slept

October 23

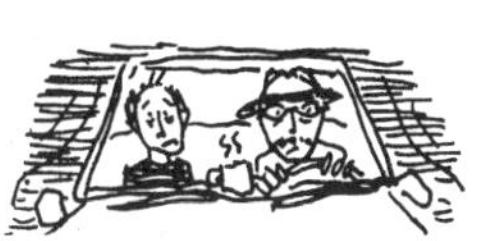

We set out for the "red eye" ferry at 5am. The pitch black of Falltime morning oozed aroundus

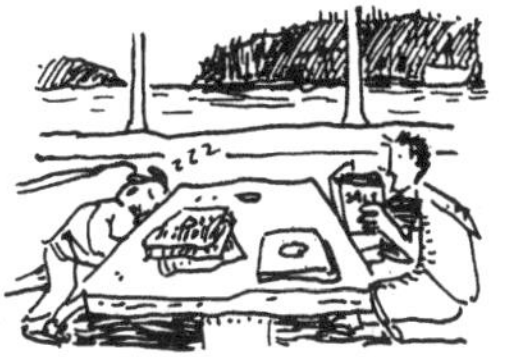

I finished "Salt" en route to Anacortes

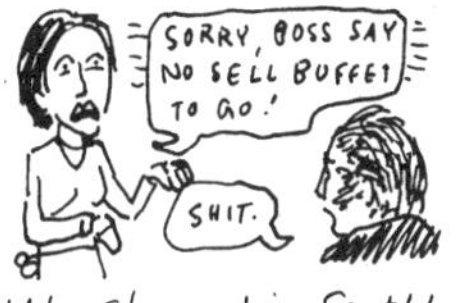
SORRY, BOSS SAY NO SELL BUFFET TO GO!
SHIT.

We stopped in Seattle to get roofing + bring Victor's dad lunch

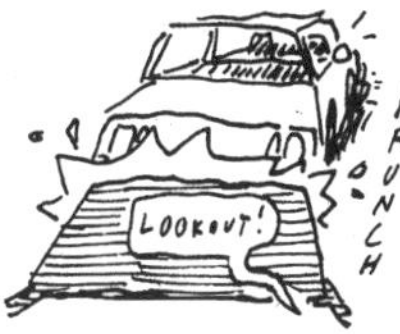
KRUNCH
LOOKOUT!

At the Queen Anne/Aurora intersection Victor smashed into the back of a lady's Volvo

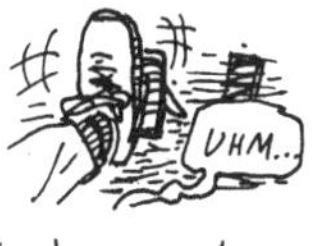
UHM...

No damage done, we pulled out, only to find we had no brakes!!

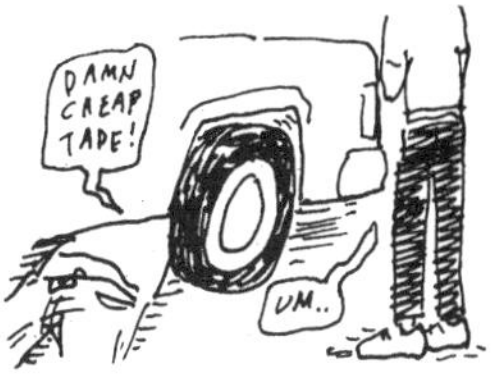
DAMN CHEAP TAPE!
UM..

Victor walked up to his brother's and got some duct tape

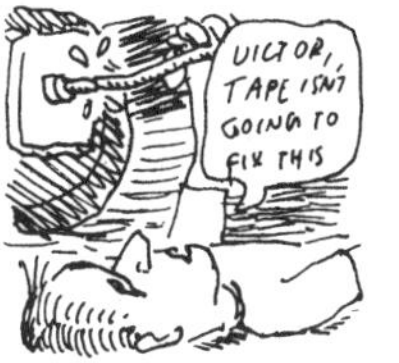
VICTOR, TAPE ISN'T GOING TO FIX THIS

I reluctantly crawled under the truck (I don't miss working on cars)

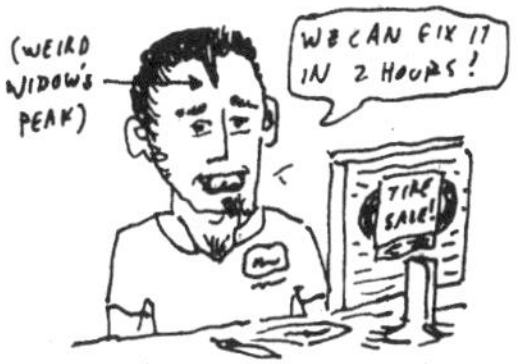
(WEIRD WIDOW'S PEAK)
WE CAN FIX IT IN 2 HOURS!
TIRE SALE!

We hobbled along with the e-brake to a nearby repair shop

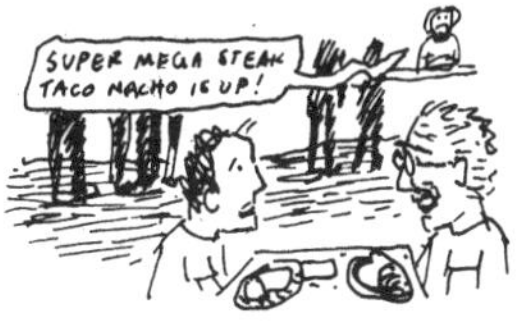
SUPER MEGA STEAK TACO NACHO IS UP!

We got some lunch and talked about how different Seattle is from Orcas- How anonymous you felt at all times

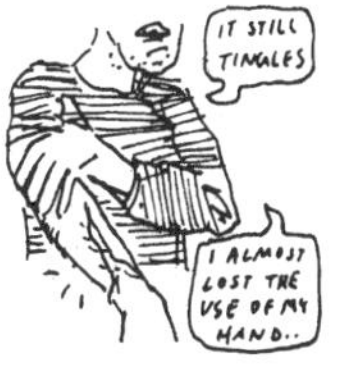
IT STILL TINGLES
I ALMOST LOST THE USE OF MY HAND..

We met Mike in Olympia — he showed us his scar from a recent drunken fall through a window

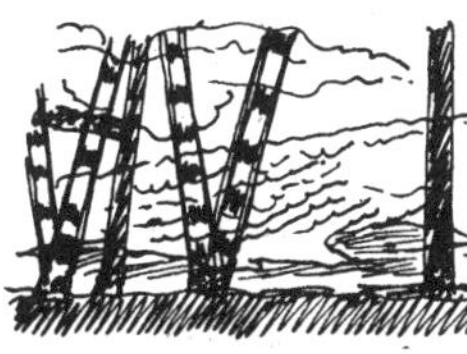

The sky was incredible coming into Portland. The weather was warm and sunny the whole day.

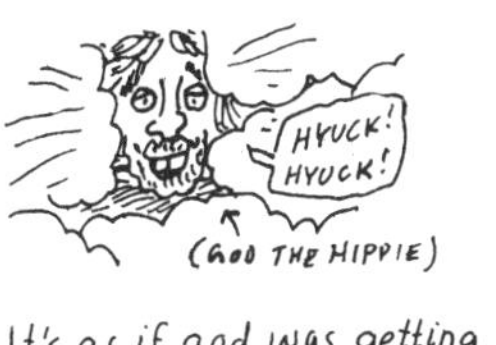
HYUCK! HYUCK!
(GOD THE HIPPIE)

It's as if god was getting a real kick out of his big cosmic joke that weather had been so dismal while I had work available

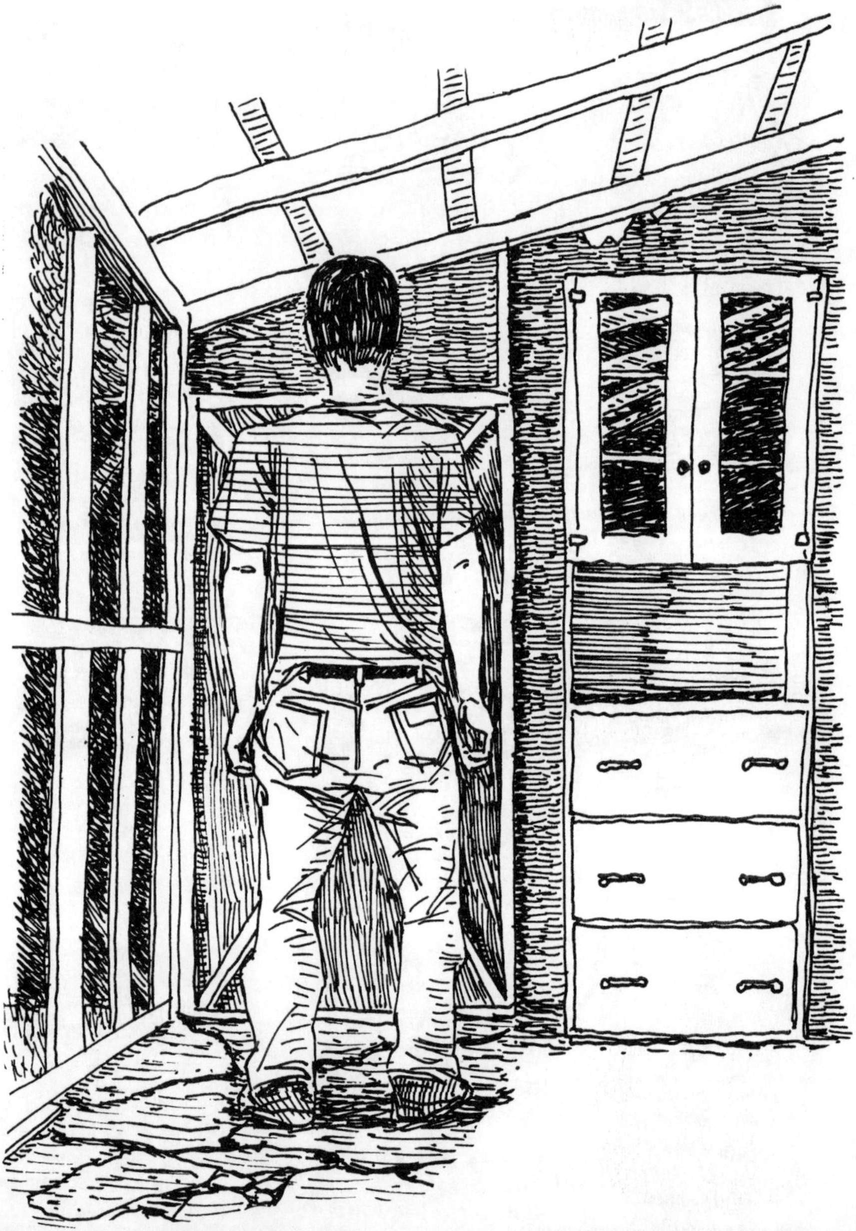

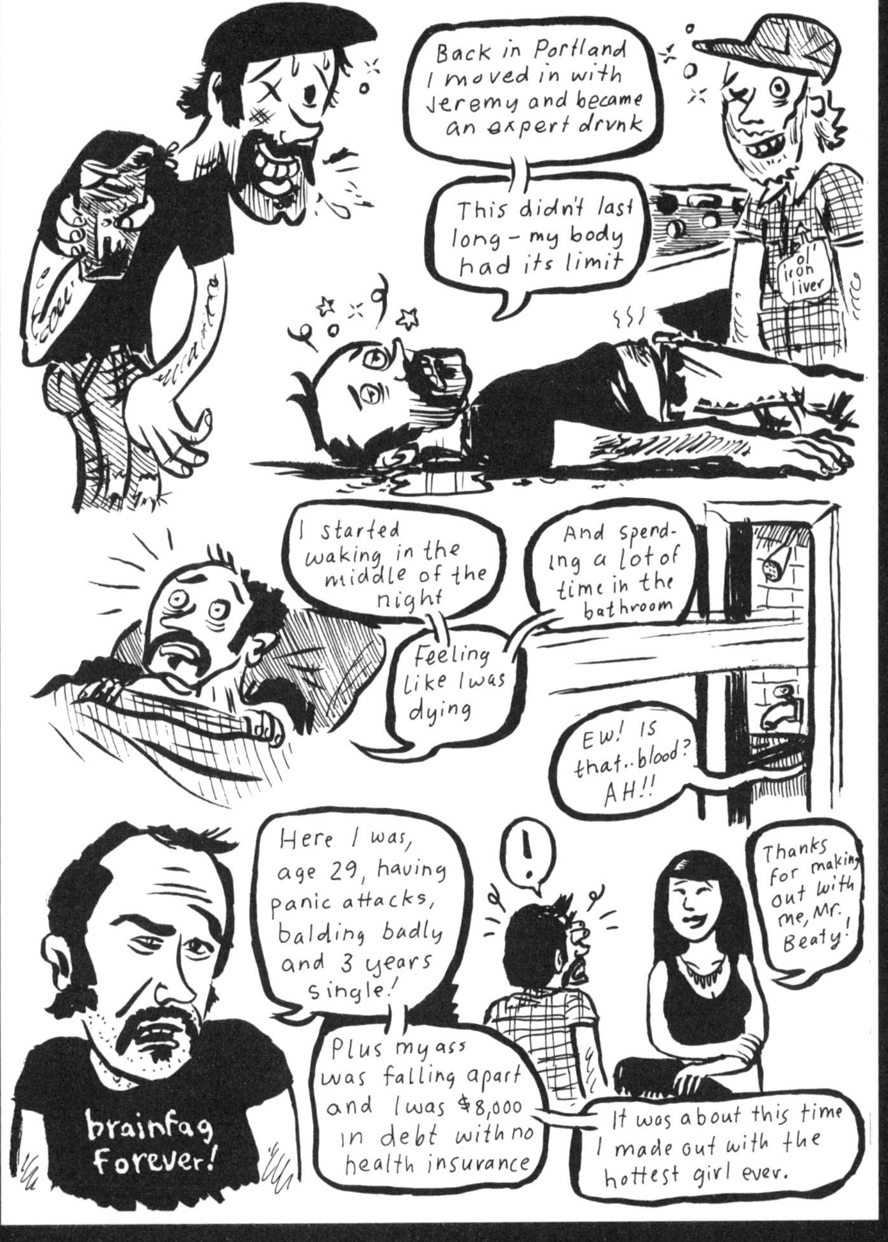

Back in Portland I moved in with Jeremy and became an expert drunk
This didn't last long - my body had its limit
ol' iron liver
I started waking in the middle of the night
Feeling like I was dying
And spending a lot of time in the bathroom
Ew! Is that..blood? AH!!
Here I was, age 29, having panic attacks, balding badly and 3 years single!
Plus my ass was falling apart and I was $8,000 in debt with no health insurance
brainfag Forever!
!
It was about this time I made out with the hottest girl ever.
Thanks for making out with me, Mr. Beaty!

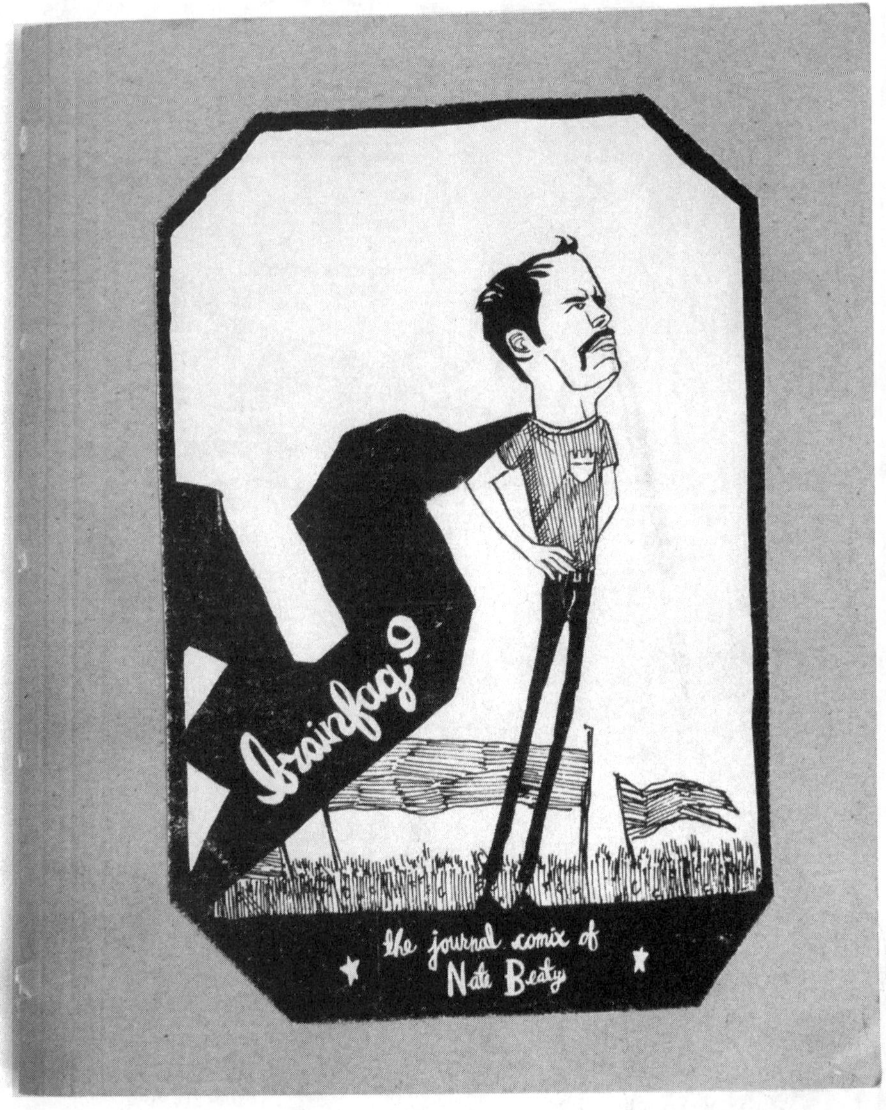
brainfag 9
the journal comix of
Nate Beaty

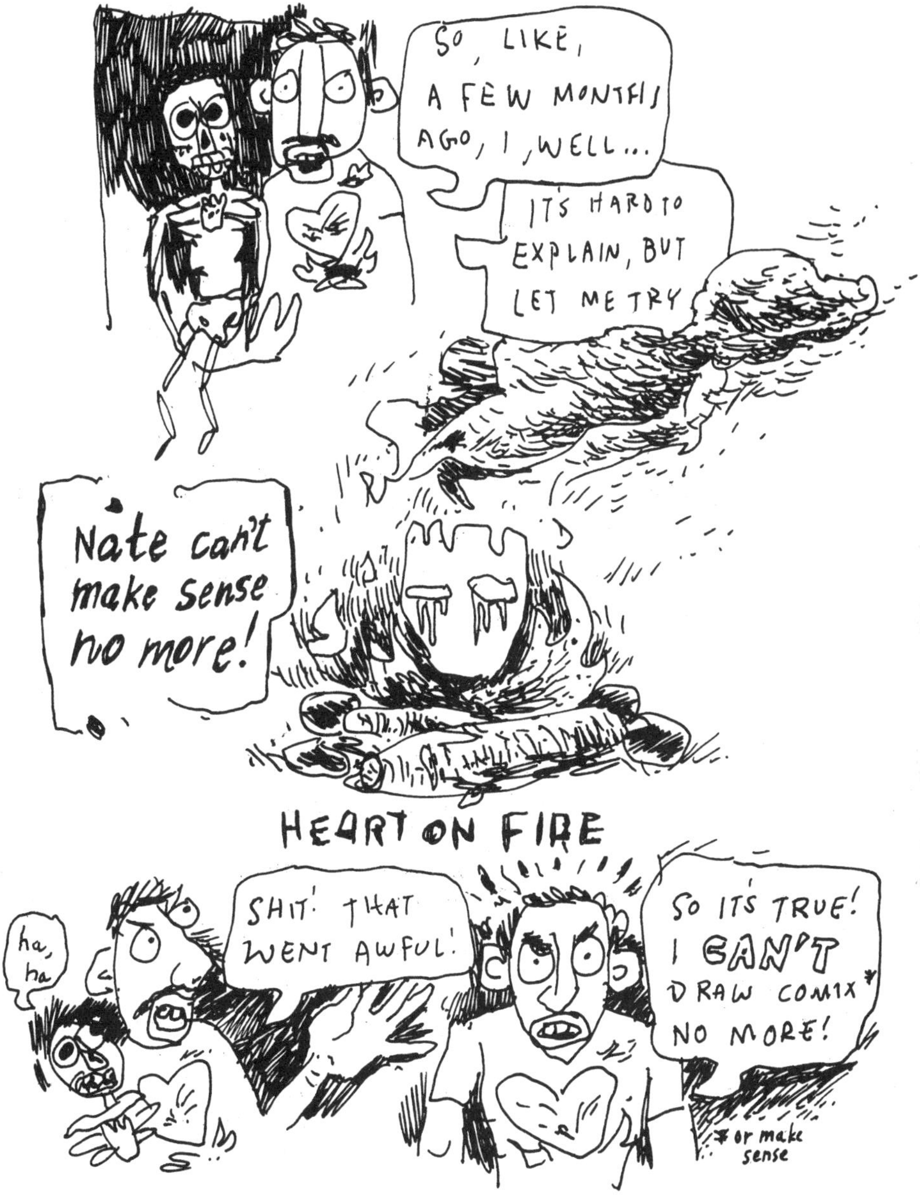

SO, LIKE, A FEW MONTHS AGO, I, WELL...
IT'S HARD TO EXPLAIN, BUT LET ME TRY
Nate can't make sense no more!
HEART ON FIRE
ha, ha
SHIT! THAT WENT AWFUL!
SO IT'S TRUE! I CAN'T DRAW COMIX* NO MORE!
*or make sense

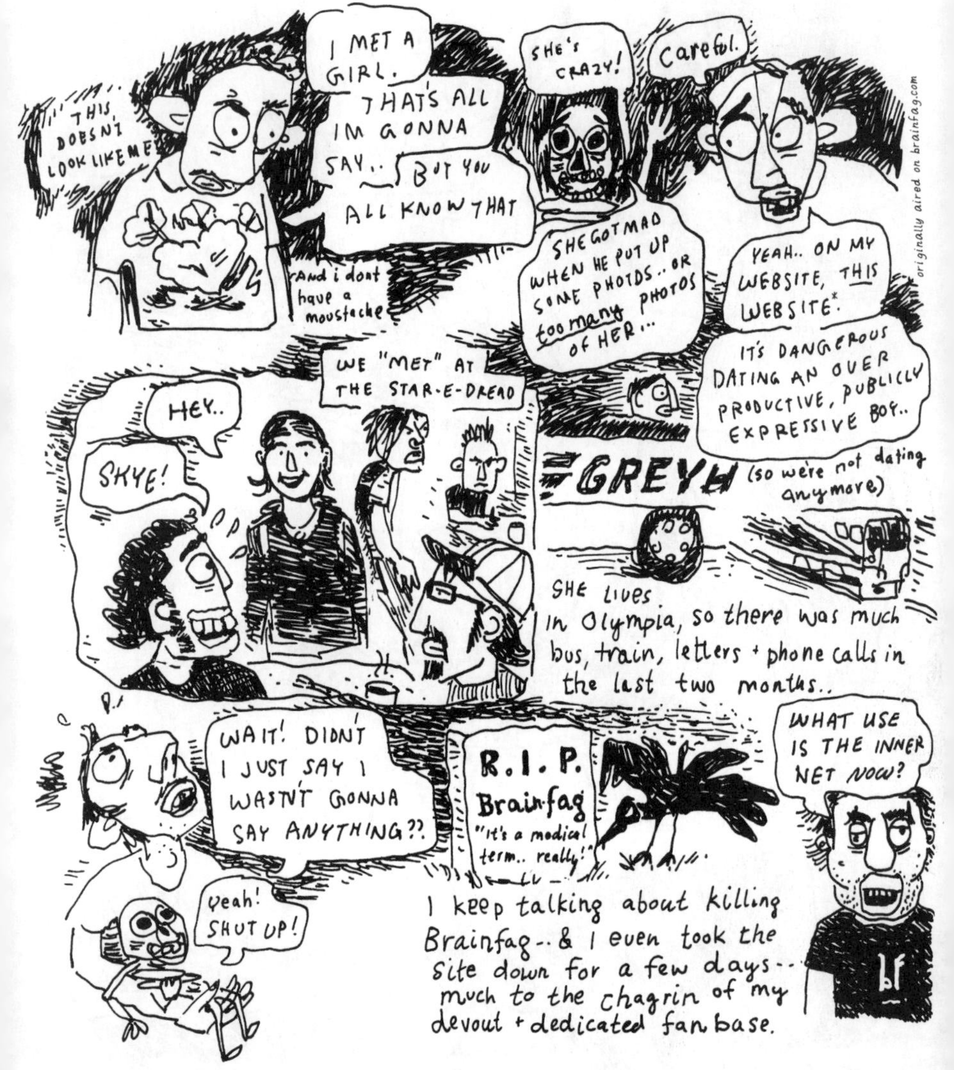
THIS DOESN'T LOOK LIKE ME
I MET A GIRL.
THAT'S ALL I'M GONNA SAY..
BUT YOU ALL KNOW THAT
And i dont have a moustache
SHE'S CRAZY!
Careful.
SHE GOT MAD WHEN HE PUT UP SOME PHOTOS.. OR too many PHOTOS OF HER...
YEAH.. ON MY WEBSITE, THIS WEBSITE*.
IT'S DANGEROUS DATING AN OVER PRODUCTIVE, PUBLICLY EXPRESSIVE BOY..
WE "MET" AT THE STAR-E-DREAD
HEY..
SKYE!
GREYH
(so we're not dating anymore)
SHE LIVES in Olympia, so there was much bus, train, letters + phone calls in the last two months..
WAIT! DIDN'T I JUST SAY I WASN'T GONNA SAY ANYTHING??
yeah! SHUT UP!
R.I.P.
Brainfag
"It's a medical term.. really!"
WHAT USE IS THE INNER NET NOW?
bf
I keep talking about killing Brainfag -.. & I even took the site down for a few days -- much to the chagrin of my devout + dedicated fan base.

originally aired on brainfag.com

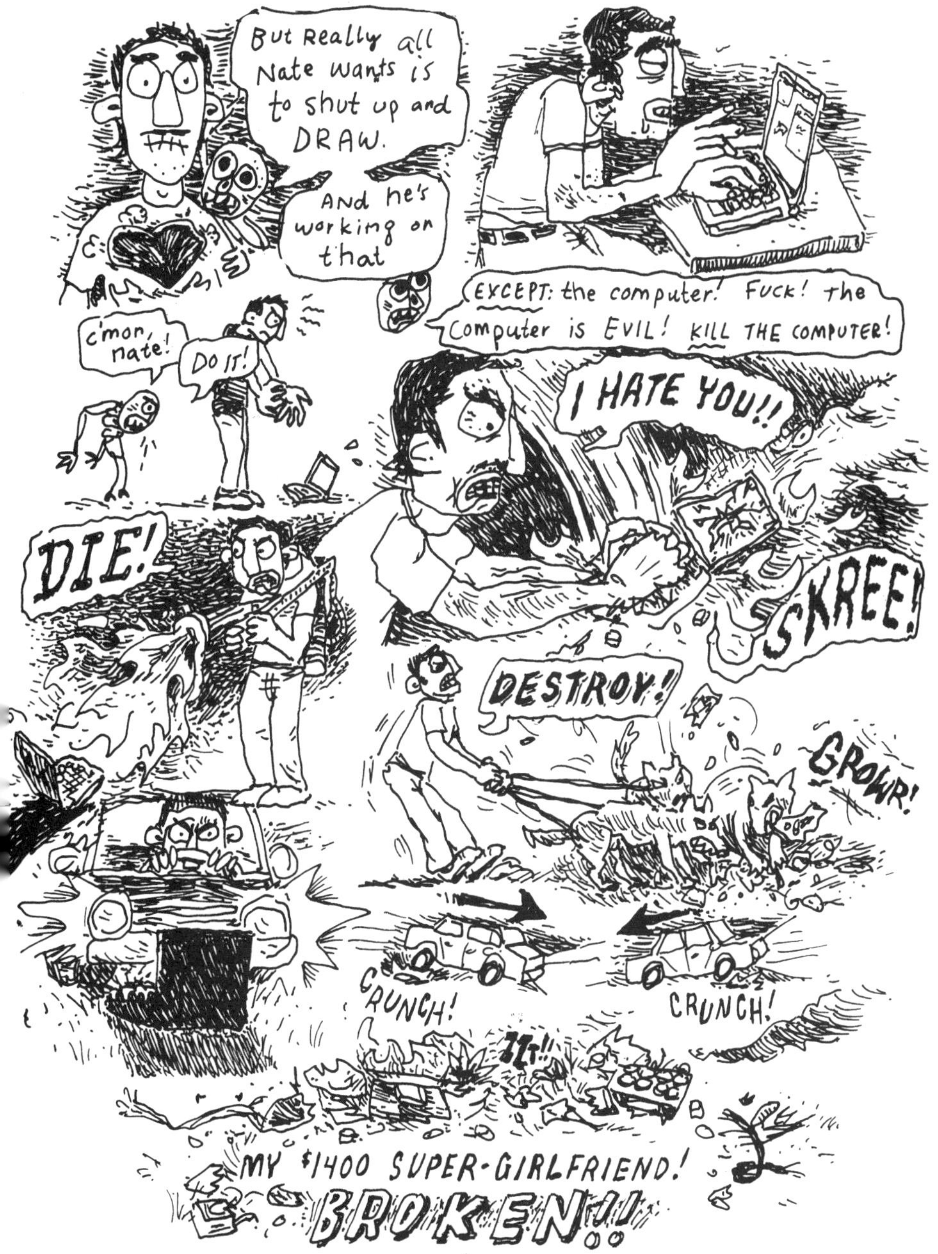

But Really all Nate wants is to shut up and DRAW.
And he's working on that
EXCEPT: the computer! Fuck! the Computer is EVIL! KILL THE COMPUTER!
c'mon, nate!
DO IT!
I HATE YOU!!
DIE!
SKREE!
DESTROY!
GROWR!
CRUNCH!
CRUNCH!
ZZT!!
MY $1400 SUPER-GIRLFRIEND!
BROKEN!!!

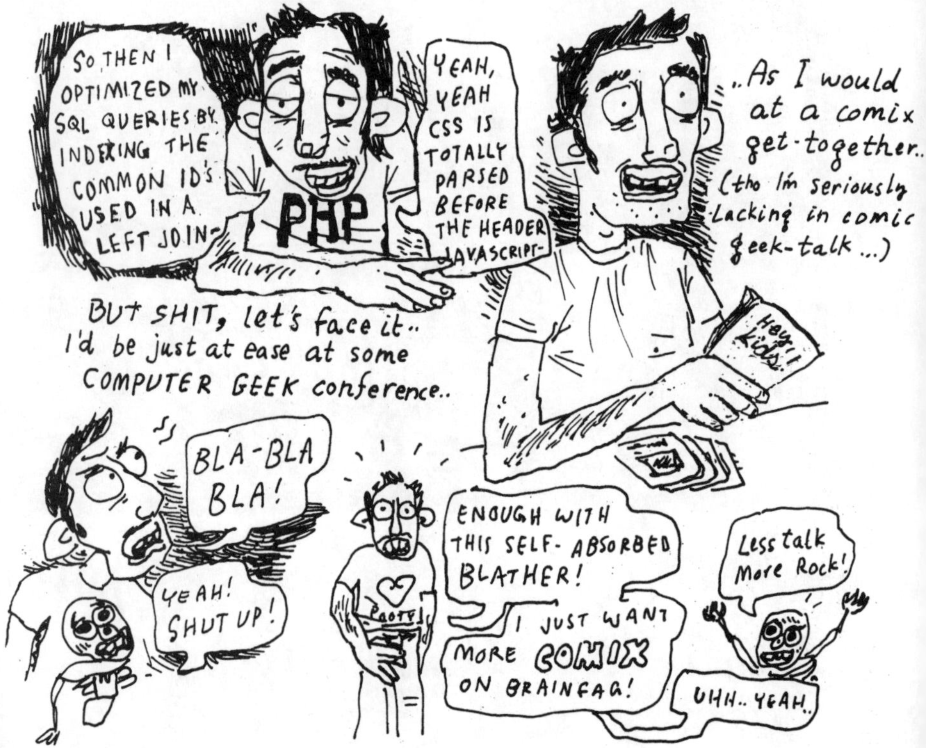
SO THEN I OPTIMIZED MY SQL QUERIES BY INDEXING THE COMMON ID'S USED IN A LEFT JOIN-
PHP
YEAH, YEAH CSS IS TOTALLY PARSED BEFORE THE HEADER JAVASCRIPT-
..As I would at a comix get-together..
(tho I'm seriously Lacking in comic geek-talk ...)
BUT SHIT, let's face it.. I'd be just at ease at some COMPUTER GEEK conference..
Hey! kids!
BLA-BLA BLA!
YEAH! SHUT UP!
ENOUGH WITH THIS SELF-ABSORBED BLATHER!
I JUST WANT MORE COMIX ON BRAINFAG!
Less talk More Rock!
UHH.. YEAH..

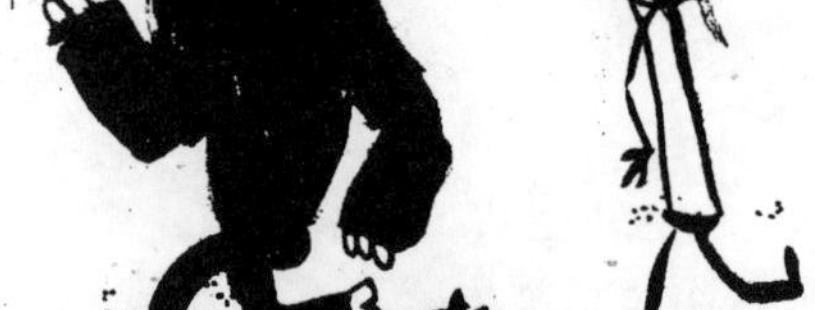
MAN.

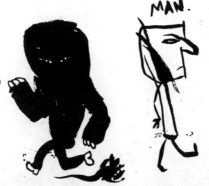

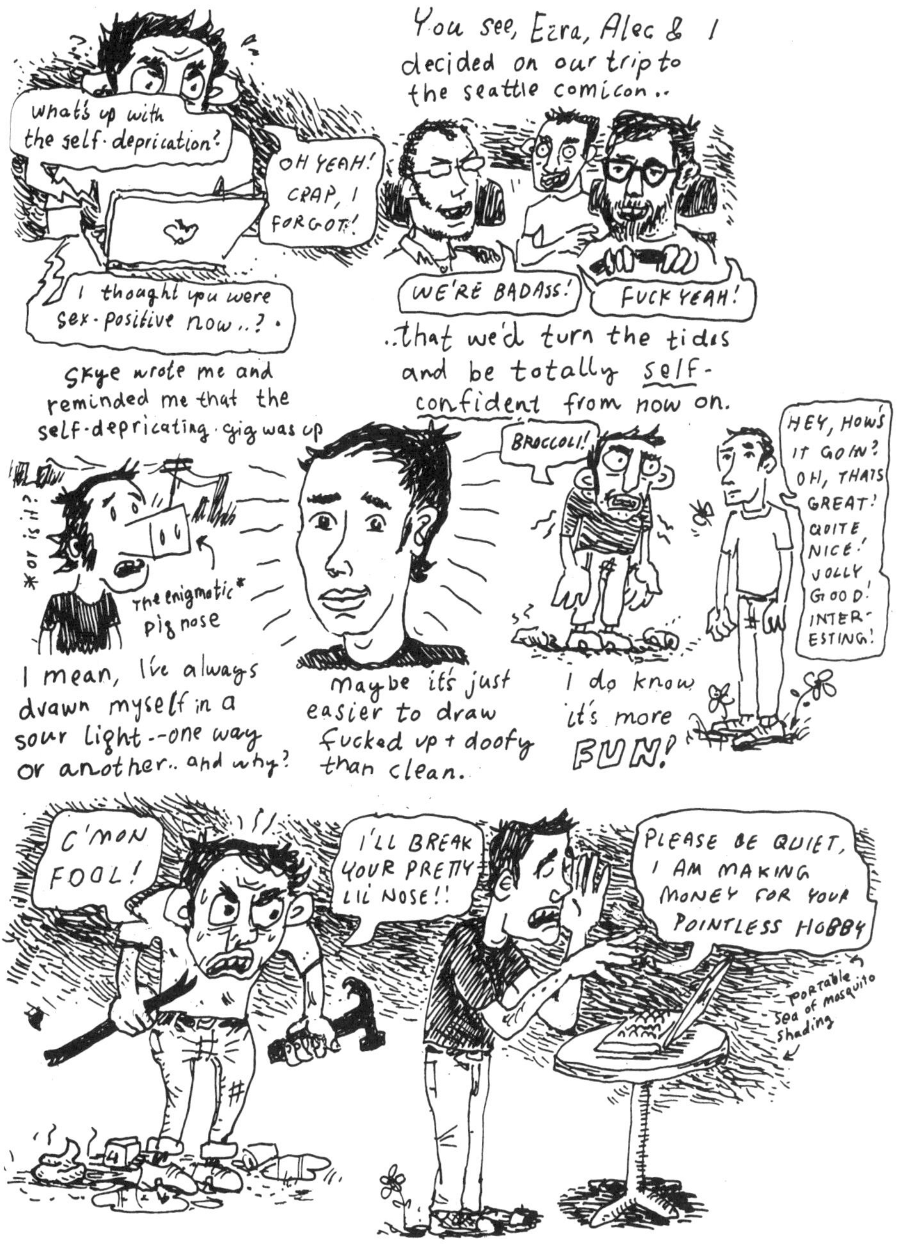
what's up with the self-deprication?
OH YEAH! CRAP, I FORGOT!
I thought you were sex-positive now..?
Skye wrote me and reminded me that the self-depricating gig was up
You see, Ezra, Alec & I decided on our trip to the seattle comicon..
WE'RE BADASS!
FUCK YEAH!
..that we'd turn the tides and be totally self-confident from now on.
*or is it?
The enigmatic* pig nose
I mean, I've always drawn myself in a sour light--one way or another.. and why?
Maybe it's just easier to draw fucked up + doofy than clean.
BROCCOLI!
HEY, HOW'S IT GOIN? OH, THATS GREAT! QUITE NICE! JOLLY GOOD! INTER-ESTING!
I do know it's more FUN!
C'MON FOOL!
I'LL BREAK YOUR PRETTY LIL NOSE!!
PLEASE BE QUIET, I AM MAKING MONEY FOR YOUR POINTLESS HOBBY
Portable sea of mosquito shading

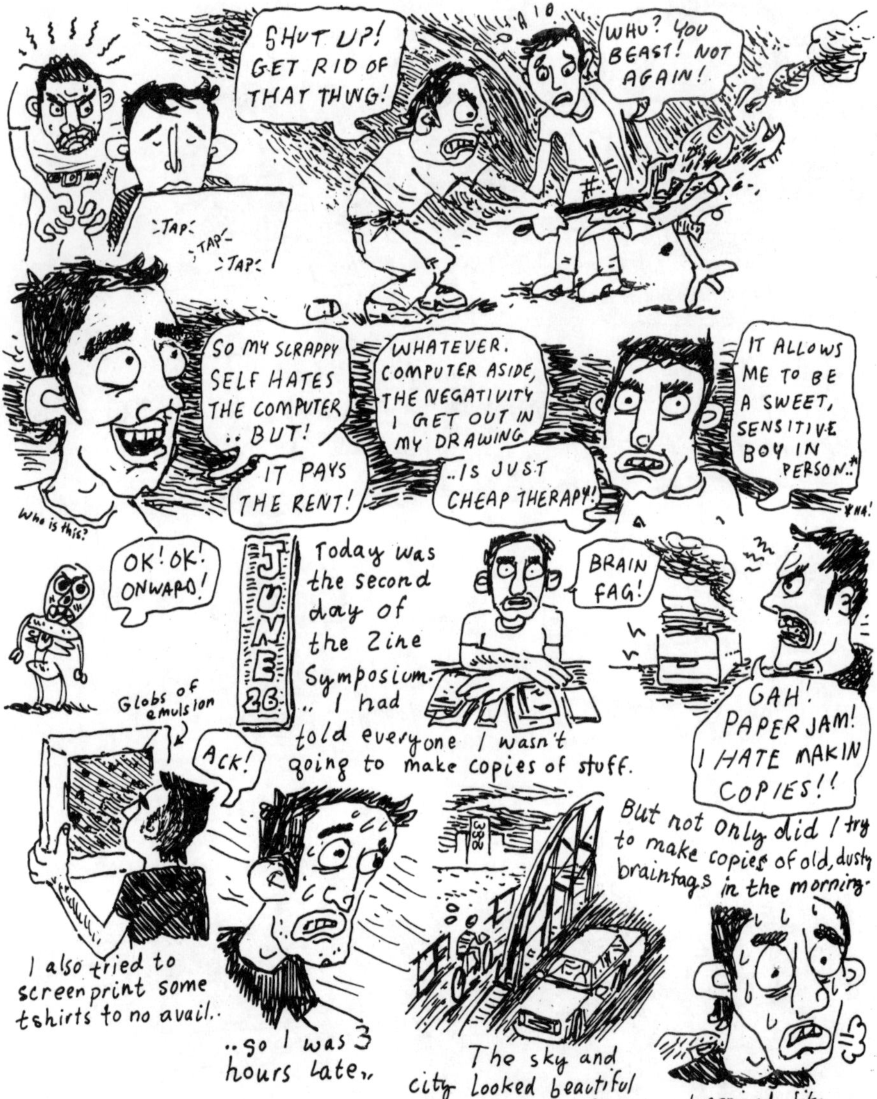
SHUT UP! GET RID OF THAT THING!
TAP
TAP
TAP
WHU? YOU BEAST! NOT AGAIN!
SO MY SCRAPPY SELF HATES THE COMPUTER .. BUT!
IT PAYS THE RENT!
WHATEVER. COMPUTER ASIDE, THE NEGATIVITY I GET OUT IN MY DRAWING
..IS JUST CHEAP THERAPY!
IT ALLOWS ME TO BE A SWEET, SENSITIVE BOY IN PERSON..*
*HA!
Who is this?
OK! OK! ONWARD!
JUNE 26
Today was the second day of the Zine Symposium. .. I had told everyone I wasn't going to make copies of stuff.
BRAIN FAG!
GAH! PAPER JAM! I HATE MAKIN COPIES!!
But not only did I try to make copies of old, dusty brainfags in the morning.
Globs of emulsion
ACK!
I also tried to screenprint some tshirts to no avail..
..so I was 3 hours late..
The sky and city looked beautiful on my sweaty, frantic ride to downtown.
I arrived like every year: wet with B.O. and super late.

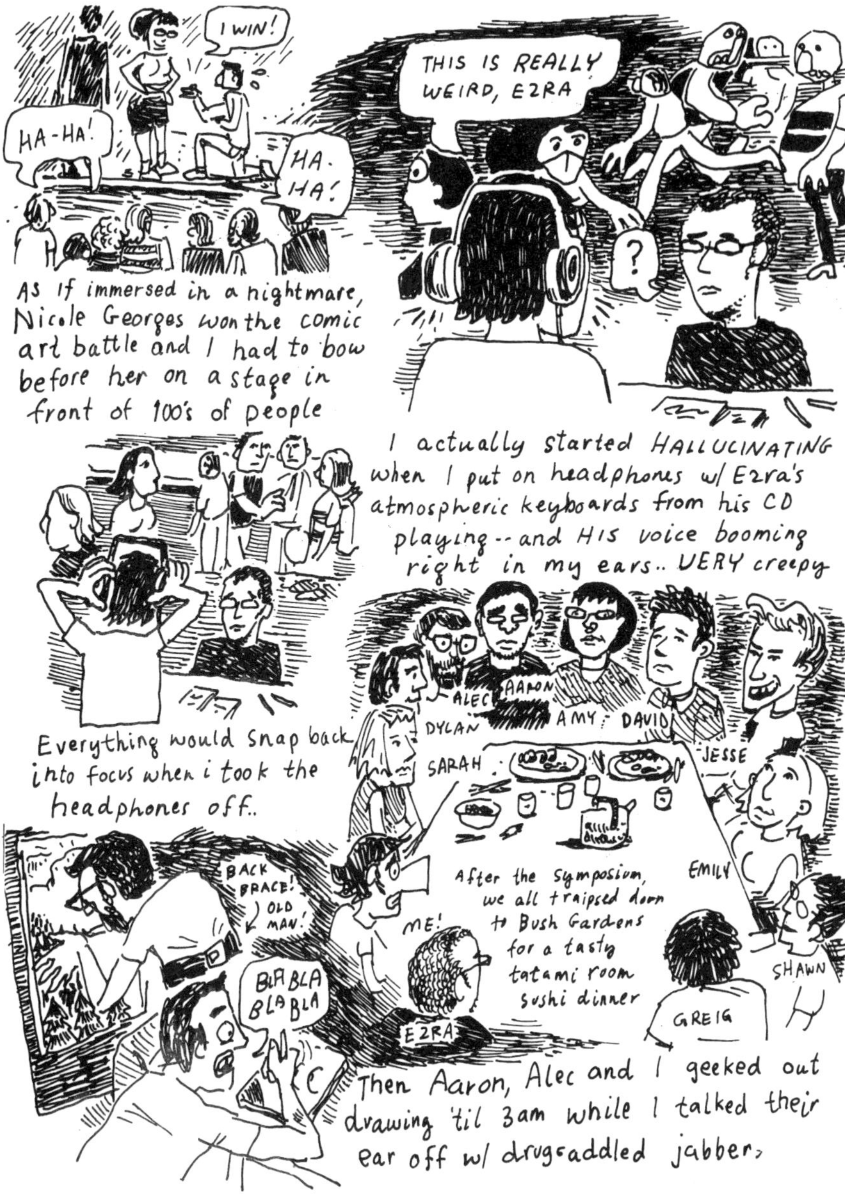
I WIN!
HA-HA!
HA-HA!
THIS IS REALLY WEIRD, EZRA
?
As if immersed in a nightmare, Nicole Georges won the comic art battle and I had to bow before her on a stage in front of 100's of people
I actually started HALLUCINATING when I put on headphones w/ Ezra's atmospheric keyboards from his CD playing -- and HIS voice booming right in my ears.. VERY creepy
Everything would snap back into focus when i took the headphones off..
ALEC
AARON
DYLAN
AMY
DAVID
JESSE
SARAH
EMILY
After the symposium, we all traipsed down to Bush Gardens for a tasty tatami room sushi dinner
ME!
SHAWN
GREIG
EZRA
BACK BRACE!
OLD MAN!
BLA BLA BLA BLA
Then Aaron, Alec and I geeked out drawing 'til 3am while I talked their ear off w/ drug-addled jabber.

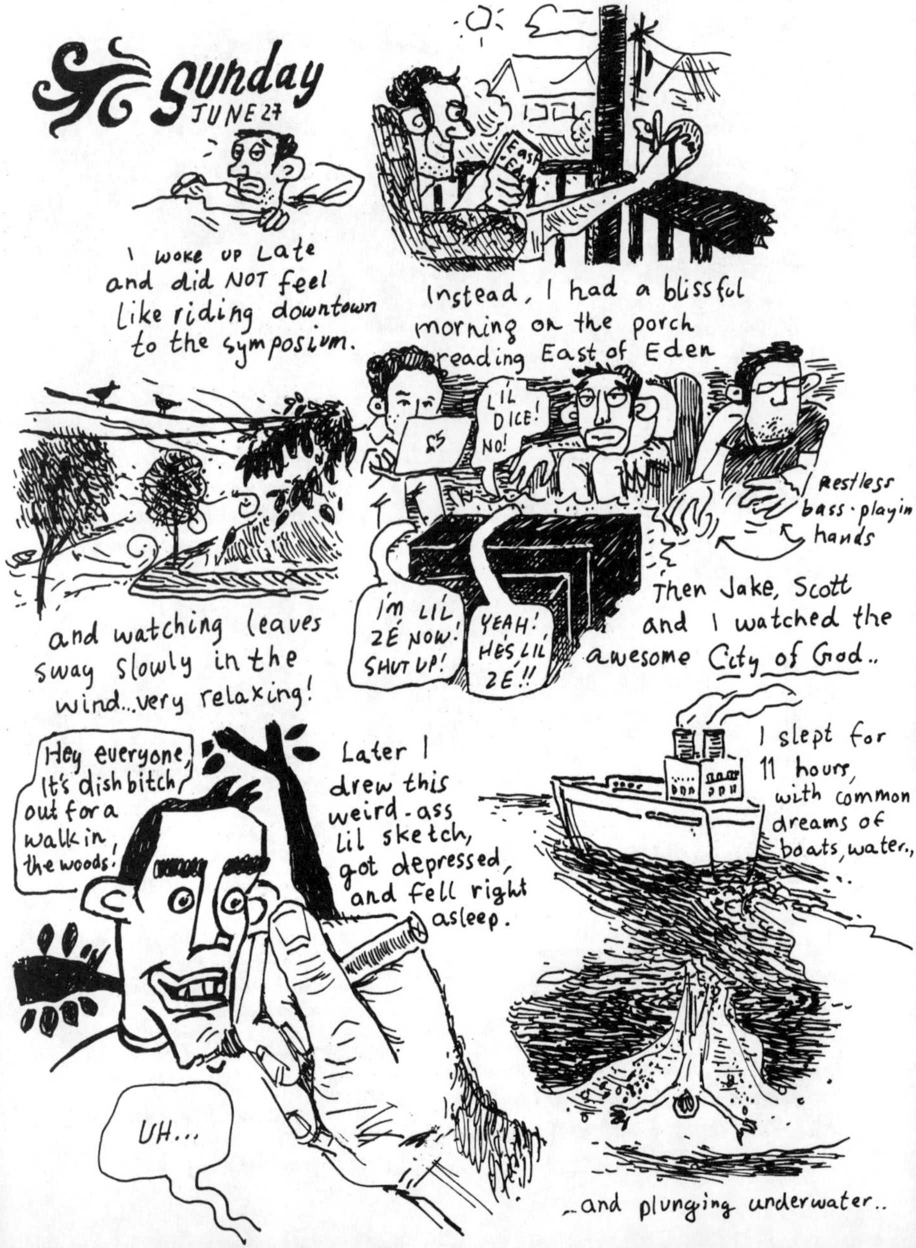
Sunday
JUNE 27
I woke up late and did NOT feel like riding downtown to the symposium.
Instead, I had a blissful morning on the porch reading East of Eden
EAST OF EDEN
and watching leaves sway slowly in the wind...very relaxing!
LIL DICE! NO!
I'M LIL ZÉ NOW! SHUT UP!
YEAH! HE'S LIL ZÉ!!
Restless bass-playin' hands
Then Jake, Scott and I watched the awesome City of God..
Hey everyone, It's dishbitch out for a walk in the woods!
UH...
Later I drew this weird-ass lil sketch, got depressed, and fell right asleep.
I slept for 11 hours, with common dreams of boats, water.,
..and plunging underwater..

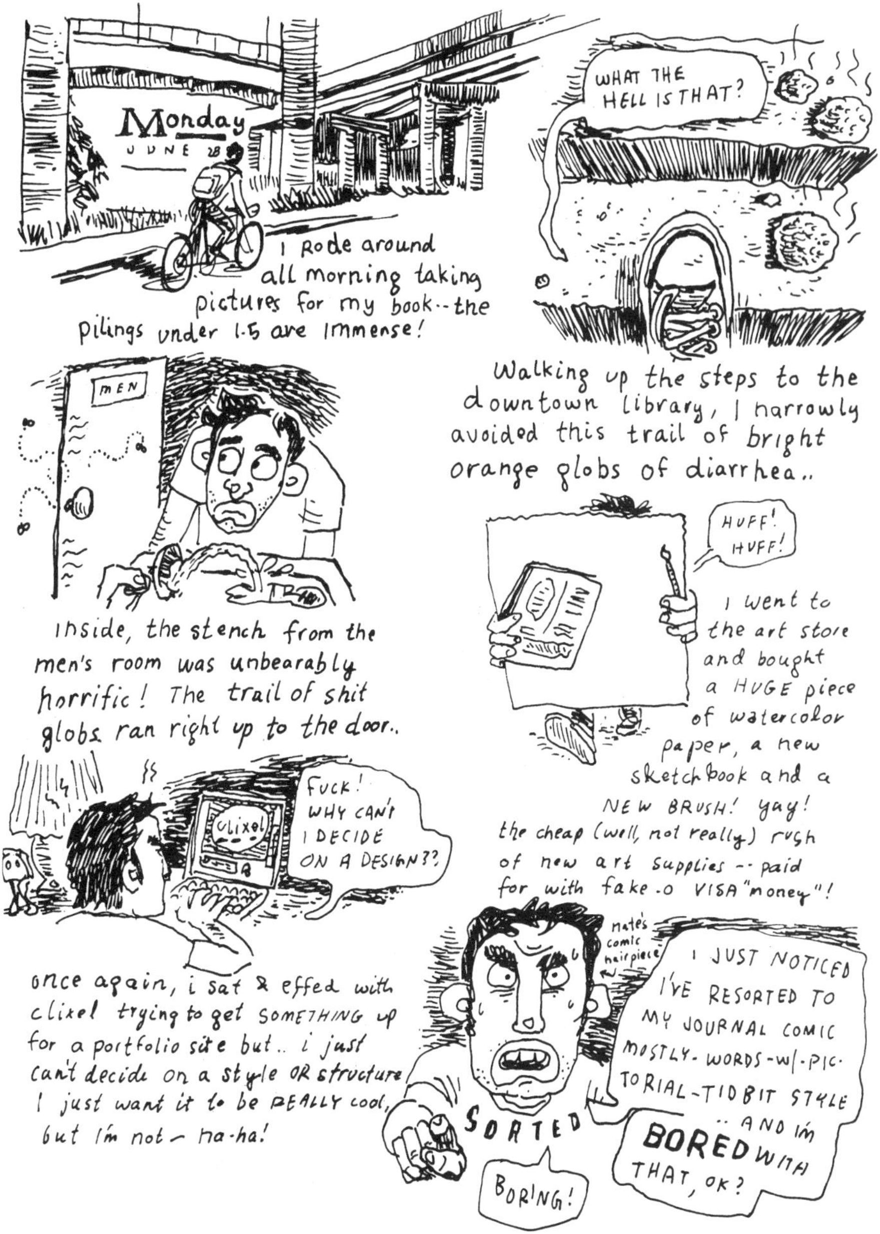
Monday
JUNE 28
I Rode around all morning taking pictures for my book.. the pilings under I-5 are immense!
WHAT THE HELL IS THAT?
Walking up the steps to the downtown library, I narrowly avoided this trail of bright orange globs of diarrhea..
MEN
inside, the stench from the men's room was unbearably horrific! The trail of shit globs ran right up to the door..
HUFF! HUFF!
I went to the art store and bought a HUGE piece of watercolor paper, a new sketchbook and a NEW BRUSH! yay!
the cheap (well, not really) rush of new art supplies -- paid for with fake-o VISA "money"!
clixel
FUCK! WHY CAN'T I DECIDE ON A DESIGN??
once again, i sat & effed with clixel trying to get SOMETHING up for a portfolio site but.. i just can't decide on a style OR structure I just want it to be REALLY cool, but i'm not - ha-ha!
nate's comic hairpiece
I JUST NOTICED I'VE RESORTED TO MY JOURNAL COMIC MOSTLY-WORDS-W/-PICTORIAL-TIDBIT STYLE .. AND I'M BORED WITH THAT, OK?
SORTED
BORING!

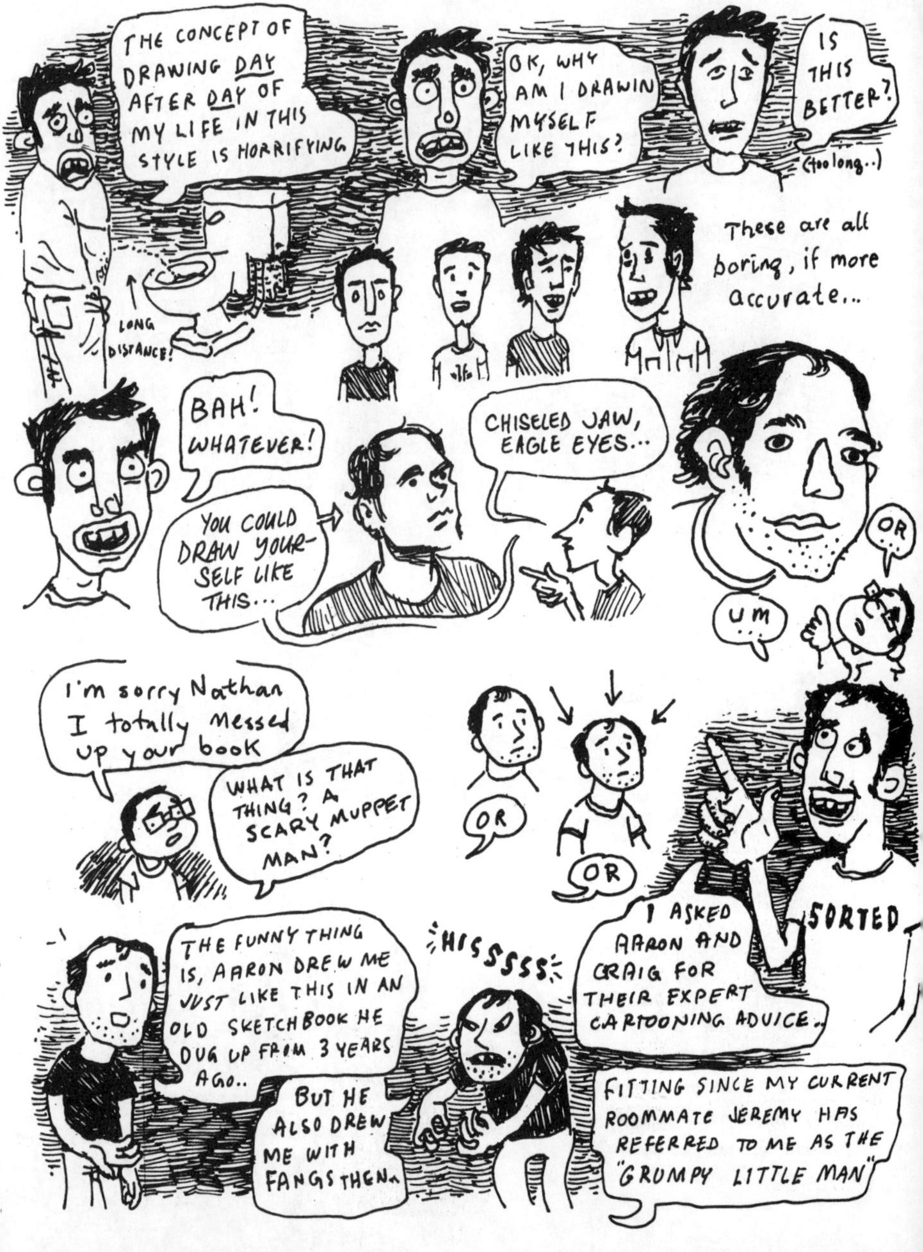
THE CONCEPT OF DRAWING DAY AFTER DAY OF MY LIFE IN THIS STYLE IS HORRIFYING
LONG DISTANCE!
OK, WHY AM I DRAWIN MYSELF LIKE THIS?
IS THIS BETTER?
(too long..)
These are all boring, if more accurate...
BAH! WHATEVER!
YOU COULD DRAW YOURSELF LIKE THIS...
CHISELED JAW, EAGLE EYES...
OR
UM
I'm sorry Nathan I totally messed up your book
WHAT IS THAT THING? A SCARY MUPPET MAN?
OR
OR
I ASKED AARON AND CRAIG FOR THEIR EXPERT CARTOONING ADVICE..
SORTED
THE FUNNY THING IS, AARON DREW ME JUST LIKE THIS IN AN OLD SKETCHBOOK HE DUG UP FROM 3 YEARS AGO..
HISSSSS
BUT HE ALSO DREW ME WITH FANGS THEN.
FITTING SINCE MY CURRENT ROOMMATE JEREMY HAS REFERRED TO ME AS THE "GRUMPY LITTLE MAN"

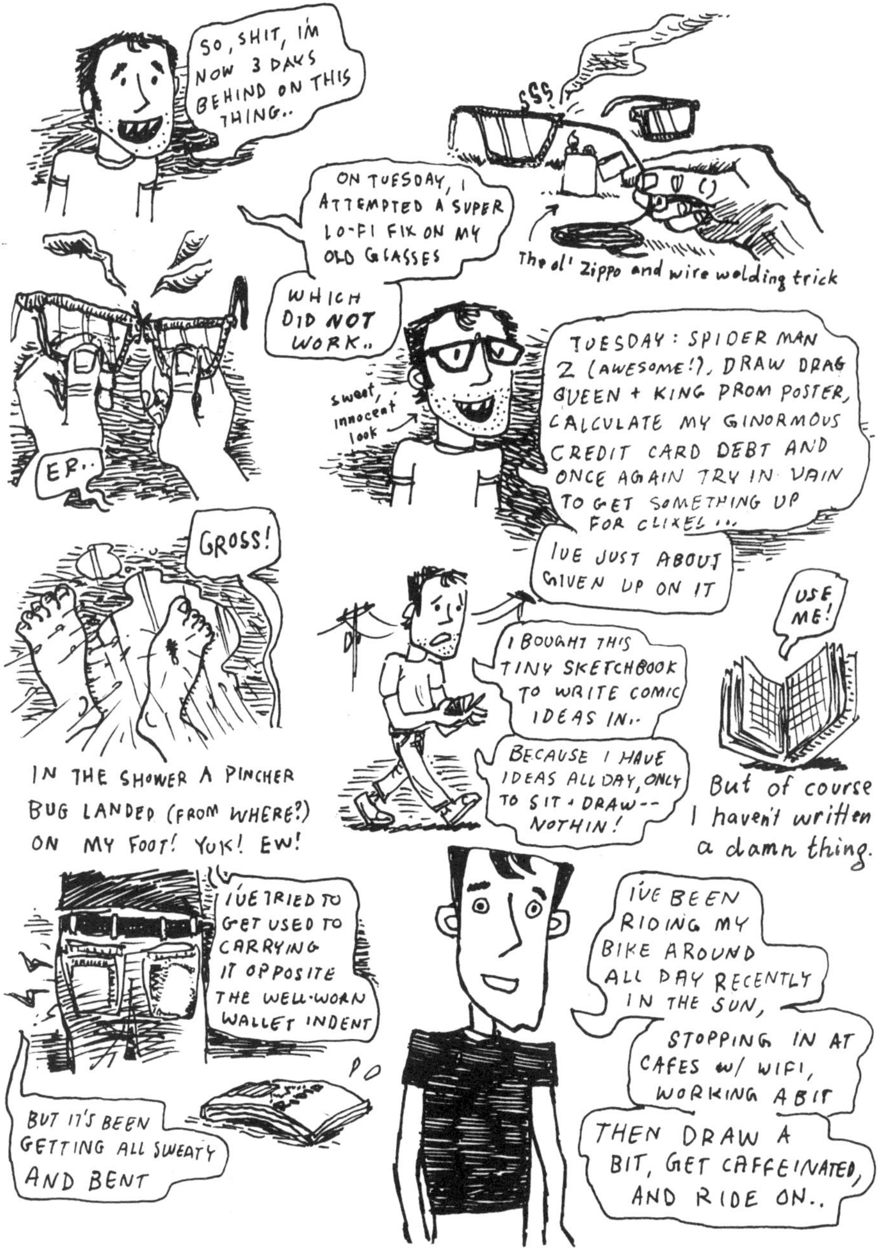

SO, SHIT, I'M NOW 3 DAYS BEHIND ON THIS THING..
SSS
The ol' Zippo and wire welding trick
ON TUESDAY, I ATTEMPTED A SUPER LO-FI FIX ON MY OLD GLASSES
WHICH DID NOT WORK..
ER..
TUESDAY: SPIDER MAN 2 (AWESOME!), DRAW DRAG QUEEN + KING PROM POSTER, CALCULATE MY GINORMOUS CREDIT CARD DEBT AND ONCE AGAIN TRY IN VAIN TO GET SOMETHING UP FOR CLIXEL..
sweet, innocent look
GROSS!
IVE JUST ABOUT GIVEN UP ON IT
USE ME!
I BOUGHT THIS TINY SKETCHBOOK TO WRITE COMIC IDEAS IN..
BECAUSE I HAVE IDEAS ALL DAY, ONLY TO SIT + DRAW-- NOTHIN!
IN THE SHOWER A PINCHER BUG LANDED (FROM WHERE?) ON MY FOOT! YUK! EW!
But of course I haven't written a damn thing.
IVE TRIED TO GET USED TO CARRYING IT OPPOSITE THE WELL-WORN WALLET INDENT
BUT IT'S BEEN GETTING ALL SWEATY AND BENT
IVE BEEN RIDING MY BIKE AROUND ALL DAY RECENTLY IN THE SUN,
STOPPING IN AT CAFES w/ WIFI, WORKING A BIT
THEN DRAW A BIT, GET CAFFEINATED, AND RIDE ON..

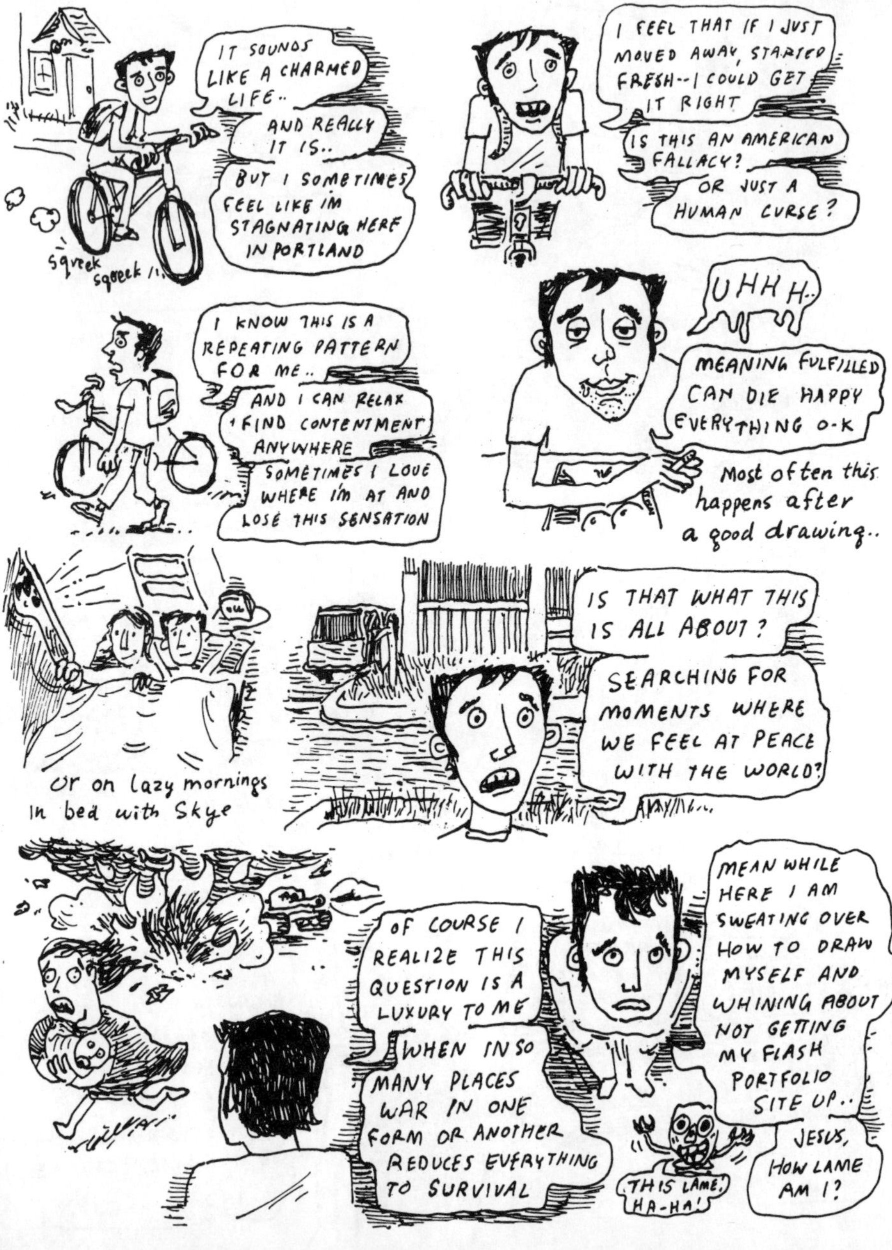
IT SOUNDS LIKE A CHARMED LIFE..
AND REALLY IT IS..
BUT I SOMETIMES FEEL LIKE IM STAGNATING HERE IN PORTLAND
sqreek
sqeek
I FEEL THAT IF I JUST MOVED AWAY, STARTED FRESH--I COULD GET IT RIGHT
IS THIS AN AMERICAN FALLACY?
OR JUST A HUMAN CURSE?
I KNOW THIS IS A REPEATING PATTERN FOR ME..
AND I CAN RELAX + FIND CONTENTMENT ANYWHERE
SOMETIMES I LOVE WHERE I'M AT AND LOSE THIS SENSATION
UHHH..
MEANING FULFILLED CAN DIE HAPPY EVERYTHING O-K
Most often this happens after a good drawing..
Or on lazy mornings in bed with Skye
IS THAT WHAT THIS IS ALL ABOUT?
SEARCHING FOR MOMENTS WHERE WE FEEL AT PEACE WITH THE WORLD?
OF COURSE I REALIZE THIS QUESTION IS A LUXURY TO ME
WHEN IN SO MANY PLACES WAR IN ONE FORM OR ANOTHER REDUCES EVERYTHING TO SURVIVAL
MEANWHILE HERE I AM SWEATING OVER HOW TO DRAW MYSELF AND WHINING ABOUT NOT GETTING MY FLASH PORTFOLIO SITE UP..
JESUS, HOW LAME AM I?
THIS LAME! HA-HA!

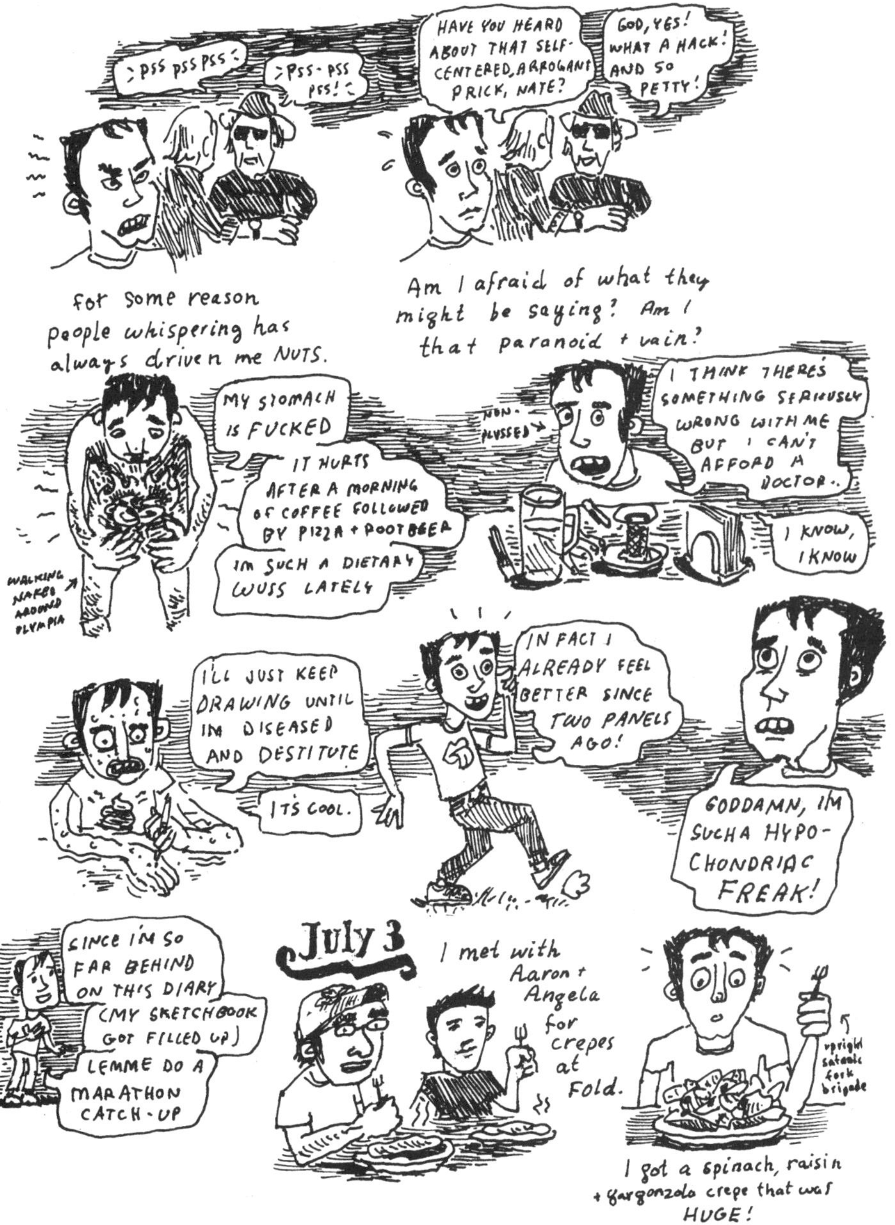

PSS PSS PSS
PSS-PSS PSS!
HAVE YOU HEARD ABOUT THAT SELF-CENTERED, ARROGANT PRICK, NATE?
GOD, YES! WHAT A HACK! AND SO PETTY!
For some reason people whispering has always driven me NUTS.
Am I afraid of what they might be saying? Am I that paranoid + vain?
MY STOMACH IS FUCKED
IT HURTS AFTER A MORNING OF COFFEE FOLLOWED BY PIZZA + ROOTBEER
IM SUCH A DIETARY WUSS LATELY
WALKING NAKED AROUND OLYMPIA
NON-PLUSSED
I THINK THERE'S SOMETHING SERIOUSLY WRONG WITH ME BUT I CAN'T AFFORD A DOCTOR..
I KNOW, I KNOW
I'LL JUST KEEP DRAWING UNTIL IM DISEASED AND DESTITUTE
IT'S COOL.
IN FACT I ALREADY FEEL BETTER SINCE TWO PANELS AGO!
GODDAMN, I'M SUCHA HYPO-CHONDRIAC FREAK!
SINCE I'M SO FAR BEHIND ON THIS DIARY (MY SKETCHBOOK GOT FILLED UP) LEMME DO A MARATHON CATCH-UP
July 3
I met with Aaron + Angela for crepes at Fold.
upright satanic fork brigade
I got a spinach, raisin + gorgonzola crepe that was HUGE!

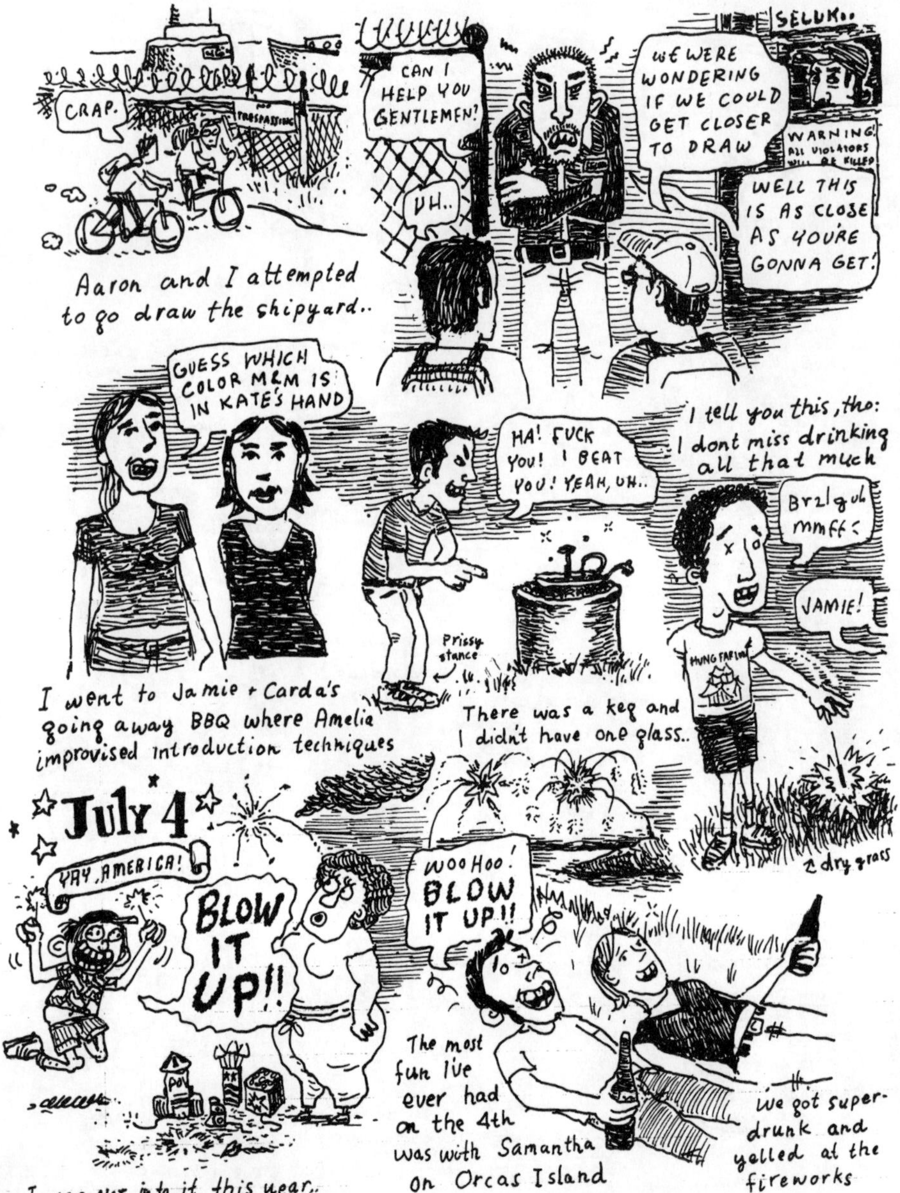
CRAP.
NO TRESPASSING
Aaron and I attempted to go draw the shipyard..
CAN I HELP YOU GENTLEMEN?
UH..
WE WERE WONDERING IF WE COULD GET CLOSER TO DRAW
SELUK..
WARNING! ALL VIOLATORS WILL BE KILLED
WELL THIS IS AS CLOSE AS YOU'RE GONNA GET!
GUESS WHICH COLOR M&M IS IN KATE'S HAND
HA! FUCK YOU! I BEAT YOU! YEAH, UH..
Prissy stance
I went to Jamie + Carda's going away BBQ where Amelia improvised introduction techniques
I tell you this, tho: I dont miss drinking all that much
Brzlguh mmff<
JAMIE!
HUNG FAR LOW
There was a keg and I didn't have one glass..
dry grass
July 4
YAY, AMERICA!
BLOW IT UP!!
WOO HOO! BLOW IT UP!!
The most fun I've ever had on the 4th was with Samantha on Orcas Island
We got super-drunk and yelled at the fireworks
I was NOT into it this year..

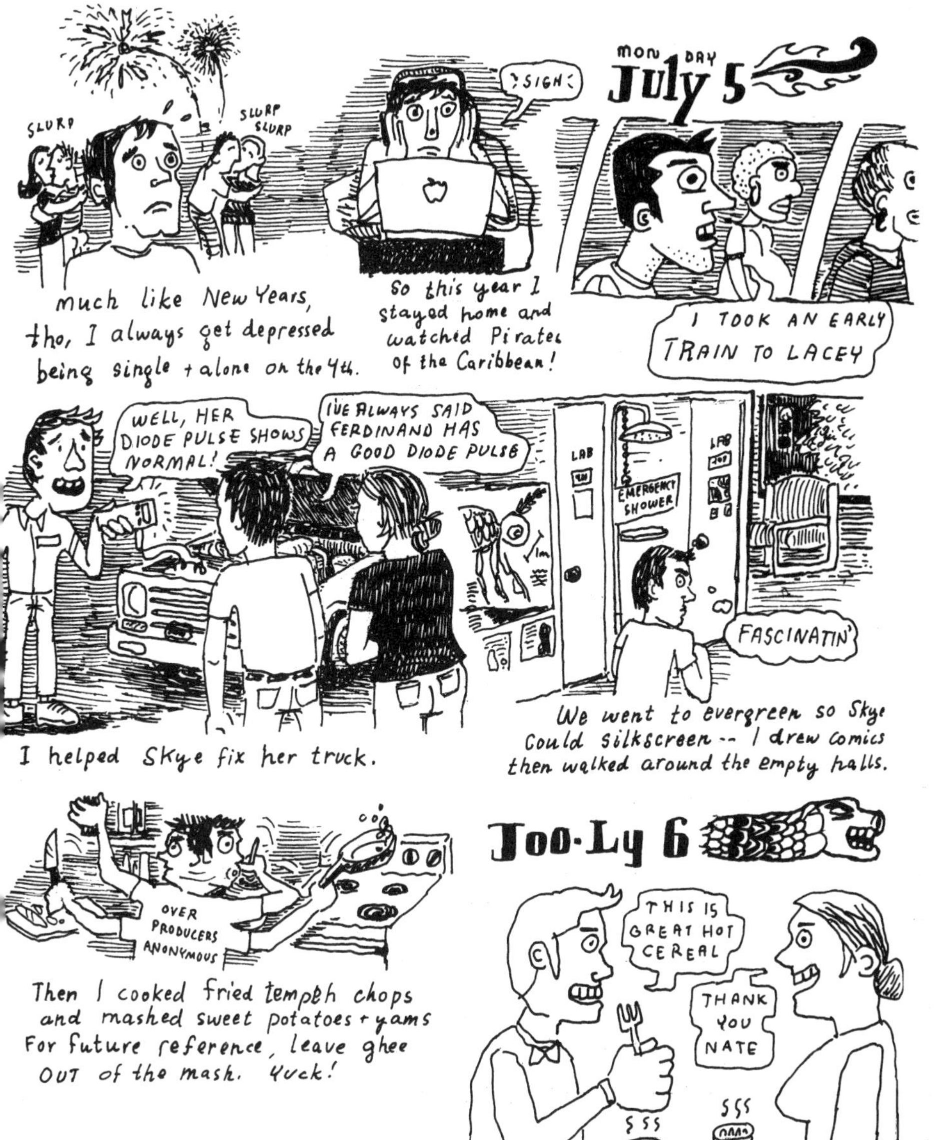
SLURP
SLURP
SLURP
much like New Years, tho, I always get depressed being single + alone on the 4th.
SIGH
So this year I stayed home and watched Pirates of the Caribbean!
MON DAY
July 5
I TOOK AN EARLY TRAIN TO LACEY
WELL, HER DIODE PULSE SHOWS NORMAL!
I'VE ALWAYS SAID FERDINAND HAS A GOOD DIODE PULSE
I helped Skye fix her truck.
LAB
LAB
EMERGENCY SHOWER
FASCINATIN'
We went to evergreen so Skye Could silkscreen -- I drew comics then walked around the empty halls.
OVER PRODUCERS ANONYMOUS
Then I cooked fried tempeh chops and mashed sweet potatoes + yams For future reference, leave ghee OUT of the mash. Yuck!
Joo-Ly 6
THIS IS GREAT HOT CEREAL
THANK YOU NATE

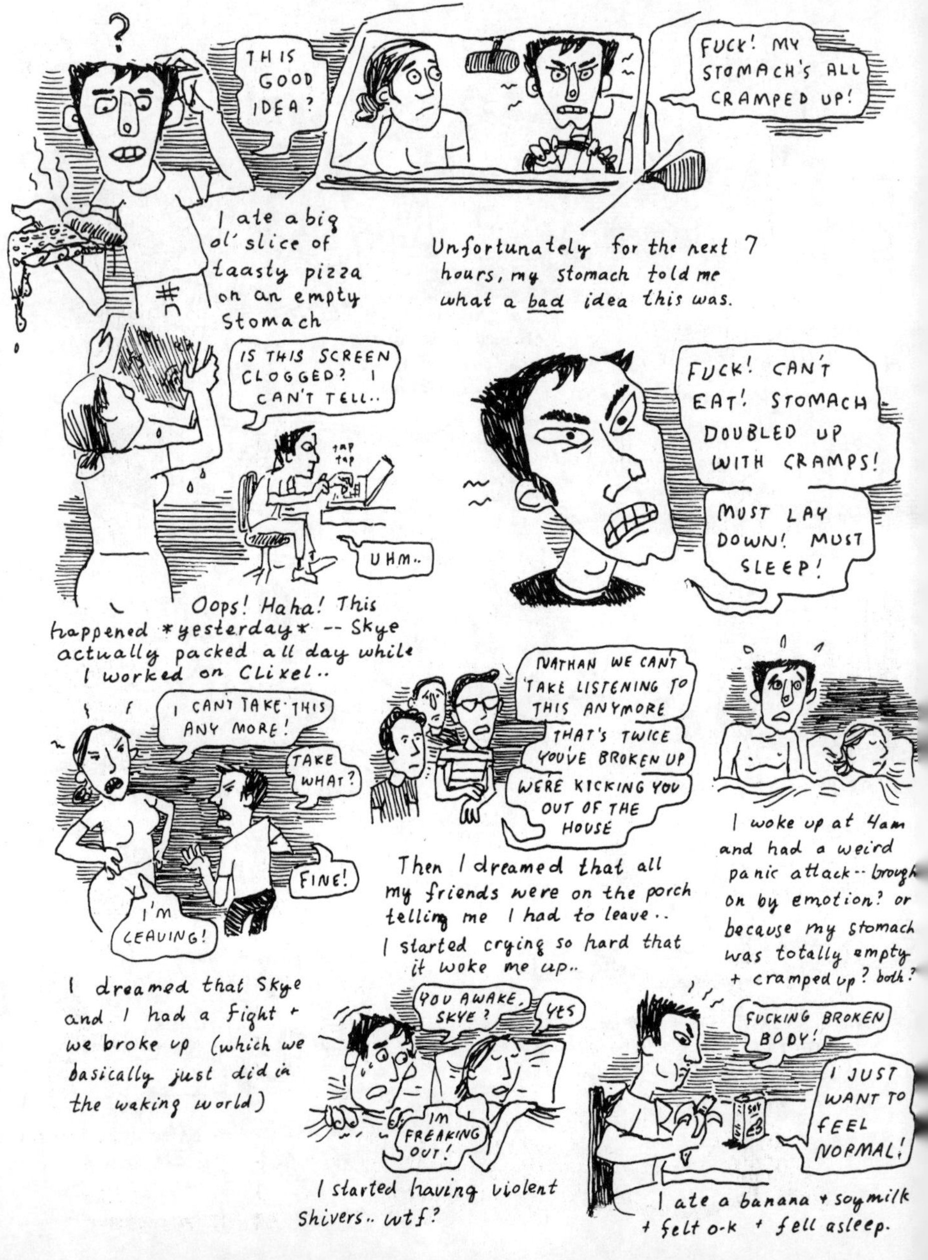
?
THIS GOOD IDEA?
I ate a big ol' slice of taasty pizza on an empty stomach
FUCK! MY STOMACH'S ALL CRAMPED UP!
Unfortunately for the next 7 hours, my stomach told me what a bad idea this was.
IS THIS SCREEN CLOGGED? I CAN'T TELL..
TAP TAP
UHM..
Oops! Haha! This happened *yesterday* -- Skye actually packed all day while I worked on Clixel..
FUCK! CAN'T EAT! STOMACH DOUBLED UP WITH CRAMPS!
MUST LAY DOWN! MUST SLEEP!
I CAN'T TAKE THIS ANY MORE!
TAKE WHAT?
FINE!
I'M LEAVING!
I dreamed that Skye and I had a fight + we broke up (which we basically just did in the waking world)
NATHAN WE CAN'T TAKE LISTENING TO THIS ANYMORE
THAT'S TWICE YOU'VE BROKEN UP
WE'RE KICKING YOU OUT OF THE HOUSE
Then I dreamed that all my friends were on the porch telling me I had to leave.. I started crying so hard that it woke me up..
I woke up at 4am and had a weird panic attack -- brough on by emotion? or because my stomach was totally empty + cramped up? both?
YOU AWAKE, SKYE?
YES
IM FREAKING OUT!
I started having violent shivers.. wtf?
FUCKING BROKEN BODY!
I JUST WANT TO FEEL NORMAL!
SOY
I ate a banana + soymilk + felt o-k + fell asleep.

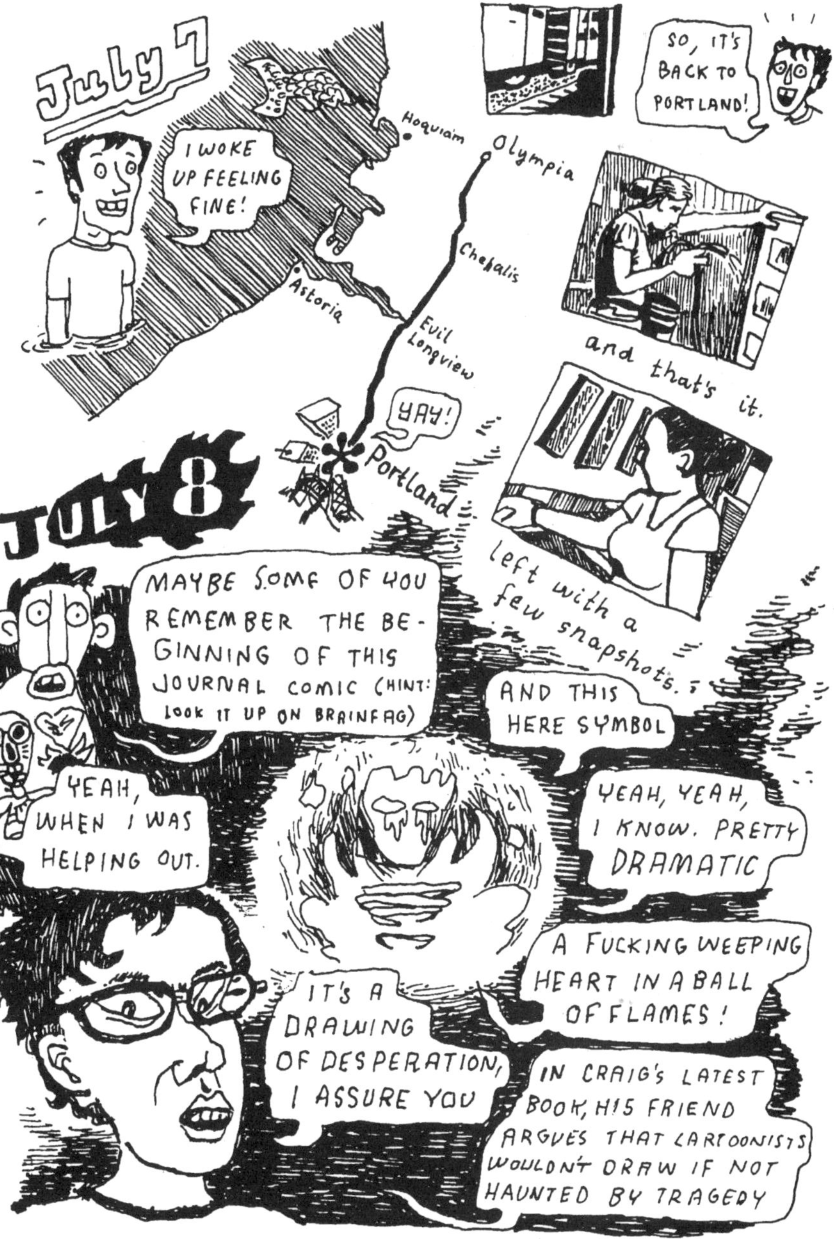

July 7
I WOKE UP FEELING FINE!
Hoquiam
Olympia
Chehalis
Astoria
Evil Longview
YAY!
Portland
SO, IT'S BACK TO PORTLAND!
and that's it.
left with a few snapshots.
JULY 8
MAYBE SOME OF YOU REMEMBER THE BEGINNING OF THIS JOURNAL COMIC (HINT: LOOK IT UP ON BRAINFAG)
AND THIS HERE SYMBOL
YEAH, WHEN I WAS HELPING OUT.
YEAH, YEAH, I KNOW. PRETTY DRAMATIC
A FUCKING WEEPING HEART IN A BALL OF FLAMES!
IT'S A DRAWING OF DESPERATION, I ASSURE YOU
IN CRAIG'S LATEST BOOK, HIS FRIEND ARGUES THAT CARTOONISTS WOULDN'T DRAW IF NOT HAUNTED BY TRAGEDY

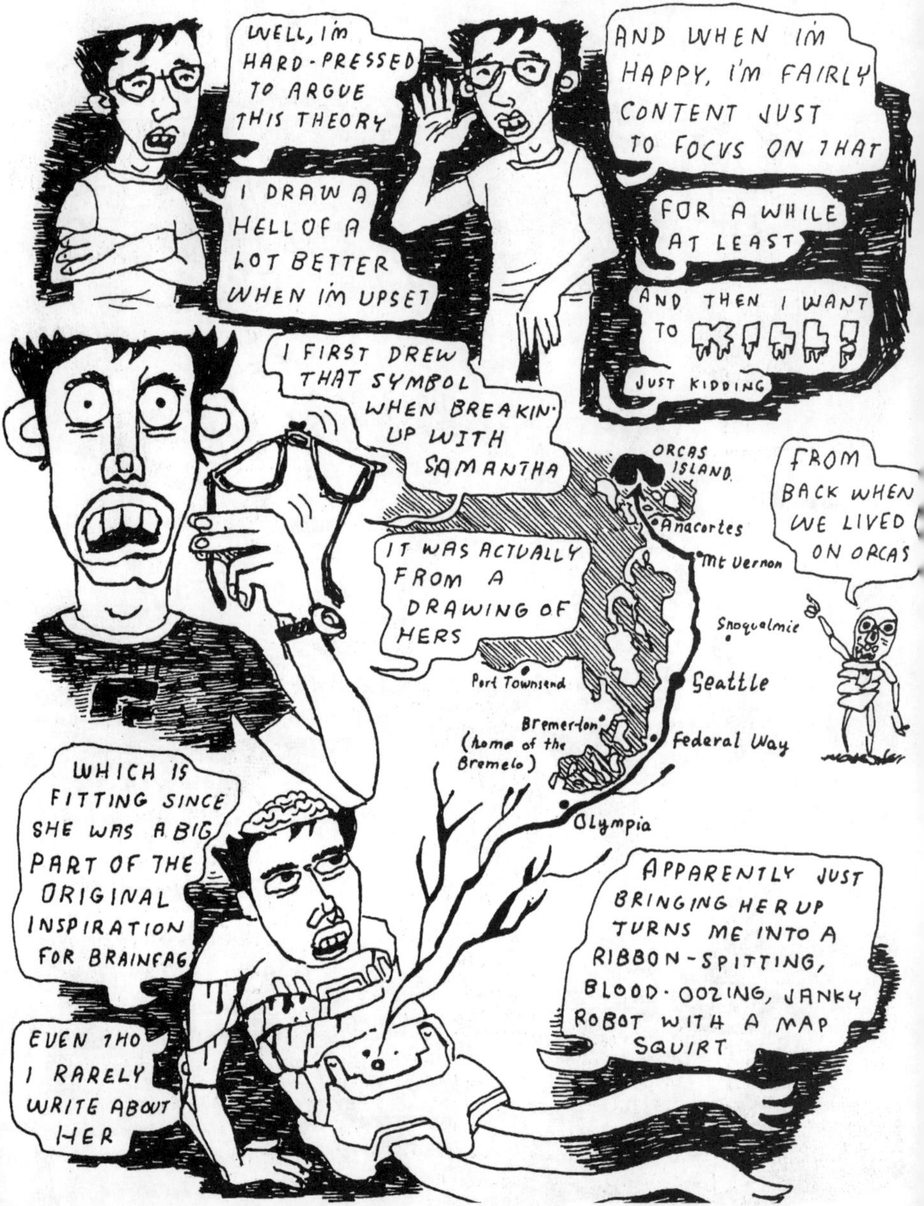
WELL, I'M HARD-PRESSED TO ARGUE THIS THEORY
I DRAW A HELL OF A LOT BETTER WHEN I'M UPSET
AND WHEN I'M HAPPY, I'M FAIRLY CONTENT JUST TO FOCUS ON THAT
FOR A WHILE AT LEAST
AND THEN I WANT TO KILL!
JUST KIDDING
I FIRST DREW THAT SYMBOL WHEN BREAKIN' UP WITH SAMANTHA
IT WAS ACTUALLY FROM A DRAWING OF HERS
ORCAS ISLAND
Anacortes
Mt Vernon
Snoqualmie
Port Townsend
Seattle
Bremerton (home of the Bremelo)
Federal Way
Olympia
FROM BACK WHEN WE LIVED ON ORCAS
WHICH IS FITTING SINCE SHE WAS A BIG PART OF THE ORIGINAL INSPIRATION FOR BRAINFAG
EVEN THO I RARELY WRITE ABOUT HER
APPARENTLY JUST BRINGING HER UP TURNS ME INTO A RIBBON-SPITTING, BLOOD-OOZING, JANKY ROBOT WITH A MAP SQUIRT

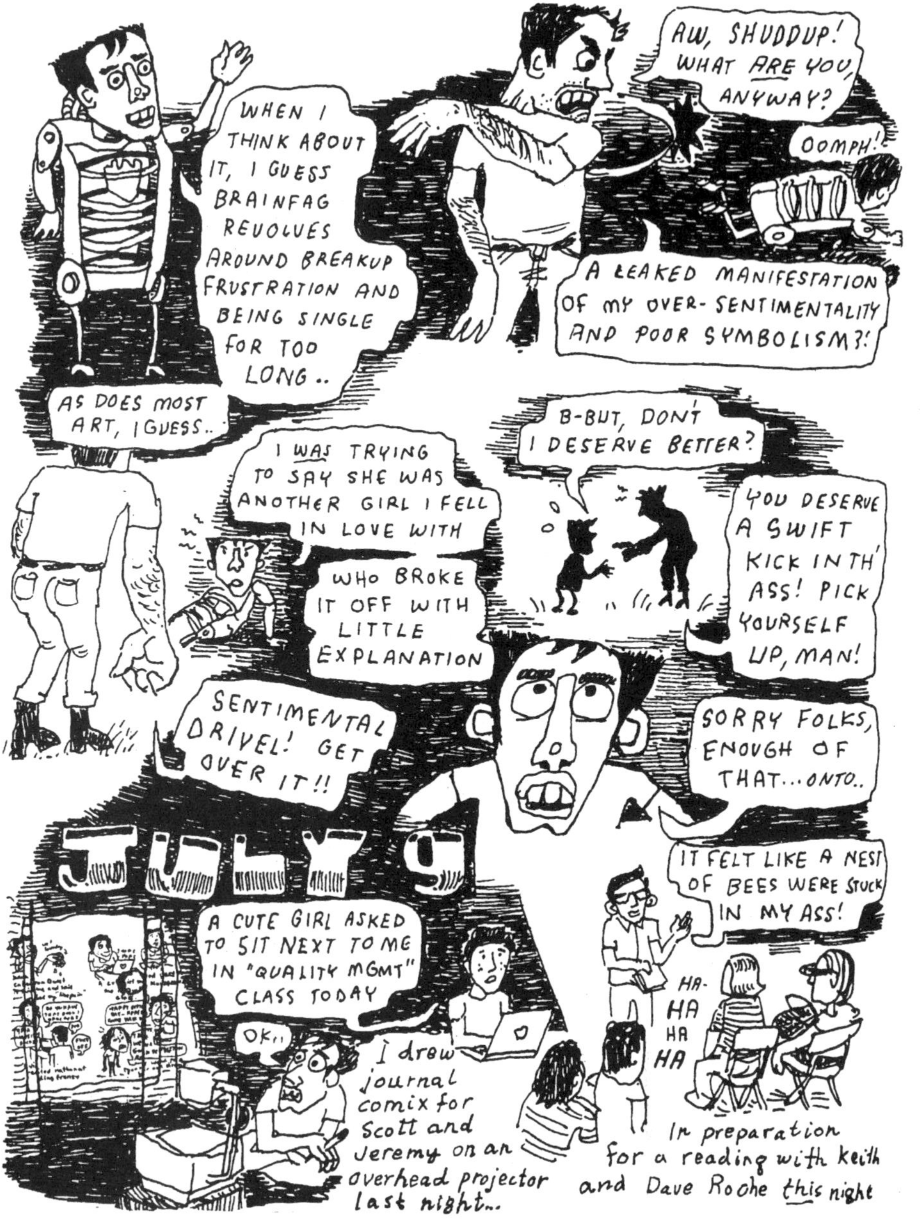
WHEN I THINK ABOUT IT, I GUESS BRAINFAG REVOLVES AROUND BREAKUP FRUSTRATION AND BEING SINGLE FOR TOO LONG..
AS DOES MOST ART, I GUESS..
AW, SHUDDUP! WHAT ARE YOU, ANYWAY?
OOMPH!
A LEAKED MANIFESTATION OF MY OVER-SENTIMENTALITY AND POOR SYMBOLISM?!
I WAS TRYING TO SAY SHE WAS ANOTHER GIRL I FELL IN LOVE WITH
WHO BROKE IT OFF WITH LITTLE EXPLANATION
B-BUT, DON'T I DESERVE BETTER?
YOU DESERVE A SWIFT KICK IN TH' ASS! PICK YOURSELF UP, MAN!
SENTIMENTAL DRIVEL! GET OVER IT!!
SORRY FOLKS, ENOUGH OF THAT...ONTO..
JULY 9
A CUTE GIRL ASKED TO SIT NEXT TO ME IN "QUALITY MGMT" CLASS TODAY
OK..
IT FELT LIKE A NEST OF BEES WERE STUCK IN MY ASS!
HA- HA HA HA
I drew journal comix for Scott and Jeremy on an overhead projector last night...
In preparation for a reading with keith and Dave Roche this night

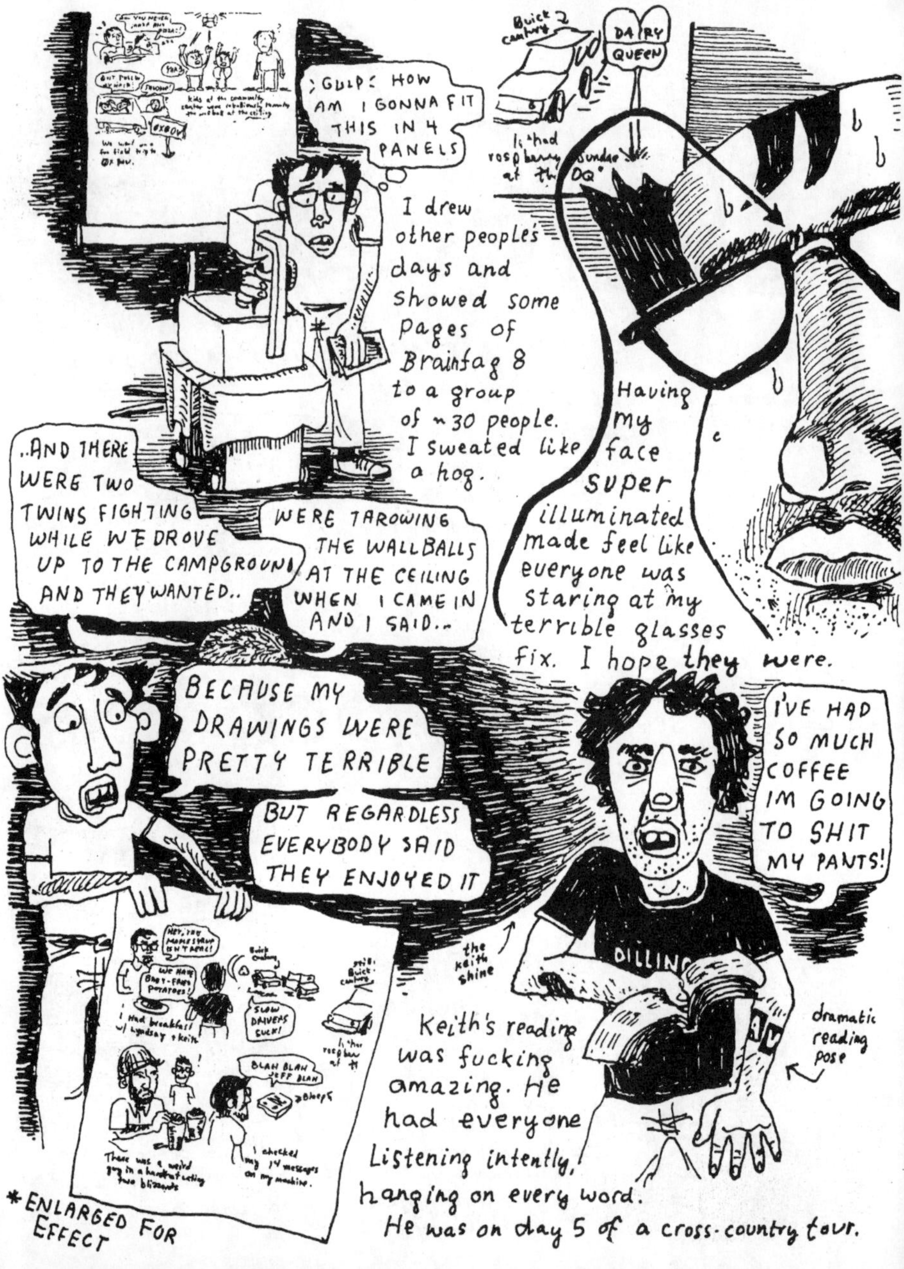
;GULP; HOW AM I GONNA FIT THIS IN 4 PANELS
I drew other people's days and showed some pages of Brainfag 8 to a group of ~30 people. I sweated like a hog.
DAIRY QUEEN
Having my face super illuminated made feel like everyone was staring at my terrible glasses fix. I hope they were.
..AND THERE WERE TWO TWINS FIGHTING WHILE WE DROVE UP TO THE CAMPGROUND AND THEY WANTED..
WERE THROWING THE WALLBALLS AT THE CEILING WHEN I CAME IN AND I SAID..
BECAUSE MY DRAWINGS WERE PRETTY TERRIBLE
BUT REGARDLESS EVERYBODY SAID THEY ENJOYED IT
I'VE HAD SO MUCH COFFEE IM GOING TO SHIT MY PANTS!
the keith shine
DILLING
dramatic reading pose
Keith's reading was fucking amazing. He had everyone Listening intently, hanging on every word.
He was on day 5 of a cross-country tour.
SLOW DRIVERS SUCK!
BLAH BLAH JEFF BLAH
* ENLARGED FOR EFFECT

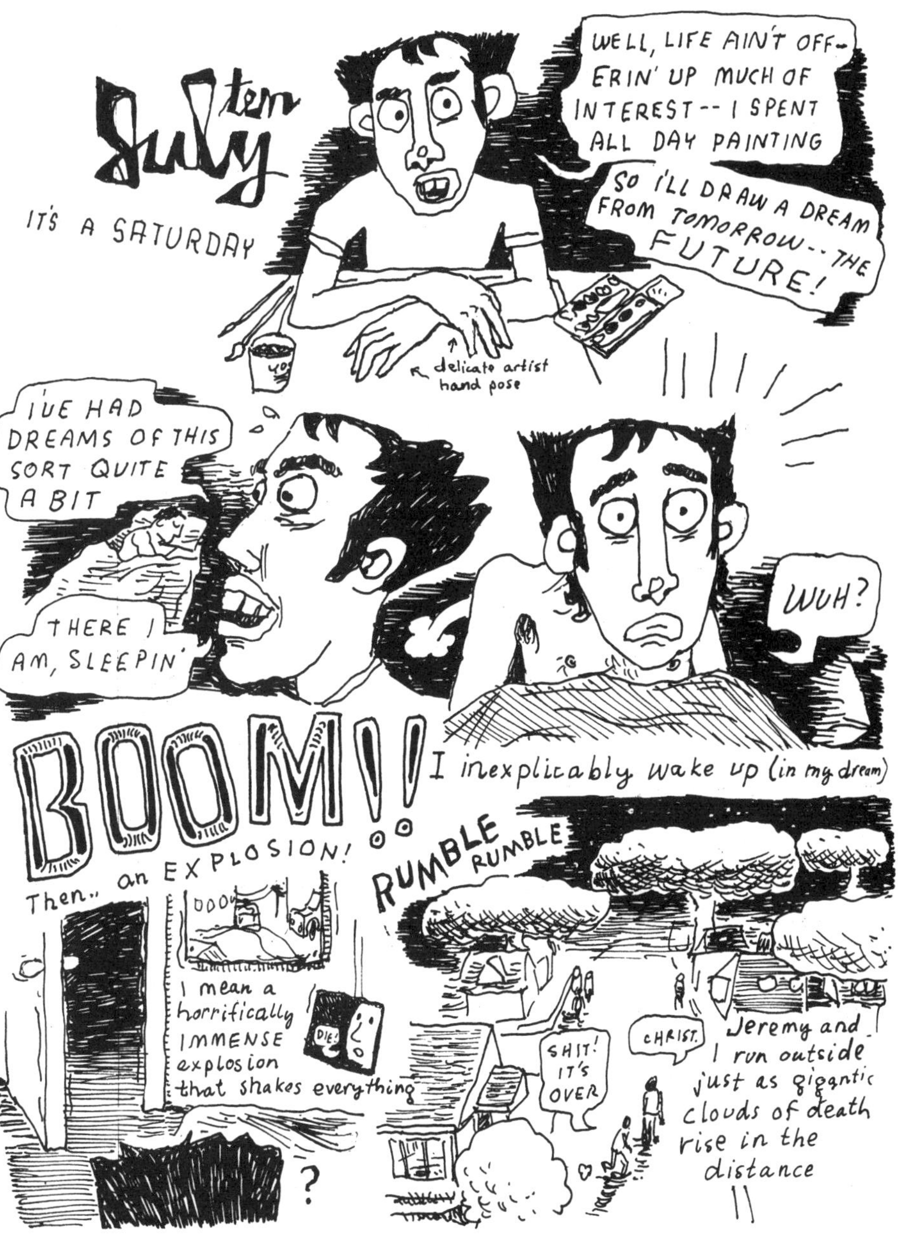

July 8 tem
IT'S A SATURDAY
WELL, LIFE AIN'T OFF-ERIN' UP MUCH OF INTEREST -- I SPENT ALL DAY PAINTING
SO I'LL DRAW A DREAM FROM TOMORROW -- THE FUTURE!
delicate artist hand pose
I'VE HAD DREAMS OF THIS SORT QUITE A BIT
THERE I AM, SLEEPIN'
WUH?
BOOM!!
I inexplicably wake up (in my dream)
Then.. an EXPLOSION!
RUMBLE RUMBLE
I mean a horrifically IMMENSE explosion that shakes everything
DIE!
?
SHIT! IT'S OVER
CHRIST.
Jeremy and I run outside just as gigantic clouds of death rise in the distance

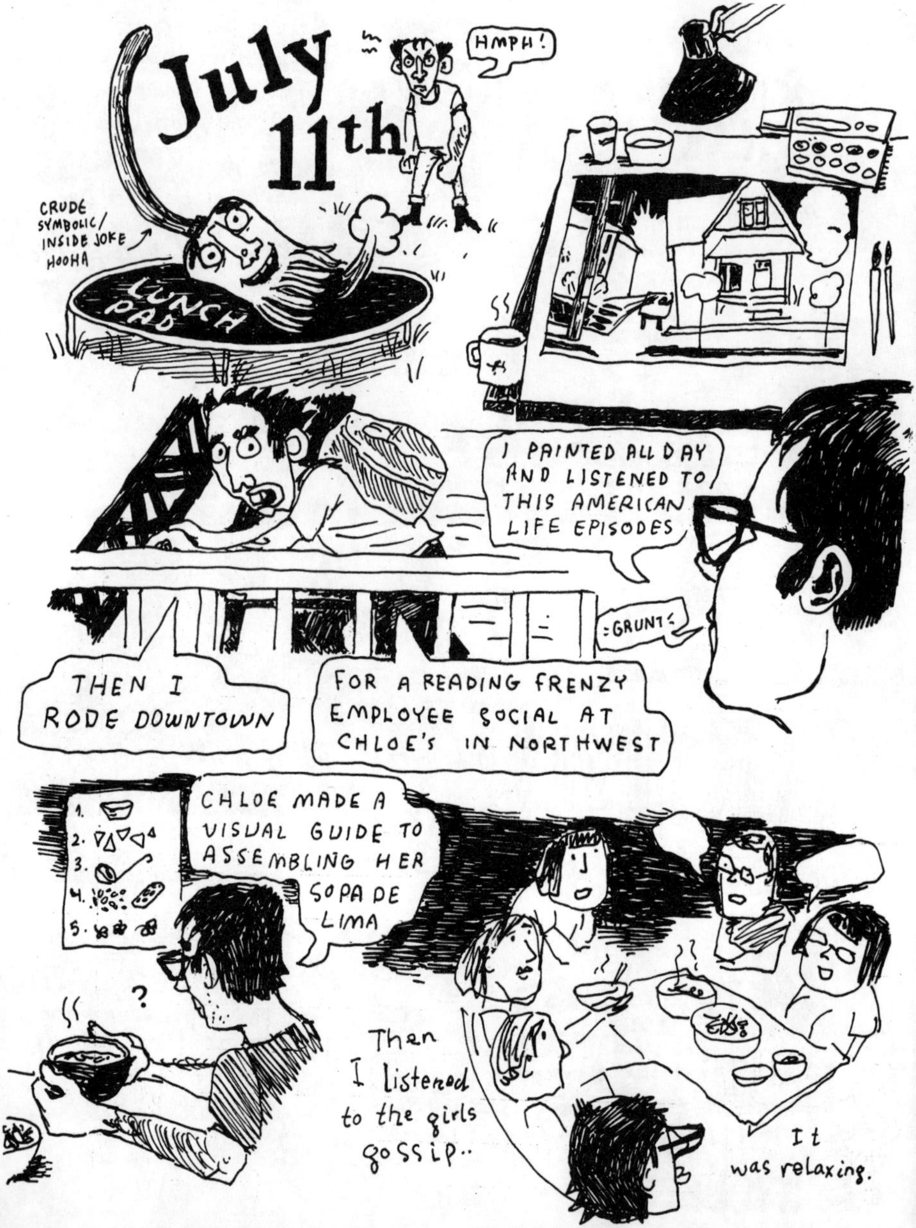
July 11th
HMPH!
CRUDE SYMBOLIC/ INSIDE JOKE HOOHA
LUNCH PAD
I PAINTED ALL DAY AND LISTENED TO THIS AMERICAN LIFE EPISODES
GRUNT
THEN I RODE DOWNTOWN
FOR A READING FRENZY EMPLOYEE SOCIAL AT CHLOE'S IN NORTHWEST
CHLOE MADE A VISUAL GUIDE TO ASSEMBLING HER SOPA DE LIMA
1.
2.
3.
4.
5.
?
Then I listened to the girls gossip..
It was relaxing.

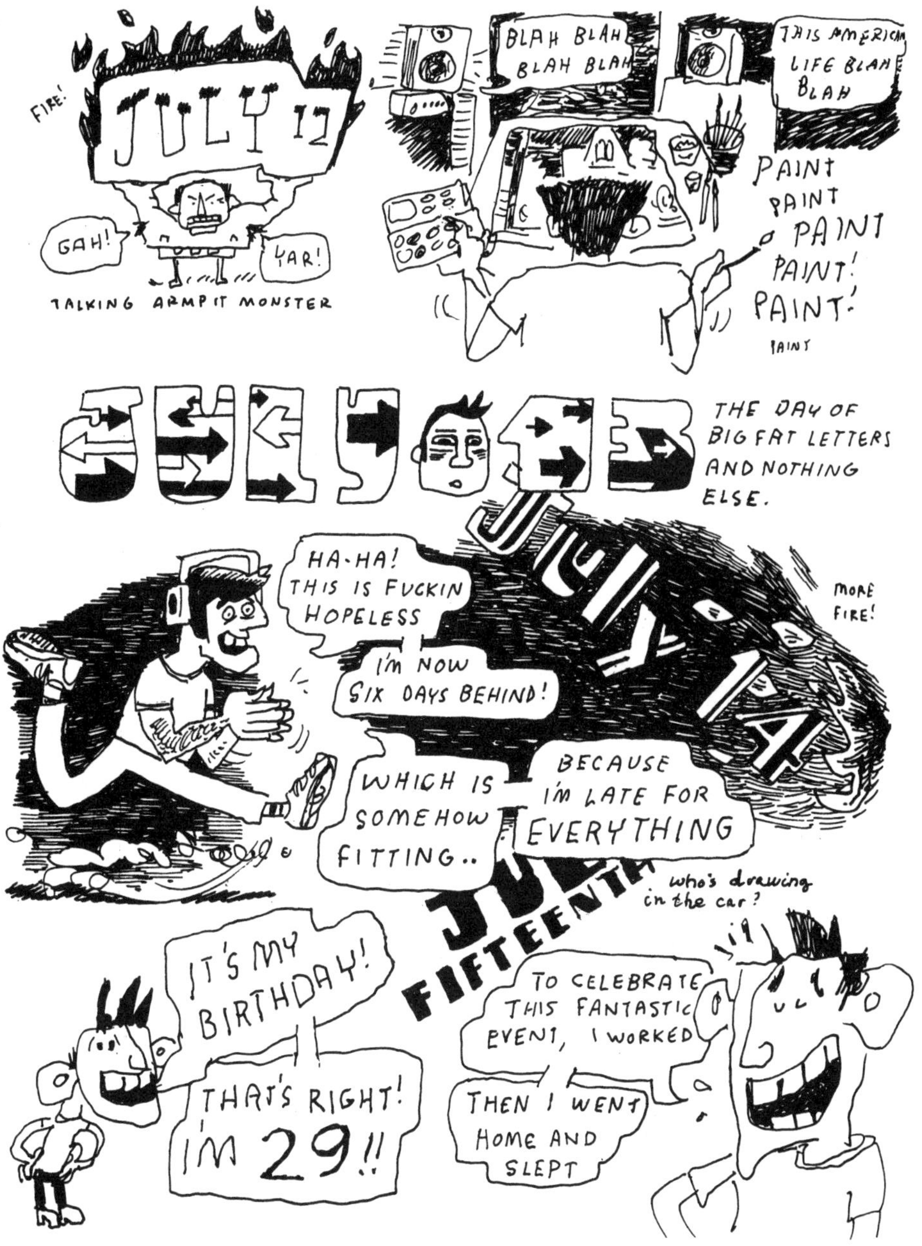
FIRE!
JULY 12
GAH!
YAR!
TALKING ARMPIT MONSTER
BLAH BLAH BLAH BLAH
THIS AMERICAN LIFE BLAH BLAH
PAINT
PAINT
PAINT
PAINT!
PAINT!
PAINT
JULY 13
THE DAY OF BIG FAT LETTERS AND NOTHING ELSE.
JULY 14
MORE FIRE!
HA-HA! THIS IS FUCKIN HOPELESS
I'M NOW SIX DAYS BEHIND!
WHICH IS SOMEHOW FITTING..
BECAUSE I'M LATE FOR EVERYTHING
JULY FIFTEENTH
who's drawing in the car?
IT'S MY BIRTHDAY!
THAT'S RIGHT! I'M 29!!
TO CELEBRATE THIS FANTASTIC EVENT, I WORKED
THEN I WENT HOME AND SLEPT

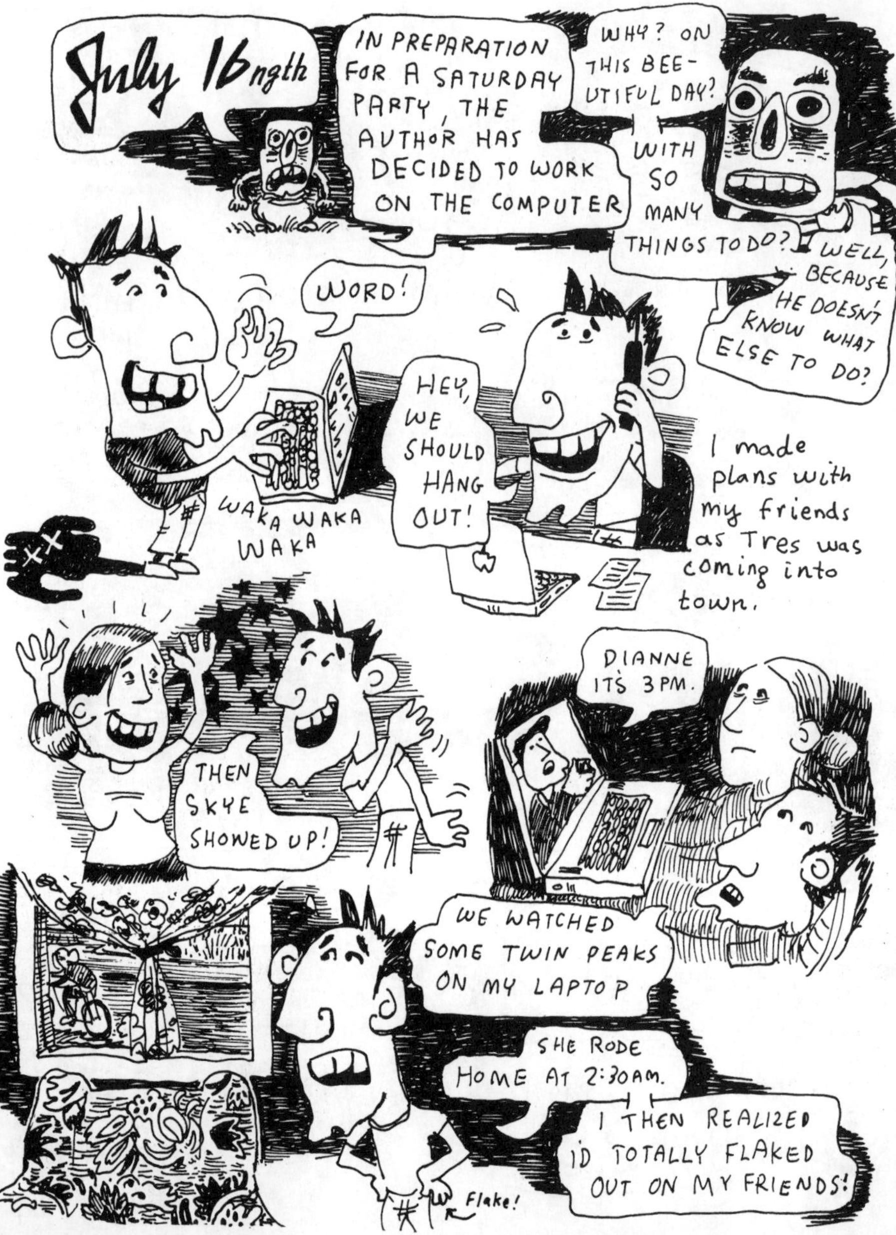

July 16ngth
IN PREPARATION FOR A SATURDAY PARTY, THE AUTHOR HAS DECIDED TO WORK ON THE COMPUTER
WHY? ON THIS BEE-UTIFUL DAY?
WITH SO MANY THINGS TO DO?
WELL, BECAUSE HE DOESN'T KNOW WHAT ELSE TO DO?
WORD!
WAKA WAKA WAKA
HEY, WE SHOULD HANG OUT!
I made plans with my friends as Tres was coming into town.
THEN SKYE SHOWED UP!
DIANNE ITS 3PM.
WE WATCHED SOME TWIN PEAKS ON MY LAPTOP
SHE RODE HOME AT 2:30AM.
I THEN REALIZED I'D TOTALLY FLAKED OUT ON MY FRIENDS!
Flake!

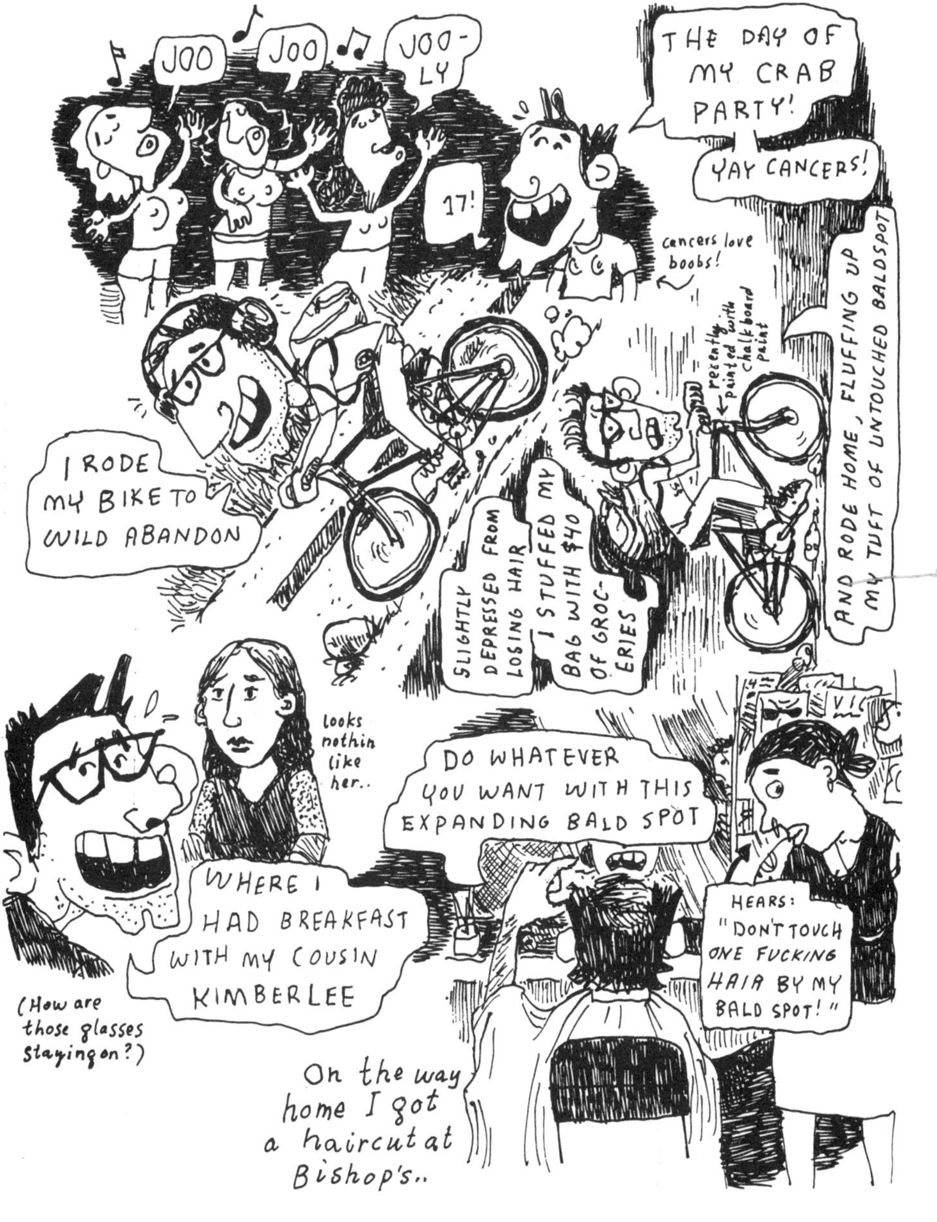
JOO
JOO
JOO-LY
17!
THE DAY OF MY CRAB PARTY!
YAY CANCERS!
cancers love boobs!
I RODE MY BIKE TO WILD ABANDON
recently painted with chalkboard paint
SLIGHTLY DEPRESSED FROM LOSING HAIR
I STUFFED MY BAG WITH $40 OF GROC-ERIES
AND RODE HOME, FLUFFING UP MY TUFT OF UNTOUCHED BALDSPOT
looks nothin like her..
WHERE I HAD BREAKFAST WITH MY COUSIN KIMBERLEE
(How are those glasses staying on?)
DO WHATEVER YOU WANT WITH THIS EXPANDING BALD SPOT
HEARS: "DON'T TOUCH ONE FUCKING HAIR BY MY BALD SPOT!"
On the way home I got a haircut at Bishop's..

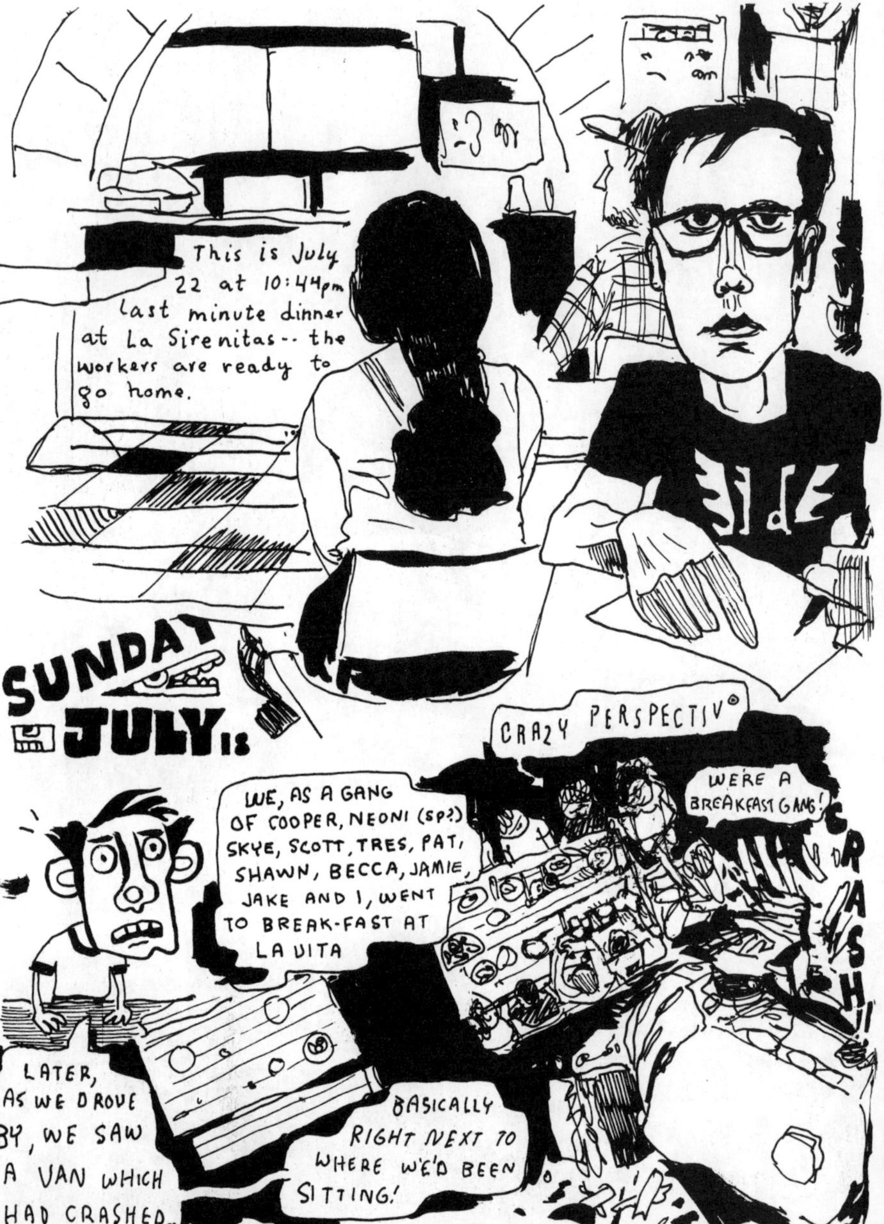

This is July 22 at 10:44pm last minute dinner at La Sirenitas -- the workers are ready to go home.
SUNDAY JULY 18
CRAZY PERSPECTIV
WE, AS A GANG OF COOPER, NEONI (SP?) SKYE, SCOTT, TRES, PAT, SHAWN, BECCA, JAMIE, JAKE AND I, WENT TO BREAK-FAST AT LA VITA
WE'RE A BREAKFAST GANG!
CRASH!!
LATER, AS WE DROVE BY, WE SAW A VAN WHICH HAD CRASHED...
BASICALLY RIGHT NEXT TO WHERE WE'D BEEN SITTING!

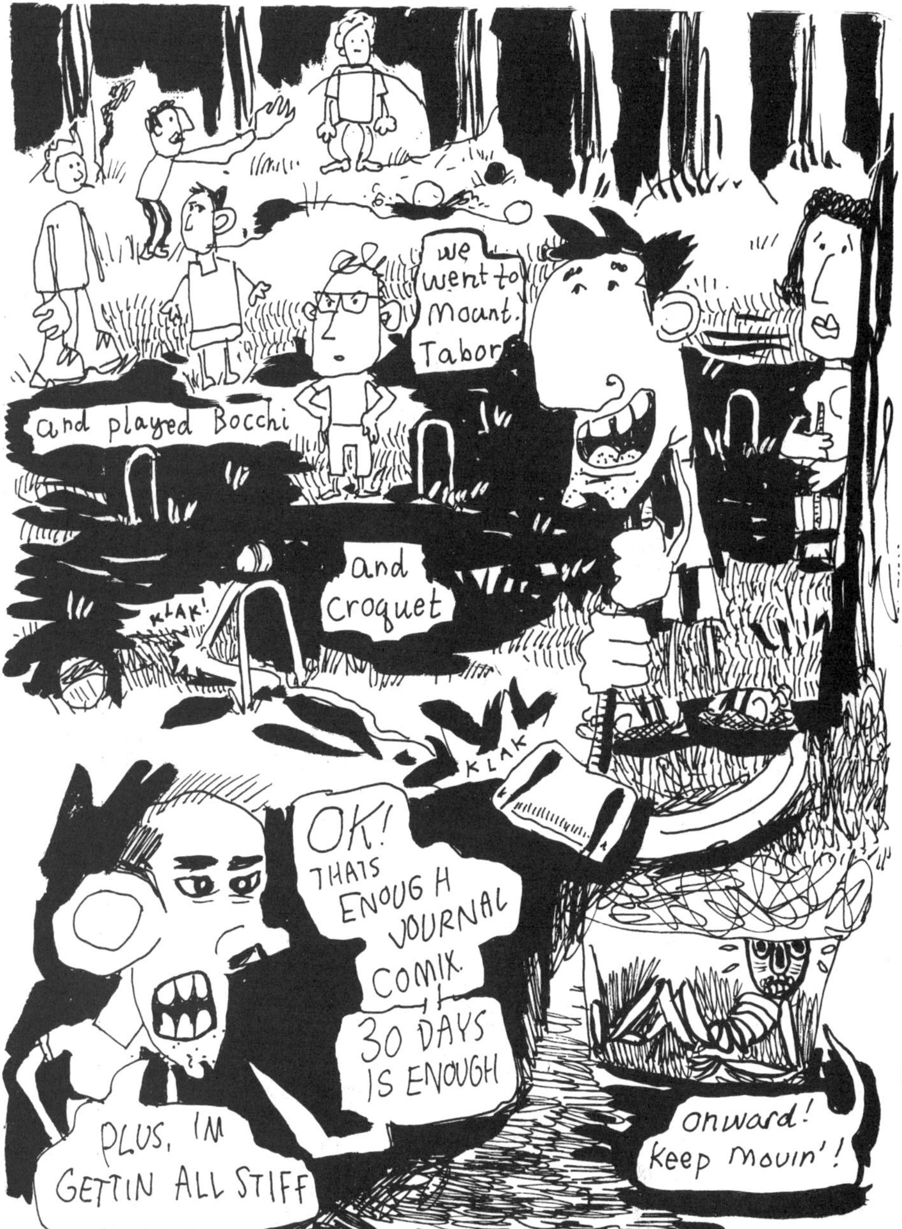
we went to Mount Tabor
and played Bocchi
and Croquet
KLAK!
KLAK
OK! THATS ENOUGH JOURNAL COMIX
30 DAYS IS ENOUGH
PLUS, IM GETTIN ALL STIFF
onward! Keep movin'!

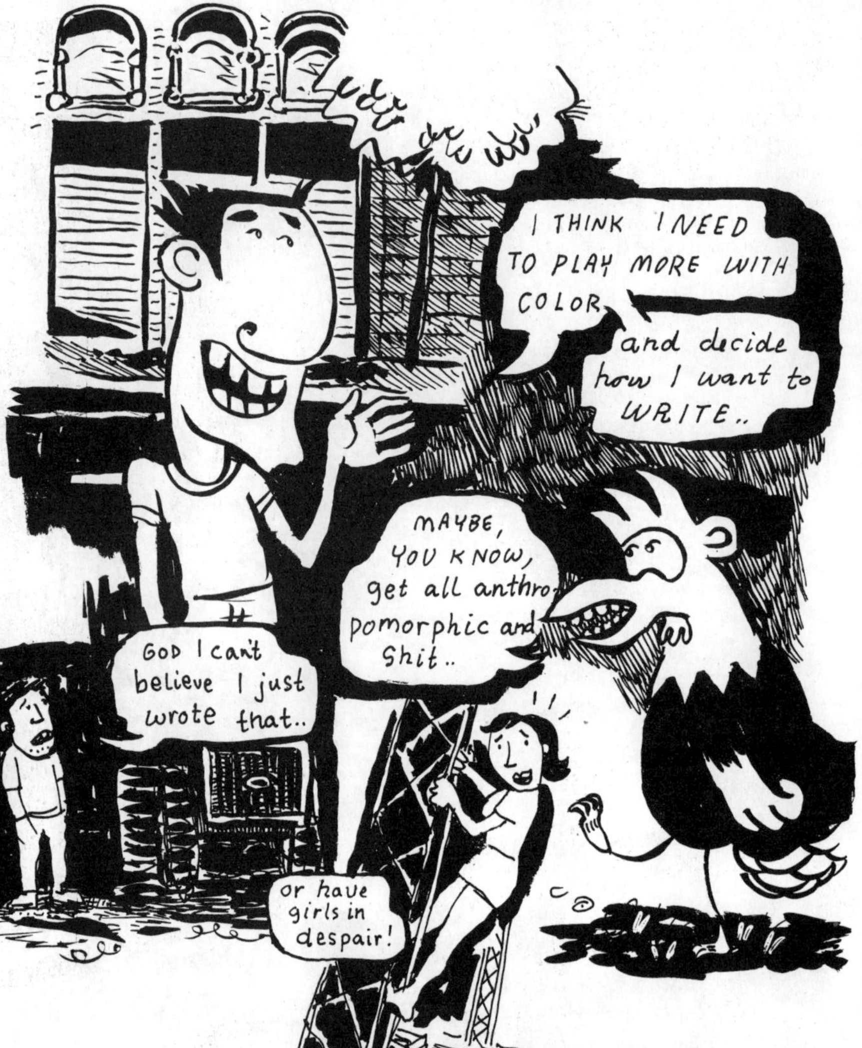
I THINK I NEED TO PLAY MORE WITH COLOR.
and decide how I want to WRITE..
MAYBE, YOU KNOW, get all anthro-pomorphic and Shit..
GOD I can't believe I just wrote that..
or have girls in despair!

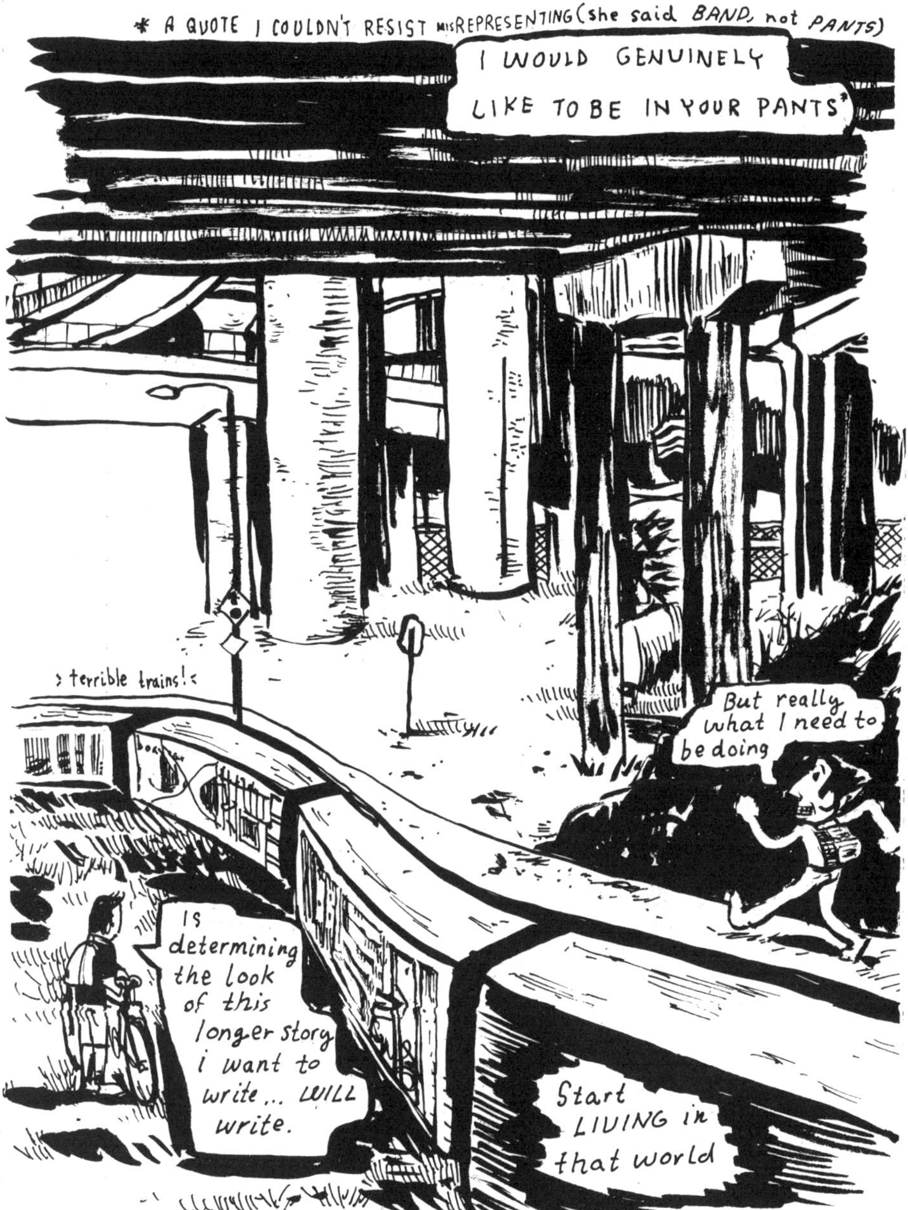
* A QUOTE I COULDN'T RESIST misREPRESENTING (she said BAND, not PANTS)
I WOULD GENUINELY LIKE TO BE IN YOUR PANTS*
: terrible trains! :
But really what I need to be doing
is determining the look of this longer story i want to write... WILL write.
Start LIVING in that world

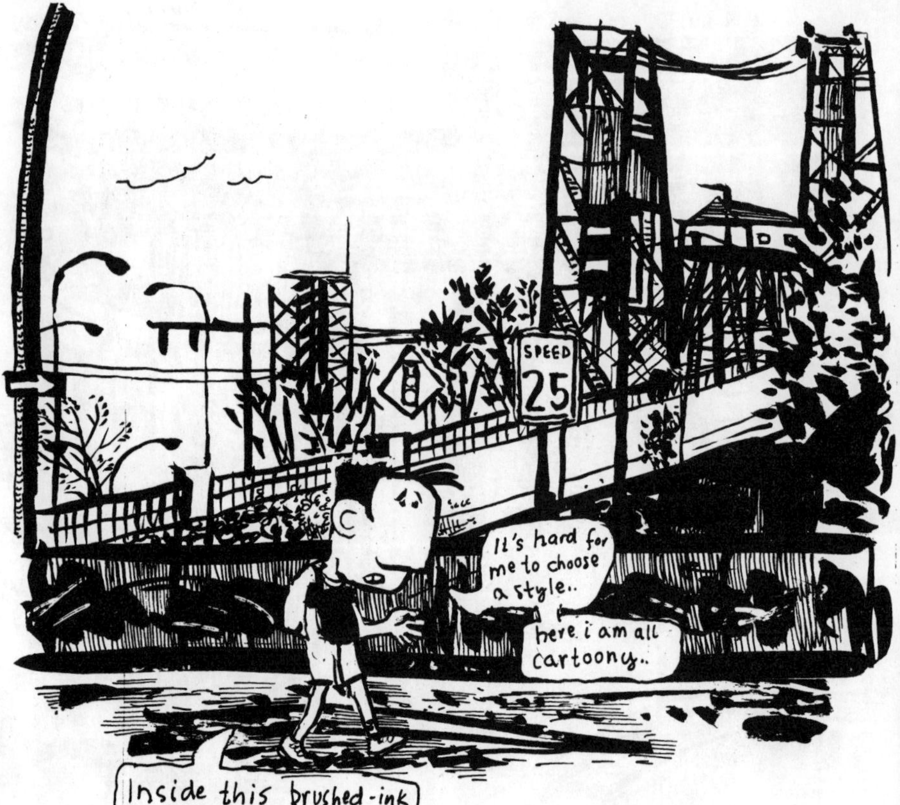
SPEED
25
It's hard for me to choose a style..
here i am all cartoony..
Inside this brushed-ink background.. ugh!

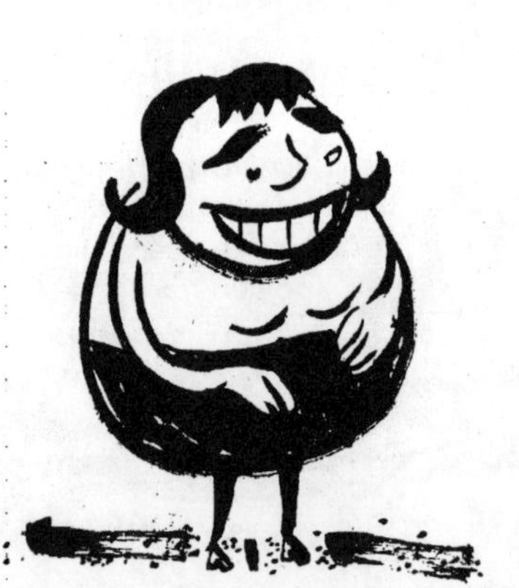

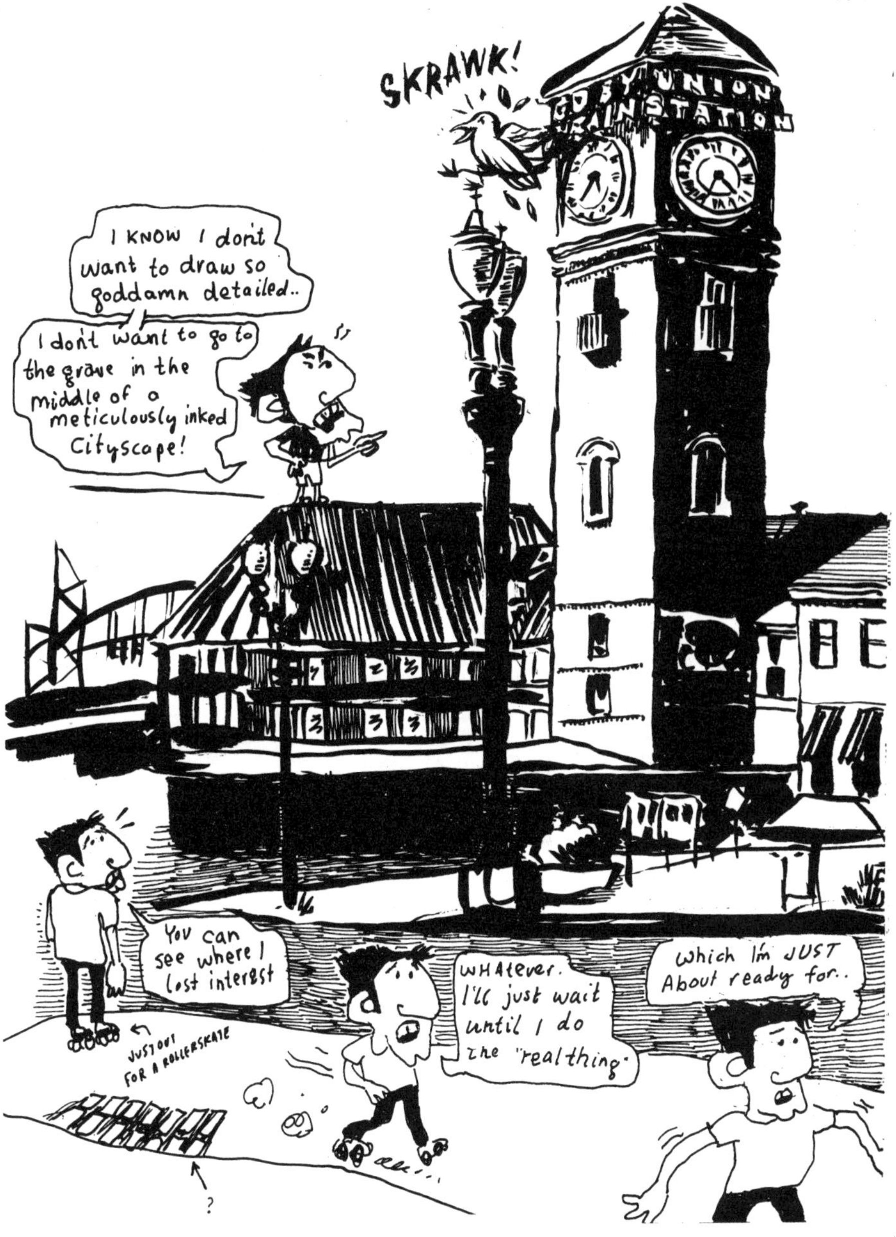
SKRAWK!
UNION STATION
I KNOW I don't want to draw so goddamn detailed..
I don't want to go to the grave in the middle of a meticulously inked Cityscape!
You can see where I lost interest
JUST OUT FOR A ROLLERSKATE
?
WHAtever. I'll just wait until I do the "real thing"
Which I'm JUST About ready for..

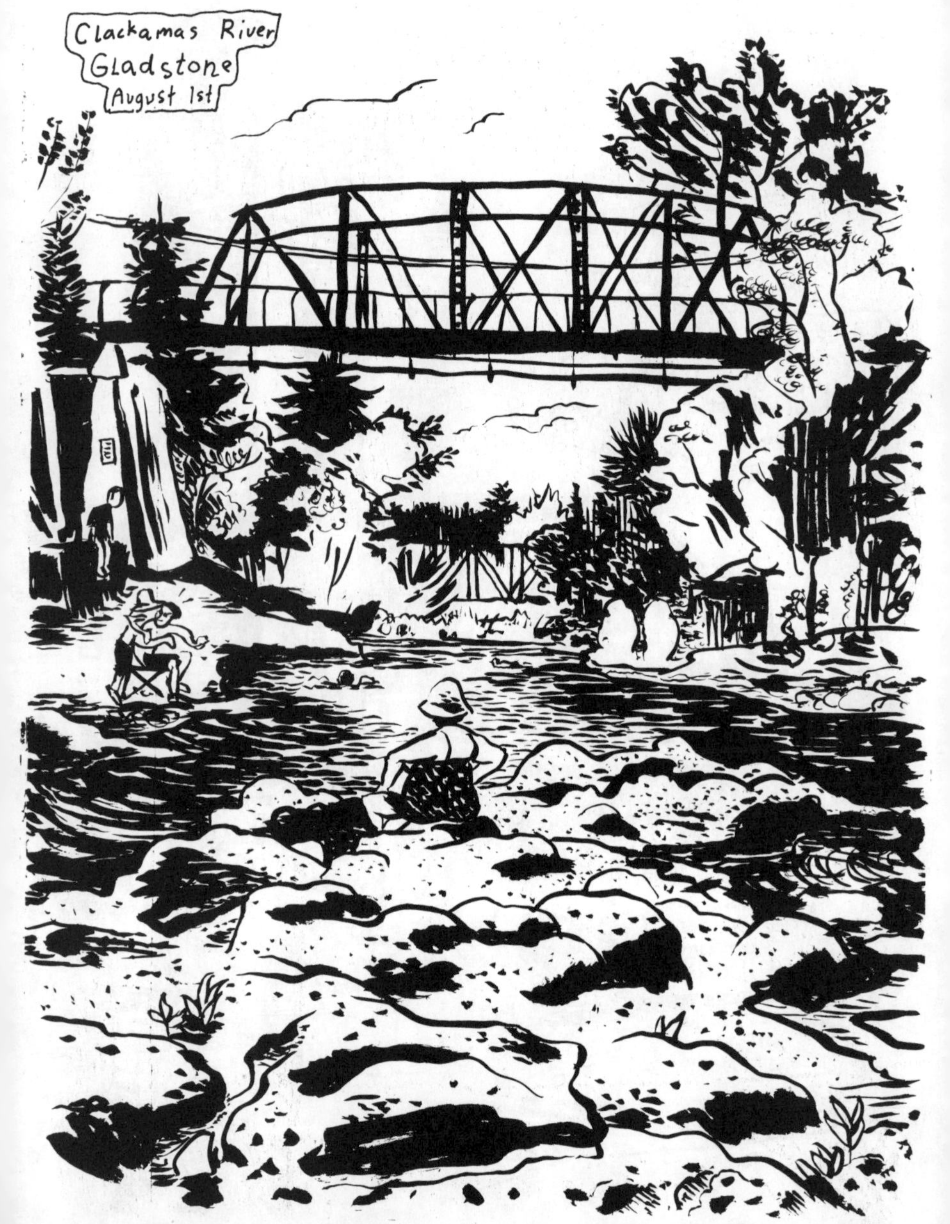
Clackamas River
Gladstone
August 1st

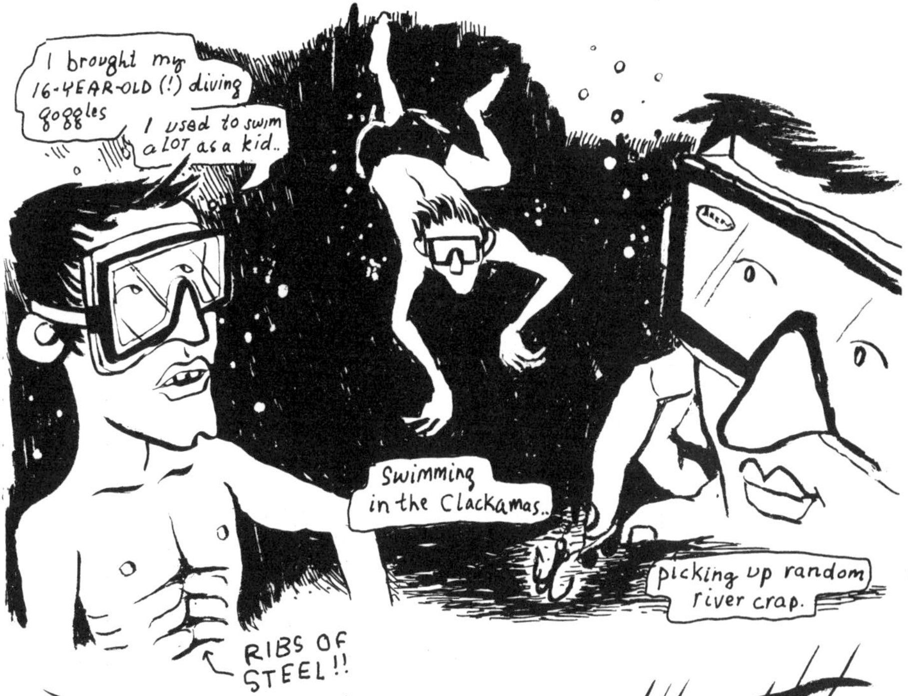
I brought my 16-YEAR-OLD (!) diving goggles
I used to swim a LOT as a kid..
Swimming in the Clackamas..
picking up random river crap.
RIBS OF STEEL!!

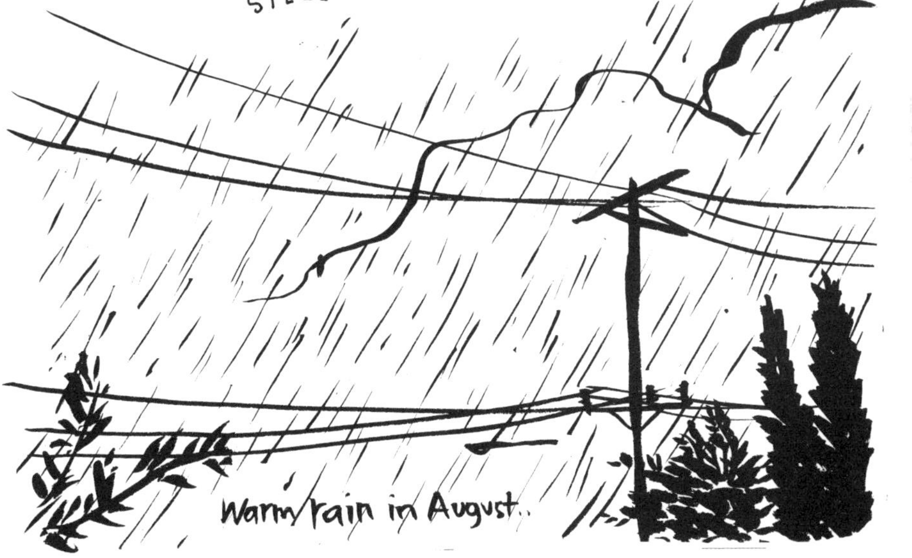
Warm rain in August..

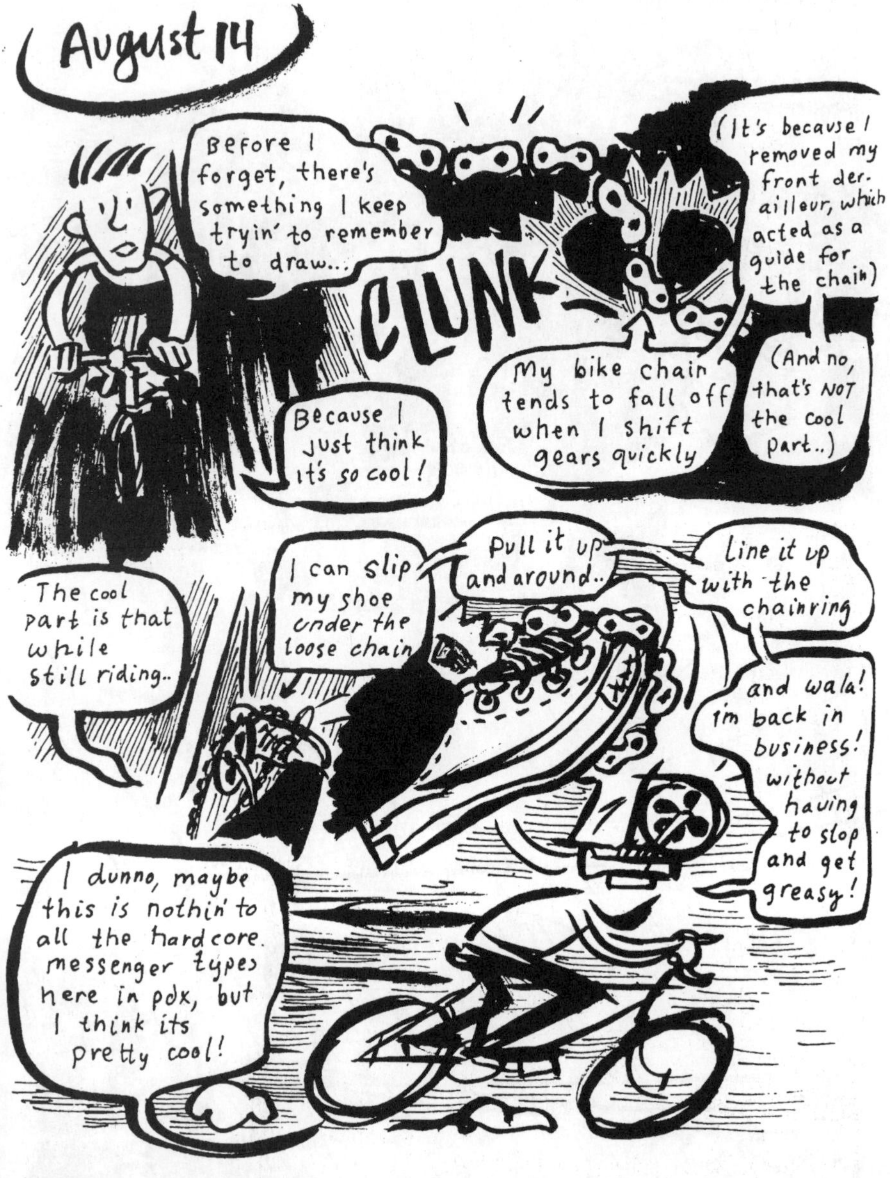

August 14
Before I forget, there's something I keep tryin' to remember to draw...
Because I just think it's so cool!
CLUNK
(It's because I removed my front derailleur, which acted as a guide for the chain)
My bike chain tends to fall off when I shift gears quickly
(And no, that's NOT the cool part..)
The cool part is that while still riding..
I can slip my shoe under the loose chain
Pull it up and around..
Line it up with the chainring
and wala! im back in business! without having to stop and get greasy!
I dunno, maybe this is nothin' to all the hardcore messenger types here in pdx, but I think its pretty cool!

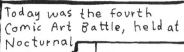

Today was the fourth Comic Art Battle, held at Nocturnal

This time toted as the fated battle between Alternative and Mainstream

The competition was fierce!

The crowd was relentless!

This battle had a cameraman + a digital projector!

At one point total chaos ensued and people were drawin' on the floor..

ACK! dumb boxes!

CANT DRAW THIS SMALL WITH THIS BRU

And Uh...

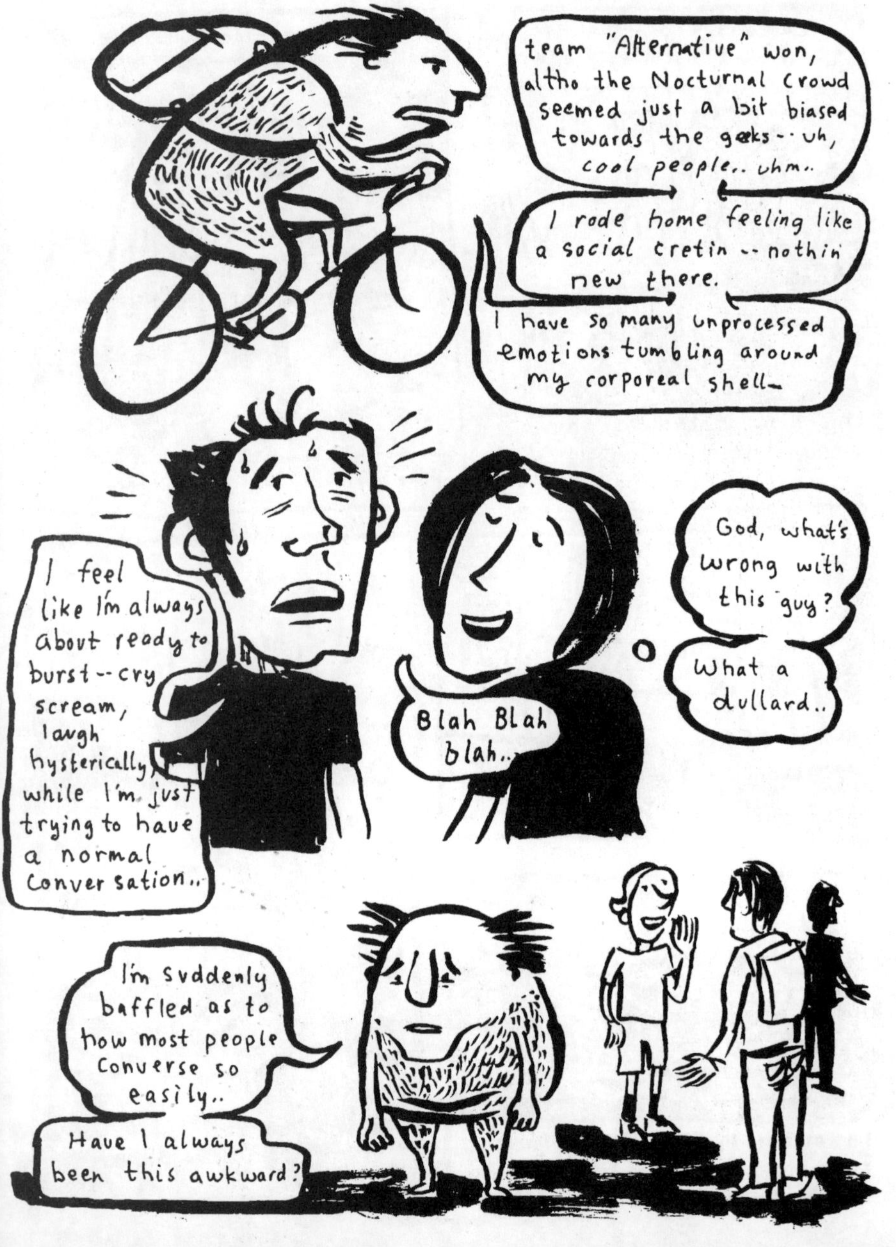
team "Alternative" won, altho the Nocturnal crowd seemed just a bit biased towards the geeks -- uh, cool people.. uhm..
I rode home feeling like a social cretin -- nothin' new there.
I have so many unprocessed emotions tumbling around my corporeal shell-
I feel like I'm always about ready to burst -- cry scream, laugh hysterically, while I'm just trying to have a normal conversation..
Blah Blah blah..
God, what's wrong with this guy?
What a dullard..
I'm suddenly baffled as to how most people converse so easily..
Have I always been this awkward?

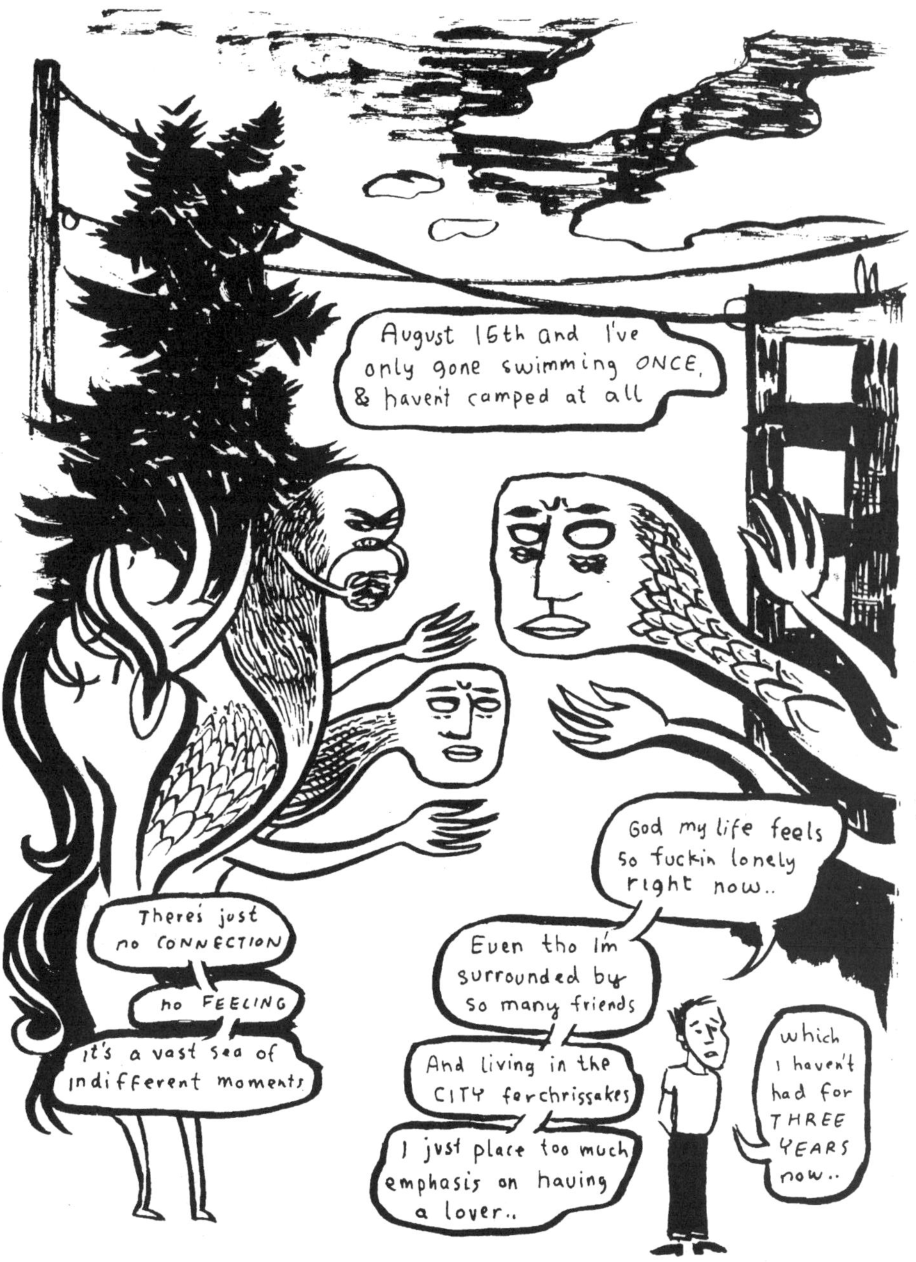
August 15th and I've only gone swimming ONCE, & haven't camped at all
There's just no CONNECTION
no FEELING
it's a vast sea of indifferent moments
God my life feels so fuckin lonely right now..
Even tho I'm surrounded by so many friends
And living in the CITY forchrissakes
I just place too much emphasis on having a lover..
which I haven't had for THREE YEARS now..

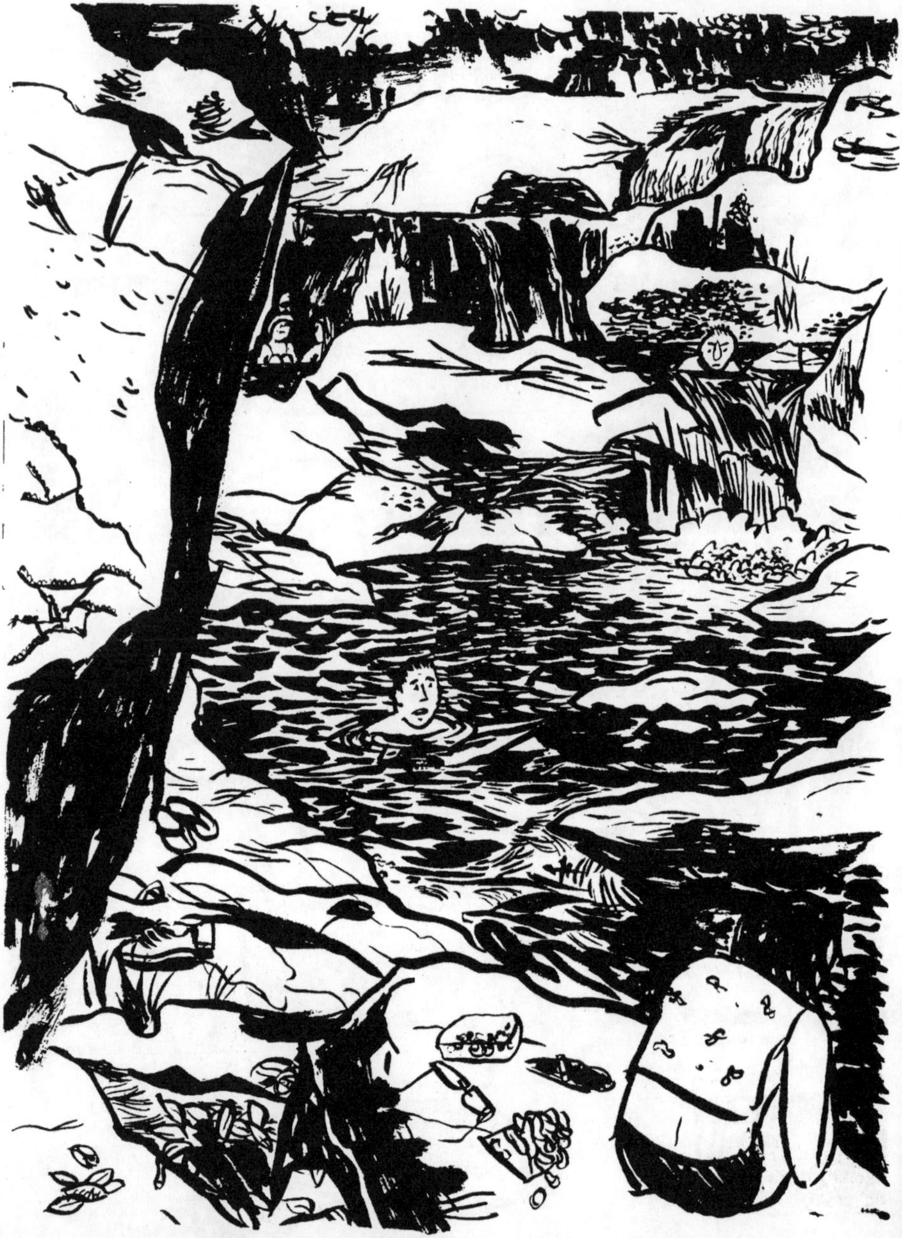

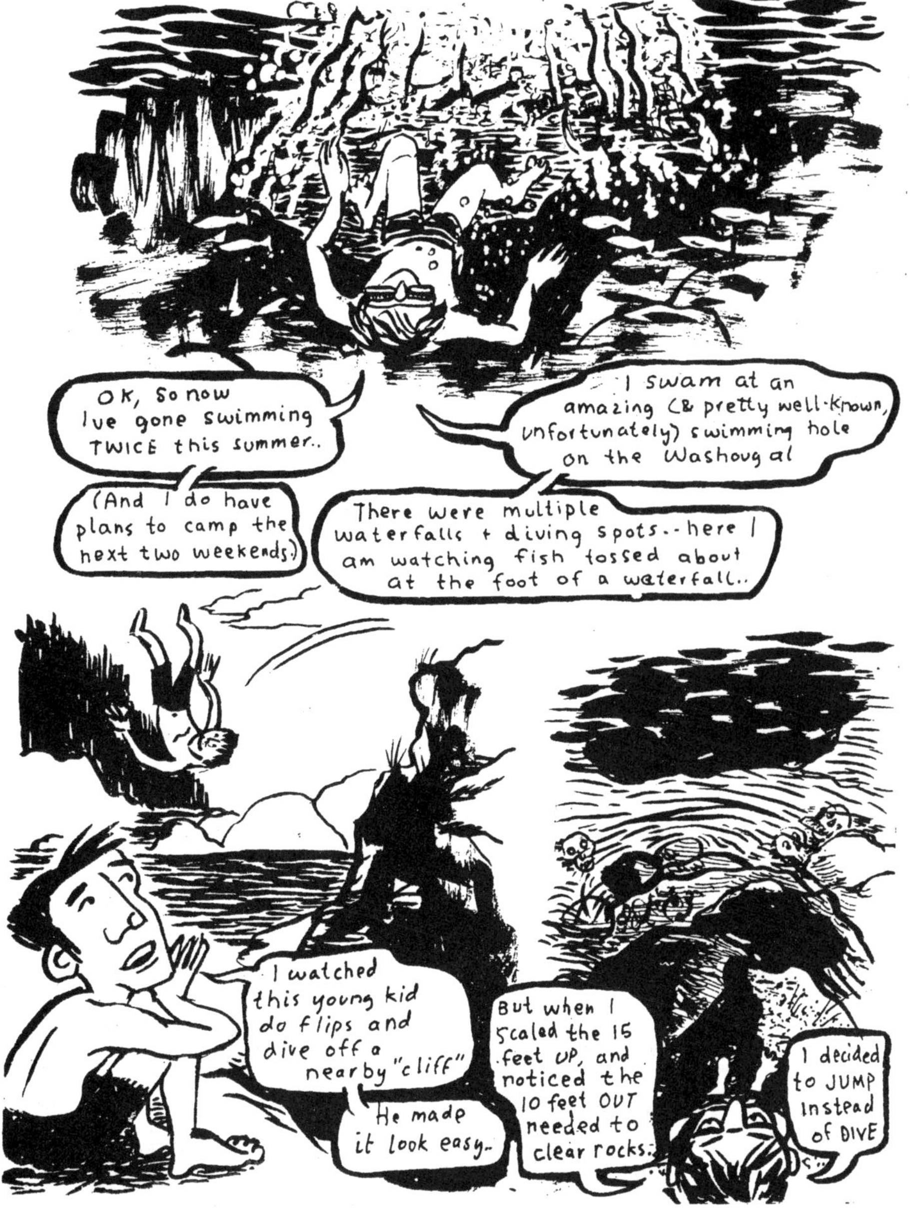

OK, so now I've gone swimming TWICE this summer..
(And I do have plans to camp the next two weekends.)
I swam at an amazing (& pretty well-known, unfortunately) swimming hole on the Washougal
There were multiple waterfalls + diving spots.- here I am watching fish tossed about at the foot of a waterfall..
I watched this young kid do flips and dive off a nearby "cliff"
He made it look easy..
But when I scaled the 15 feet UP, and noticed the 10 feet OUT needed to clear rocks:
I decided to JUMP instead of DIVE

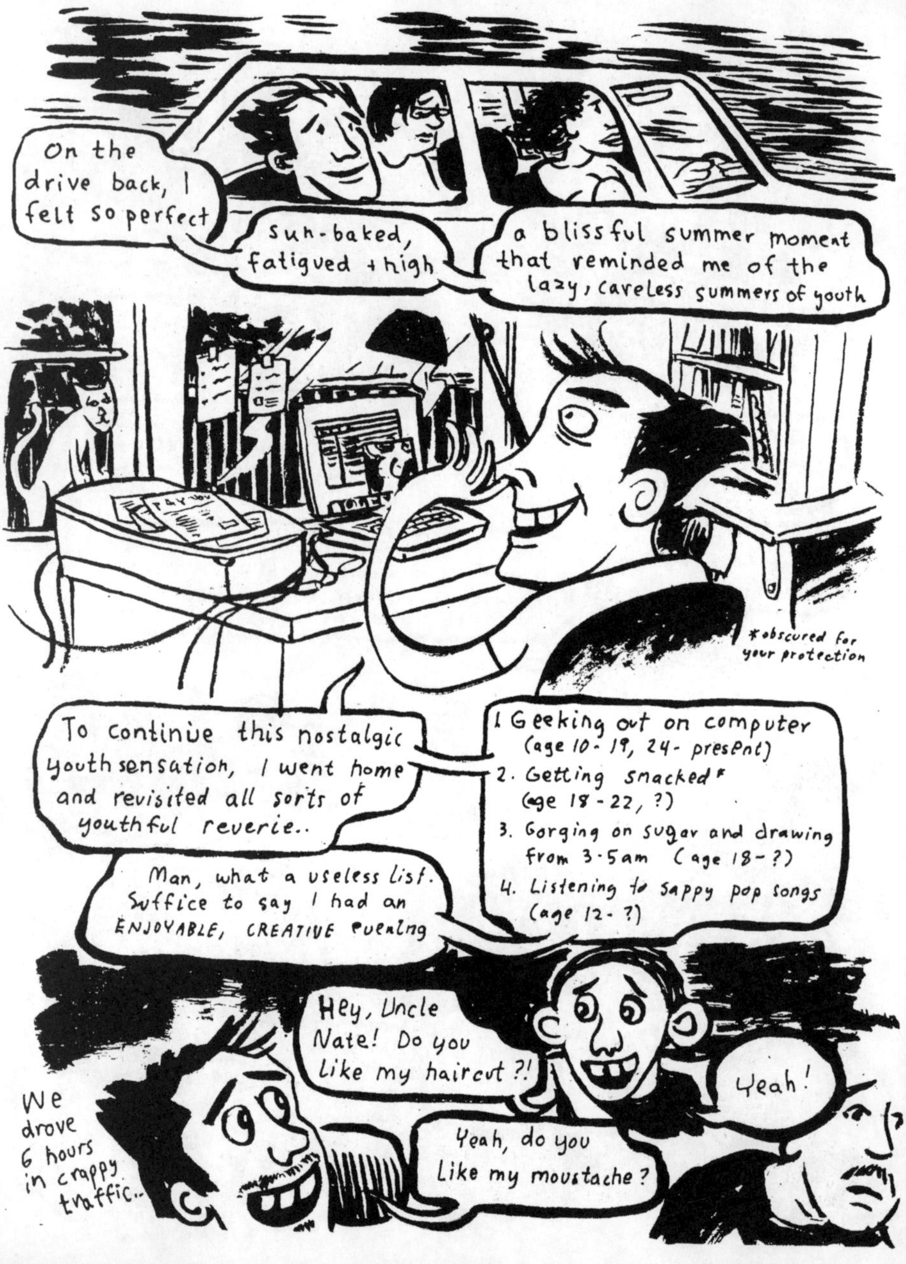
On the drive back, I felt so perfect
sun-baked, fatigued + high
a blissful summer moment that reminded me of the lazy, careless summers of youth
*obscured for your protection
To continue this nostalgic youth sensation, I went home and revisited all sorts of youthful reverie..
1. Geeking out on computer (age 10-19, 24-present)
2. Getting smacked* (age 18-22, ?)
3. Gorging on sugar and drawing from 3-5am (age 18-?)
4. Listening to sappy pop songs (age 12-?)
Man, what a useless list. Suffice to say I had an ENJOYABLE, CREATIVE evening
We drove 6 hours in crappy traffic..
Hey, Uncle Nate! Do you like my haircut?!
Yeah!
Yeah, do you like my moustache?

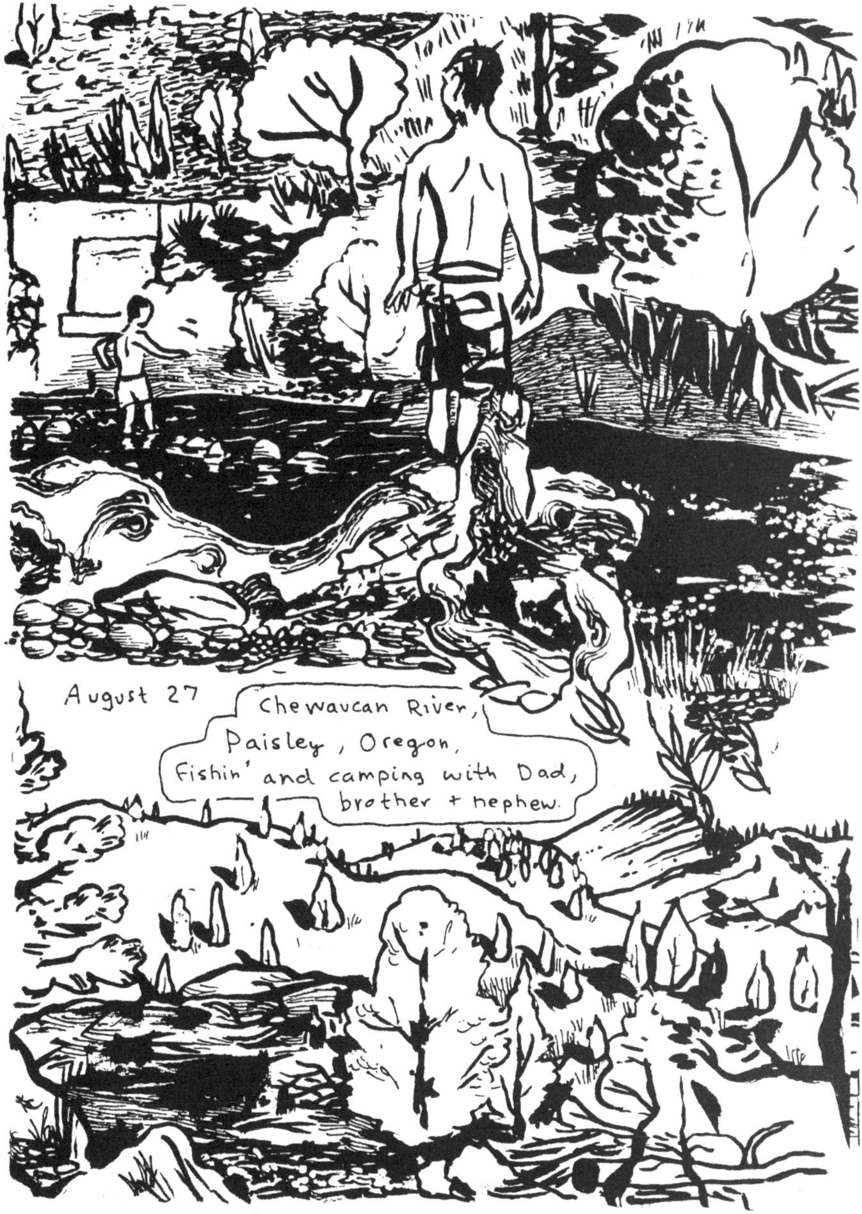
August 27
Chewaucan River, Paisley, Oregon, Fishin' and camping with Dad, brother + nephew.

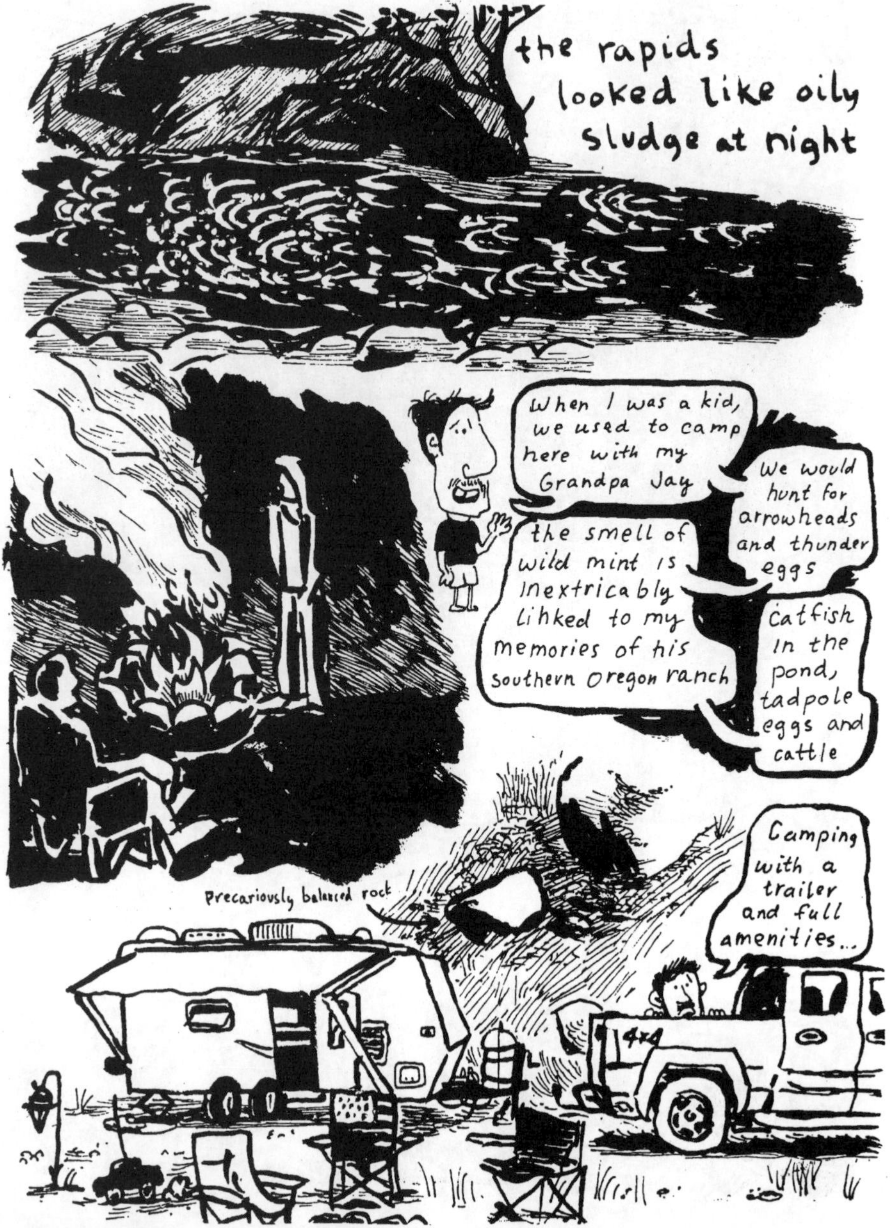
the rapids looked like oily sludge at night
When I was a kid, we used to camp here with my Grandpa Jay
We would hunt for arrowheads and thunder eggs
the smell of wild mint is inextricably linked to my memories of his southern Oregon ranch
Catfish in the pond, tadpole eggs and cattle
Precariously balanced rock
Camping with a trailer and full amenities...
4x4

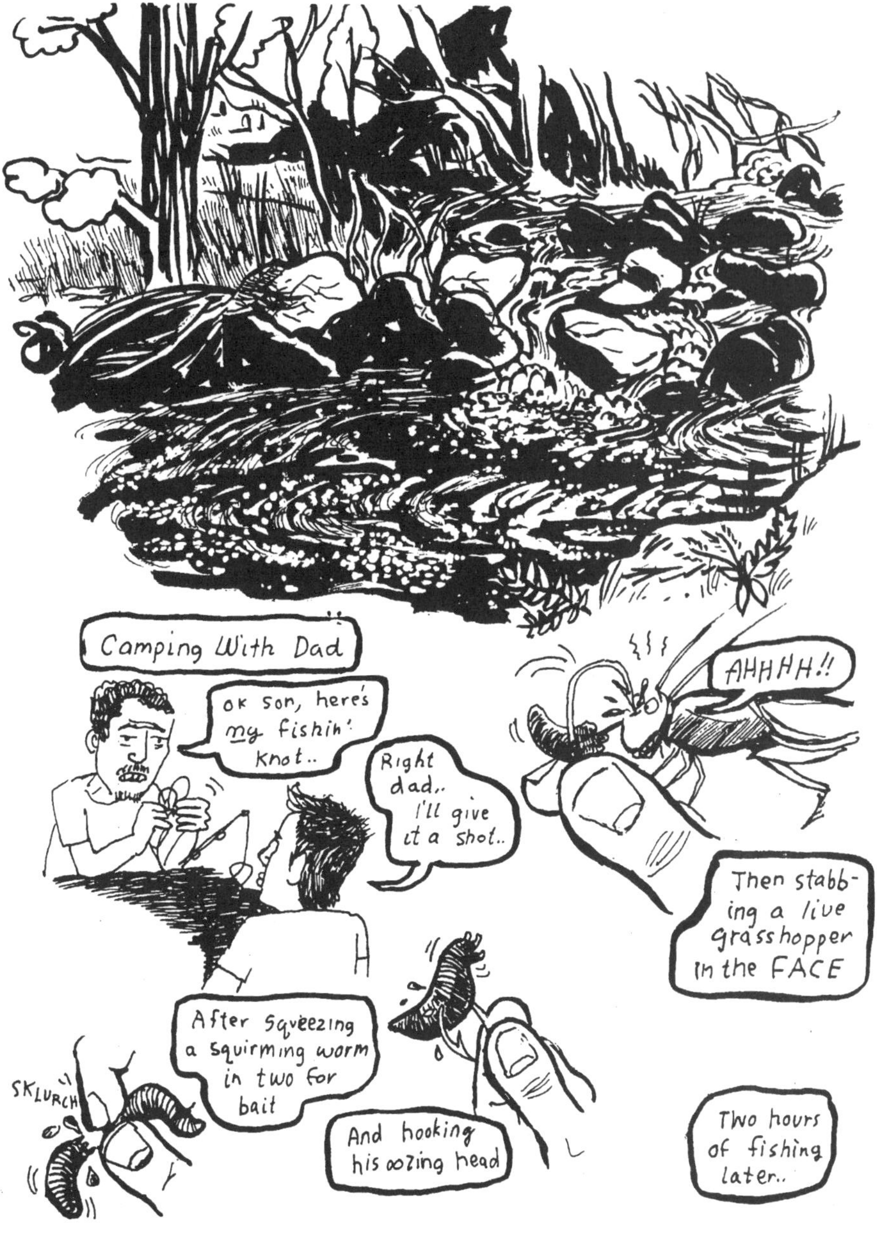
Camping With Dad
ok son, here's my fishin' knot..
Right dad.. I'll give it a shot..
After squeezing a squirming worm in two for bait
SKLURCH
And hooking his oozing head
AHHHH!!
Then stabbing a live grasshopper in the FACE
Two hours of fishing later..

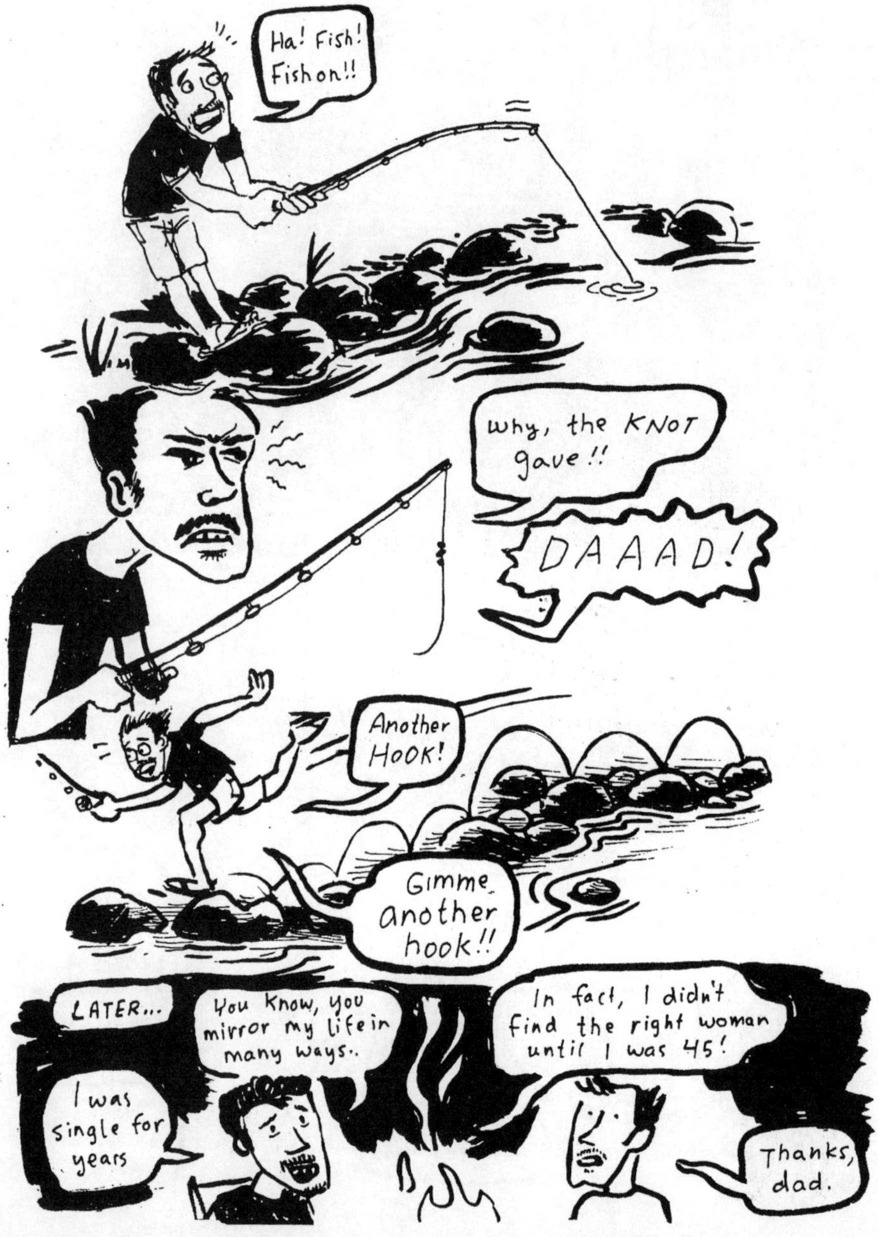
Ha! Fish! Fish on!!
why, the KNOT gave!!
DAAAD!
Another HOOK!
Gimme another hook!!
LATER...
You know, you mirror my life in many ways..
In fact, I didn't find the right woman until I was 45!
I was single for years
Thanks, dad.

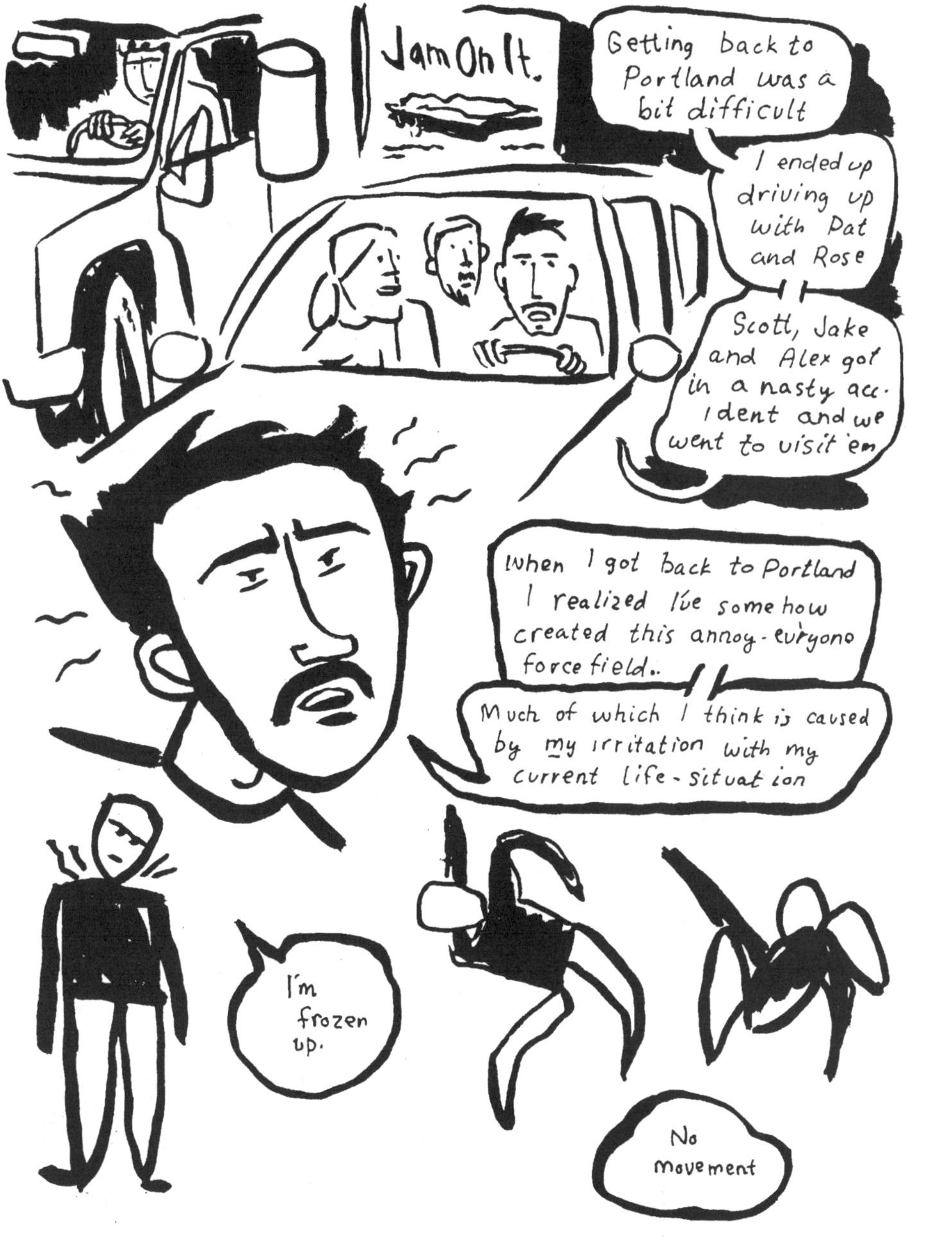
Jam On It.
Getting back to Portland was a bit difficult
I ended up driving up with Pat and Rose
Scott, Jake and Alex got in a nasty acc-ident and we went to visit 'em
When I got back to Portland I realized I've somehow created this annoy-evryono force field..
Much of which I think is caused by my irritation with my current life-situation
I'm frozen up.
No movement

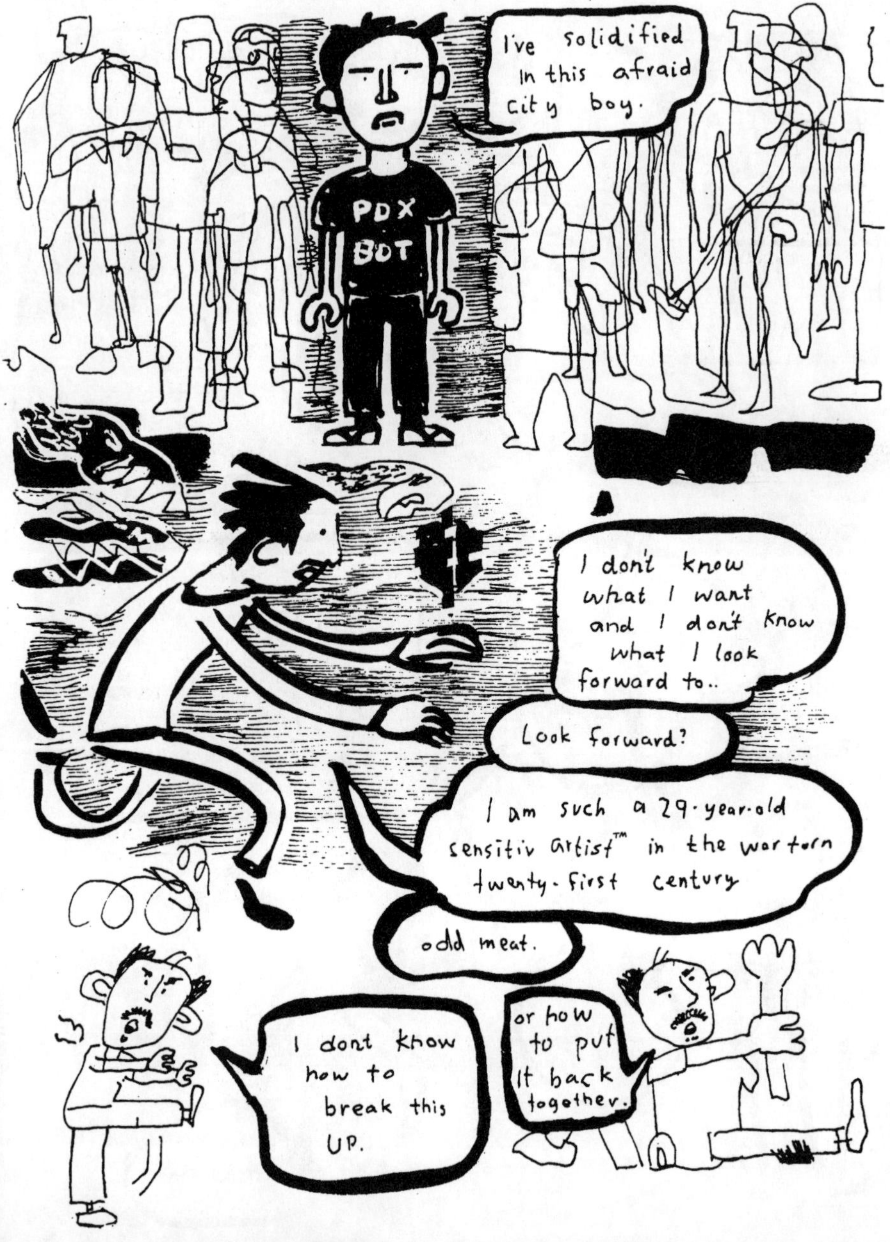

I've solidified in this afraid city boy.
PDX BOT
I don't know what I want and I don't know what I look forward to..
Look forward?
I am such a 29-year-old sensitiv artist™ in the wartorn twenty-first century
odd meat.
I dont know how to break this UP.
or how to put it back together.

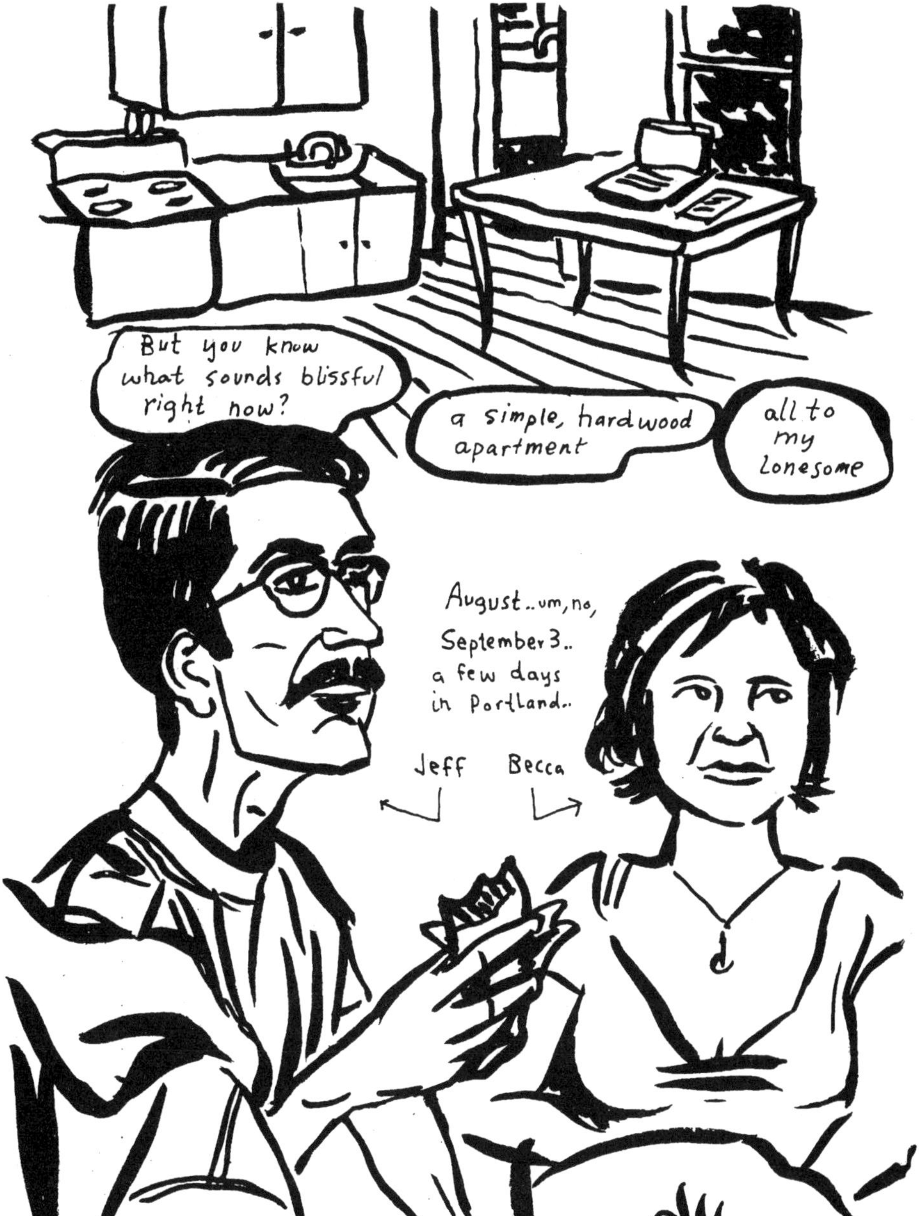
But you know what sounds blissful right now?
a simple, hardwood apartment
all to my lonesome
August..um, no, September 3.. a few days in Portland..
Jeff
Becca

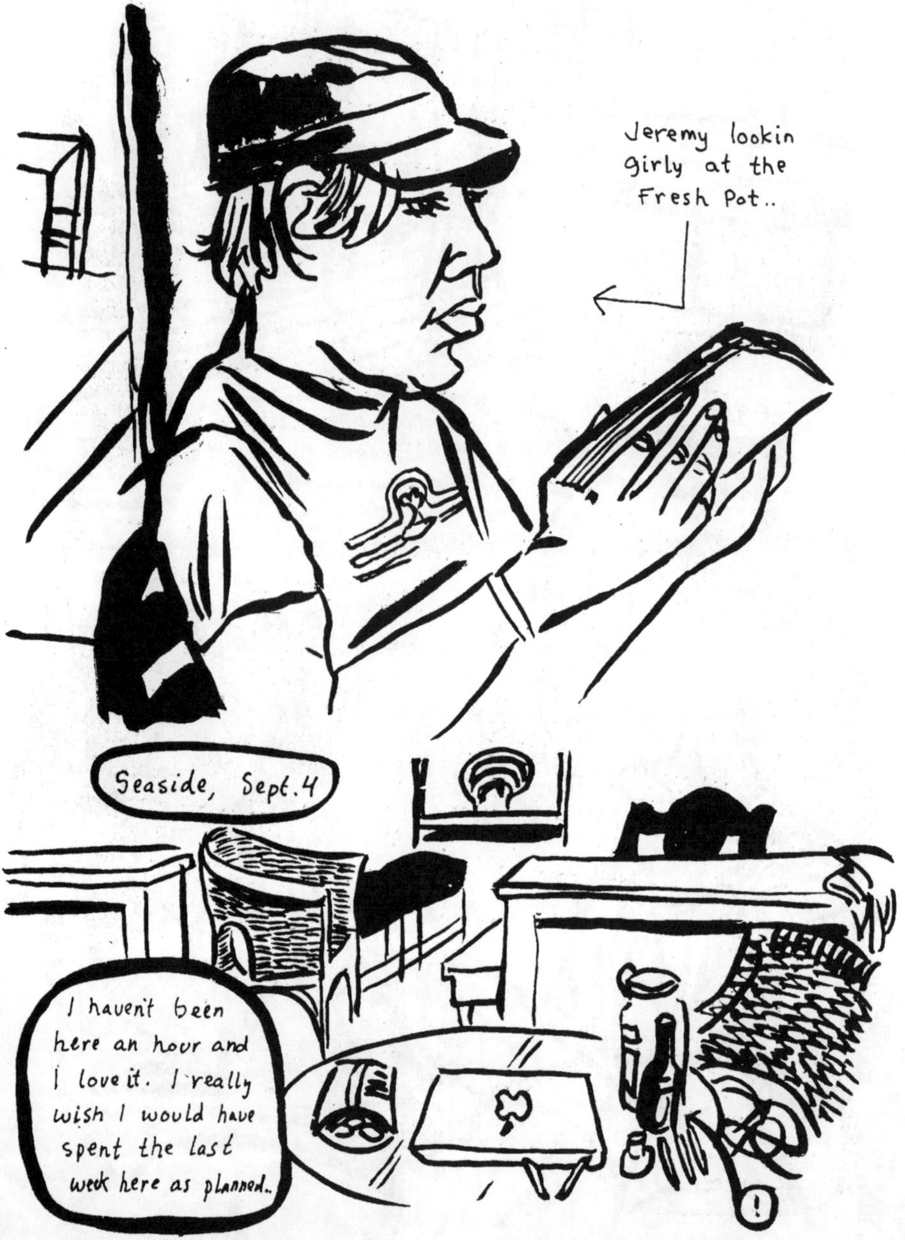
Jeremy lookin girly at the Fresh Pot..
Seaside, Sept. 4
I haven't been here an hour and I love it. I really wish I would have spent the last week here as planned..
!

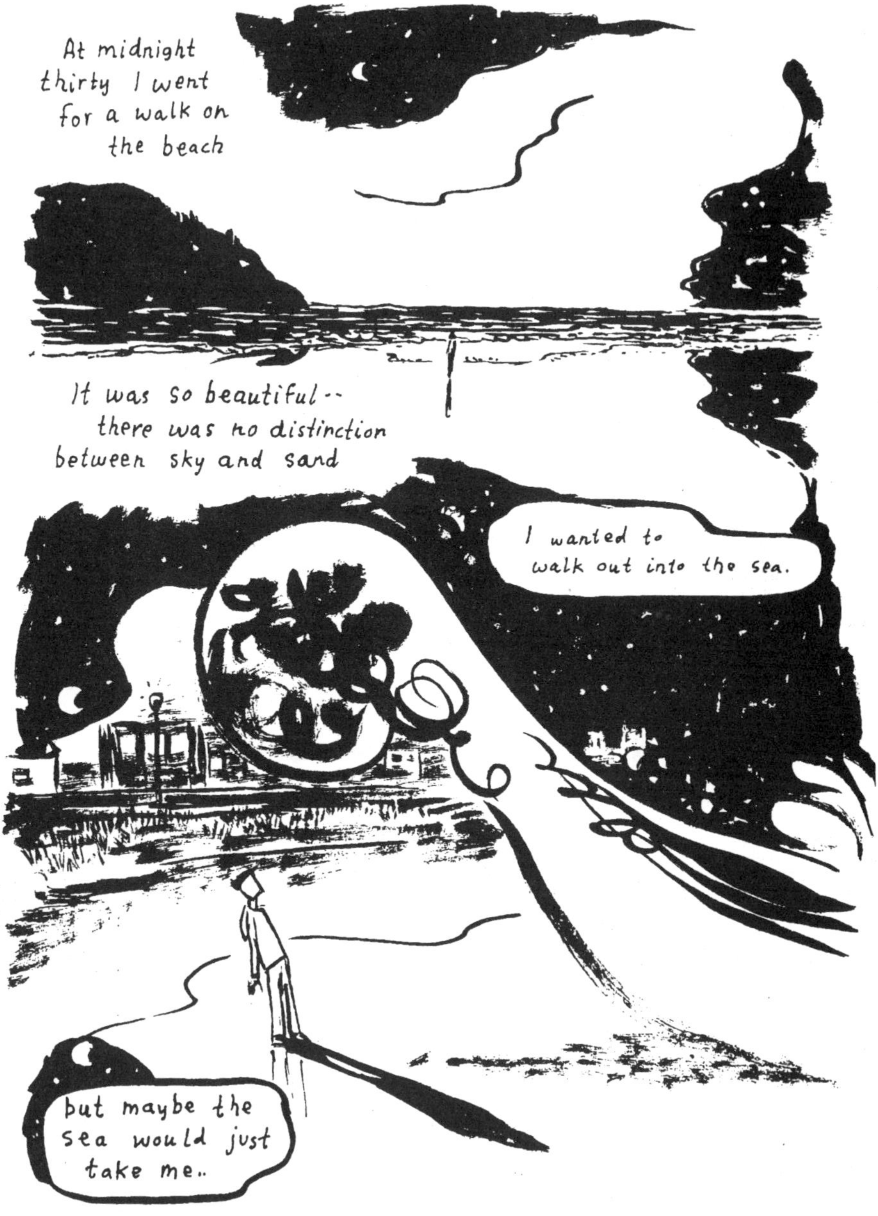
At midnight thirty I went for a walk on the beach
It was so beautiful.. there was no distinction between sky and sand
I wanted to walk out into the sea.
but maybe the sea would just take me..

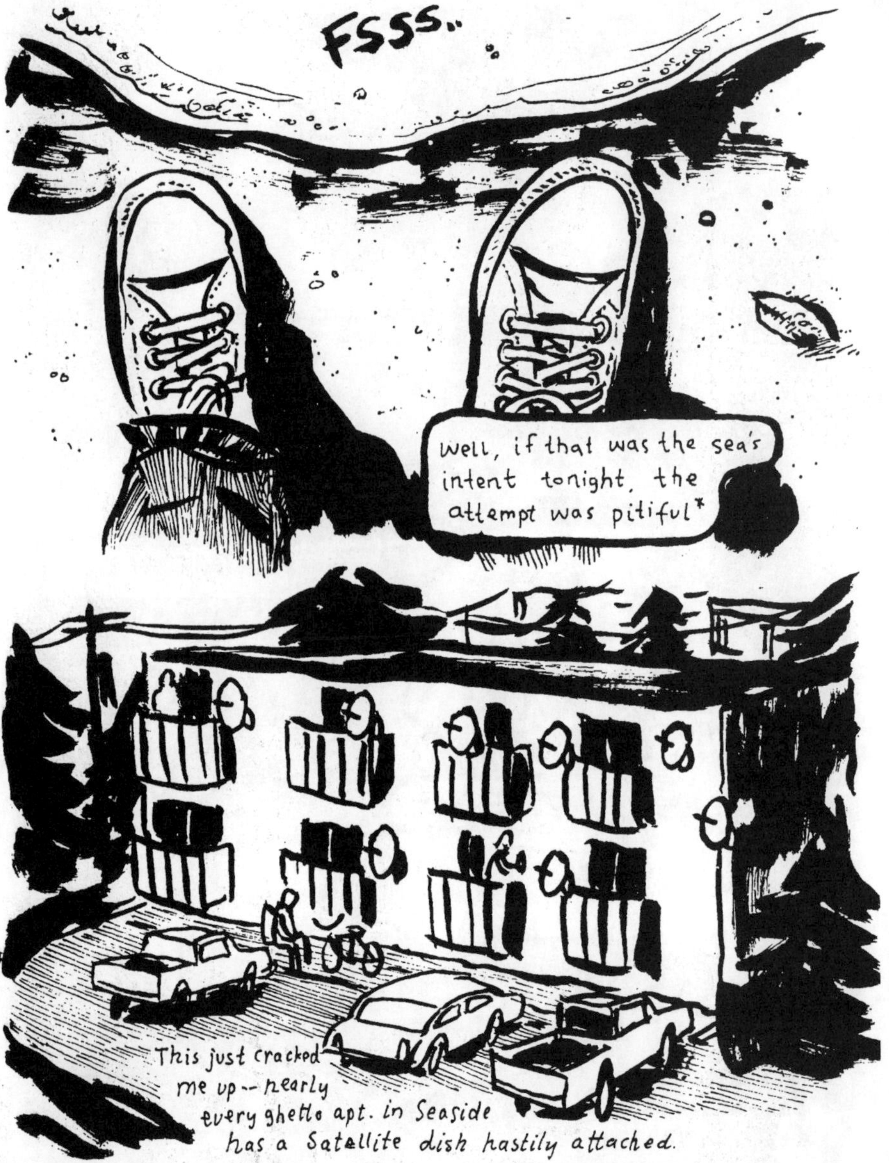
FSSS..
well, if that was the sea's intent tonight, the attempt was pitiful*
This just cracked me up -- nearly every ghetto apt. in Seaside has a Satellite dish hastily attached.

* did YOUR brain immediately offer Tom Waits lyrics?

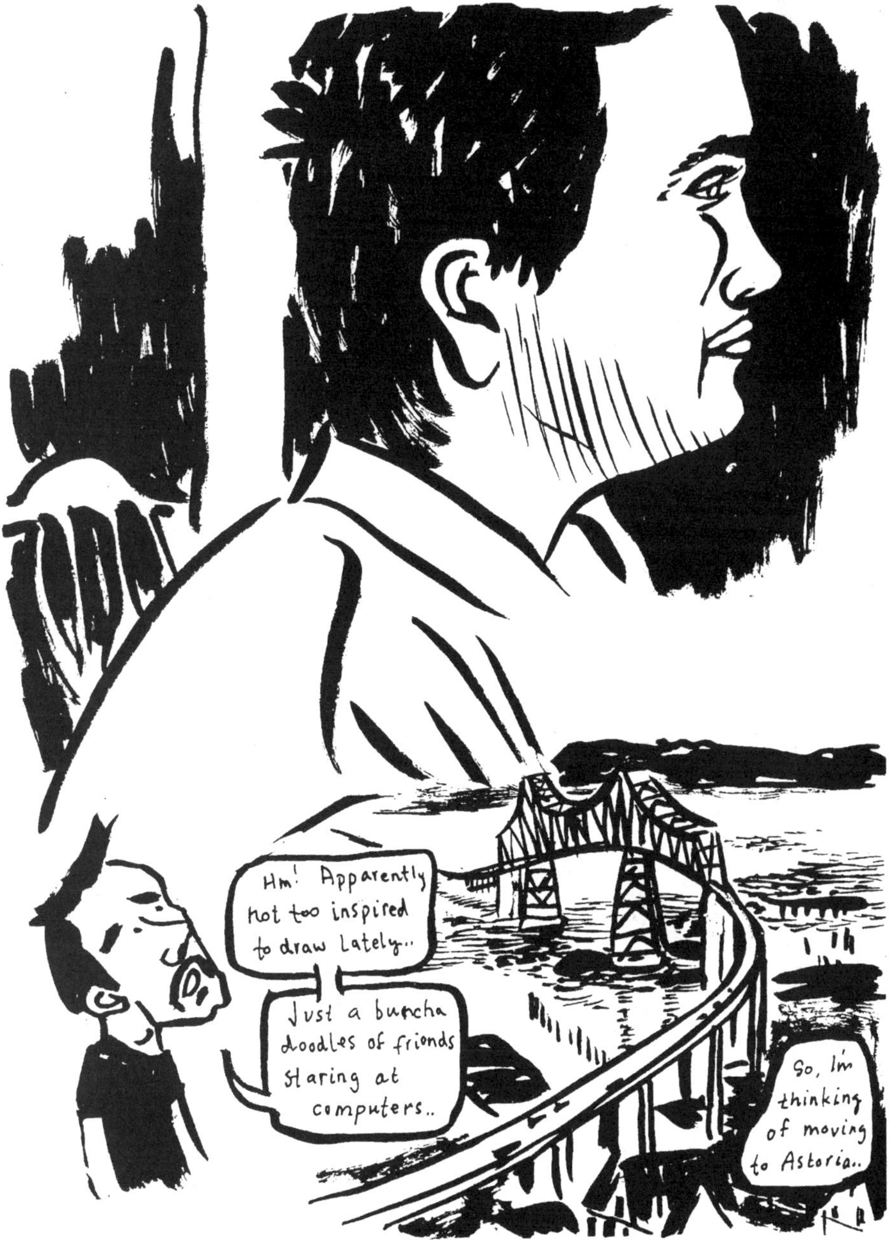
Hm! Apparently not too inspired to draw Lately..
Just a buncha doodles of friends staring at computers..
So, I'm thinking of moving to Astoria..

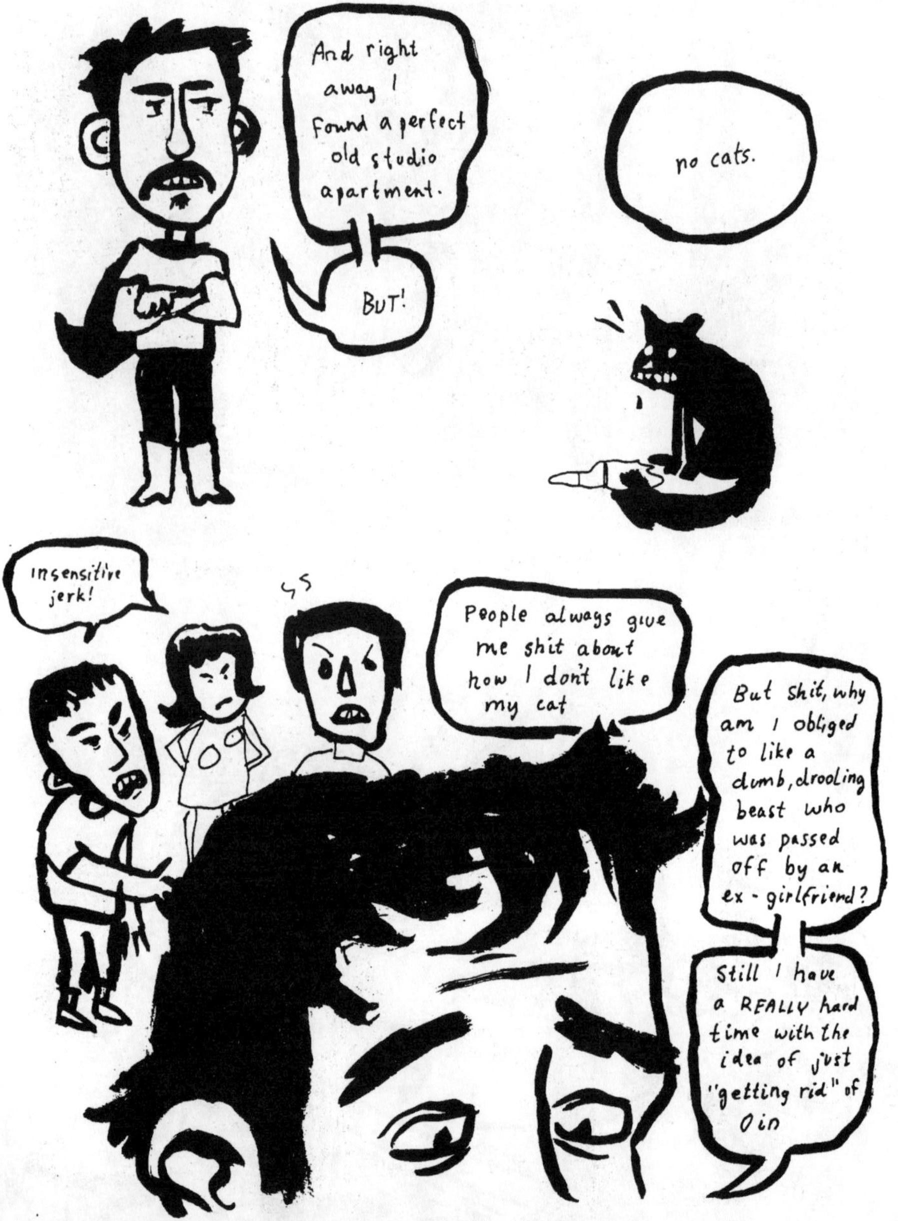

And right away I found a perfect old studio apartment.
BUT!
no cats.
insensitive jerk!
People always give me shit about how I don't like my cat
But shit, why am I obliged to like a dumb, drooling beast who was passed off by an ex-girlfriend?
Still I have a REALLY hard time with the idea of just "getting rid" of Oin

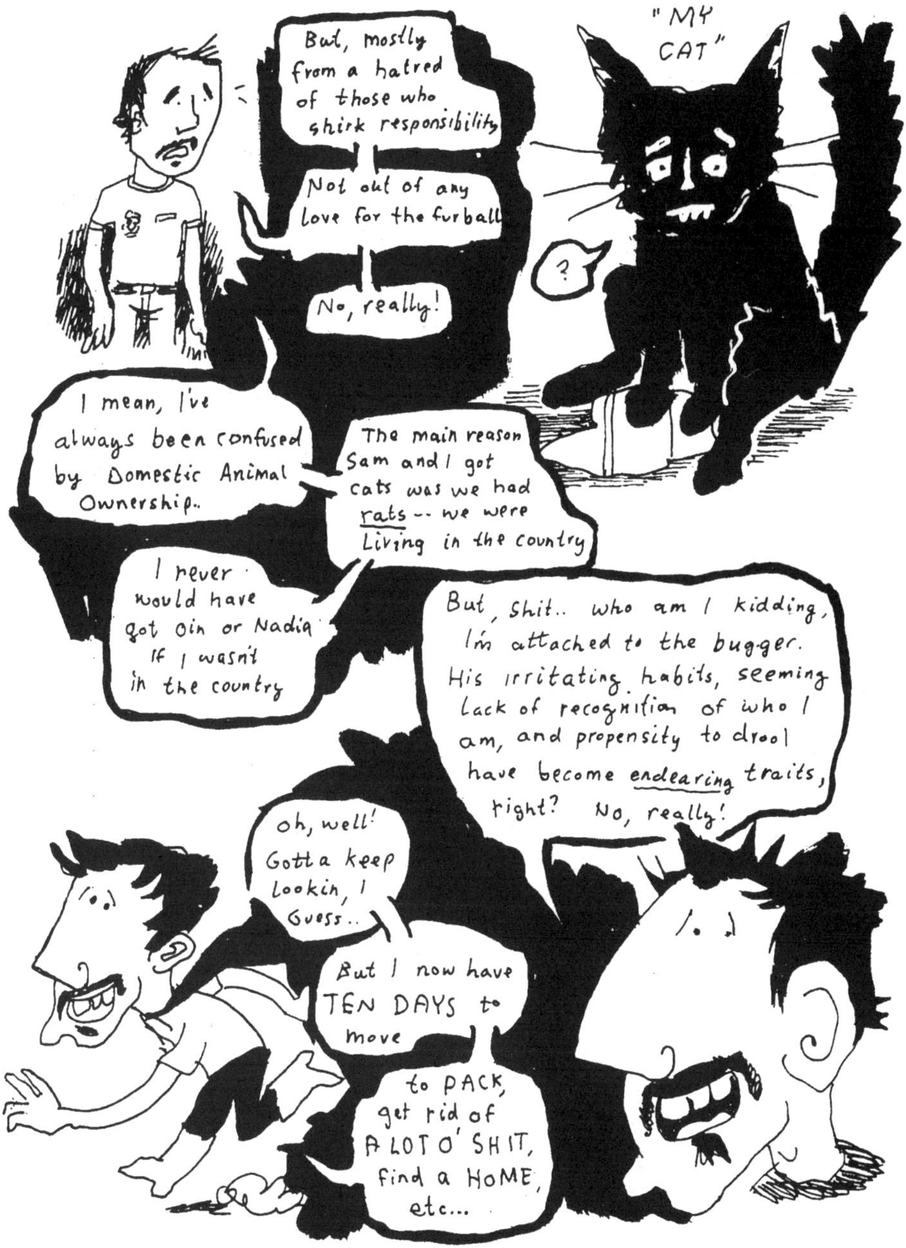
But, mostly from a hatred of those who shirk responsibility
Not out of any love for the furball
No, really!
"MY CAT"
?
I mean, I've always been confused by Domestic Animal Ownership..
The main reason Sam and I got cats was we had rats -- we were Living in the country
I never would have got Oin or Nadia If I wasn't in the country
But, shit.. who am I kidding, I'm attached to the bugger. His irritating habits, seeming lack of recognition of who I am, and propensity to drool have become endearing traits, right? No, really!
Oh, well! Gotta keep lookin, I Guess..
But I now have TEN DAYS to move
to PACK, get rid of A LOT O' SHIT, find a HOME, etc...

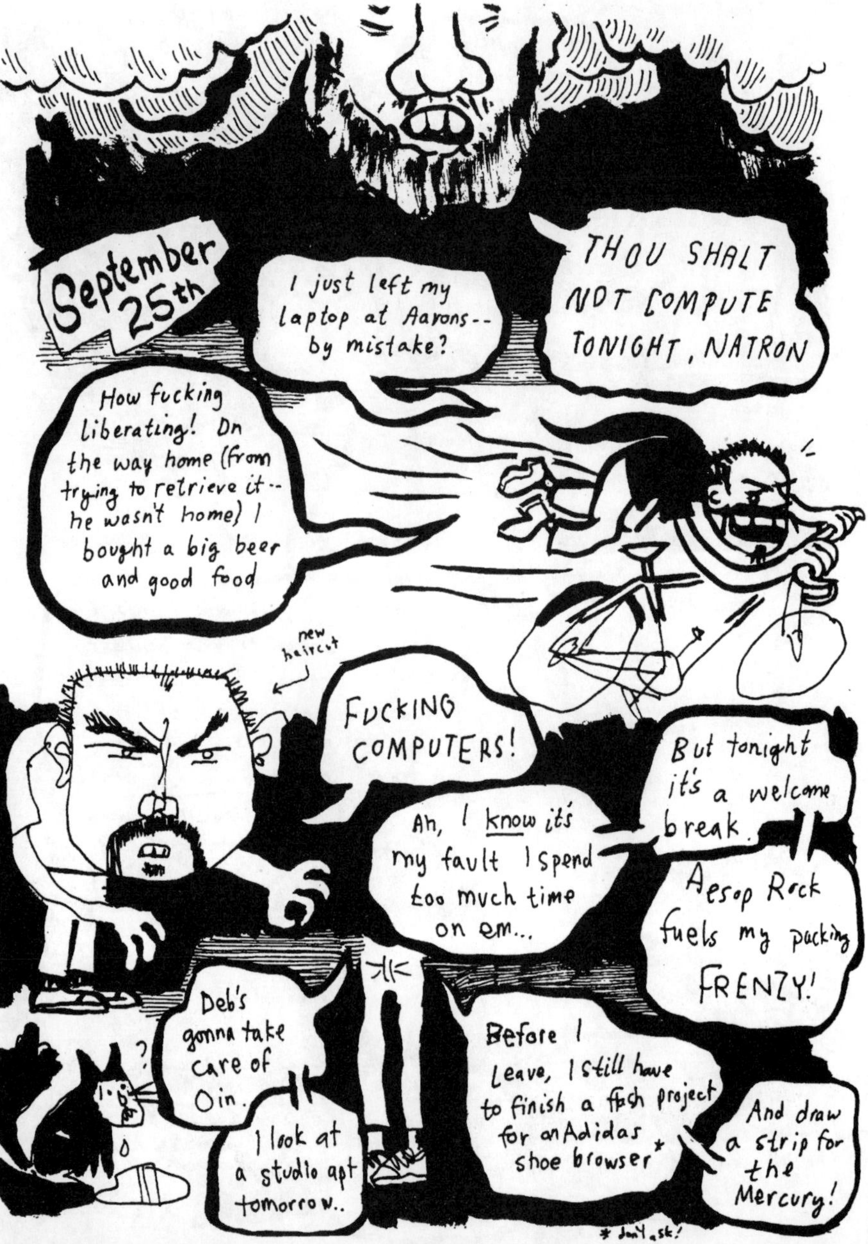
September 25th
I just left my laptop at Aarons-- by mistake?
THOU SHALT NOT COMPUTE TONIGHT, NATRON
How fucking liberating! On the way home (from trying to retrieve it-- he wasn't home) I bought a big beer and good food
new haircut
FUCKING COMPUTERS!
Ah, I know it's my fault I spend too much time on em...
But tonight it's a welcome break.
Aesop Rock fuels my packing FRENZY!
Deb's gonna take care of Oin.
?
I look at a studio apt tomorrow..
Before I leave, I still have to finish a flash project for an Adidas shoe browser*
And draw a strip for the Mercury!
* don't ask!

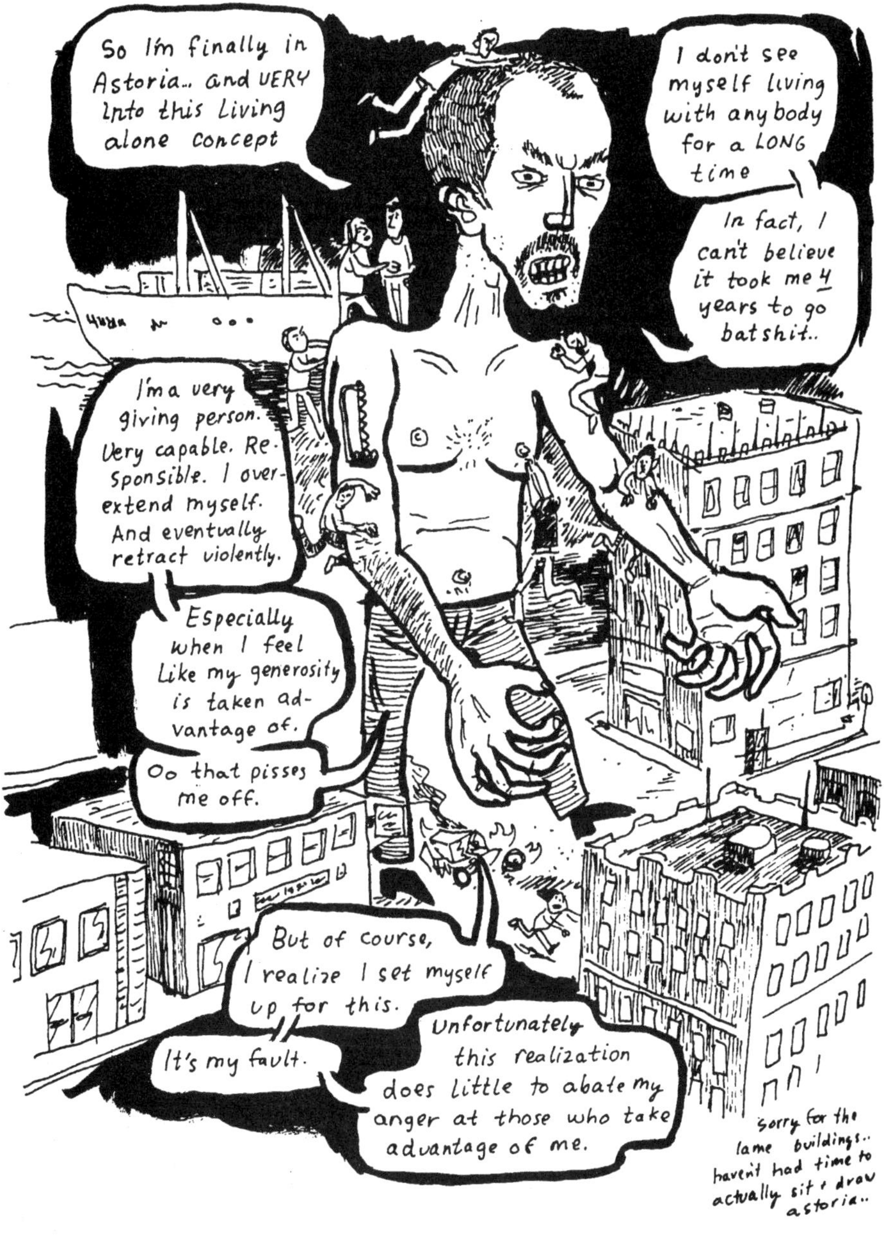
So I'm finally in Astoria.. and VERY Into this Living alone concept
I don't see myself living with anybody for a LONG time
In fact, I can't believe it took me 4 years to go batshit..
I'm a very giving person. Very capable. Responsible. I over-extend myself. And eventually retract violently.
Especially when I feel Like my generosity is taken advantage of.
Oo that pisses me off.
But of course, I realize I set myself up for this.
It's my fault.
Unfortunately this realization does little to abate my anger at those who take advantage of me.
sorry for the lame buildings.. haven't had time to actually sit + draw astoria..

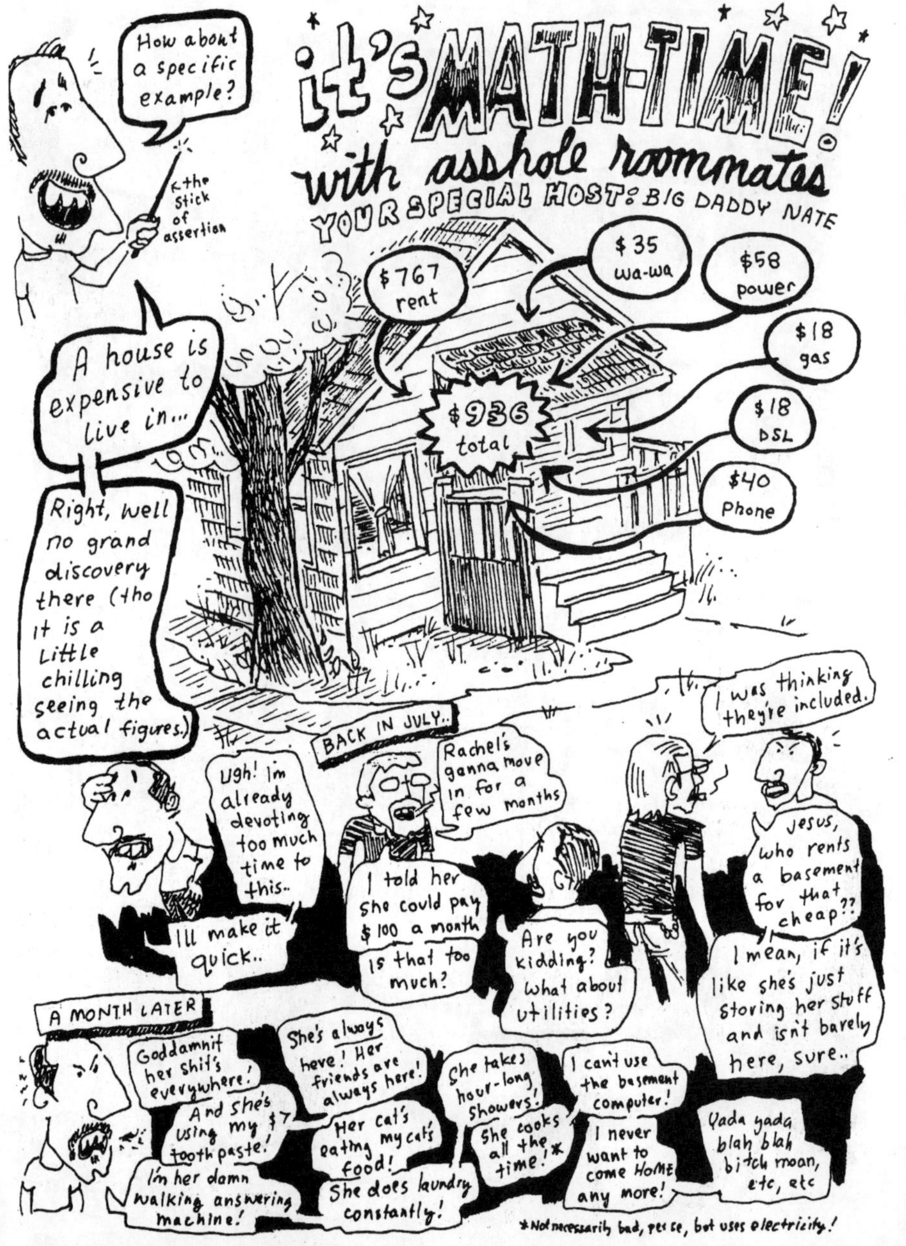

How about a specific example?
it's MATH-TIME!
with asshole roommates
YOUR SPECIAL HOST: BIG DADDY NATE
← the stick of assertion
A house is expensive to live in...
$767 rent
$35 wa-wa
$58 power
$18 gas
$18 DSL
$40 phone
$936 total
Right, well no grand discovery there (tho it is a little chilling seeing the actual figures.)
BACK IN JULY..
Ugh! I'm already devoting too much time to this..
I'll make it quick..
Rachel's gonna move in for a few months
I told her she could pay $100 a month
Is that too much?
I was thinking they're included.
Are you kidding? What about utilities?
Jesus, who rents a basement for that cheap??
I mean, if it's like she's just storing her stuff and isn't barely here, sure..
A MONTH LATER
Goddamnit her shit's everywhere!
And she's using my $7 toothpaste!
I'm her damn walking answering machine!
She's always here! Her friends are always here!
Her cat's eating my cat's food!
She does laundry constantly!
She takes hour-long showers!
She cooks all the time!*
I can't use the basement computer!
I never want to come HOME any more!
Yada yada blah blah bitch moan, etc, etc
*Not necessarily bad, per se, but uses electricity!

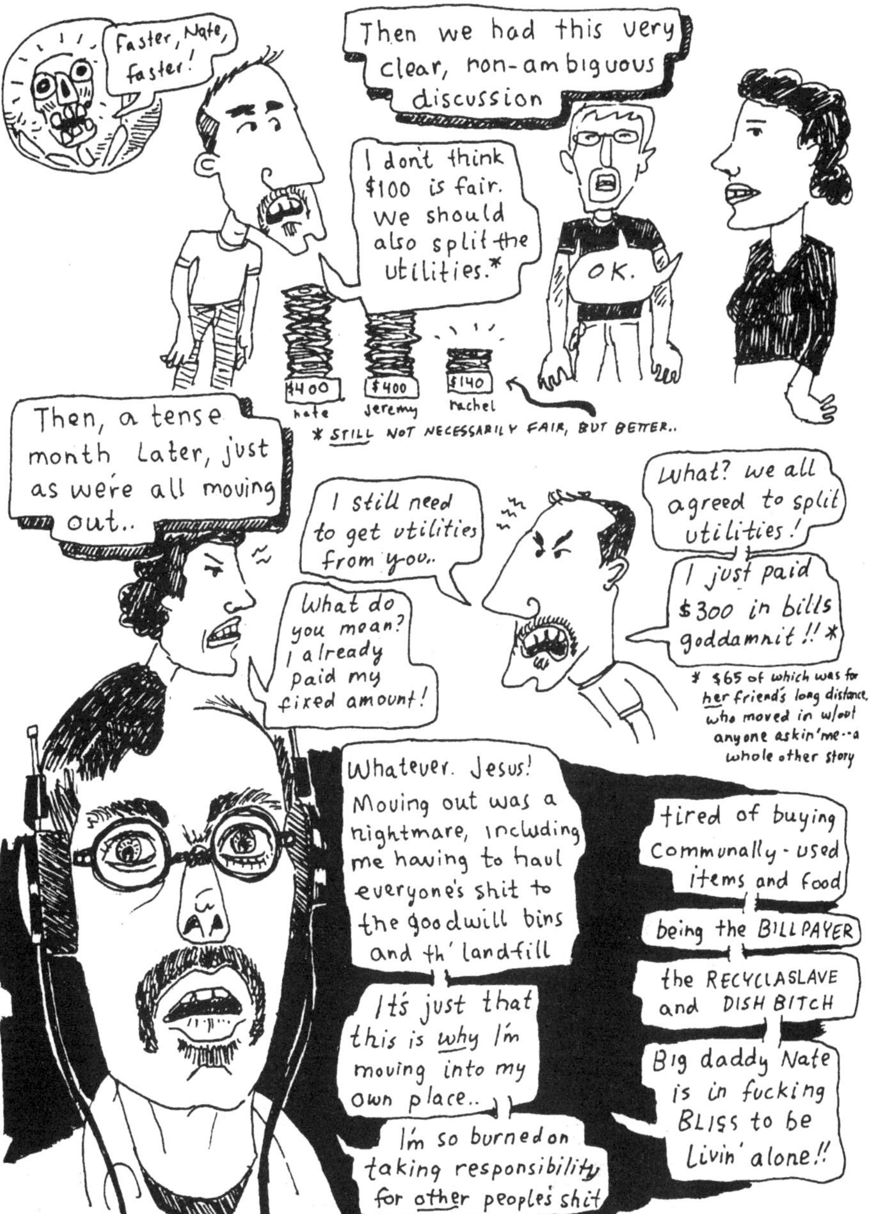
Faster, Nate, faster!
Then we had this very clear, non-ambiguous discussion
I don't think $100 is fair. We should also split the utilities.*
OK.
$400 nate
$400 Jeremy
$140 rachel
* STILL NOT NECESSARILY FAIR, BUT BETTER..
Then, a tense month later, just as we're all moving out..
I still need to get utilities from you..
What do you mean? I already paid my fixed amount!
What? we all agreed to split utilities!
I just paid $300 in bills goddamnit!! *
* $65 of which was for her friend's long distance, who moved in w/out anyone askin' me--a whole other story
Whatever. Jesus! Moving out was a nightmare, including me having to haul everyone's shit to the goodwill bins and th' landfill
It's just that this is why I'm moving into my own place..
I'm so burned on taking responsibility for other people's shit
tired of buying communally-used items and food
being the BILLPAYER
the RECYCLASLAVE and DISH BITCH
Big daddy Nate is in fucking BLISS to be Livin' alone!!

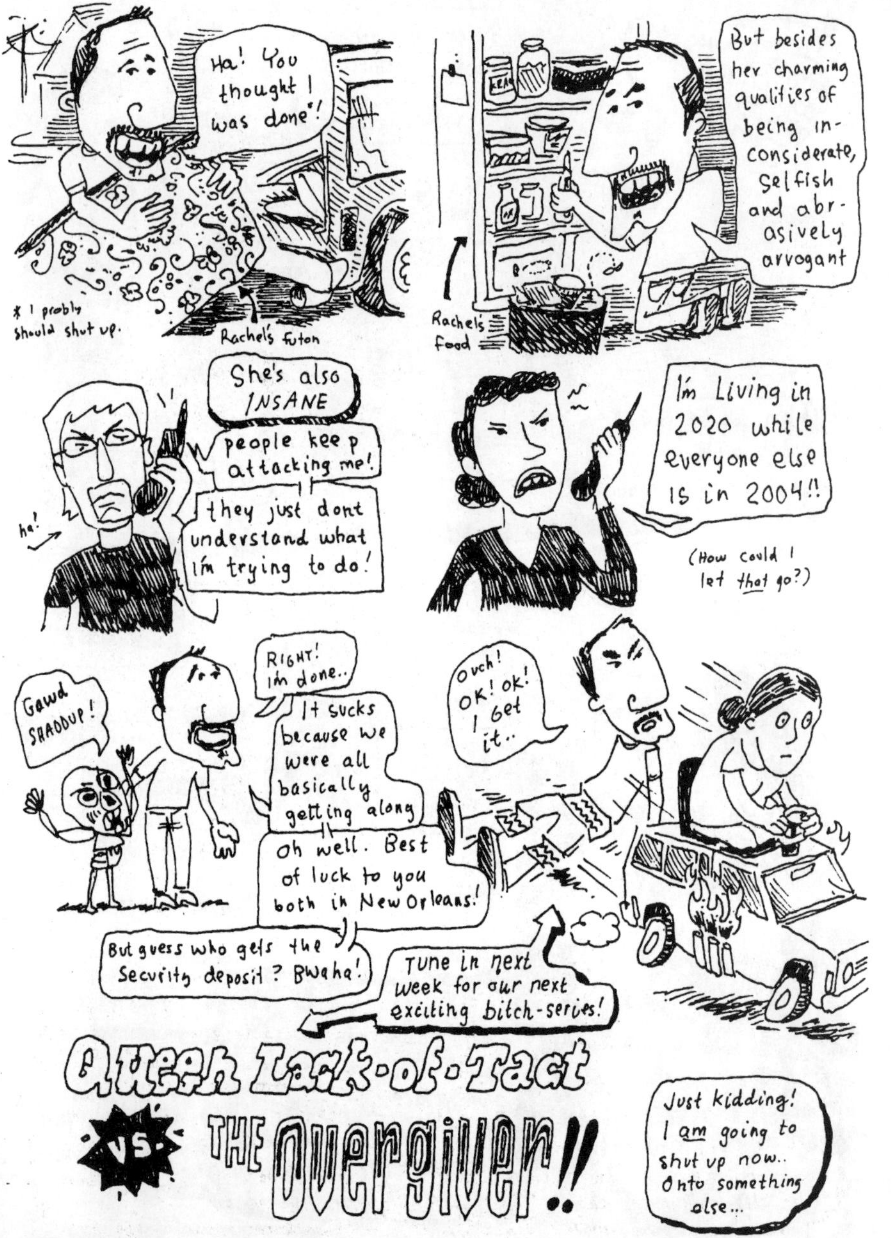

Ha! You thought I was done*!
* I probly should shut up.
Rachel's futon
But besides her charming qualities of being inconsiderate, selfish and abrasively arrogant
Rachel's food
She's also INSANE
people keep attacking me!
they just dont understand what I'm trying to do!
ha!
I'm Living in 2020 while everyone else is in 2004!!
(How could I let that go?)
Gawd SHADDUP!
RIGHT! I'm done..
It sucks because we were all basically getting along
Oh well. Best of luck to you both in New Orleans!
But guess who gets the security deposit? Bwaha!
Ouch! OK! ok! I Get it..
Tune in next week for our next exciting bitch-series!
Queen Lack-of-Tact
VS.
THE Overgiver!!
Just kidding! I am going to shut up now.. Onto something else...

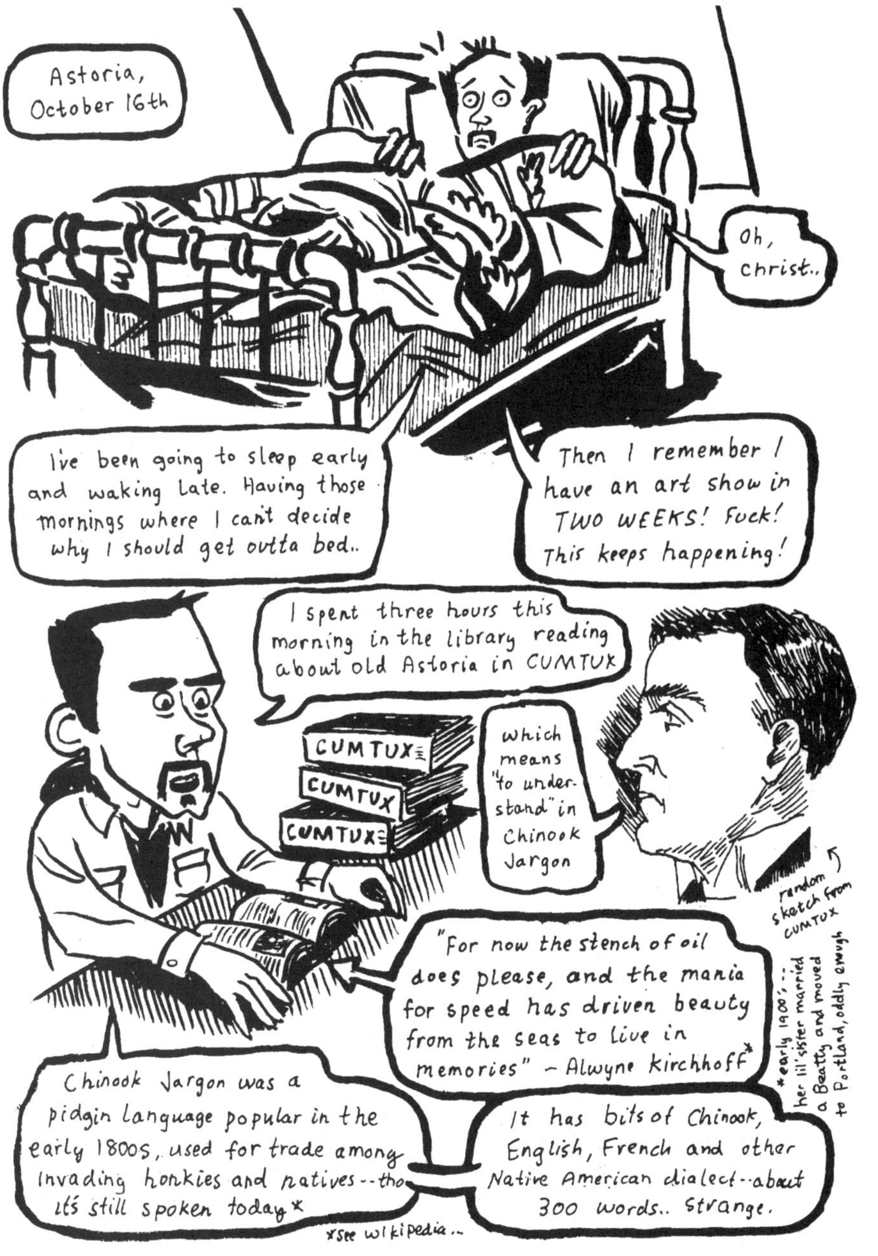

Astoria, October 16th
Oh, christ..
I've been going to sleep early and waking late. Having those mornings where I can't decide why I should get outta bed..
Then I remember I have an art show in TWO WEEKS! Fuck! This keeps happening!
I spent three hours this morning in the library reading about old Astoria in CUMTUX
CUMTUX
CUMTUX
CUMTUX
which means "to understand" in Chinook Jargon
random sketch from CUMTUX
"For now the stench of oil does please, and the mania for speed has driven beauty from the seas to live in memories" – Alwyne Kirchhoff*
*early 1900's -- her lil' sister married a Beatty and moved to Portland, oddly enough
Chinook Jargon was a pidgin language popular in the early 1800s, used for trade among invading honkies and natives -- tho it's still spoken today*
*see wikipedia..
It has bits of Chinook, English, French and other Native American dialect -- about 300 words.. Strange.

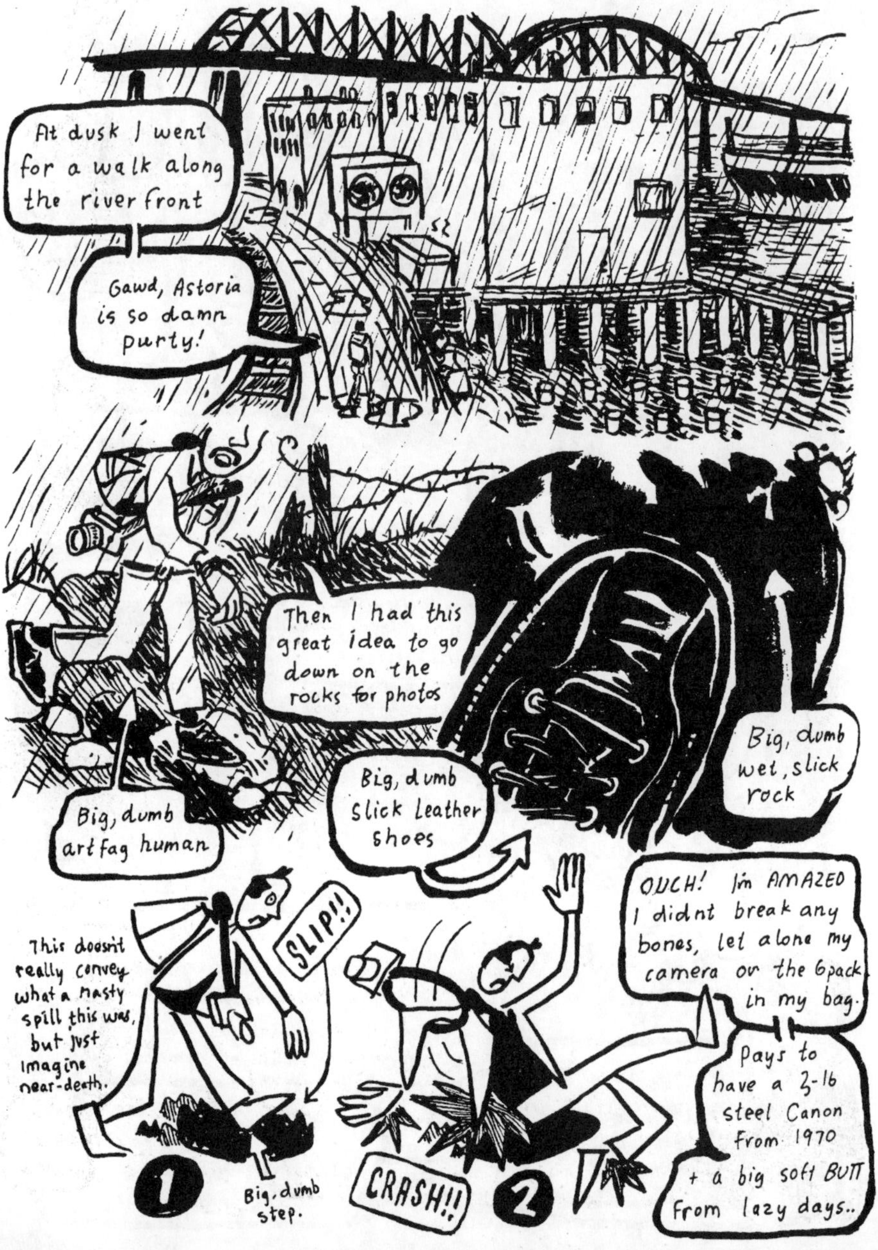
At dusk I went for a walk along the river front
Gawd, Astoria is so damn purty!
Then I had this great idea to go down on the rocks for photos
Big, dumb art fag human
Big, dumb slick leather shoes
Big, dumb wet, slick rock
This doesn't really convey what a nasty spill this was, but just imagine near-death.
SLIP!!
1
Big, dumb step.
CRASH!!
2
OUCH! I'm AMAZED I didnt break any bones, let alone my camera or the 6pack in my bag.
Pays to have a 3-lb steel Canon from 1970 + a big soft BUTT from lazy days..

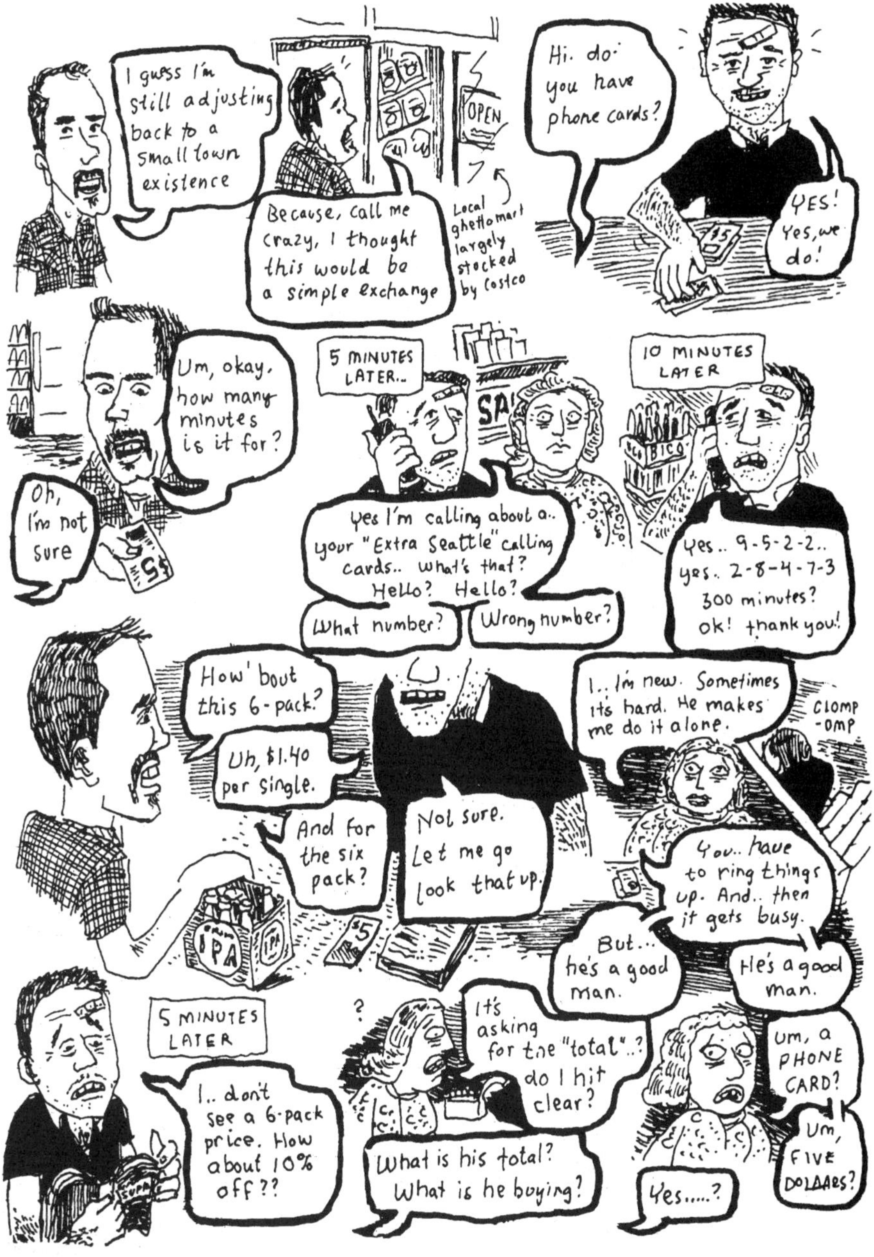

I guess I'm still adjusting back to a small town existence
Because, call me crazy, I thought this would be a simple exchange
OPEN
Local ghettomart largely stocked by Costco
Hi. do you have phone cards?
YES! Yes, we do!
Um, okay, how many minutes is it for?
Oh, I'm not sure
$5
5 MINUTES LATER..
Yes I'm calling about a.. your "Extra Seattle" calling cards.. what's that? Hello? Hello?
What number?
Wrong number?
10 MINUTES LATER
Yes.. 9-5-2-2.. yes.. 2-8-4-7-3 300 minutes? ok! thank you!
How' bout this 6-pack?
Uh, $1.40 per single.
And for the six pack?
Not sure. Let me go look that up.
IPA
$5
I.. I'm new. Sometimes its hard. He makes me do it alone.
CLOMP -OMP
You.. have to ring things up. And.. then it gets busy.
But... he's a good man.
He's a good man.
5 MINUTES LATER
I.. don't see a 6-pack price. How about 10% off??
?
It's asking for the "total"..? do I hit clear?
What is his total? What is he buying?
Um, a PHONE CARD?
Um, FIVE DOLLARS?
Yes.....?

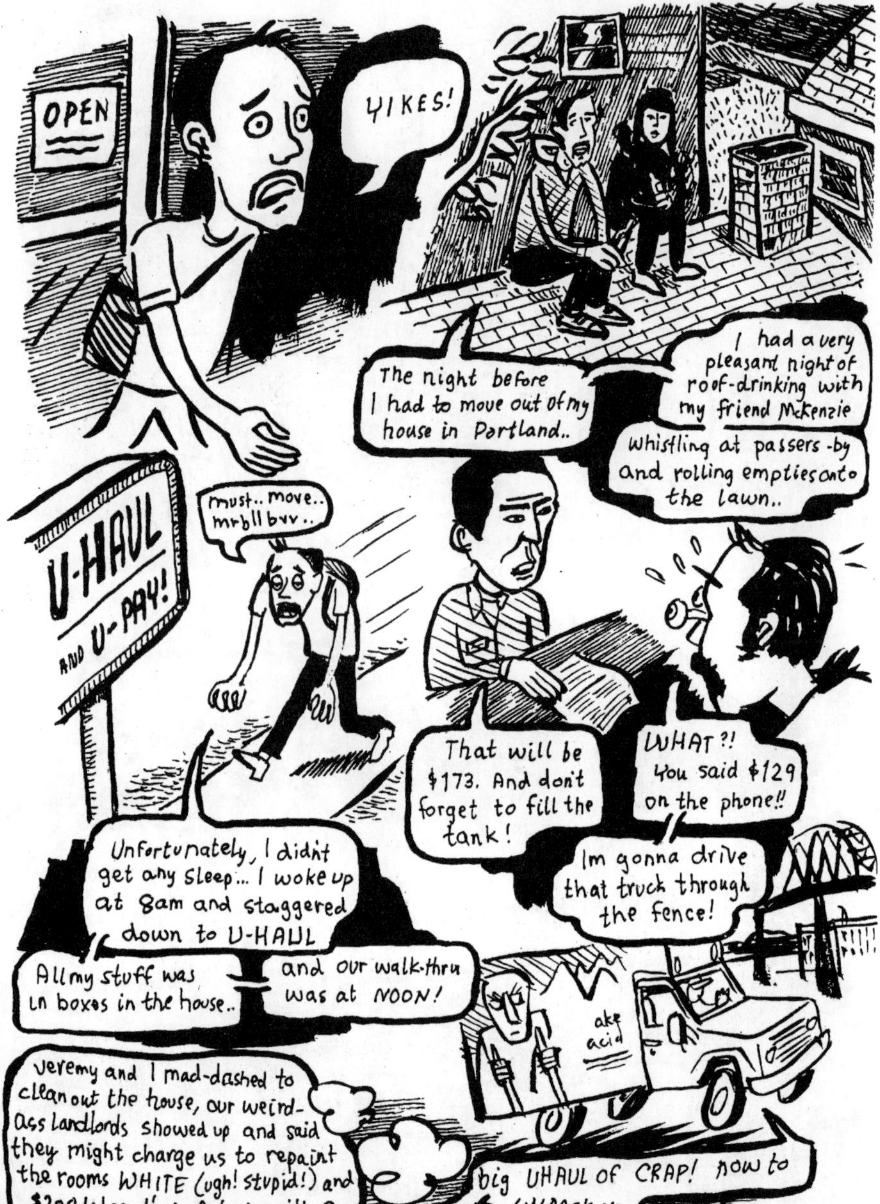
OPEN
YIKES!
The night before I had to move out of my house in Portland..
I had a very pleasant night of roof-drinking with my friend McKenzie
whistling at passers-by and rolling empties onto the lawn..
U-HAUL AND U-PAY!
must.. move.. mrbll bvv..
Unfortunately, I didn't get any sleep... I woke up at 8am and staggered down to U-HAUL
All my stuff was in boxes in the house..
and our walk-thru was at NOON!
That will be $173. And don't forget to fill the tank!
WHAT?! You said $129 on the phone!!
Im gonna drive that truck through the fence!
ake acid
Jeremy and I mad-dashed to clean out the house, our weird-ass landlords showed up and said they might charge us to repaint the rooms WHITE (ugh! stupid!) and $200 later, I'm in Astoria with a
big UHAUL OF CRAP! now to UNPACK..

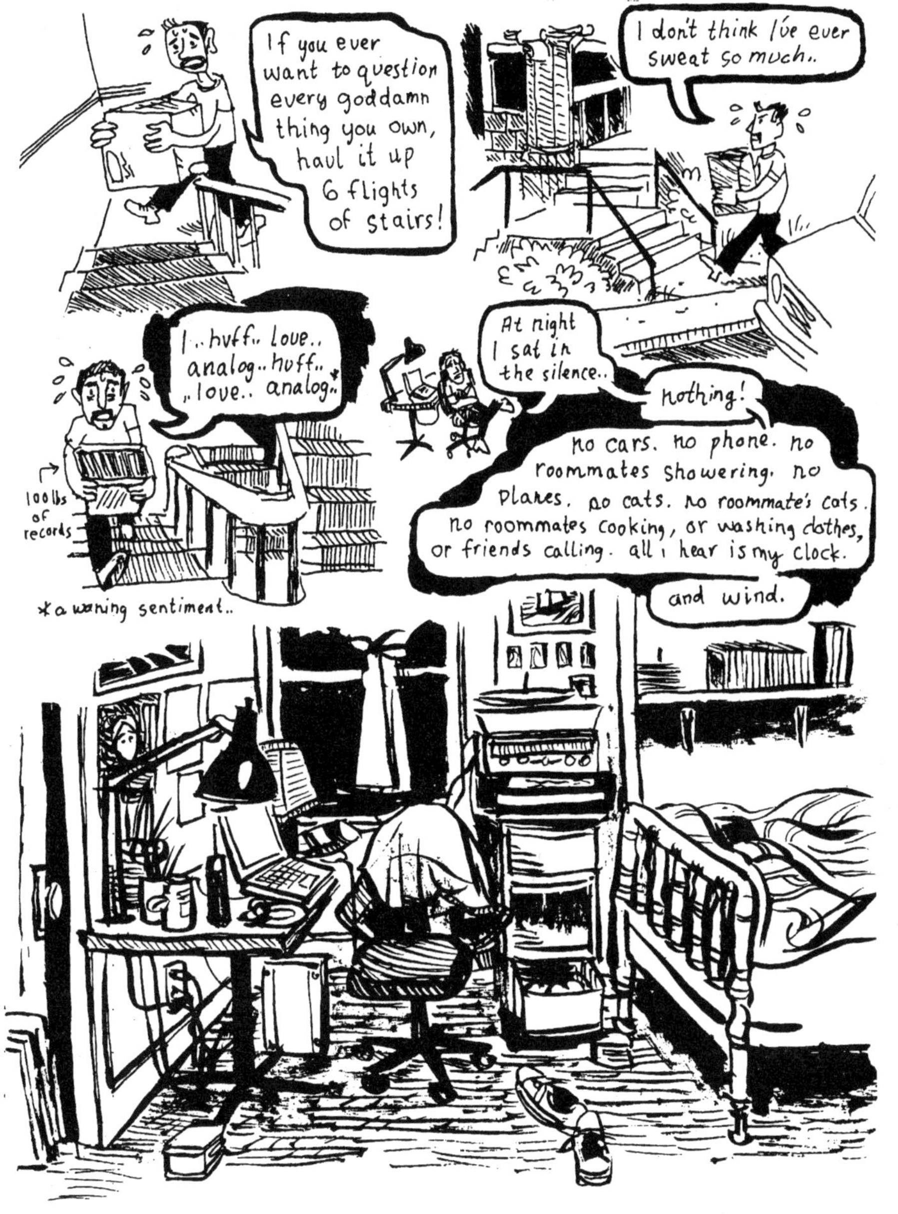
If you ever want to question every goddamn thing you own, haul it up 6 flights of stairs!
I don't think I've ever sweat so much..
I..huff.. love.. analog..huff.. ..love.. analog..*
100lbs of records
*a waning sentiment..
At night I sat in the silence..
nothing!
no cars. no phone. no roommates showering. no planes. no cats. no roommate's cats. no roommates cooking, or washing clothes, or friends calling. all i hear is my clock.
and wind.

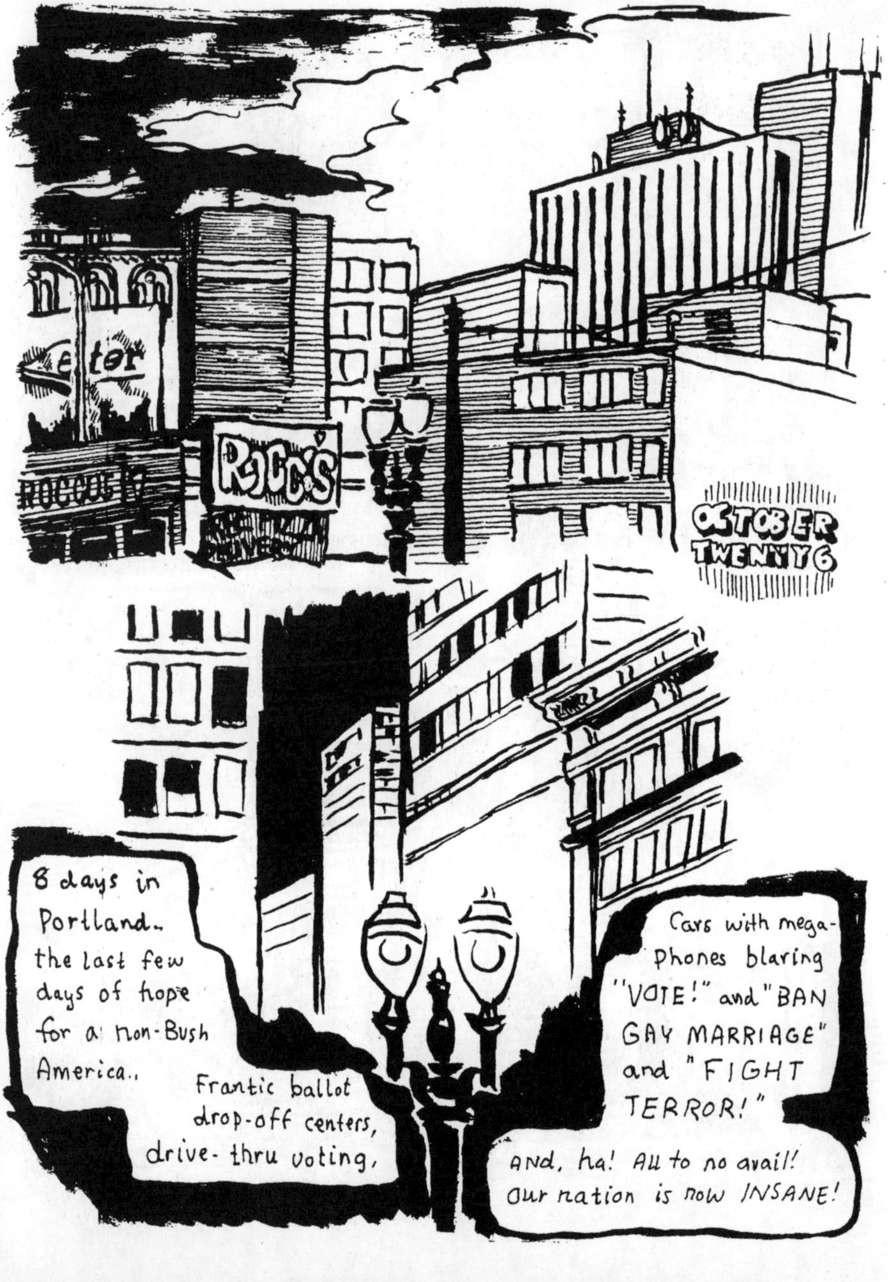
OCTOBER TWENTY 6
8 days in Portland.. the last few days of hope for a non-Bush America..
Frantic ballot drop-off centers, drive-thru voting,
Cars with mega-phones blaring "VOTE!" and "BAN GAY MARRIAGE" and "FIGHT TERROR!"
AND, ha! All to no avail! Our nation is now INSANE!

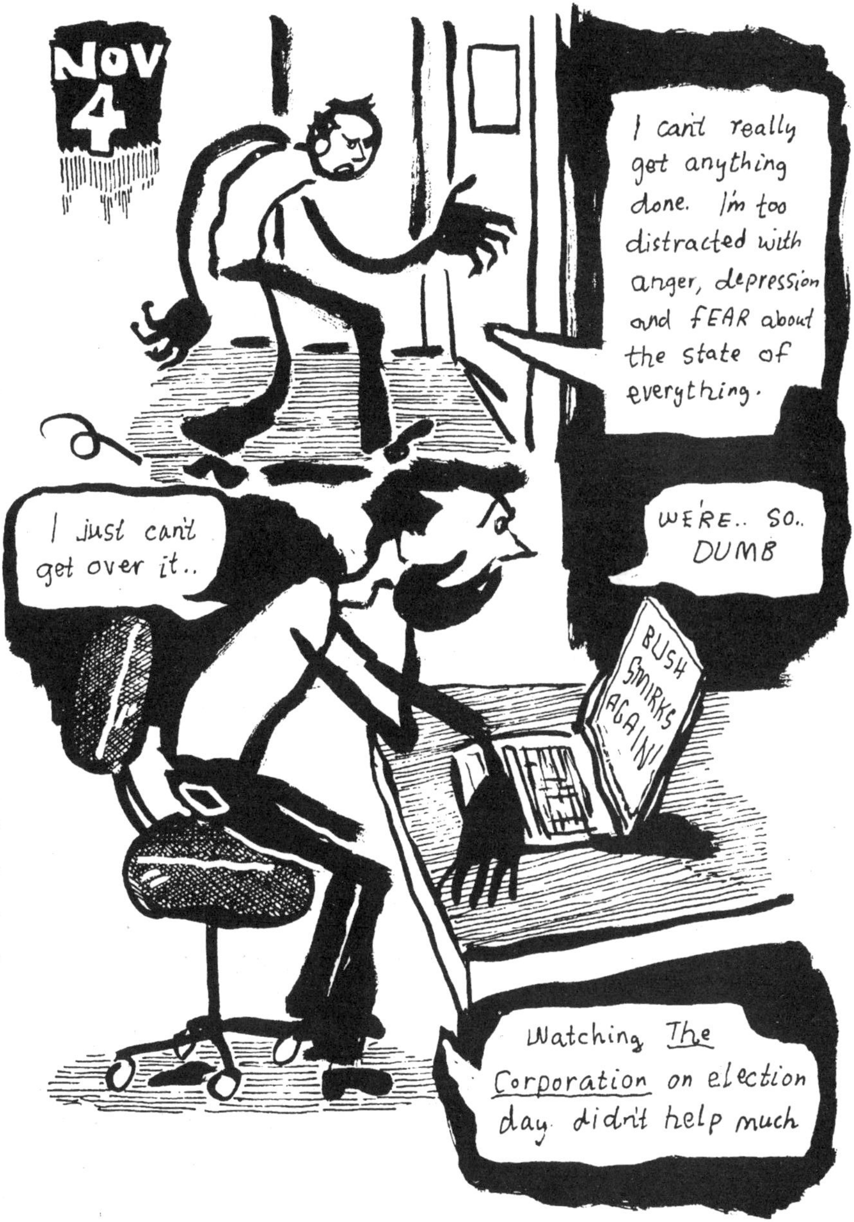
NOV 4
I can't really get anything done. I'm too distracted with anger, depression and FEAR about the state of everything.
I just can't get over it..
WE'RE.. SO.. DUMB
BUSH SMIRKS AGAIN!
Watching The Corporation on election day didn't help much

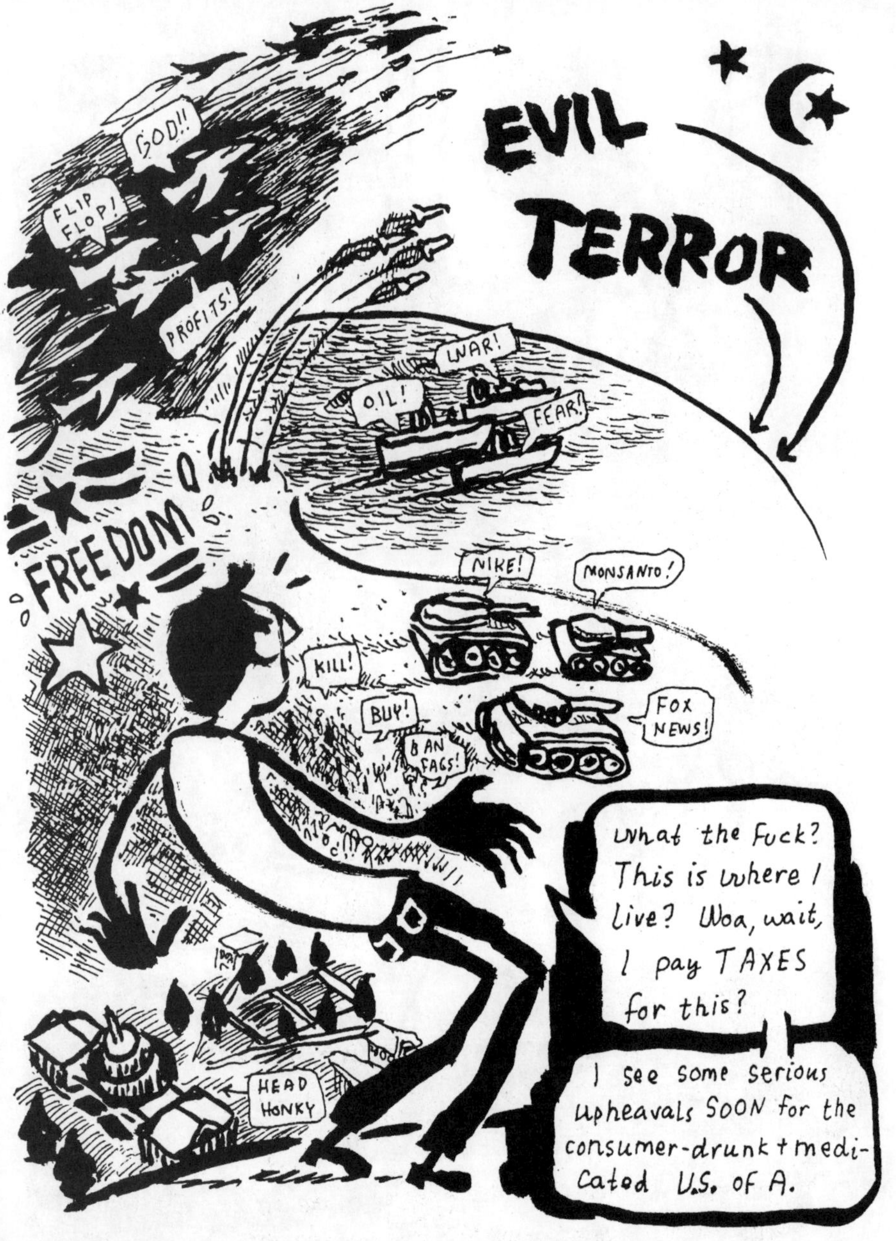
GOD!!
FLIP FLOP!
PROFITS!
EVIL
TERROR
WAR!
OIL!
FEAR!
FREEDOM
NIKE!
MONSANTO!
KILL!
BUY!
FOX NEWS!
BAN FAGS!
What the Fuck? This is where I live? Woa, wait, I pay TAXES for this?
I see some serious upheavals SOON for the consumer-drunk + medicated U.S. of A.
HEAD HONKY

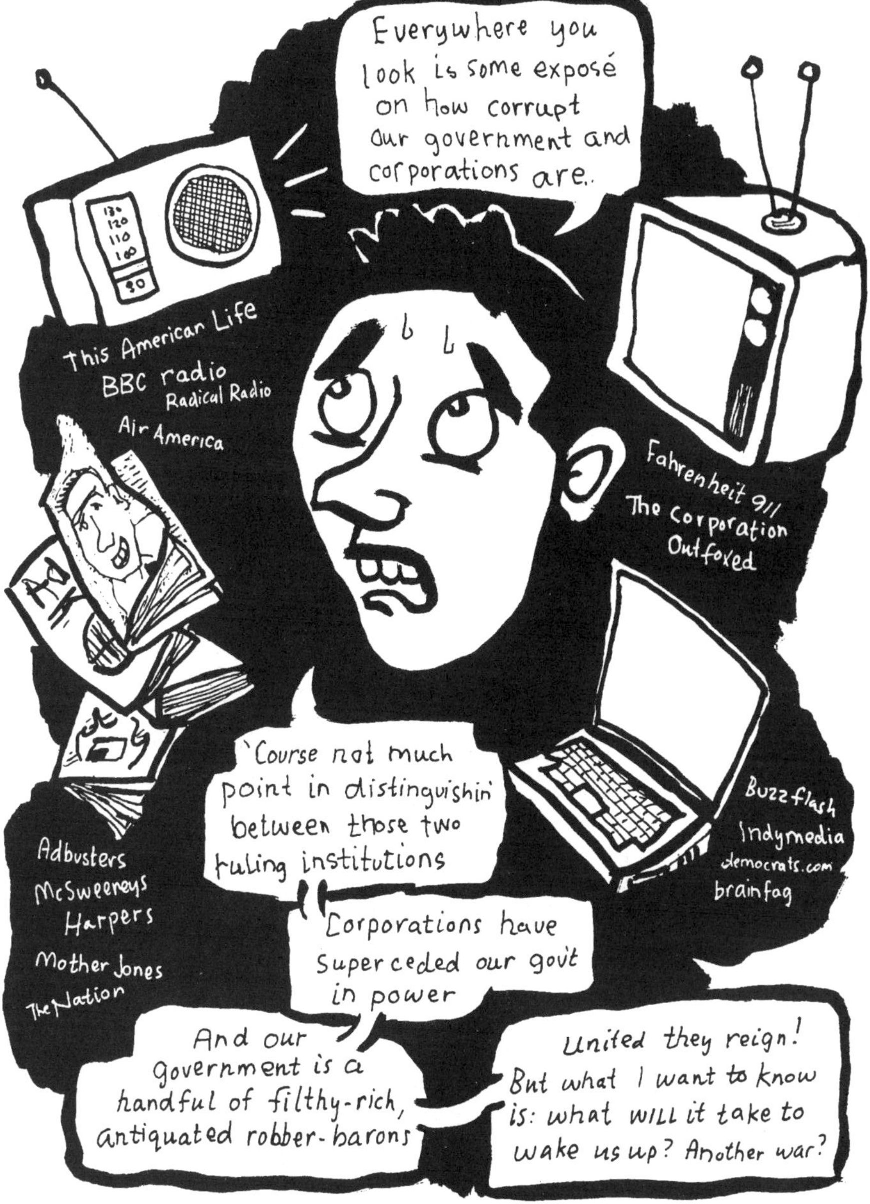
Everywhere you look is some exposé on how corrupt our government and corporations are.
130 120 110 100 90
This American Life
BBC radio
Radical Radio
Air America
Fahrenheit 9/11
The Corporation
Outfoxed
`Course not much point in distinguishin' between those two ruling institutions
Buzzflash
Indymedia
democrats.com
brainfag
Adbusters
McSweeneys
Harpers
Mother Jones
The Nation
Corporations have superceded our gov't in power
And our government is a handful of filthy-rich, antiquated robber-barons
United they reign! But what I want to know is: what will it take to wake us up? Another war?

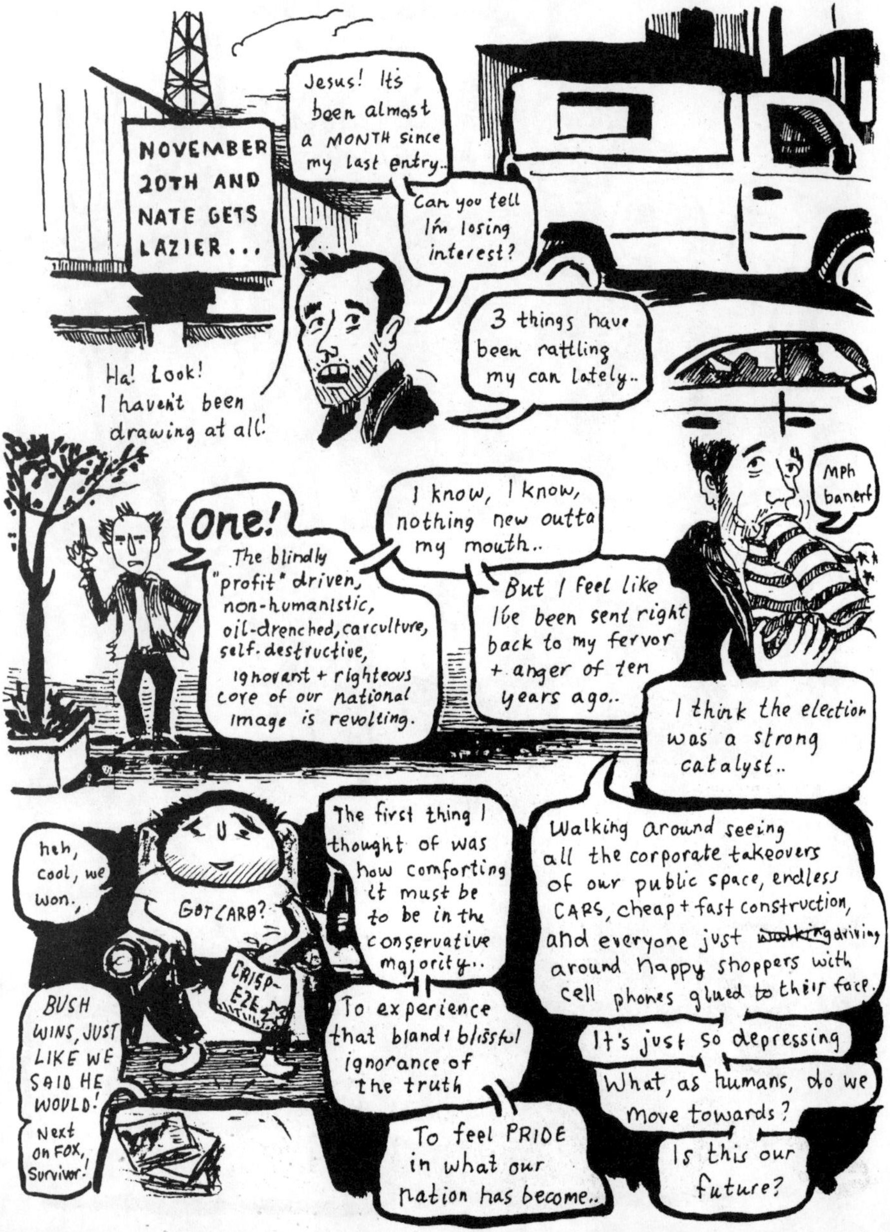

NOVEMBER 20TH AND NATE GETS LAZIER...
Jesus! It's been almost a MONTH since my last entry..
Can you tell I'm losing interest?
Ha! Look! I haven't been drawing at all!
3 things have been rattling my can lately..
One! The blindly "profit" driven, non-humanistic, oil-drenched, carculture, self-destructive, ignorant + righteous core of our national image is revolting.
I know, I know, nothing new outta my mouth..
But I feel like I've been sent right back to my fervor + anger of ten years ago..
Mph banerf
I think the election was a strong catalyst..
heh, cool, we won.
GOT CARB?
CRISP-EZE
BUSH WINS, JUST LIKE WE SAID HE WOULD!
Next on FOX, Survivor!
The first thing I thought of was how comforting it must be to be in the conservative majority..
To experience that bland + blissful ignorance of the truth
To feel PRIDE in what our nation has become..
Walking around seeing all the corporate takeovers of our public space, endless CARS, cheap + fast construction, and everyone just ~~walking~~ driving around happy shoppers with cell phones glued to their face.
It's just so depressing
What, as humans, do we move towards?
Is this our future?

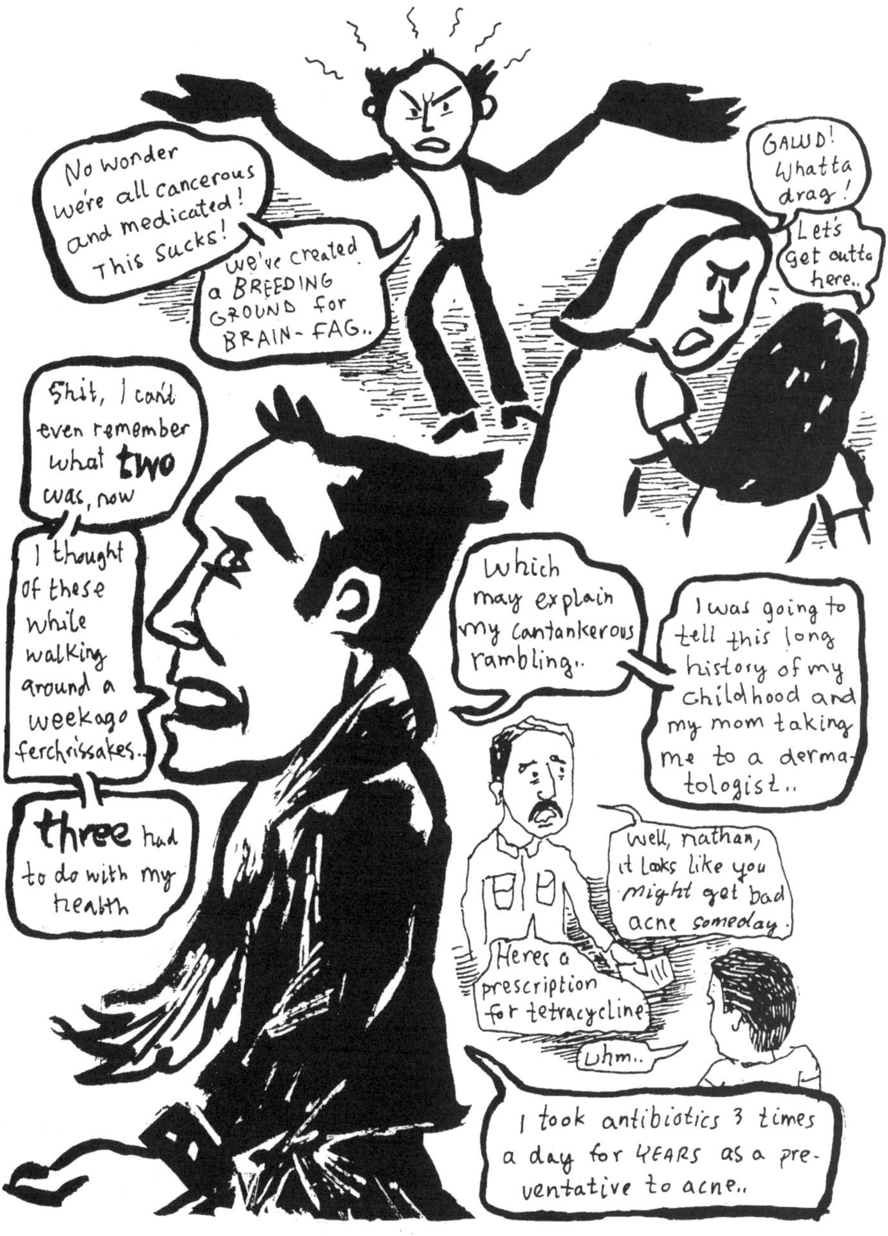
No wonder we're all cancerous and medicated! This Sucks!
We've created a BREEDING GROUND for BRAIN-FAG..
GAWD! Whatta drag!
Let's get outta here..
Shit, I can't even remember what TWO was, now
I thought of these while walking around a weekago ferchrissakes..
THREE had to do with my health
Which may explain my cantankerous rambling..
I was going to tell this long history of my childhood and my mom taking me to a dermatologist..
Well, nathan, it looks like you might get bad acne someday.
Heres a prescription for tetracycline
Uhm..
I took antibiotics 3 times a day for YEARS as a preventative to acne..

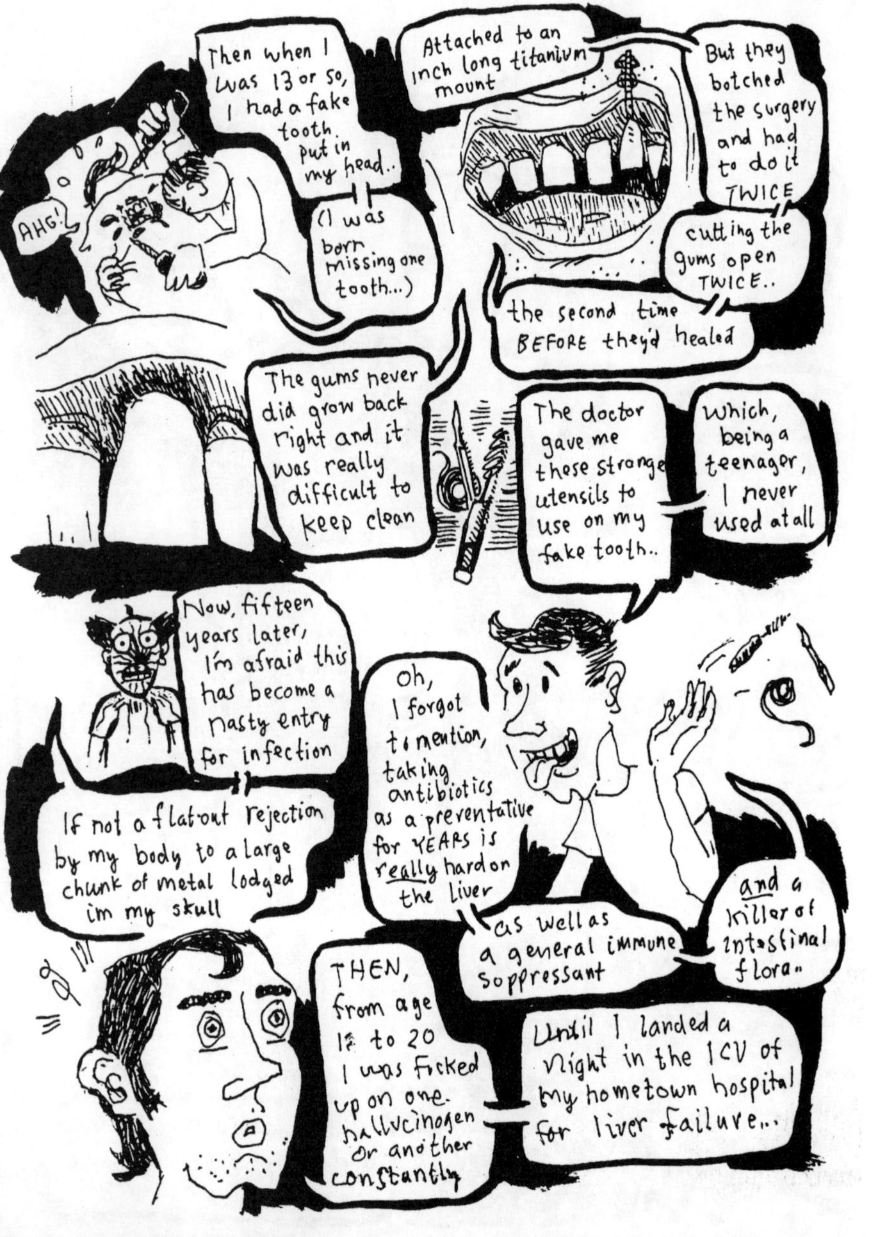
Then when I was 13 or so, I had a fake tooth put in my head..
AHG!
(I was born missing one tooth...)
Attached to an inch long titanium mount
But they botched the surgery and had to do it TWICE
cutting the gums open TWICE..
the second time BEFORE they'd healed
The gums never did grow back right and it was really difficult to keep clean
The doctor gave me these strange utensils to use on my fake tooth..
which, being a teenager, I never used at all
Now, fifteen years later, I'm afraid this has become a nasty entry for infection
If not a flat-out rejection by my body to a large chunk of metal lodged im my skull
Oh, I forgot to mention, taking antibiotics as a preventative for YEARS is really hard on the liver
as well as a general immune soppressant
and a killer of intestinal flora..
THEN, from age 15 to 20 I was fucked up on one hallucinogen or another constantly
Until I landed a night in the ICU of my hometown hospital for liver failure...

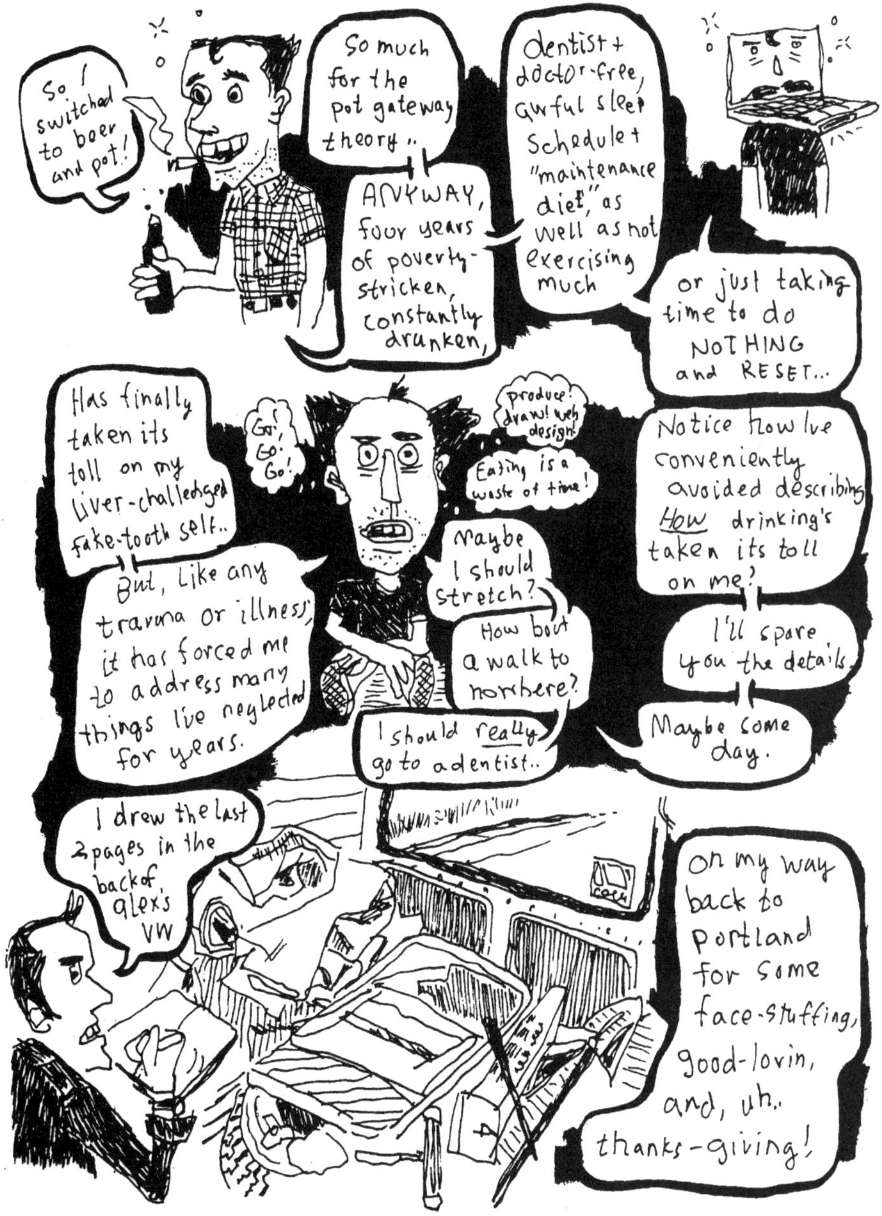
So I switched to beer and pot!
So much for the pot gateway theory..
ANYWAY, four years of poverty-stricken, constantly drunken,
dentist + doctor-free, awful sleep schedule + "maintenance diet", as well as not exercising much
or just taking time to do NOTHING and RESET...
Has finally taken its toll on my liver-challedged fake-tooth self..
But, like any trauma or illness, it has forced me to address many things I've neglected for years.
Go! Go! Go!
produce! draw! web design!
Eating is a waste of time!
Maybe I should stretch?
How bout a walk to nowhere?
I should really go to a dentist..
Notice how I've conveniently avoided describing HOW drinking's taken its toll on me?
I'll spare you the details.
Maybe some day.
I drew the last 2 pages in the back of alex's VW
On my way back to portland for some face-stuffing, good-lovin, and, uh.. thanks-giving!

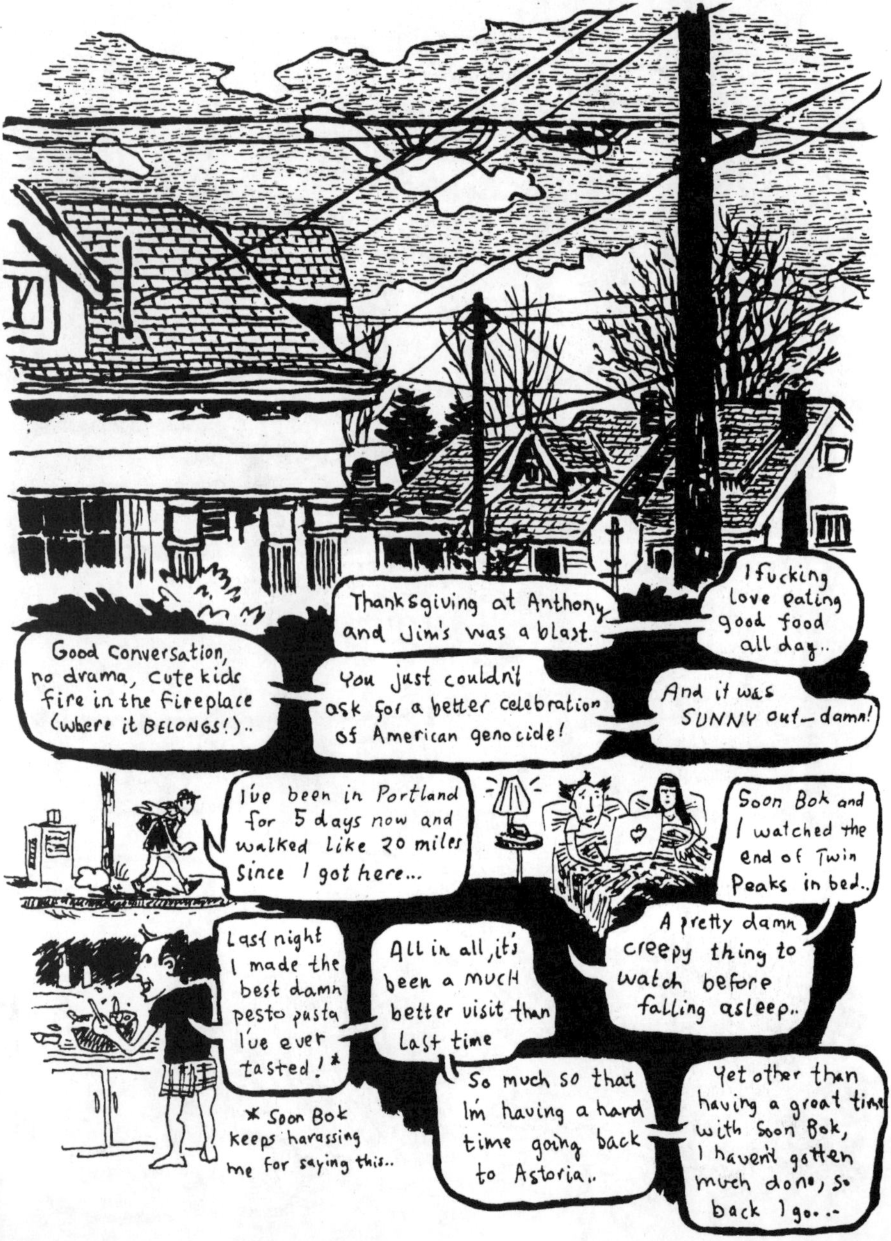

Thanksgiving at Anthony and Jim's was a blast.
I fucking love eating good food all day..
Good conversation, no drama, cute kids fire in the fireplace (where it BELONGS!)..
You just couldn't ask for a better celebration of American genocide!
And it was SUNNY out—damn!
I've been in Portland for 5 days now and walked like 20 miles since I got here...
Soon Bok and I watched the end of Twin Peaks in bed..
A pretty damn creepy thing to watch before falling asleep..
Last night I made the best damn pesto pasta I've ever tasted! *
All in all, it's been a MUCH better visit than last time
So much so that I'm having a hard time going back to Astoria..
Yet other than having a great time with Soon Bok, I haven't gotten much done, so back I go..-
* Soon Bok keeps harassing me for saying this..

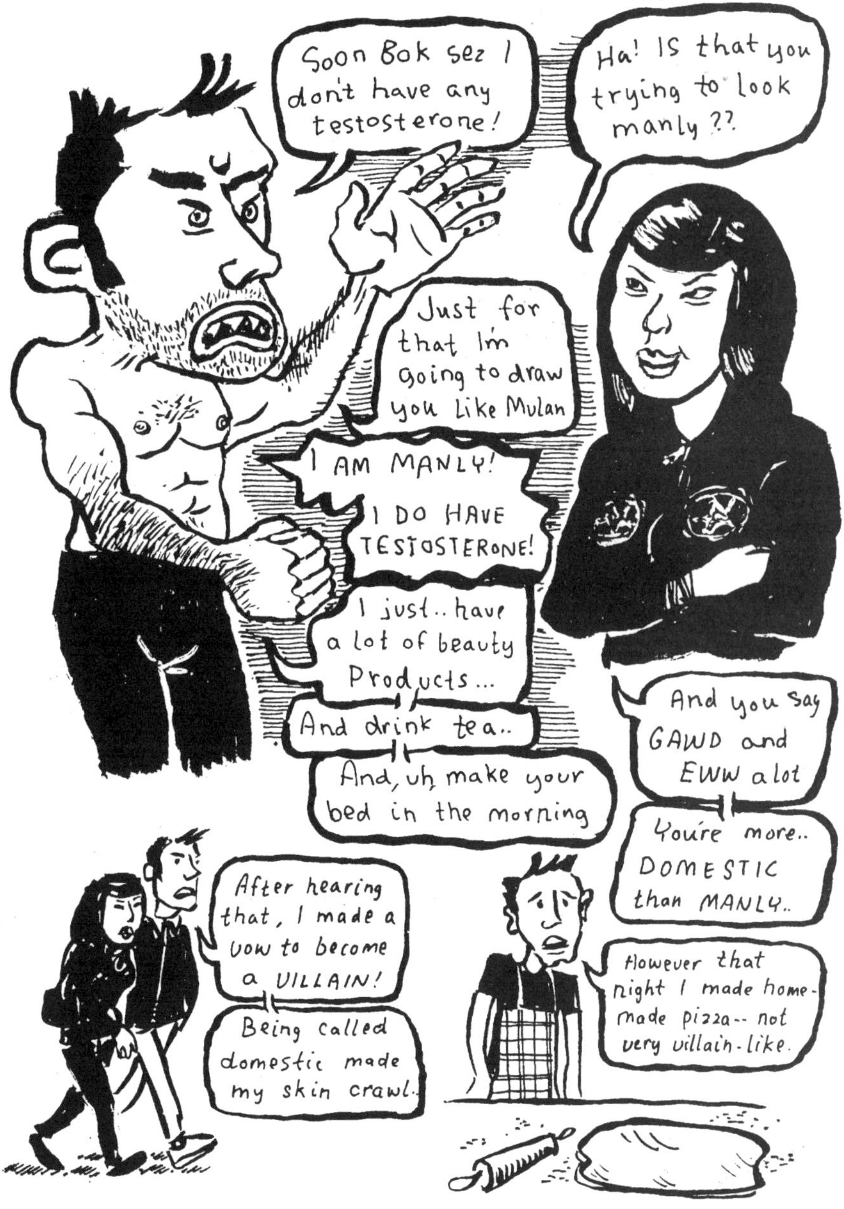
Soon Bok sez I don't have any testosterone!
Ha! Is that you trying to look manly ??
Just for that I'm going to draw you like Mulan
I AM MANLY!
I DO HAVE TESTOSTERONE!
I just.. have a lot of beauty Products...
And drink tea..
And, uh, make your bed in the morning
And you say GAWD and EWW a lot
You're more.. DOMESTIC than MANLY..
After hearing that, I made a vow to become a VILLAIN!
Being called domestic made my skin crawl..
However that night I made home-made pizza-- not very villain-like.

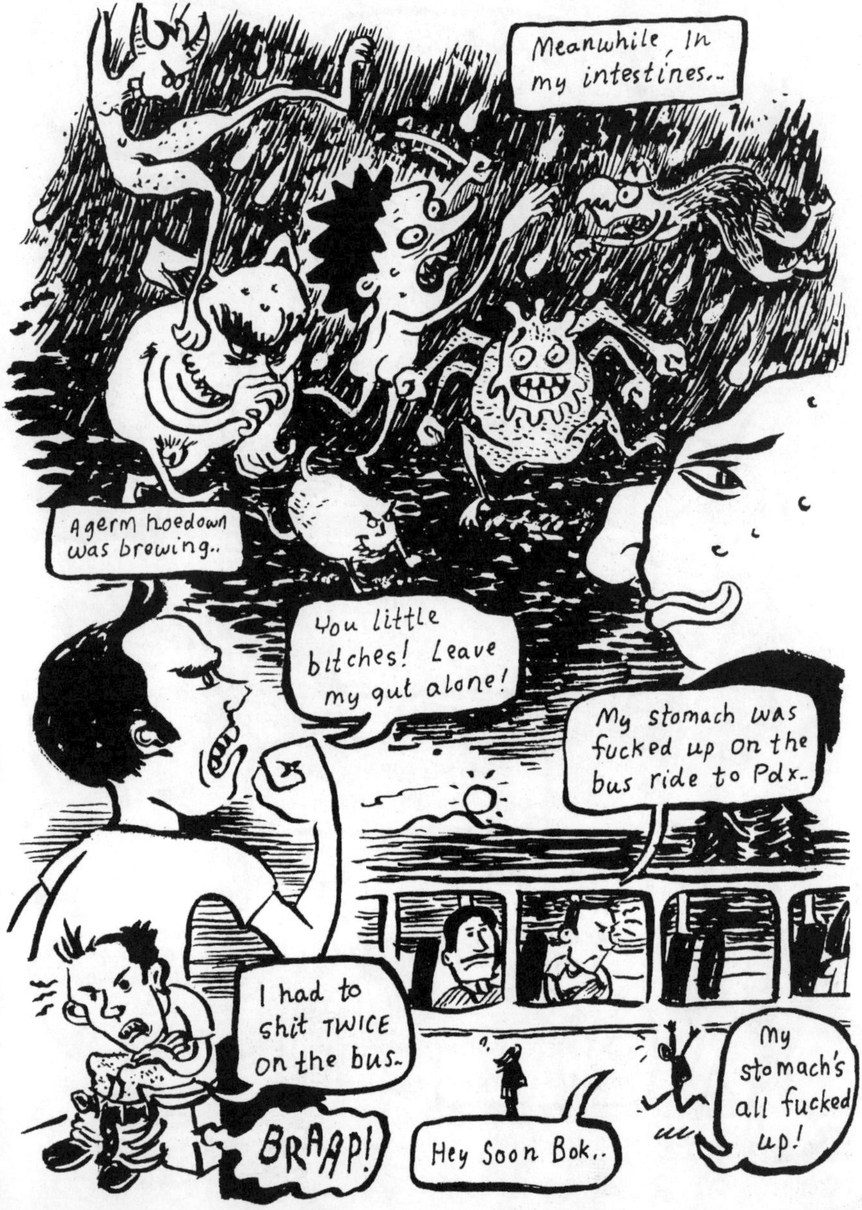
Meanwhile, In my intestines..
Agerm hoedown was brewing..
You little bitches! Leave my gut alone!
My stomach was fucked up on the bus ride to Pdx..
I had to shit TWICE on the bus..
BRAAP!
Hey Soon Bok..
My stomach's all fucked up!

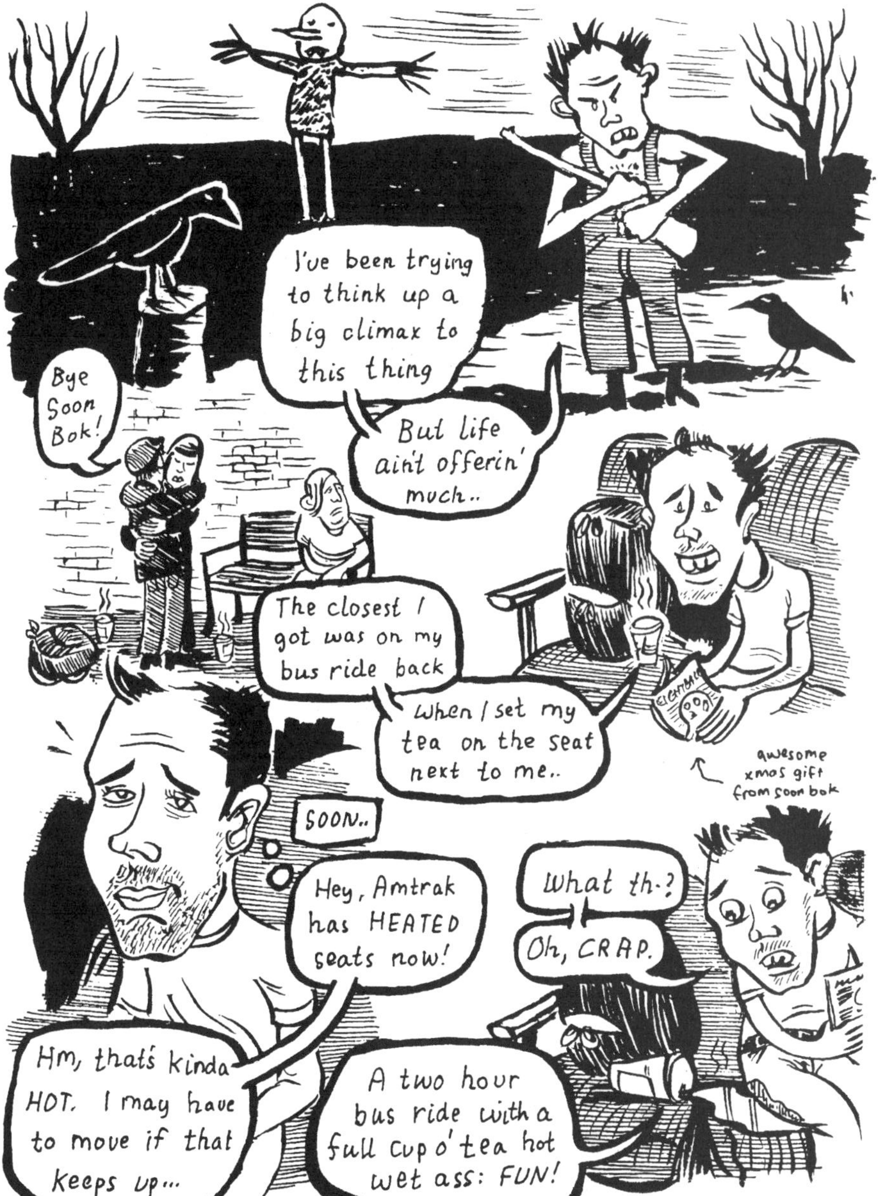
I've been trying to think up a big climax to this thing
But life ain't offerin' much..
Bye Soon Bok!
The closest I got was on my bus ride back
When I set my tea on the seat next to me..
awesome xmas gift from soon bok
SOON..
Hey, Amtrak has HEATED seats now!
Hm, that's kinda HOT. I may have to move if that keeps up...
What th-?
Oh, CRAP.
A two hour bus ride with a full cup o' tea hot wet ass: FUN!

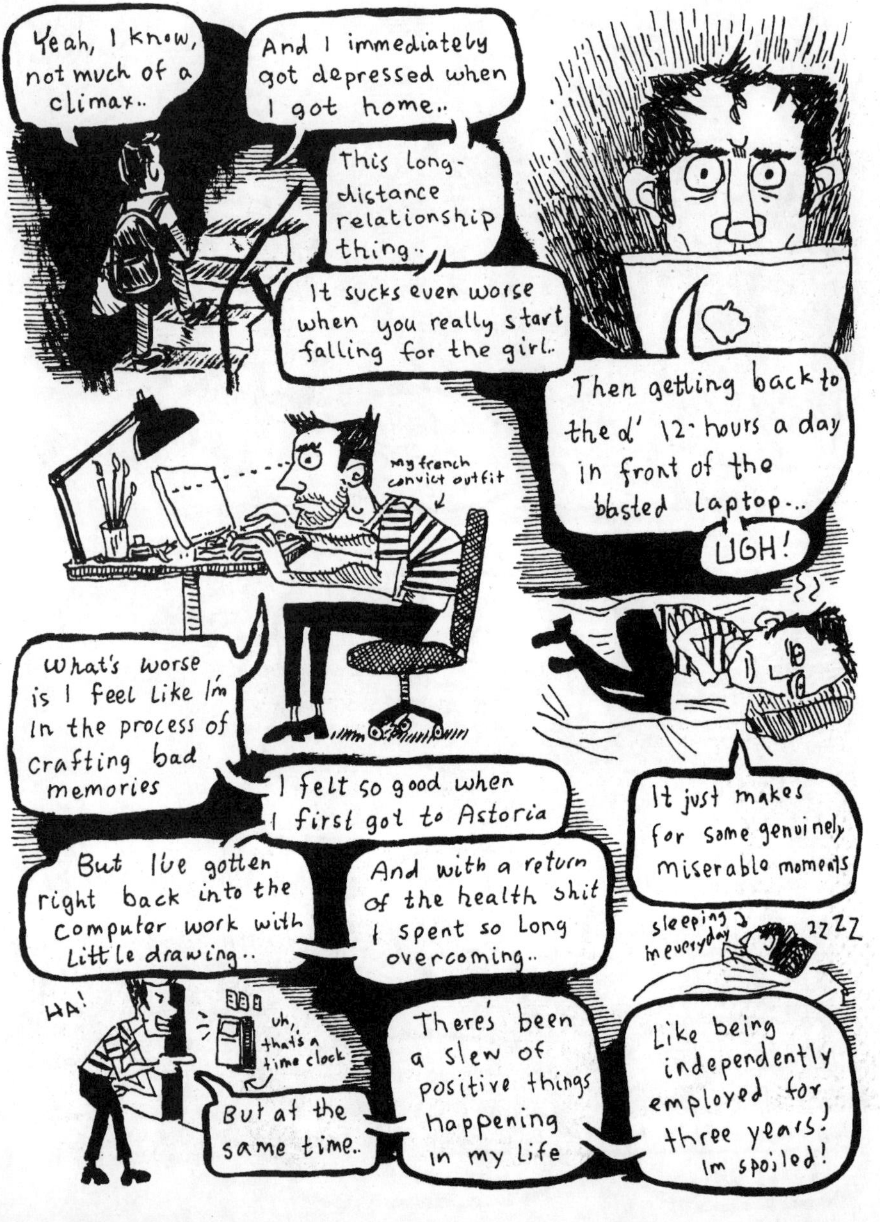

Yeah, I know, not much of a climax..
And I immediately got depressed when I got home..
This long-distance relationship thing..
It sucks even worse when you really start falling for the girl..
Then getting back to the ol' 12-hours a day in front of the blasted laptop...
UGH!
my french convict outfit
What's worse is I feel like I'm in the process of crafting bad memories
I felt so good when I first got to Astoria
It just makes for some genuinely miserable moments
But I've gotten right back into the computer work with little drawing..
And with a return of the health shit I spent so long overcoming..
sleeping in everyday
ZZZ
HA!
uh, that's a time clock
But at the same time..
There's been a slew of positive things happening in my life
Like being independently employed for three years! Im spoiled!

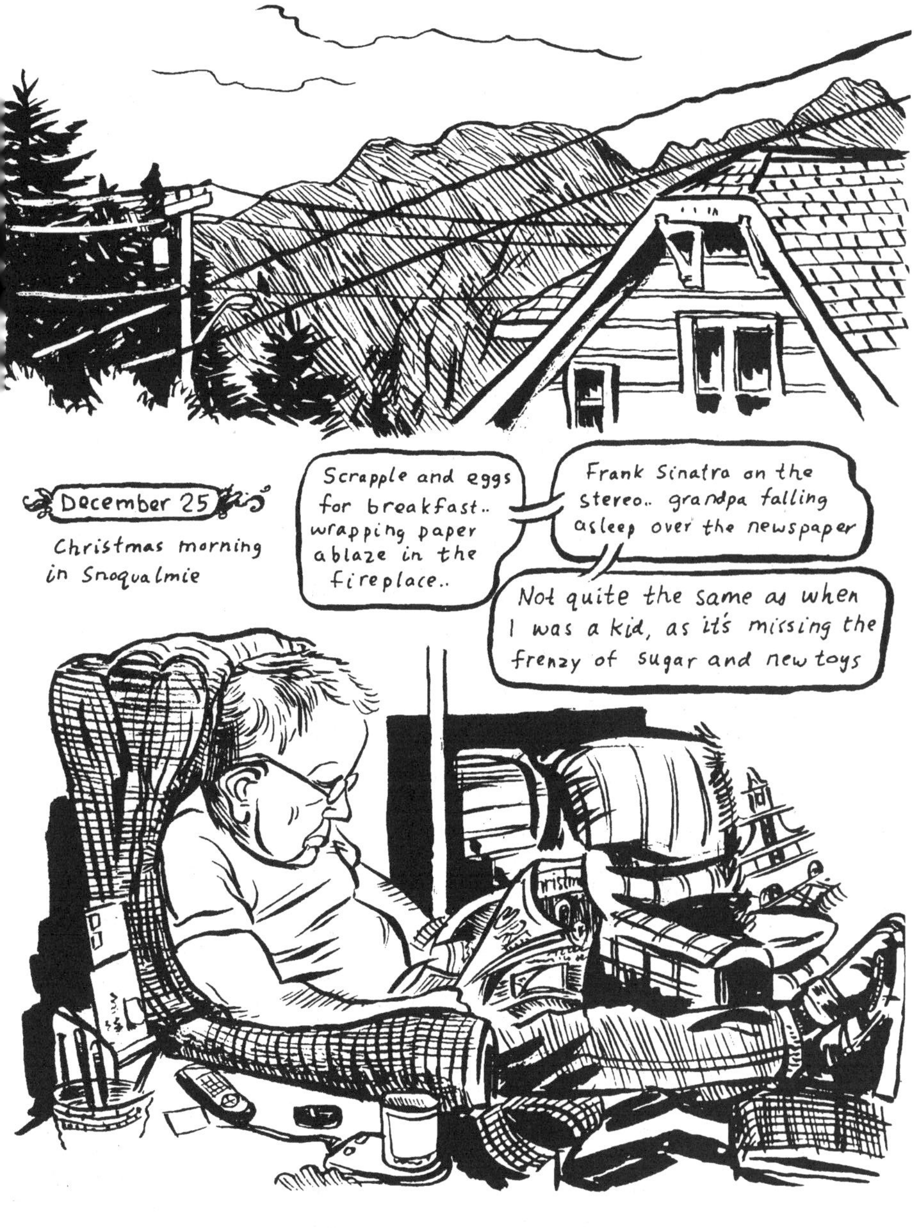
December 25
Christmas morning in Snoqualmie
Scrapple and eggs for breakfast.. wrapping paper ablaze in the fireplace..
Frank Sinatra on the stereo.. grandpa falling asleep over the newspaper
Not quite the same as when I was a kid, as it's missing the frenzy of sugar and new toys

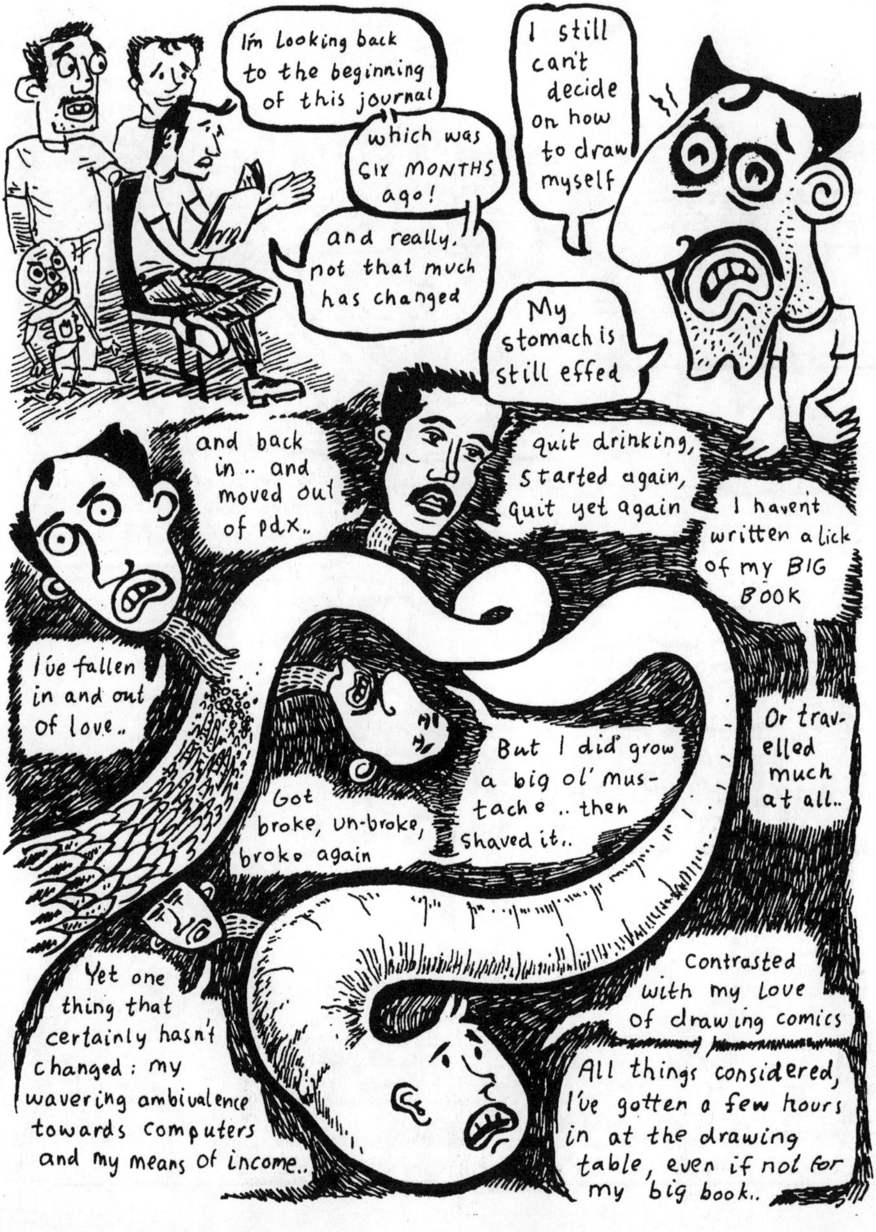
I'm Looking back to the beginning of this journal
which was SIX MONTHS ago!
and really, not that much has changed
I still can't decide on how to draw myself
My stomach is still effed
and back in .. and moved out of pdx..
quit drinking, started again, quit yet again
I havent written a lick of my BIG BOOK
I've fallen in and out of love..
Or travelled much at all..
But I did grow a big ol' mustache .. then shaved it..
Got broke, un-broke, broke again
Yet one thing that certainly hasn't changed: my wavering ambivalence towards computers and my means of income..
Contrasted with my Love of drawing comics
All things considered, I've gotten a few hours in at the drawing table, even if not for my big book..

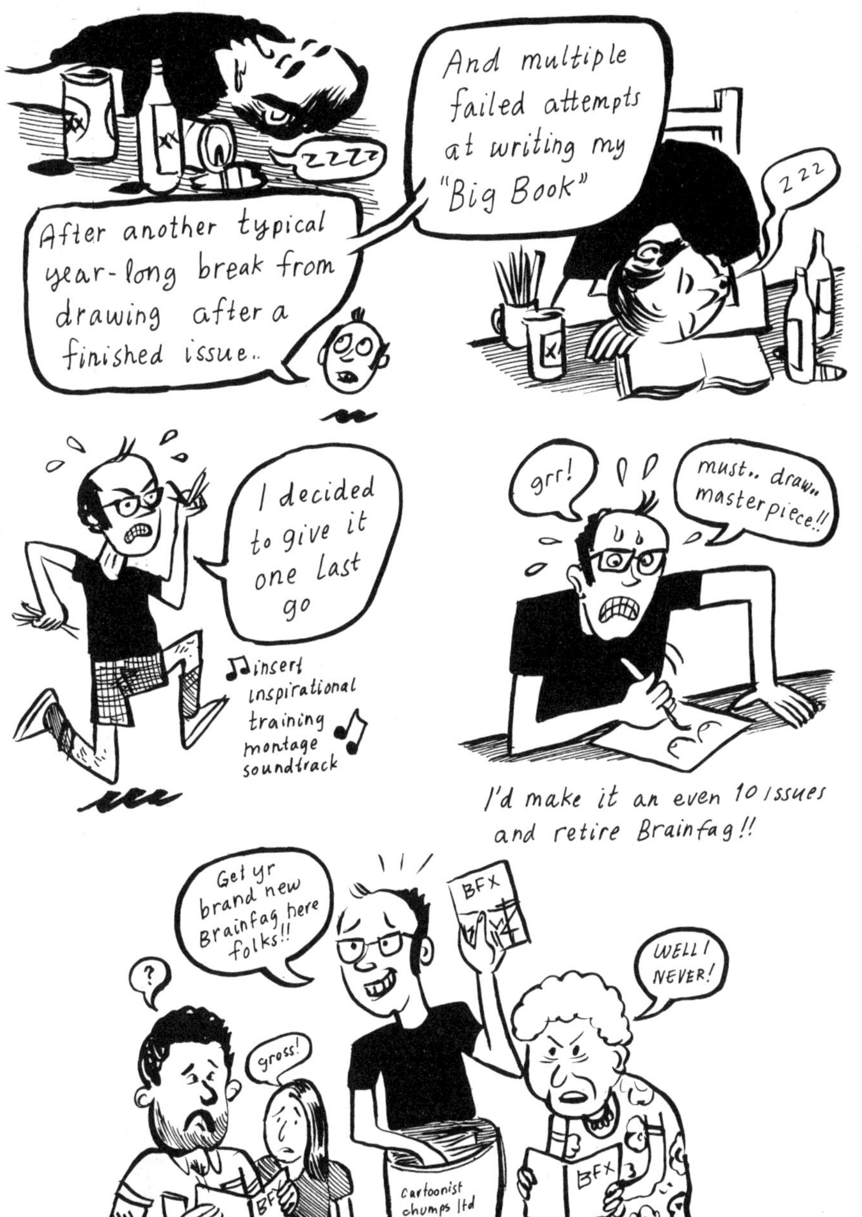
ZZZZ
After another typical year-long break from drawing after a finished issue..
And multiple failed attempts at writing my "Big Book"
ZZZ
I decided to give it one last go
insert inspirational training montage soundtrack
grr!
must.. draw.. masterpiece!!
I'd make it an even 10 issues and retire Brainfag!!
Get yr brand new Brainfag here folks!!
BFX
?
WELL I NEVER!
gross!
cartoonist chumps ltd
BFX
BFX 3

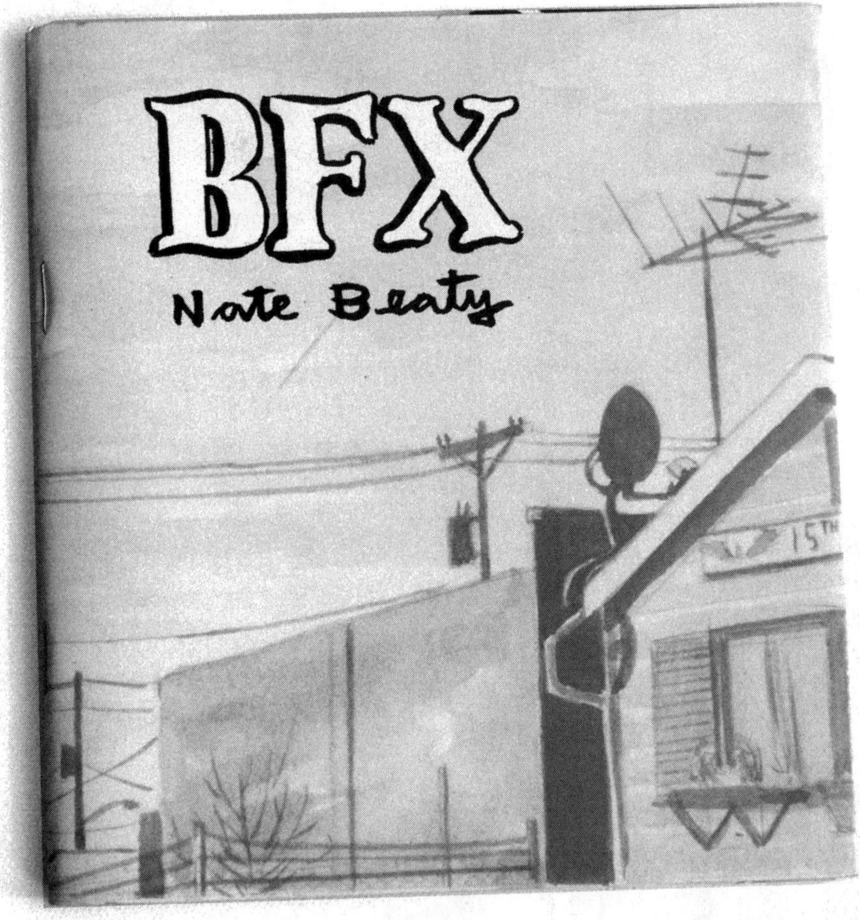
BFX
Nate Beaty
15TH

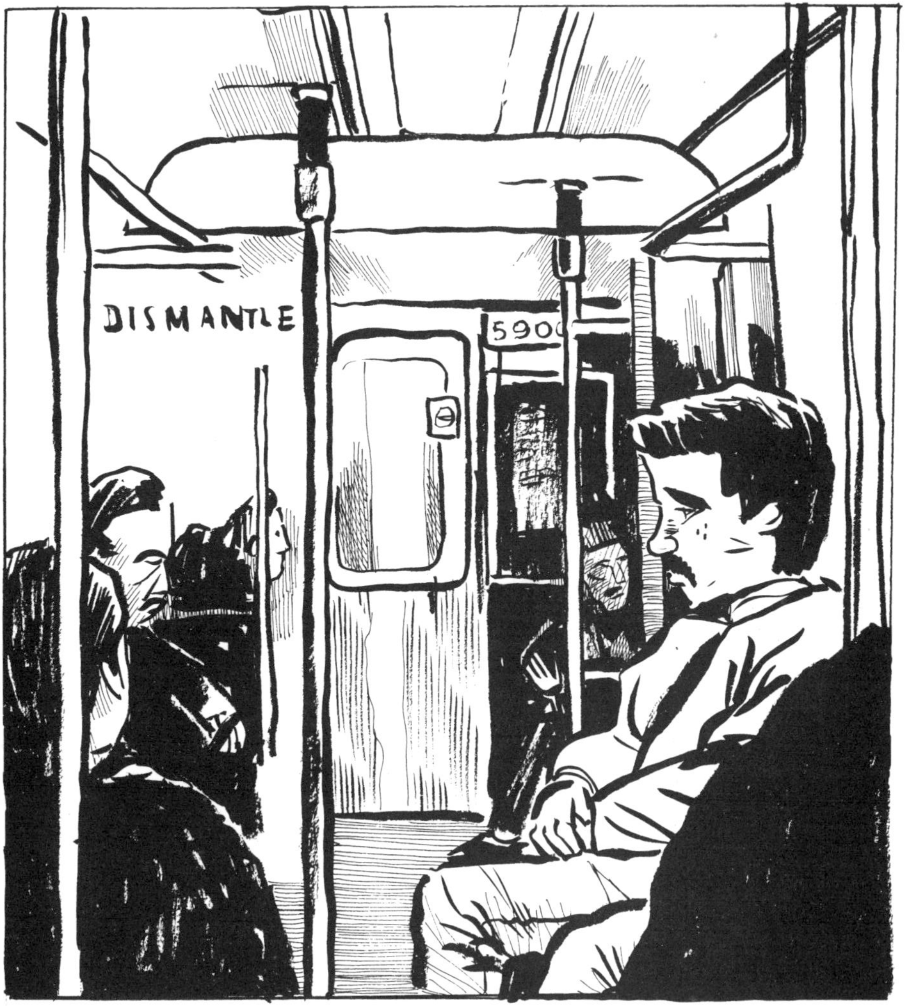
DISMANTLE
5900

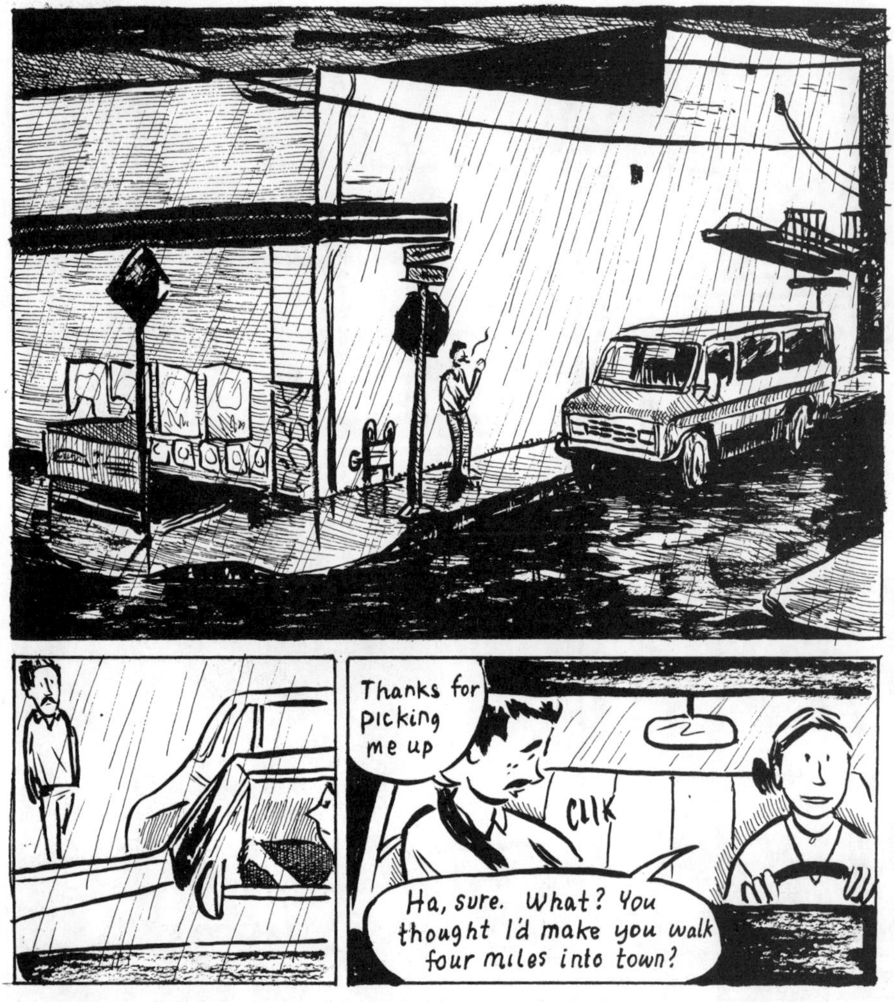
Thanks for picking me up
CLIK
Ha, sure. What? You thought I'd make you walk four miles into town?

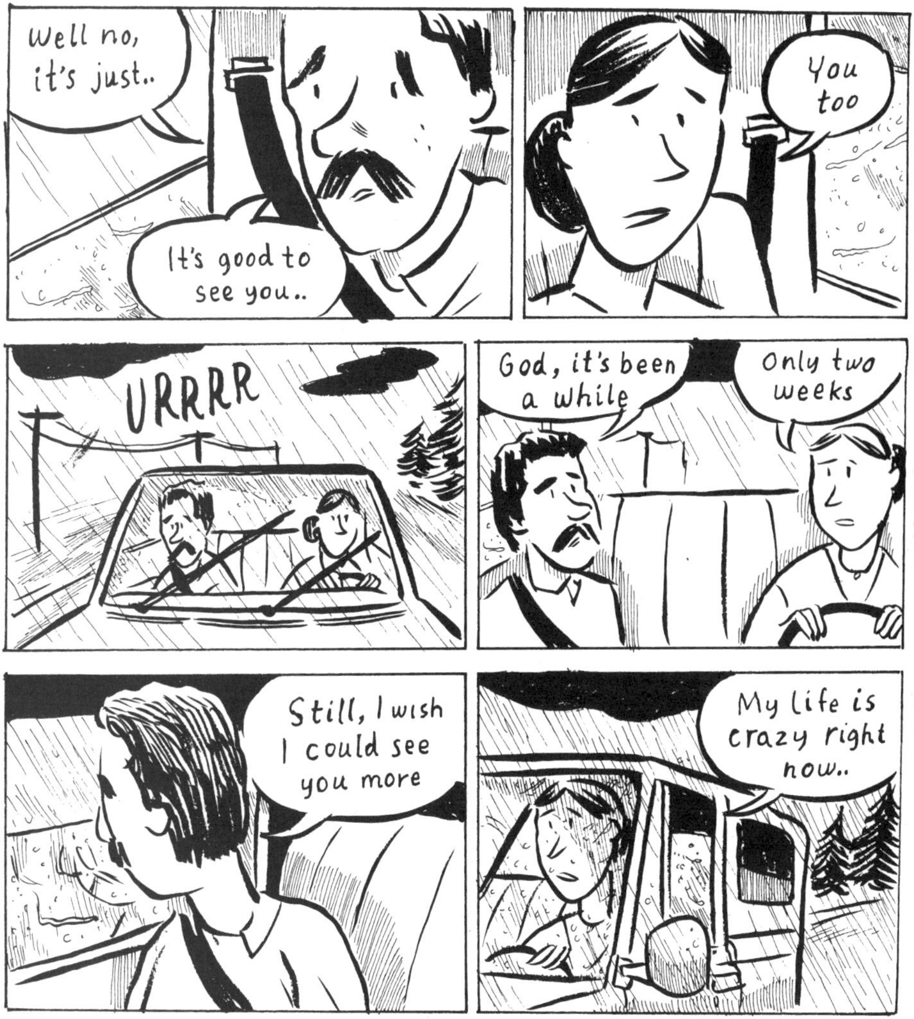
Well no, it's just..
It's good to see you..
You too
URRRR
God, it's been a while
Only two weeks
Still, I wish I could see you more
My life is crazy right now..

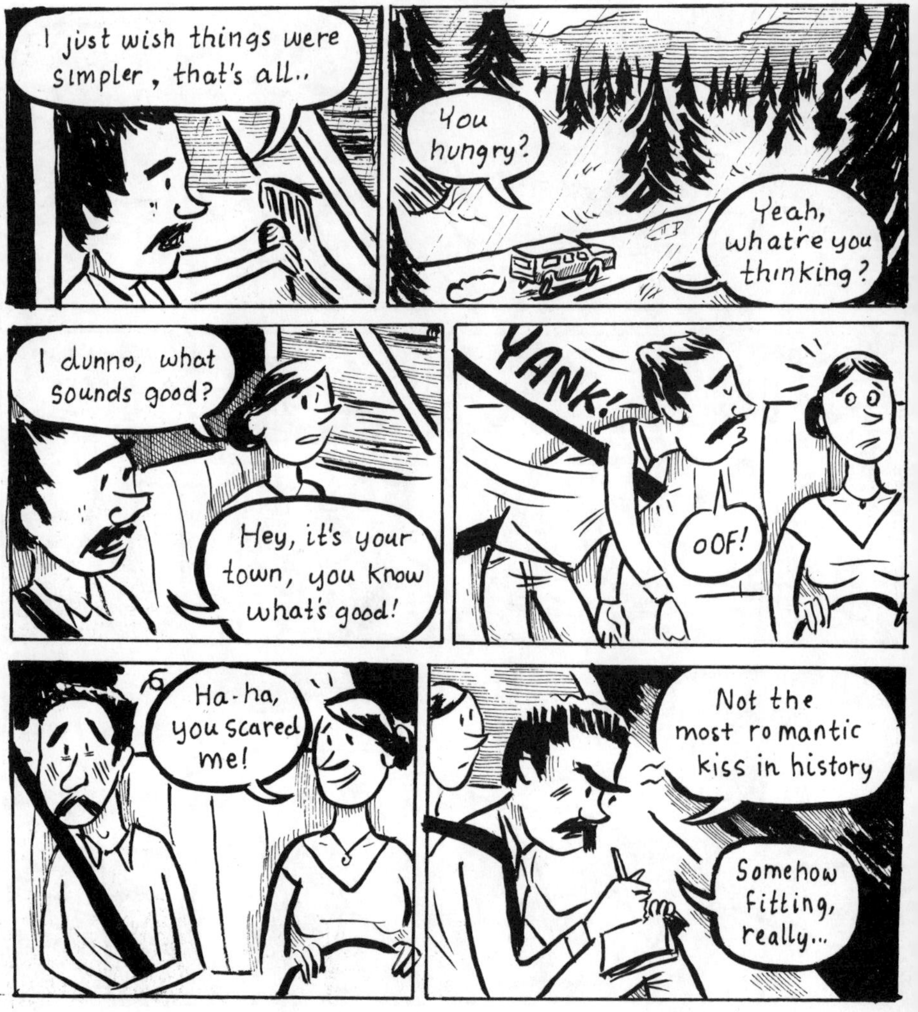
I just wish things were simpler, that's all..
You hungry?
Yeah, whatre you thinking?
I dunno, what sounds good?
Hey, it's your town, you know what's good!
YANK!
OOF!
Ha-ha, you scared me!
Not the most romantic kiss in history
Somehow fitting, really...

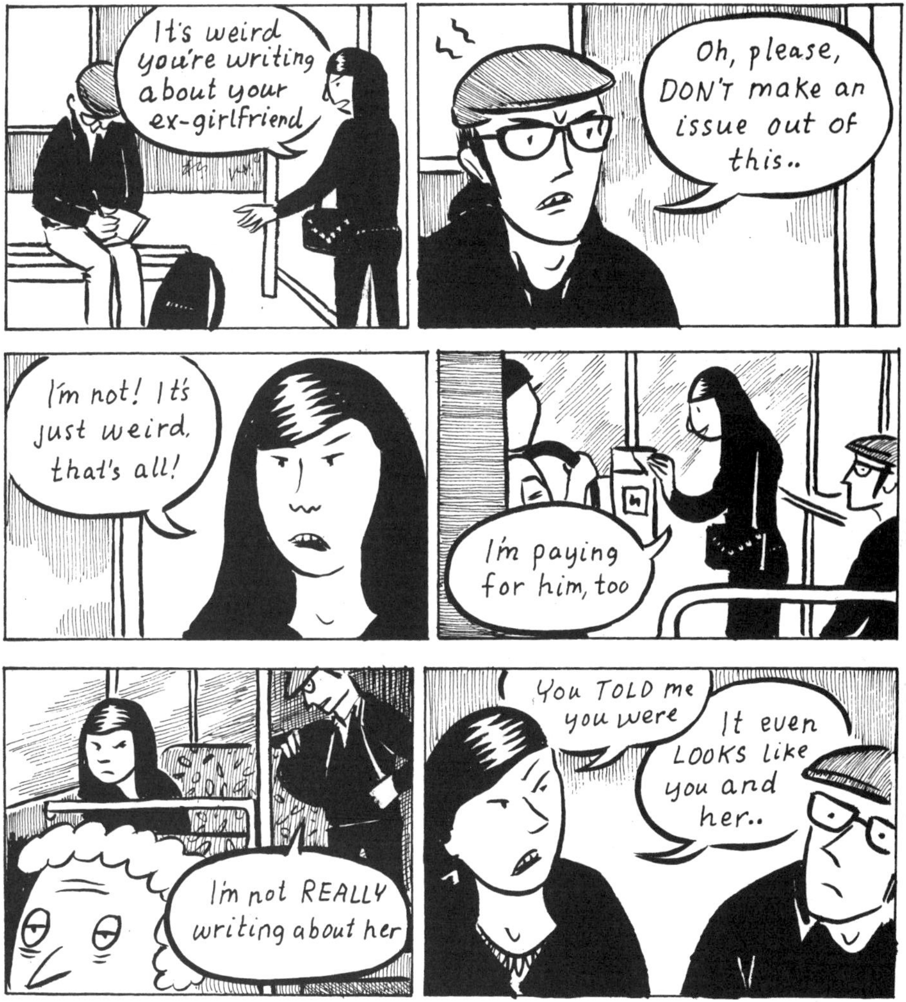
It's weird you're writing about your ex-girlfriend
Oh, please, DON'T make an issue out of this..
I'm not! It's just weird, that's all!
I'm paying for him, too
I'm not REALLY writing about her
You TOLD me you were
It even LOOKS like you and her..

What? I don't have a moustache and I'm not THAT ugly!
Ha ha!
Is it gonna hurt?
KOJIS
Bla bla bla
?
Where's my food?
It's ok! You can draw!
You sure?

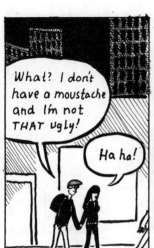

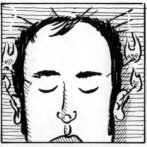

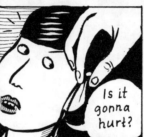

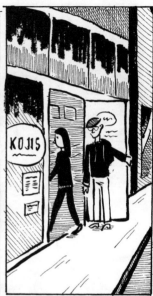

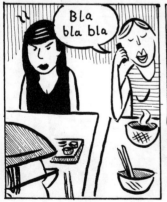

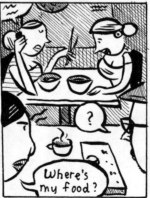

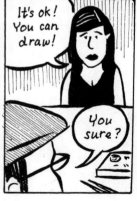

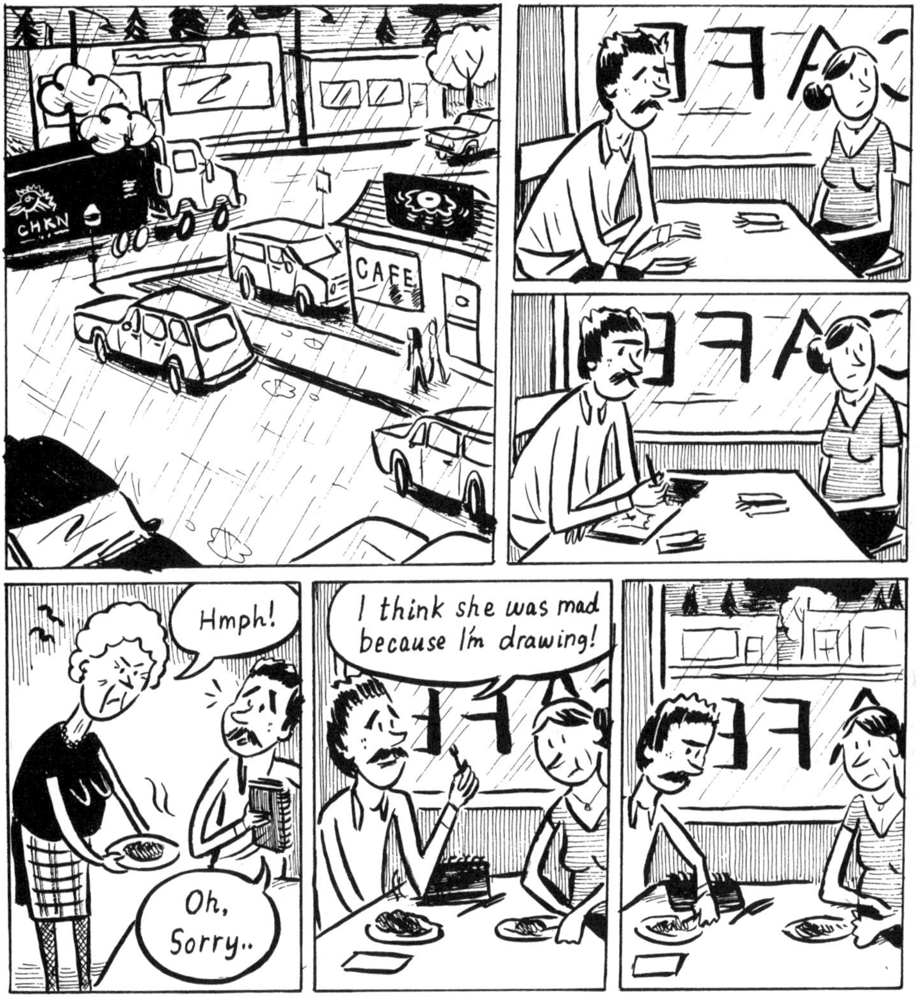
CHKN
CAFE
Hmph!
Oh, Sorry..
I think she was mad because I'm drawing!

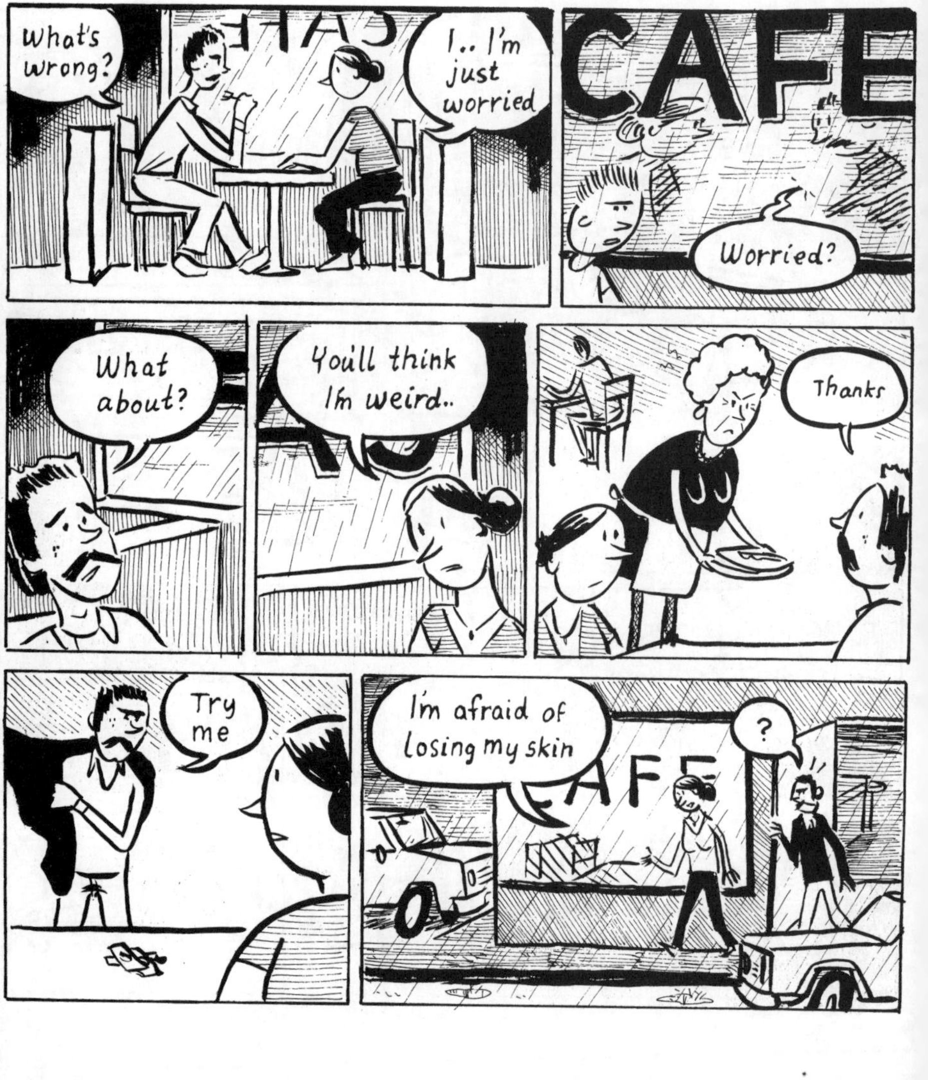
What's wrong?
I.. I'm just worried
CAFE
Worried?
What about?
You'll think I'm weird..
Thanks
Try me
I'm afraid of losing my skin
?
CAFE

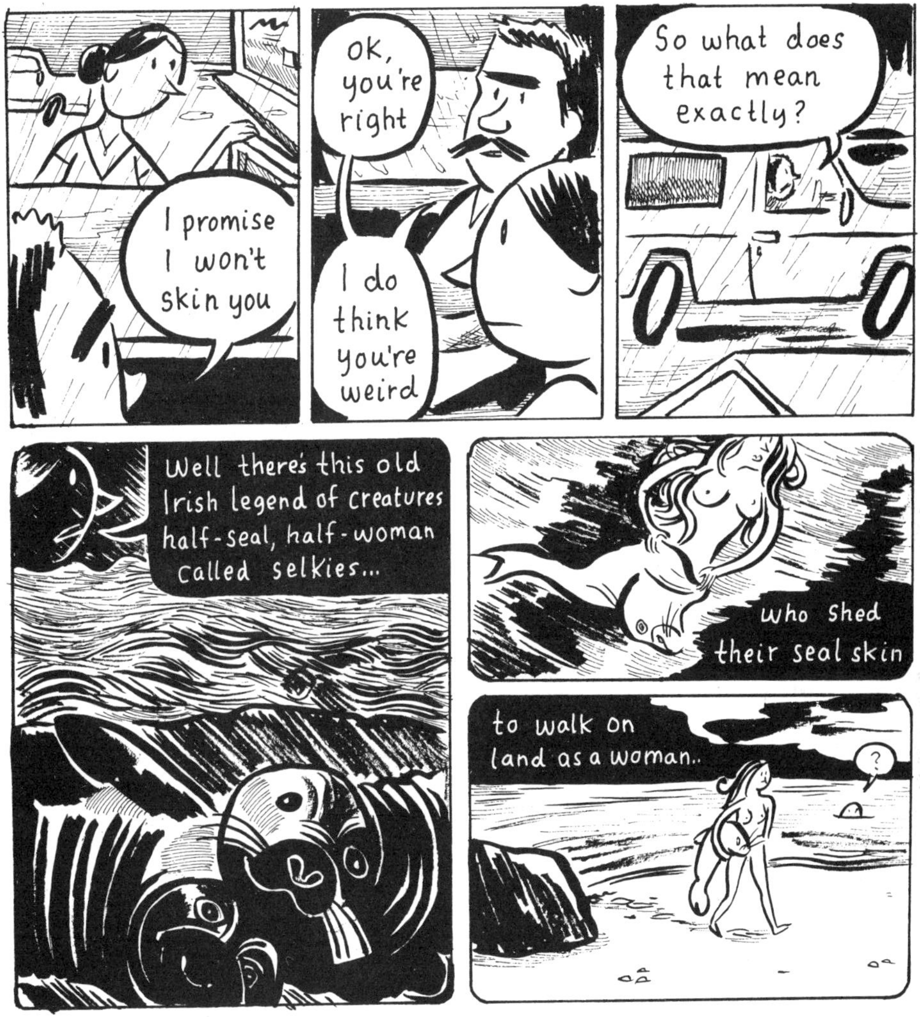
I promise I won't skin you
ok, you're right
I do think you're weird
So what does that mean exactly?
Well there's this old Irish legend of creatures half-seal, half-woman called selkies...
who shed their seal skin
to walk on land as a woman..
?

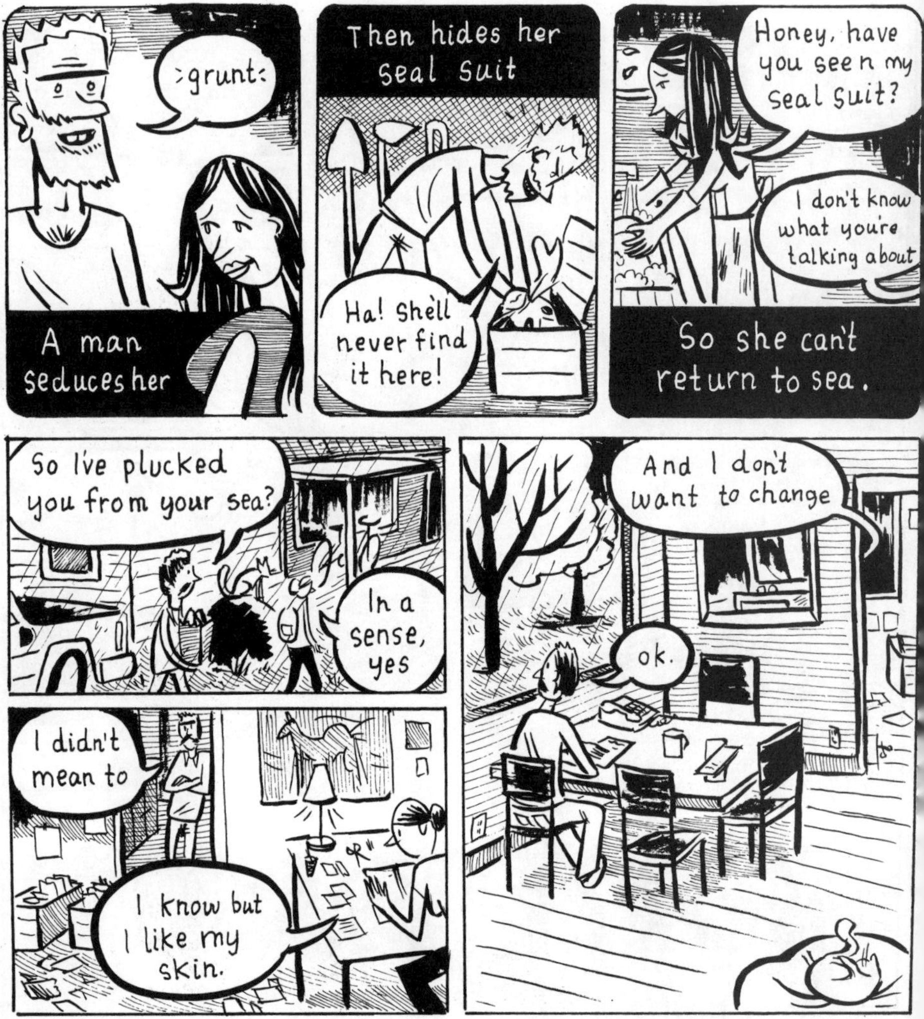

:grunt:
A man seduces her
Then hides her seal suit
Ha! She'll never find it here!
Honey, have you seen my seal suit?
I don't know what you're talking about
So she can't return to sea.
So I've plucked you from your sea?
In a sense, yes
And I don't want to change
ok.
I didn't mean to
I know but I like my skin.

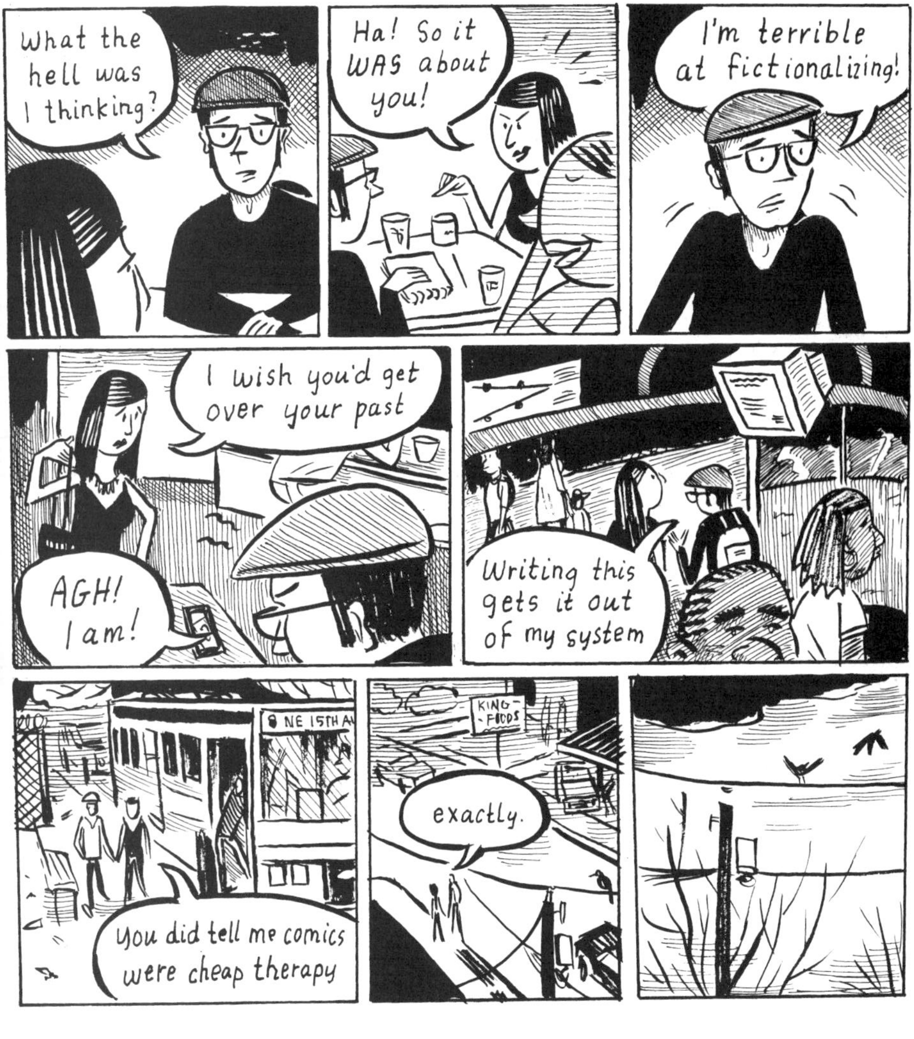

What the hell was I thinking?
Ha! So it WAS about you!
I'm terrible at fictionalizing!
I wish you'd get over your past
AGH! I am!
Writing this gets it out of my system
NE 15TH A
You did tell me comics were cheap therapy
KING-FOODS
exactly.

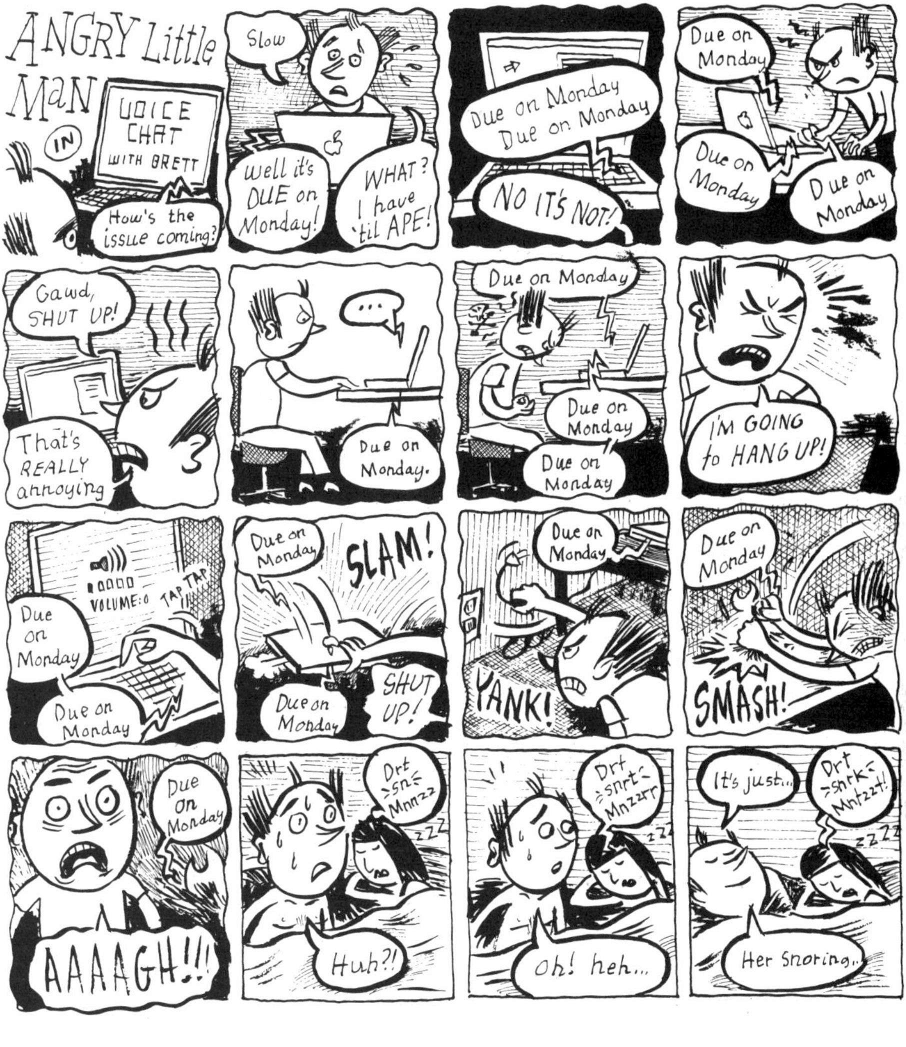

ANGRY Little Man
IN
VOICE CHAT WITH BRETT
How's the issue coming?
Slow
Well it's DUE on Monday!
WHAT? I have 'til APE!
Due on Monday Due on Monday
NO IT'S NOT!
Due on Monday
Due on Monday
Due on Monday
Gawd, SHUT UP!
That's REALLY annoying
...
Due on Monday.
Due on Monday
Due on Monday
Due on Monday
I'M GOING to HANG UP!
VOLUME: 0
TAP TAP
Due on Monday
Due on Monday
Due on Monday
SLAM!
Due on Monday
SHUT UP!
Due on Monday
YANK!
Due on Monday
SMASH!
Due on Monday
AAAAGH!!!
Drt sn Mnnzz
Huh?!
Drt snrt Mnzzrr
Oh! heh...
It's just...
Drt snrk Mntzzt!
Her snoring...

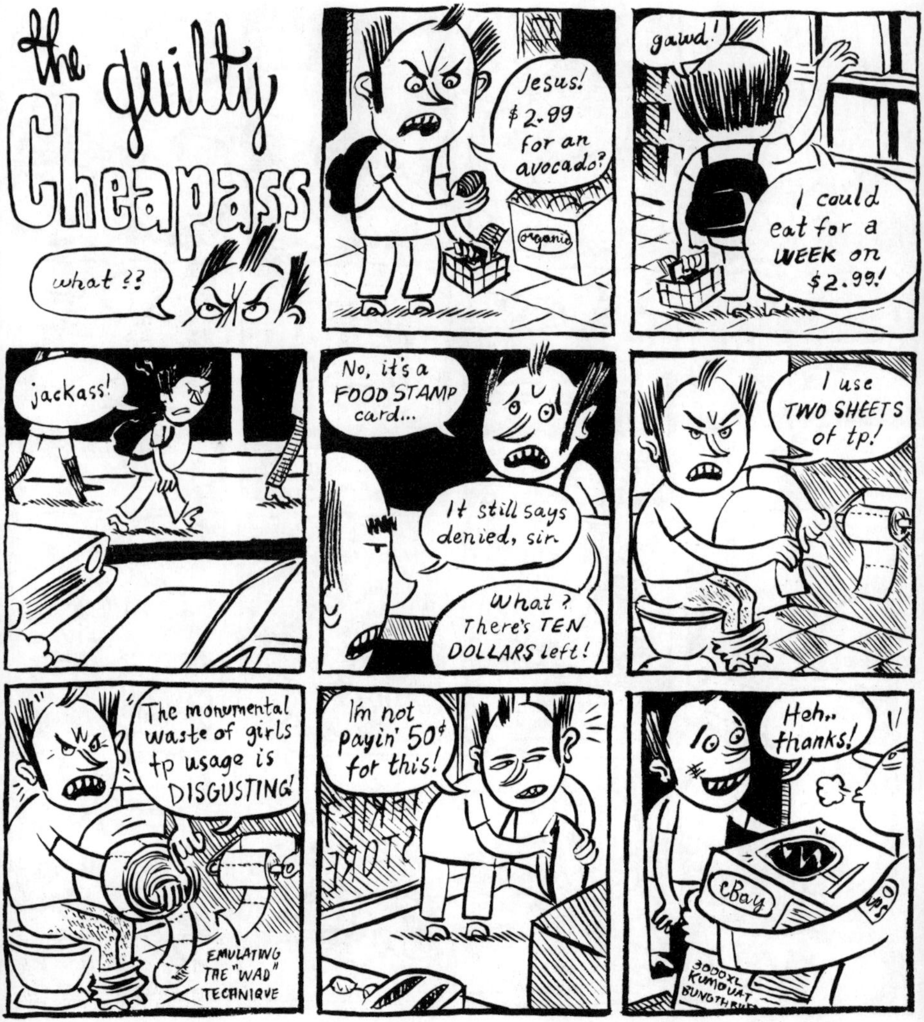
the guilty Cheapass
what ??
Jesus! $2.99 for an avocado?
organic
gawd!
I could eat for a WEEK on $2.99!
jackass!
No, it's a FOOD STAMP card...
It still says denied, sir
What? There's TEN DOLLARS left!
I use TWO SHEETS of tp!
The monumental waste of girls tp usage is DISGUSTING!
EMULATING THE "WAD" TECHNIQUE
I'm not payin' 50¢ for this!
Heh.. thanks!
eBay
ups
3000XL
KUMQUAT

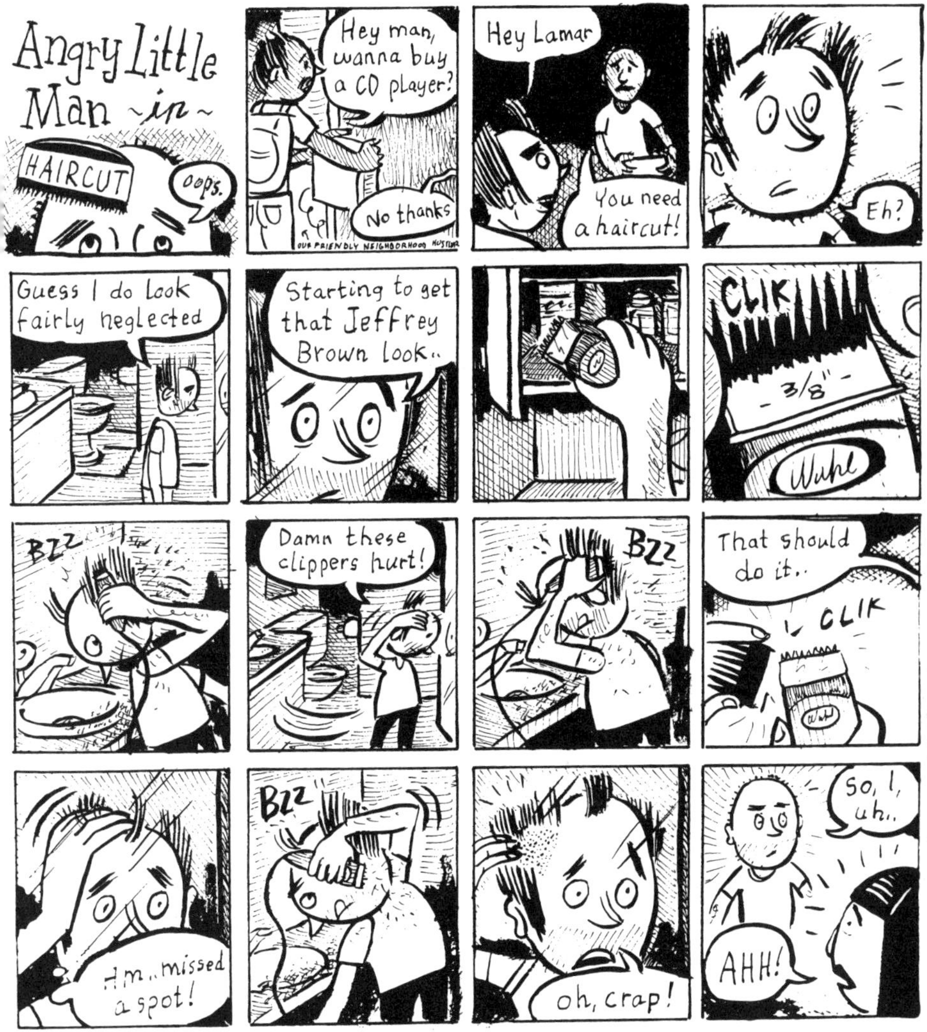
Angry Little Man ~in~
HAIRCUT
oops.
Hey man, wanna buy a CD player?
No thanks
OUR FRIENDLY NEIGHBORHOOD HUSTLER
Hey Lamar
You need a haircut!
Eh?
Guess I do look fairly neglected
Starting to get that Jeffrey Brown look..
CLIK
3/8"
Wahl
BZZ
Damn these clippers hurt!
BZZ
That should do it..
CLIK
Hm.. missed a spot!
BZZ
oh, crap!
So, I, uh..
AHH!

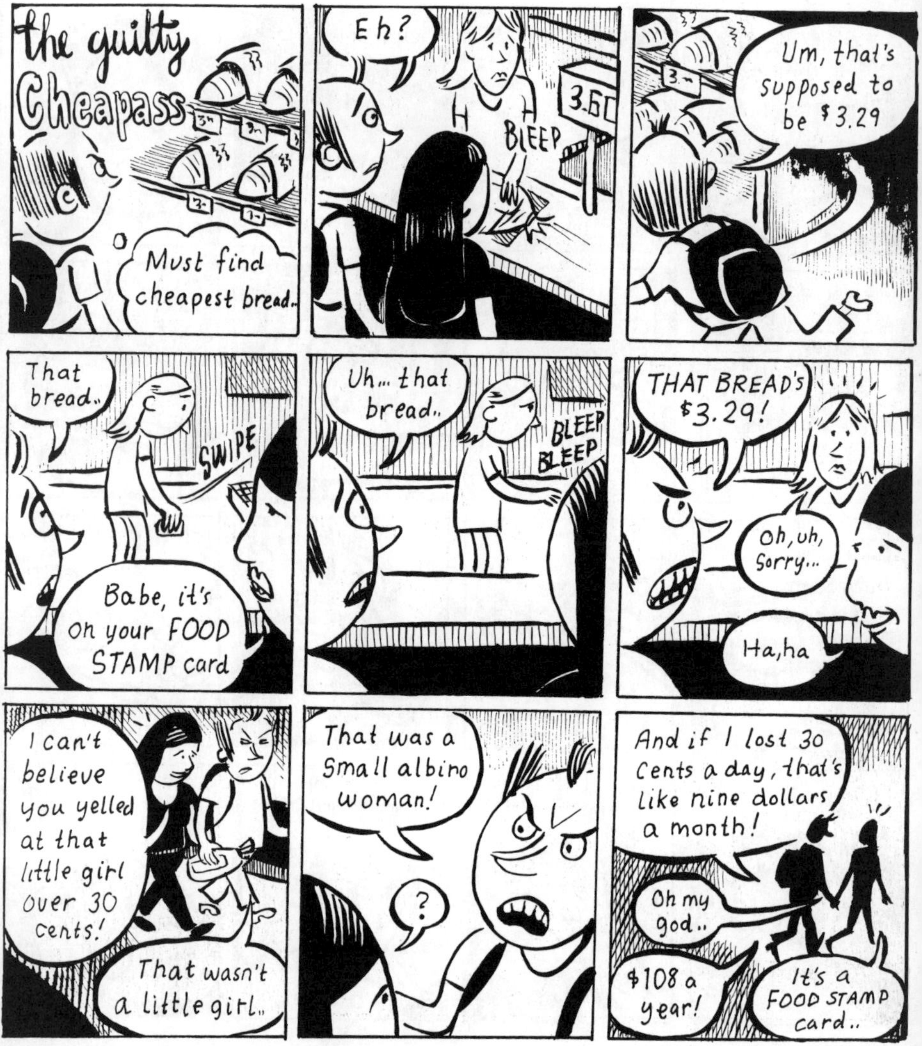
the guilty Cheapass
Must find cheapest bread..
Eh?
BLEEP
3.60
Um, that's supposed to be $3.29
That bread..
SWIPE
Babe, it's on your FOOD STAMP card
Uh... that bread..
BLEEP BLEEP
THAT BREAD'S $3.29!
Oh, uh, sorry...
Ha, ha
I can't believe you yelled at that little girl over 30 cents!
That wasn't a little girl..
That was a small albino woman!
?
And if I lost 30 cents a day, that's like nine dollars a month!
Oh my god..
$108 a year!
It's a FOOD STAMP card..

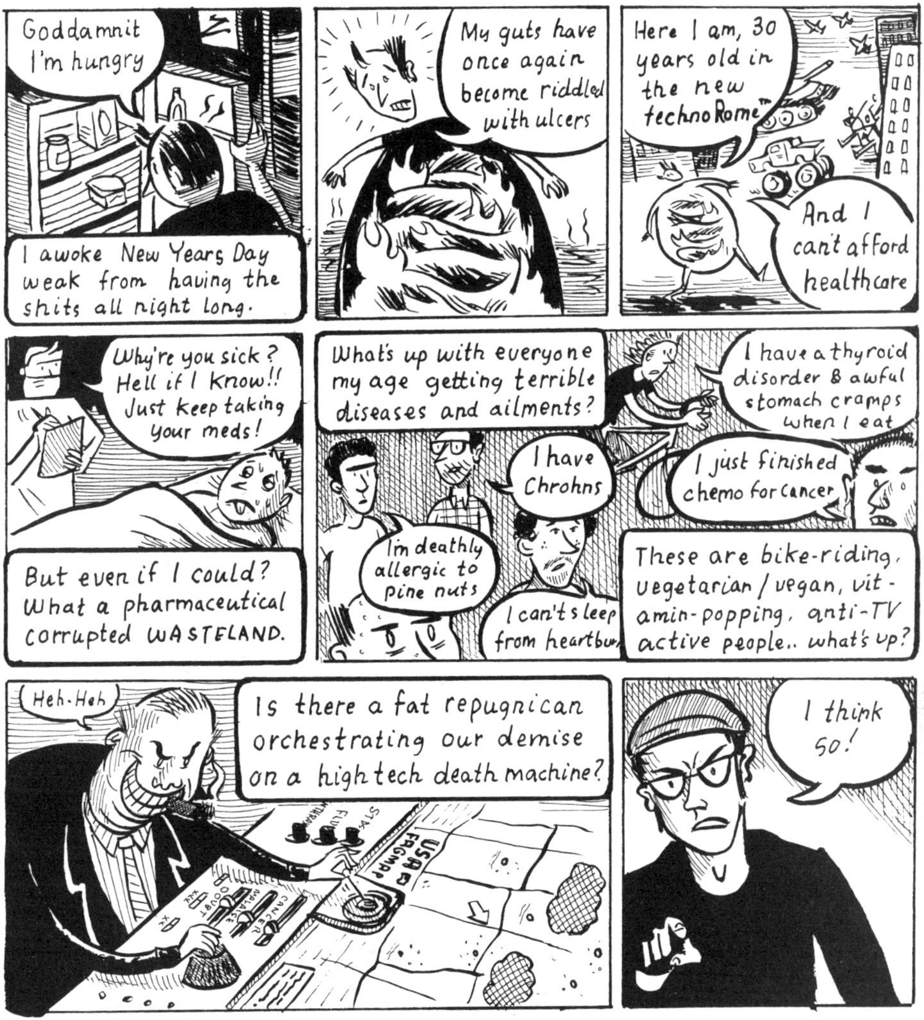
Goddamnit I'm hungry
I awoke New Years Day weak from having the shits all night long.
My guts have once again become riddled with ulcers
Here I am, 30 years old in the new technoRome™
And I can't afford healthcare
Why're you sick? Hell if I know!! Just keep taking your meds!
But even if I could? What a pharmaceutical corrupted WASTELAND.
What's up with everyone my age getting terrible diseases and ailments?
I have a thyroid disorder & awful stomach cramps when I eat
I have Chrohns
I just finished chemo for cancer
I'm deathly allergic to pine nuts
I can't sleep from heartburn
These are bike-riding, vegetarian / vegan, vit-amin-popping, anti-TV active people.. what's up?
Heh-Heh
Is there a fat repugnican orchestrating our demise on a high tech death machine?
CANCER
DOUBT
I think so!

Because last year I joined the ranks..
I was diagnosed with Ulcerative Colitis
Which is a lot like Crohns
An IBD① with urgent diarrhea, rapid weight loss and cramps
① INFLAMMATORY BOWEL DISEASE
FOOD
It's not pretty
It's not fun either
I decided to go to a new naturopath
ALAMED, CLINIC
Blind Onion
?
Come on in, Nathan
Have a seat
?!
I'm gonna read you a poem!
..I laid out pictures of you and rubbed against them..
It made me itch
Here's your prescription for prednisone and antibiotics
I then remembered why I self-medicate..

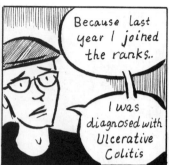

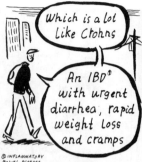

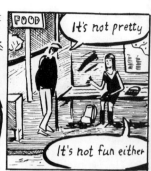

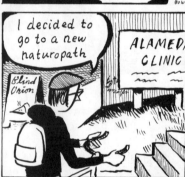

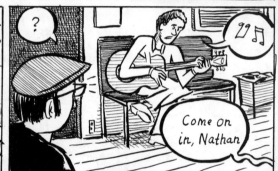

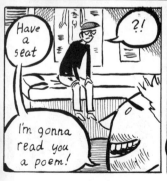

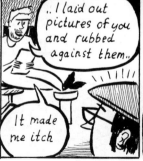

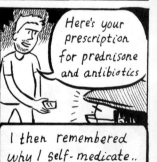

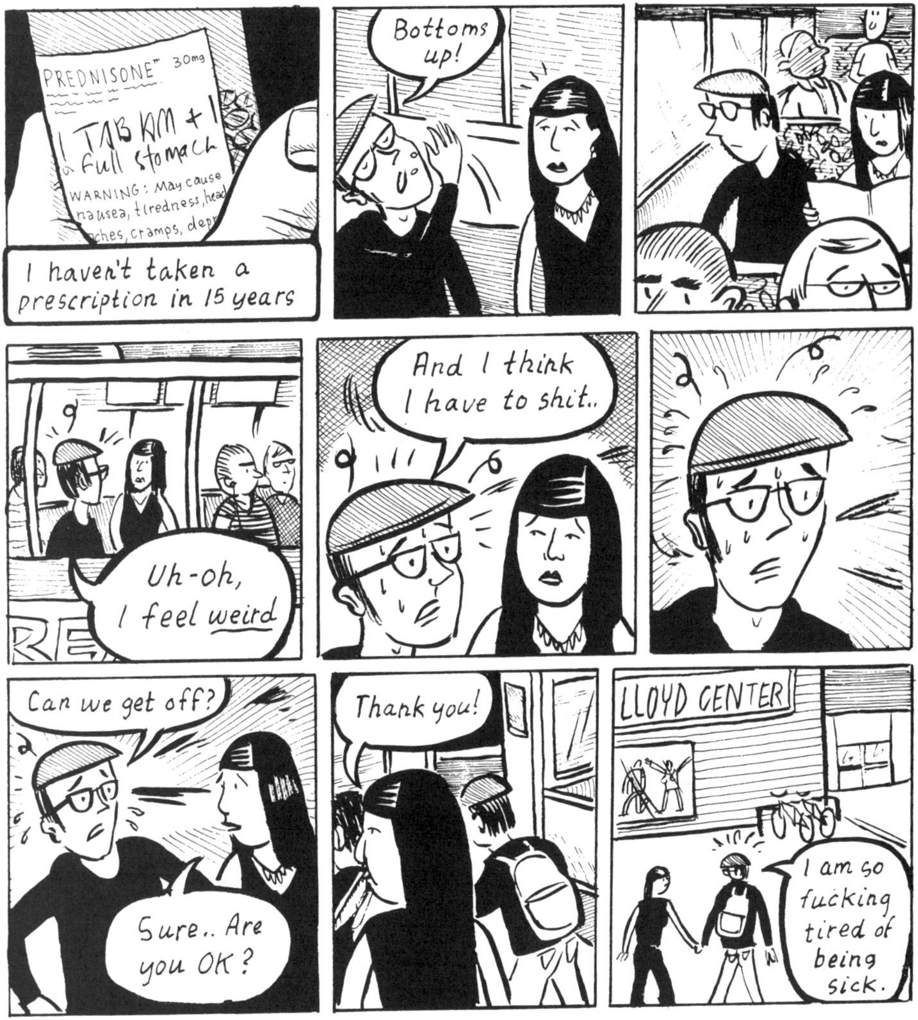

PREDNISONE™ 30mg
1 TAB AM + 1
full stomach
WARNING: May cause nausea, tiredness, headaches, cramps, dep
I haven't taken a prescription in 15 years
Bottoms up!
Uh-oh, I feel weird
And I think I have to shit..
Can we get off?
Sure.. Are you OK?
Thank you!
LLOYD CENTER
I am so fucking tired of being sick.

FOOT SPANK
FOREVER YOUNG AND HOT
Jesus! Four miles of mall just to find a shitter!
Gross!
McMeat $1
lovin' fat
46
WAH
STROOMS
Gak!
Never mind, I couldn't go!
?

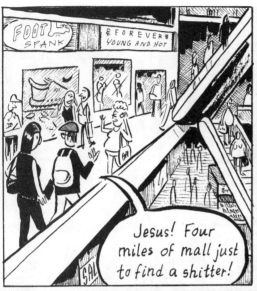

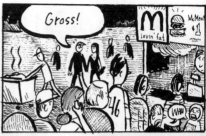

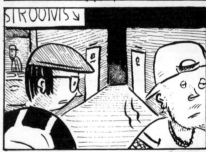

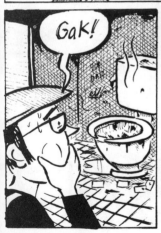

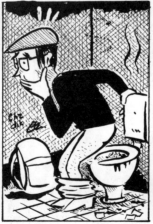

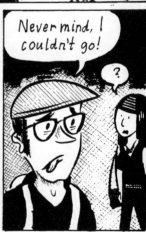

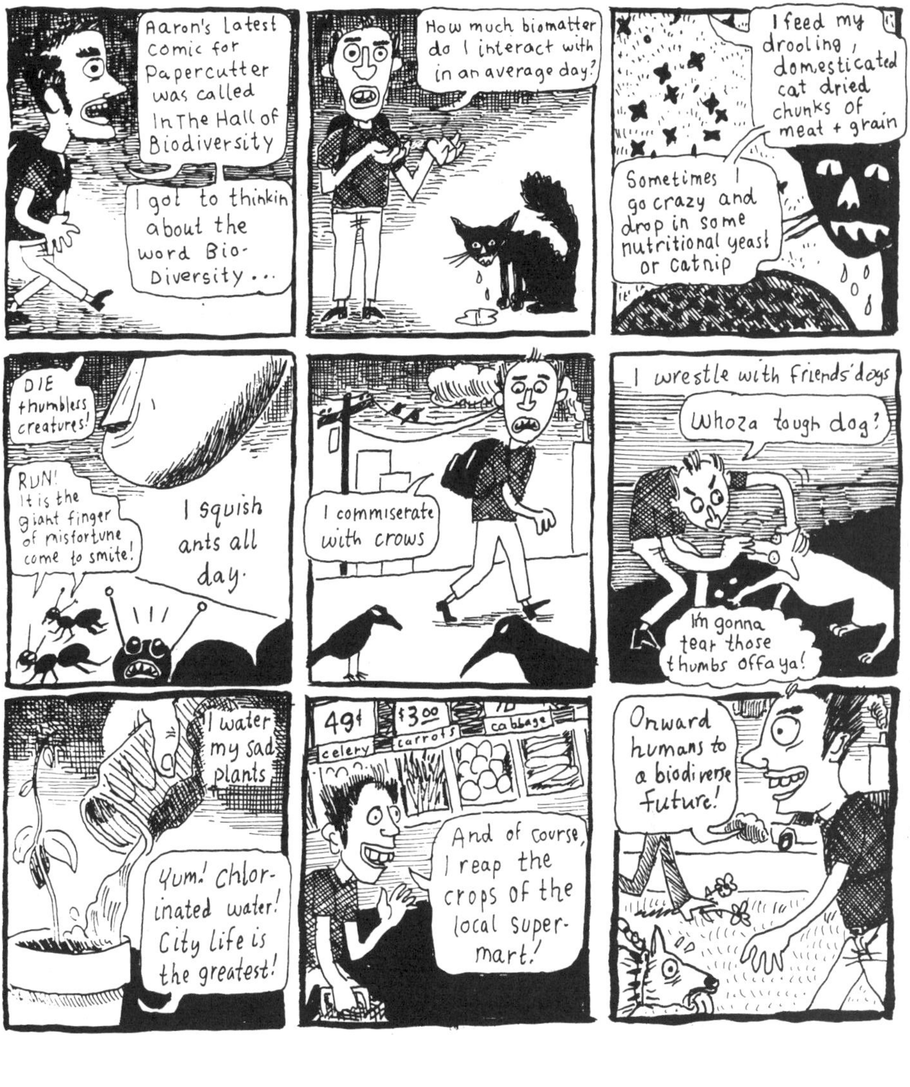
Aaron's latest comic for Papercutter was called In The Hall of Biodiversity
I got to thinkin about the word Bio-Diversity...
How much biomatter do I interact with in an average day?
I feed my drooling, domesticated cat dried chunks of meat + grain
Sometimes I go crazy and drop in some nutritional yeast or catnip
DIE thumbless creatures!
RUN! It is the giant finger of misfortune come to smite!
I squish ants all day.
I commiserate with crows
I wrestle with friends' dogs
Whoza tough dog?
I'm gonna tear those thumbs offa ya!
I water my sad plants
Yum! Chlor-inated water! City life is the greatest!
49¢
celery
$3.00
carrots
cabbage
And of course, I reap the crops of the local super-mart!
Onward humans to a biodiverse future!

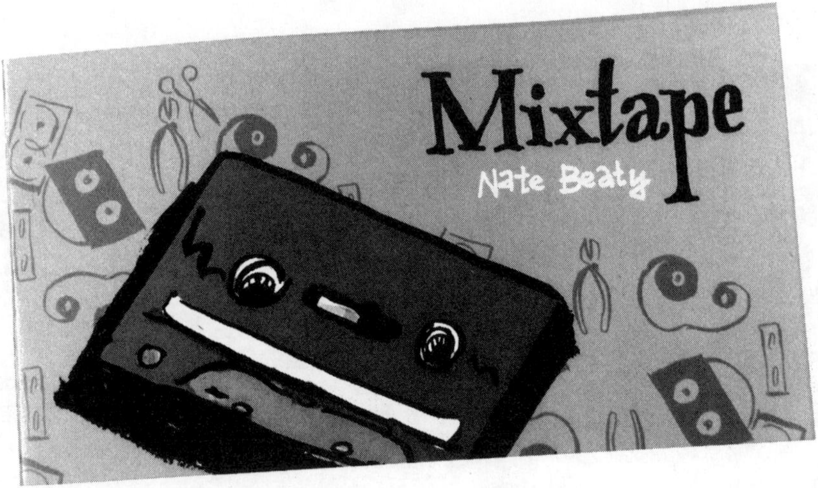
Mixtape
Nate Beaty

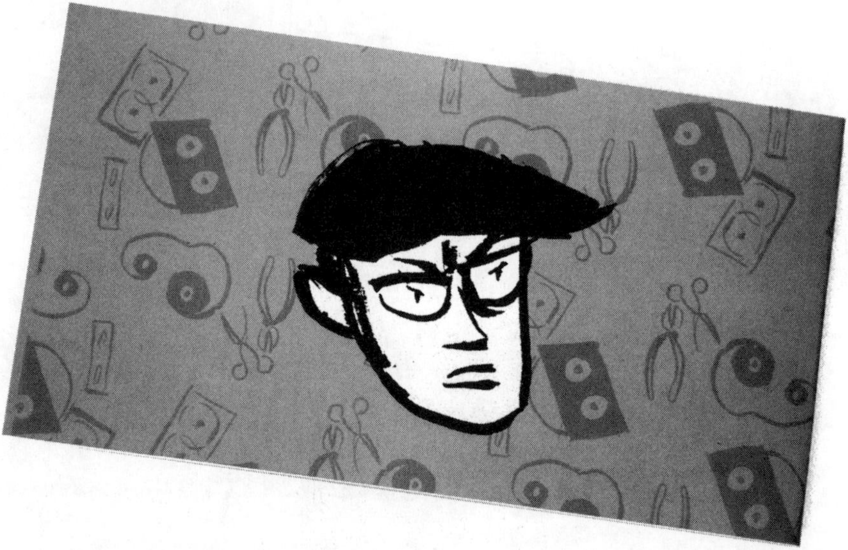

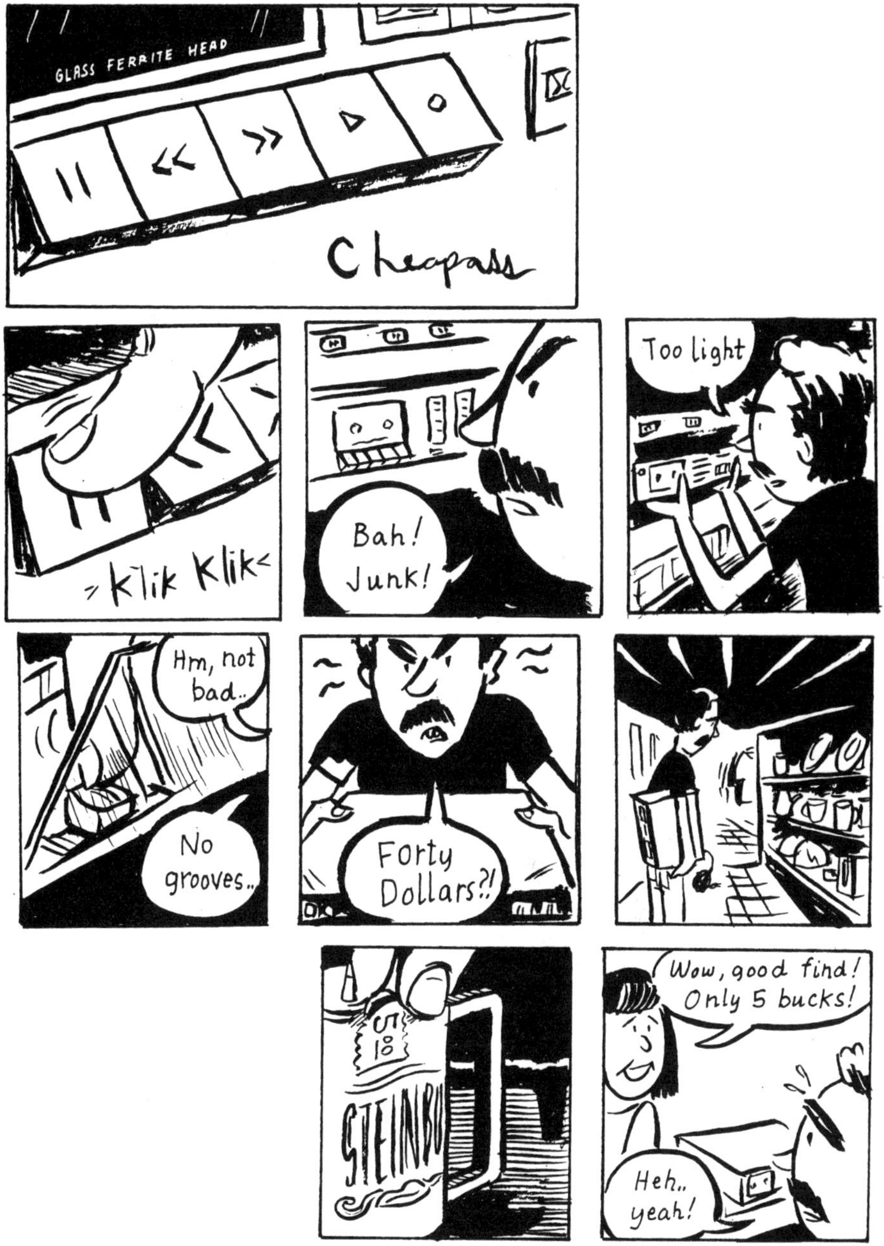
GLASS FERRITE HEAD
Cheapass
klik klik
Bah! Junk!
Too light
Hm, not bad..
No grooves..
Forty Dollars?!
STEINBU
Wow, good find! Only 5 bucks!
Heh.. yeah!

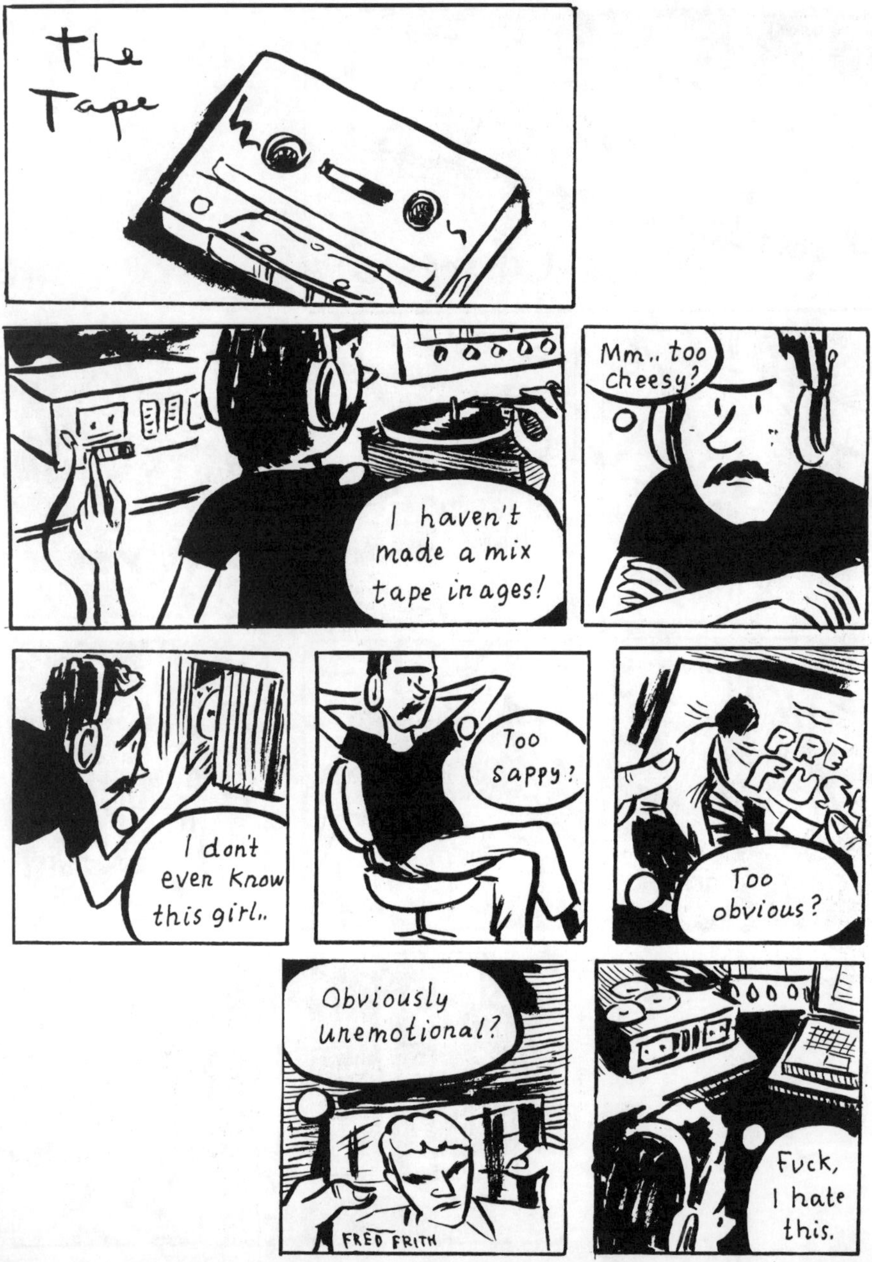
The Tape
I haven't made a mix tape in ages!
Mm.. too cheesy?
I don't even know this girl..
Too sappy?
Too obvious?
Obviously unemotional?
FRED FRITH
Fuck, I hate this.

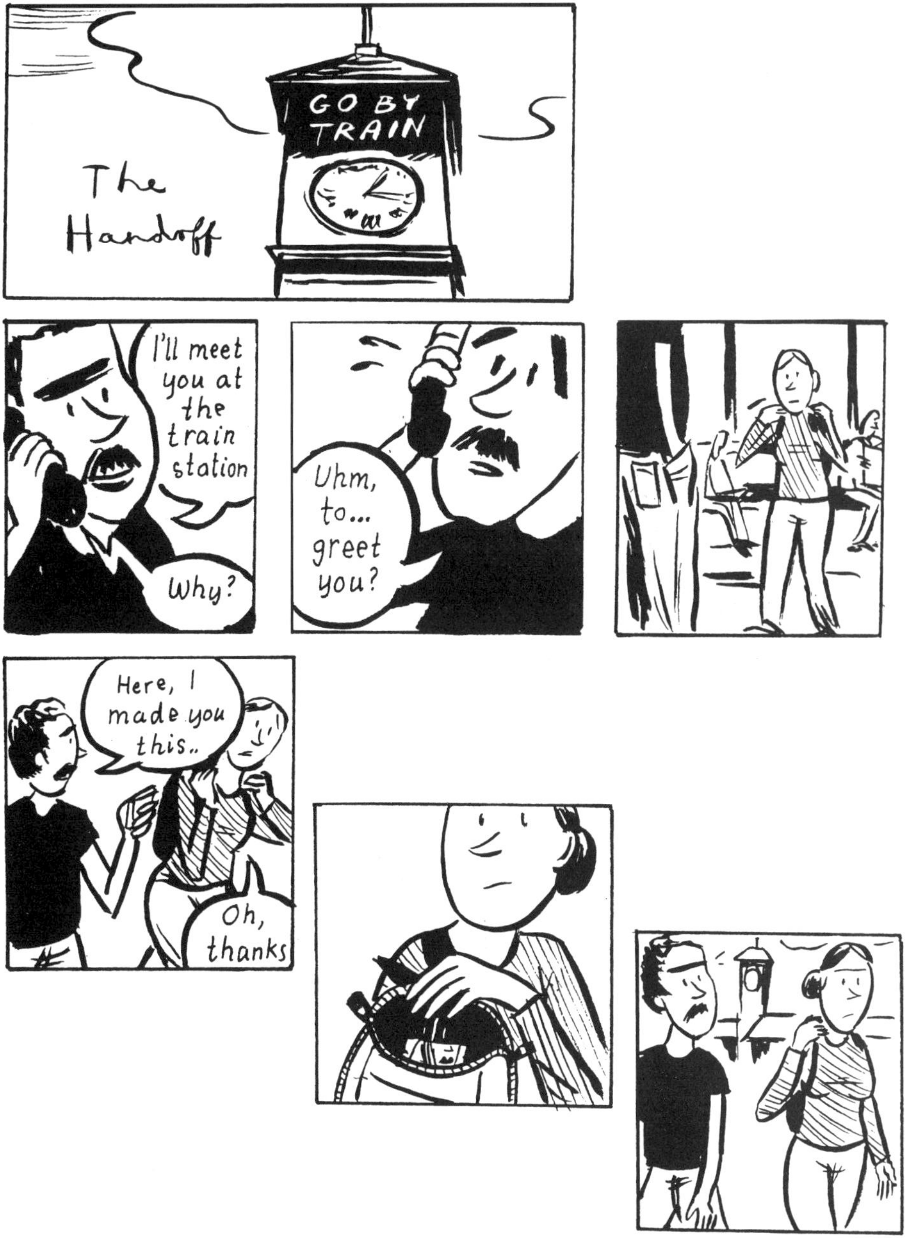
GO BY TRAIN
The Handoff
I'll meet you at the train station
Why?
Uhm, to... greet you?
Here, I made you this..
Oh, thanks

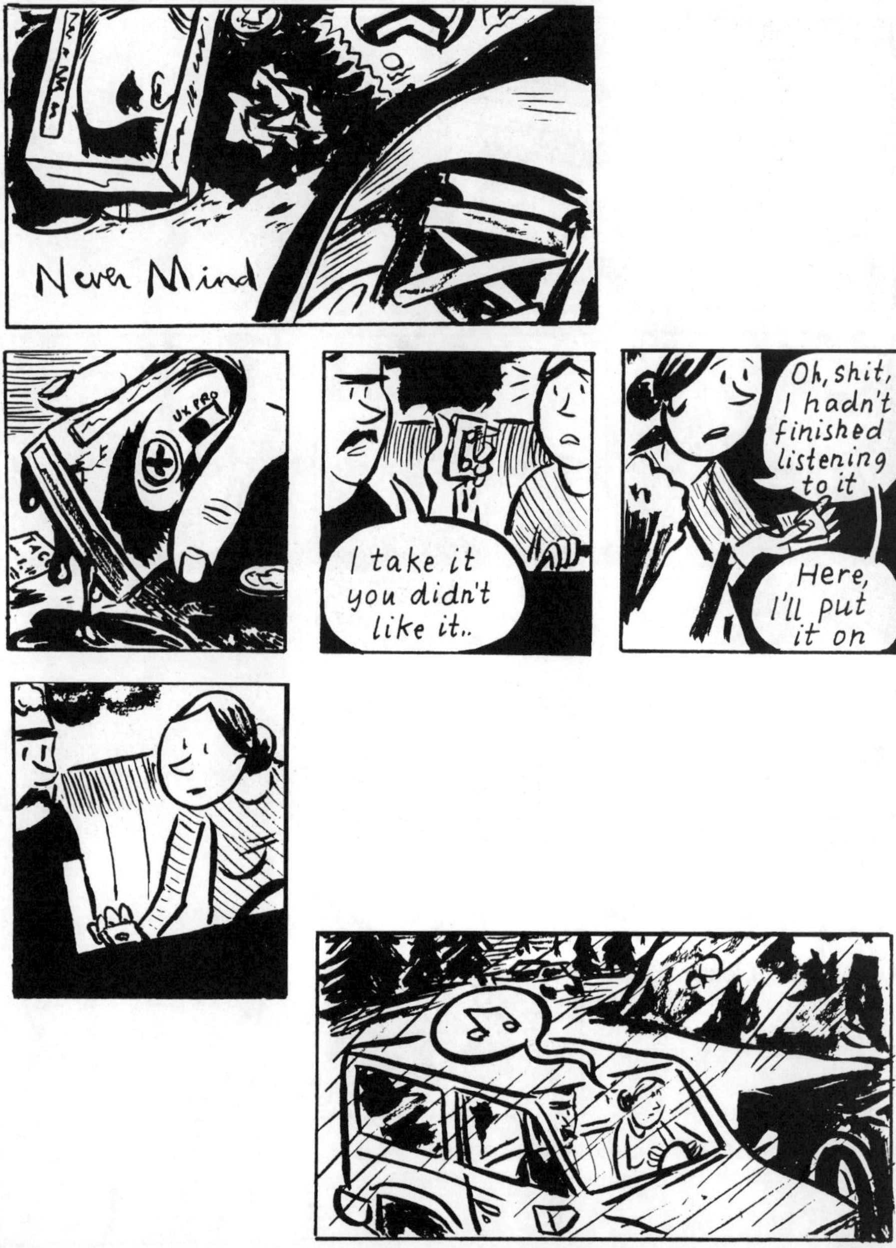
Never Mind
I take it you didn't like it..
Oh, shit, I hadn't finished listening to it
Here, I'll put it on

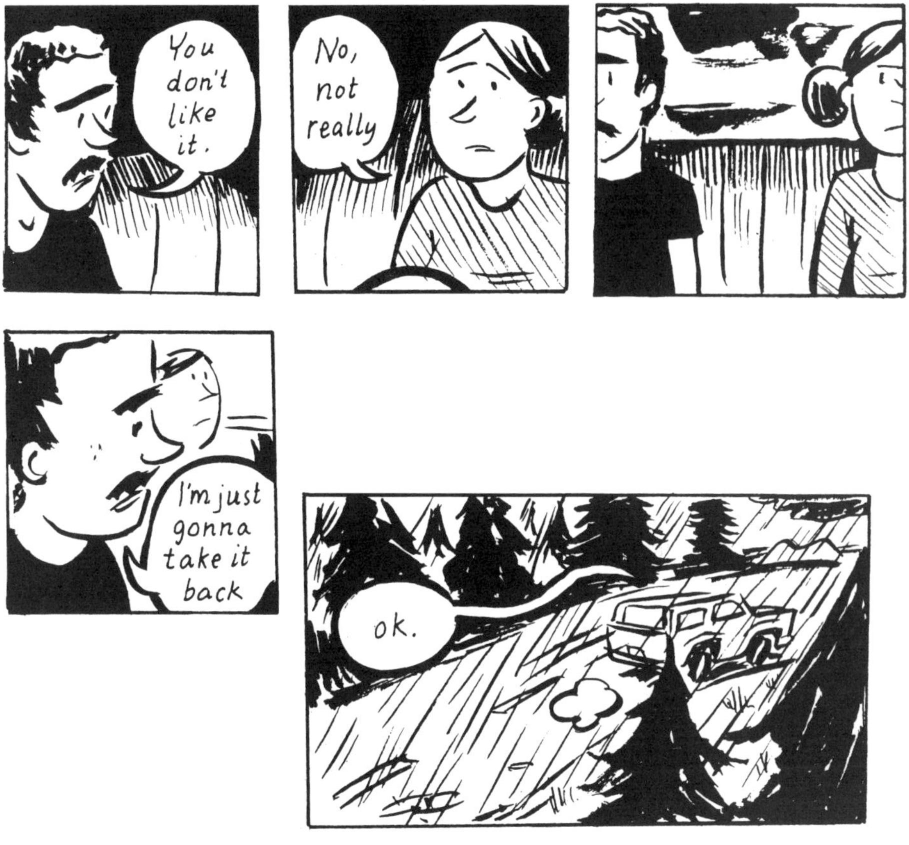
You don't like it.
No, not really
I'm just gonna take it back
ok.

Mix tape was drawn Apr '06 as an epilogue of sorts to BFX.

I haven't made a mixtape since.

Good night,
Dear
Readers..

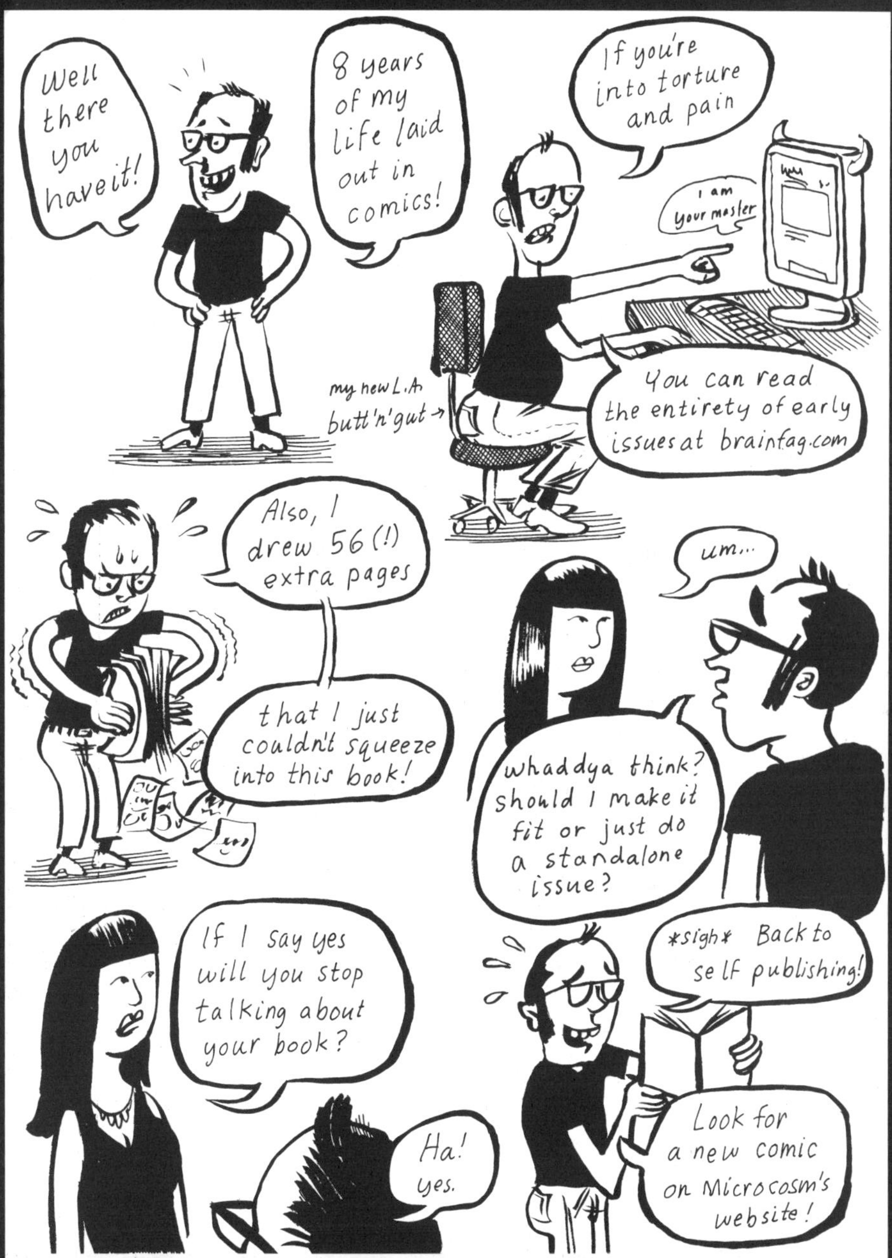

Well there you have it!
8 years of my life laid out in comics!
If you're into torture and pain
I am your master
You can read the entirety of early issues at brainfag.com
my new L.A butt'n'gut
Also, I drew 56 (!) extra pages
that I just couldn't squeeze into this book!
um...
whaddya think? should I make it fit or just do a standalone issue?
If I say yes will you stop talking about your book?
Ha! yes.
sigh Back to self publishing!
Look for a new comic on Microcosm's website!

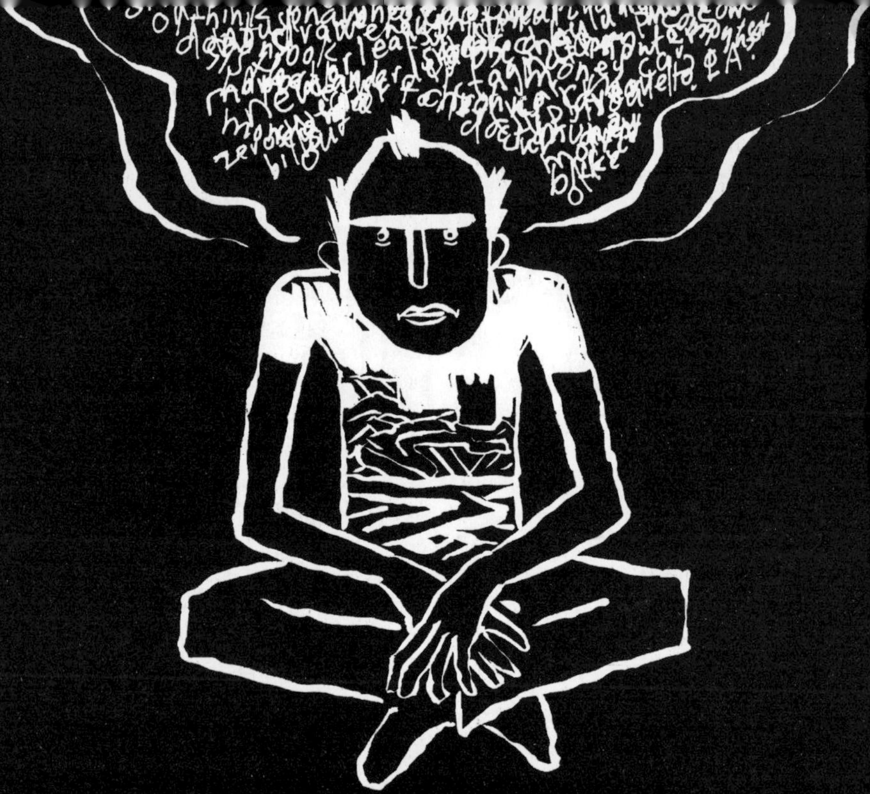

Ye Olde Thanks!

Aaron "ANIMAL" Renier, Alec "TASKMASTER" Longstreth, Ezra "DREAMY CHOCOLATE MAN" Clayton Daniels, Greg "MAN OF MEANS" Beans, Jonathan "BROWN BAGGIN IT" Hill, Joseph "JAZZY J" Robertson, Kang "THE ASIAN HURRICANE" Soon Bok, Joe "BRAIN PILLS" Biel, This American Life, Radiolab, Ink, Paper, Music, Green tea

brainfag.com ~ microcosmpublishing.com